Fools Are Everywhere

"Oh, to be a splendid fellow like this, self-contained, ready of speech, agile beyond conception, braving the forces of society, his hand against everyone, and yet always getting the best of it!"

FOOLS

are

EVERYWHERE

THE COURT JESTER AROUND THE WORLD

Beatrice K. Otto

THE UNIVERSITY OF CHICAGO PRESS
CHICAGO AND LONDON

Beatrice Otto is a freelance consultant in London.

The University of Chicago Press, Chicago 60637
The University of Chicago Press, Ltd., London
© 2001 by The University of Chicago
All rights reserved. Published 2001
Printed in the United States of America

10 09 08 07 06 05 04 03 02 01   1 2 3 4 5

ISBN: 0-226-64091-4 (cloth)

Library of Congress Cataloging-in-Publication Data

Otto, Beatrice K.
    Fools are everywhere : the court jester around the world / Beatrice K. Otto.
        p. cm.
    Rev. of the author's thesis Cosmic caperers (doctoral—1996)
    Includes bibliographical references and index.
    ISBN 0-226-64091-4 (alk. paper)
        1. Fools and jesters—History.   2. Fools and jesters—Cross-cultural studies.
    I. Title.

GT3670 .O77 2000
792.7'028—dc21

                                                            00-044706

♾ The paper used in this publication meets the minimum requirements of the
American National Standard for Information Sciences—Permanence of Paper for
Printed Library Materials, ANSI Z39.48-1992.

To everyone who has ever made me laugh
(wittingly or unwittingly)

或笑人或笑於人笑人者
亦復笑於人笑于人者亦
復笑人人之相笑寧有
已時　古今世界一大
笑府我與若皆在其中
供人話柄不話不成人
不笑不成話不笑不話
不成世界布袋和尚
吾師乎吾師乎

馮夢龍廣笑府序
謹應歐桃友人雅囑
書於英倫
一九九四年
六月八日

Some laugh at others and some are laughed at by others; those who
laugh at others also become the butt of others' laughter while those
who are laughed at in turn laugh at others. Ah, people will never
stop laughing at one another, will they? . . . There's still all the rest
of that one great treasury of the laughable—the whole world past
and present with you and me in the middle of it as well, as part of
the pabulum. Man isn't man without talk, and talk's unthinkable
without laughter. Yes, the world wouldn't be the world without
talking and laughing. Ah, Cloth-Bag Monk, Maitreya the
Laughing Buddha, my master! Yes, you're my master!

Feng Menglong (1574–1646), Preface to the *Expanded Treasury
of Laughter*, trans. William Dolby

CONTENTS

ACKNOWLEDGMENTS

Some fools seek knowledge high and higher,
To M.A., Ph.D aspire,
Though people deem them very bright,
These fools can't understand aright.

Sebastian Brant, *Ship of Fools* (1494)

A. So you must have written a thesis then?
B. Yeah, a doctoral thesis.
A. Was it published?
B. Yup. While I was studying abroad I wrote this thesis, forty
thousand words or more, took me three whole months hard
work. . . . ha, ha.

Hou Baolin, "Chats on Drama"

At the risk of omitting some of the many people to whom I owe a debt of gratitude, I would like to thank a few by name: Reza Sabri-Tabrizi for his help with Middle Eastern jesters and his expansiveness and humor; Paul Dundas for suggesting materials on the jesters of the Indian stage and for his helpful comments; Philip Bennett, who cleared up some confusion over French medieval entertainers and then read over the sections on these and the *sotties;* Allen Hood for discussing the entertainers of Rome and Greece and reading the relevant sections; Stephan Bumbacher for suggesting numerous pertinent materials and for his enthusiasm and constant jesting. All of these gave their time and ideas generously and enthusiastically. Tommy McClellan also deserves a mention for introducing me to the jester at the End of Time as well as for bibliographic help during his stay in China.

To Jill Evans, Kerry Watt, and others at the Interlibrary Loans desk of Edinburgh University I owe a huge vote of thanks for being unfailingly efficient and cheerful in procuring materials, despite my mountain of requests. The British Library also merits praise for speed of delivery and determination in detective work—without the help of these people my bibliography would be about a quarter the size it is. In addition, my thanks go to John Moffett for high-speed bibliographic searches despite being under exam pressure.

Further afield I would like to mention Marguerite Wells for coming up trumps on Japanese jesters when I had drawn nothing but blanks; David Shulman, whose eloquent book first brought the magnificent jesters of India to my door; Lee Siegel—whose warm and colorful wit shows to what extent an eminently scholarly work can also be a Damn Good Read—for his enthusiasm and inspiration; Karl Flögel and Enid Welsford, on whose wide-ranging books I could have based the whole Western side of my research, were I not so thorough; José Moreno Villa for doing the eighteen months of "laborious work" in the National Palace archives in Madrid that I had neither the time nor the money to do; and Ren Erbei, whose careful groundwork laid the solid foundations on which the Chinese side of this book is built, thereby saving me decades of preparatory work and allowing me to proceed straight to the heart of the matter.

For practical as well as moral support, I owe much to my brothers and to John Rapley and Steve Bennett. I am also particularly grateful to Roderick Dunlop Brown, who kept a roof over my head for the duration regardless of when the rent was paid, making his home mine from the day I arrived in Edinburgh as well as allowing me unlimited access to his computer; and to my grandmother, Dorothy Stanton, whose bequest to me financed most of this dream. Another *danapati* (kindly benefactor) was Carolyn Boyes, who bought me an airline ticket to New York, ostensibly to view a single manuscript. I must also thank the British Federation of Women Graduates for providing me with an emergency grant to see me through the last month of my research.

For help with foreign languages, I am very grateful to Miklos Otto and Otto Fényi (Latin), Elizabeth Temple of Stowe (Hungarian), and Bill Dolby (German, Dutch, and Italian, not to mention Chinese). For the beautiful calligraphy on the book's epigraph, I thank He Yubin.

Much gratitude is also due to those (some of them named above) who stood by me when my work brought me into a head-on collision with what can perhaps be loosely described as the academic establishment, in a farce that will be chronicled elsewhere. I include my parents, Miklos Otto and

Diana Stanton, who in addition to having passed on to me their loud laughs, also impressed on me that on no account does one cave in to Grayness, however eminent.

In the move toward publication, this (as yet) unknown author owes her lucky break to David Brent, executive editor at the University of Chicago Press, who has been a warm, unwavering, and sensitive champion throughout. If an authorette were to fantasize about an editor, he would be it—he is all that we are told editors should be while being assured in the same breath that they never are. His patience with my questions, understanding of delays, and delicate prising out of my thoughts have made preparing this manuscript easy and stress-free. I am also grateful to Alice Bennett, manuscript editor at Chicago, who managed to combine a sharp eye with a light touch.

And as the reader appointed by Chicago, I am immensely grateful to Bill Jenner for bringing his robust intellect to bear on the manuscript and for his valuable suggestions and kind encouragement. It was with verve that he opened up the world of Chinese studies to me in the first place, apparently maintaining faith in my long-term potential even when I occasionally veered toward the edge of the rails, if never quite off them. I trust that faith has paid off in this, the first of many books.

Finally, my greatest gratitude goes to Bill Dolby, whose reputation for true scholarship and kindliness in equal measure was the magnet that brought me to Edinburgh, as it has been for others, and who agreed to supervise my work long before I was confident enough to embark on it, wholeheartedly sharing my delight in the jester. He has proved the greatest of friends in addition to being an exemplary scholar, steering me with impeccable tact, patience, and humor through uncharted waters, throwing open to me the vast archives of his mind, and handing me, piled high, the many fruits of his labors. To him is due much of the credit for this work's having blossomed into maturity and none of the blame. Besides which the countless hours spent feasting, talking, and laughing made Thursday afternoons something of a hallowed institution.

Now, this is what made me advance my argument so far into this matter of laughter, the nicest and most exciting that has ever been touched. For from one proposition I am led to another, and with a curious desire I go searching constantly, as though insatiable, all that I can grasp. I think that surely I shall never finish, and that there will always be more to say or add.

[Or c'et ce qui m'a fait, si avant anfoncer au discours de mon argumant, an cette matiere du Ris, la plus jantile & galharde qui ayt eté jamais touchee. Car d'vn propos je suis conduit à l'autre, & d'vn curieus desir je vay toujours recherchant, comme insatiable, tout ce que j'an peus comprandre. Ie panse bien que je n'auray jamais achevé, & qu'il y aura toujours à redire, ou ajouter quelque chose.]

Laurent Joubert, *Le traité du ris* (1579)[1]

Yes, there were descriptions, confessions, portraits, and memoirs of jesters. . . . It is the histories that remain silent in the face of people from the dregs of society: whores, lackeys, convicts, galley slaves, . . . louts, pimps, rogues, crooks, beggars, and buffoons. It is the history of the "elite" that is left to us.

Estebanillo González, *Vida y hechos de Estebanillo González*[2]

PROLOGUE

The Number of Fools Is Infinite

━━━ ⚃

THE ARGUMENT

It is all too often forgotten that the ancient symbol for the pre-
nascence of the world is a fool, and that foolishness, being a divine
state, is not a condition to be either proud or ashamed of.
> G. Spencer-Brown, *Laws of Form* [3]

I have always loved jesters, but then who doesn't? Put a capering juggler
with a quick patter in a town square on a sunny day and you will soon have
a crowd, with children usually outnumbered by adults. He can make fun
of the audience—make fools of them even—and nobody will mind, nor
will they mind if he makes a fool of himself. Everybody knows who he
is and what he is about, and even something of his checkered history, although the chances are nobody has ever formally taught them. People's
understanding of jesters, and their delight in them, has been kept alive
over centuries and around the world with little prompting.

Three years into studying modern Chinese, I came across a lively
translation of some ancient anecdotes concerning Chinese jesters. I could
see no real difference between their humor and function and those of their
Western counterparts. Therein lay the seed of what is proving a lifelong
passion, the first flourishing of which you hold in your hands. Originally
I intended to show the universal nature of the court jester by comparing
the magnificent traditions of jesterdom that existed in China, England,
and France, but it soon became apparent that in focusing exclusively on
this trinity I would have had to ignore splendid specimens of jesters from
elsewhere, denying myself masses of colorful evidence to support my ten-
tative theory. In setting the goalposts wider than the China-Europe pa-
rameter to include the historical and legendary jesters of the Middle East

and India (not to mention their American and African colleagues), it became clear that there was such a "model," to which the Chinese jester conformed, perhaps even taking it to its most refined form. The European jester was in some ways the exception rather than the rule.

My particular passion is the court jester. I argue that he is very much a universal character, more or less interchangeable regardless of the time or culture in which he happens to cavort—the same techniques, the same functions, the same license. His universality was something I began by exploring most tentatively, but he led me quite a dance into times and places I'd never visited. I've since been branded a "universalist," with which I'm not altogether comfortable, since it perhaps suggests that I began my research with a notion I wanted to prove, then shopped around for some evidence (jesters will do) to fit the theory. Nothing of the sort. I started because I'm mad about jesters and, knowing I could never match their sparkling, death-defying wit, I decided to give them the limelight they deserve. The universalist slant stemmed from the fact that the Chinese jesters were so similar to our Western stereotype (bar the cap and bells, which was not the daily garb of real jesters anyway).

In other words, jesters first, "universalism" second, though I will admit to a gut feeling that humor is not humanity's only constant or, as Ernst Gombrich put it, that one should be wary of treating Renaissance man as a separate species, given that he was sure "these people too liked to stay in bed in the morning."[4]

The appeal and even, I believe, the need for jesters is in all likelihood only one of many currents running through human society, such as a common desire to stay in bed in the morning and a tendency to fall in love and in lust. Those are universals. The distinctions lie in the design of the beds we long to lounge in, and in what triggers a man's "mmm" at a passing girl—in some times and places women flatten their breasts to make them sexier, in others they resort to silicone implants. That is cultural quirk.

On one level it could be argued that I cannot really know what went on between a Chinese emperor and his jester, because I was not there. Nor can it be guaranteed that my interpretation of what went on is not in any way colored by my twentieth-century European vantage point. To minimize these pitfalls, I have quoted many jester stories, rather than paraphrasing them, thereby avoiding another layer of cultural filter. That is the intellectual rationale: the real reason, of course, is that jesters speak for themselves better than I can, and more entertainingly.

One filter that cannot be avoided, even if it is minimized, is that of translation, a problem I have circumvented where possible by including the original text. Including quotations in the original also enriches the texture of the book, allowing readers to savor the evidence more directly, rather like showing the jury a photograph of the murder weapon rather than a sketch. And the visual impact of turning pages and being greeted with different languages at different stages of their evolution also reinforces the notion that the jester is at home in disparate times and places.

I do not say that the jester exists in all times and places: the crux is rather that he is not the product of any particular time or place. The preconditions for the emergence of jesters are minimal—some courtlike institution in the form of a head honcho with a partly dependent entourage. No critical mass of courtiers or pomp is needed. Lear in the wilderness had his fool if little else. This does not of course mean that every courtlike institution is bound to have a fool. Even if we had access to all records, it would be impossible to prove an unbroken line of jesters, given that records are written by different people with different priorities. That said, I cannot think of one instance of a jester's being documented with incomprehension. People do not seem to write along the lines of "the emperor revived an ancient custom and brought a thing called a 'jester' into his court" or "we visited a two-headed tribe, and the chief kept a one-headed man who made him laugh, thus proving the uniqueness of the tribe."

In other words, the jester may not be omnipresent, but he does seem omnifamiliar to anybody writing about him, even when they are describing him in a culture alien to their own. The evidence points to his having existed across the globe and across history, in most of the major civilizations of the world and many of the minor ones. And while there was certainly cross-fertilization within, let us say, the European tradition, by and large he seems to have arisen spontaneously and independently within societies without their necessarily being aware of his existence elsewhere, suggesting that he fulfills a deep and widespread social need. The frequency of his occurrence, and the diversity of the cultures he has thrived in, make it hard to see how his universal nature can easily be refuted. "This is global terrain that needs multilingual and 'multimind' explorers who *delight in unexpected links.*"[5]

When academics ask me what my field is and I say "jesters," they commonly ask which period, looking askance when I answer "any period I can find them." Sometimes it seems one is supposed to define one's field with geographic and chronological boundaries, and any attempt to traverse all terrains and times in pursuit of themes or phenomena is tantamount to trespass.[6] Yet to place a Groucho Marx quip alongside an ancient Chinese one is to show that the Chinese may not have been as remote as we think, and I have chosen to track my quarry sleuthlike wherever it takes me, borders and jurisdictions notwithstanding. A crime may be committed in PC Plod's precinct, but it might be cracked only when he hands the case over to Interpol where the big picture can be seen and transnational patterns discerned. Has scholarship become too obsessed with growing prize onions on the garden plot while ignoring the beckoning fecundity of fields beyond the fence? So let me end with a gentle kid glove challenge: after reading the evidence I put forward, show how it can be denied that the jester is universal, and from that how some other things might not also be universal, such as love, lust, and a longing for bed.

THE EVIDENCE

> Trying to understand another country merely by reading its literature results in limited knowledge even when the literature read is genuinely representative of the country's various facets. But to delete from the sampling as large and important an element of a nation's culture as its humor and satire is to create a hopelessly distorted image.
>
> Leonard Feinberg, *Asian Laughter*[7]

Although the past two centuries, and especially the past two decades, have seen a swelling corpus of impressive Western works on the court jester, these tend to concentrate on Europe, occasionally fanning out to touch on peripheral cultures but rarely giving even cursory acknowledgment of the treasure trove of China.[8] There is certainly a very deep and widespread understanding within Europe of this lively character, and the word "jester" still conjures a vivid and appealing image. With his instantly recognizable uniform of cap and bells, he has become a symbol of physical and verbal dexterity and of freedom from convention. To the Westerner he remains a familiar figure of fun capable of eliciting delight and enthusiasm.

In contrast to Europeans, the past few centuries have seen the Chinese increasingly out of touch with the richness of their own tradition of court jesters, and apart from the work of Wang Guowei, "Record of Jesters' Words" ("Youyu lu"), later superseded by Ren Erbei in his landmark *The Collected Sayings of Jesters and Actors (Youyu ji)*, there has been a dearth of works on the subject.[9] In fact, so far removed have the Chinese become from their court jesters that the Chinese words for "jester," such as *youren, paiyou,* and *lingren,* usually have to be repeated, spelled out, and explained, either being met with a blank response or interpreted as "actor" or "entertainer." Yet contemporaries of the Chinese jesters wrote about them with a careful analysis rarely matched in Europe, and in vivid detail, leaving us a hefty legacy of wit and pointed advice. Records of anecdotes regarding jesters, from improvised playlets put on by a group of jesters to comic duos to pithy one-liners of a single jester addressing himself directly to the emperor, give us a tantalizing taste of their well-aimed witticisms.

Despite the staggering similarity between Chinese and European jesters, the materials relating to them differ. To put it simply, when jesters were flourishing their exploits were recorded and commented on by some of the greatest scholars in Chinese history. The Europeans wrote and analyzed less, but what they neglected to write, they drew, painted, and carved: at the height of his popularity in Europe the jester's likeness was committed to canvas, paper, wood, and stone and could be seen in churches, palaces, and public buildings. The Chinese picture of the jester predominantly consists of words, while the European is as much visual as verbal. In China the evidence of writers and historians is matched by a signal paucity of pictorial evidence, and there is little to indicate that the Chinese jester had a costume as distinctive as that of his European counterpart; so perhaps in sartorial appearance, at least, he merged more easily into the court.

This difference in pictographic evidence—an overflowing European cornucopia compared with a relative dearth elsewhere—is one of the principal factors distinguishing the European tradition, hence the Eurocentric weighting to the illustrations in this book.[10] This, combined with the fact that the notion of folly as a human universal was more vociferously and explicitly stated in Europe, explains the close conformity of figure 1 to the European image of the jester. Had I commissioned a designer to encapsulate the book's focus on the jester as a global player, I could not have hoped for a more powerfully eloquent exponent.

> It's not for nowt the jester's global clout
> Is colorfully illustrated, amply illuminated
> By a world map in a fool's cap.

The Chinese jester crops up in some of the most important and widely read works of classical Chinese history and literature, from dynastic histories to essay collections. China's Herodotus, Sima Qian (145 – ca. 86 B.C.), devoted a chapter to them in his *Historical Records (Shiji),* providing the inspiration and the sanction for other literary giants to write about jesters. Several of the formal dynastic histories have a section of jester biographies, in addition to numerous other works of history, musicology, and

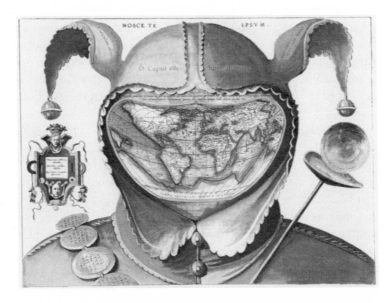

Figure 1 *The Fool's Cap World Map*

miscellaneous jottings and jestbooks that deal with them or touch on their nature or exploits, and Ban Gu's (32–92) *History of the Former Han (Hanshu)* devotes an entire chapter to Dongfang Shuo, principal jester of Emperor Wudi (r. 140–87 B.C.) of the Han.[11] In Europe some writers mentioned jesters, and Erasmus had a few nice things to say about them, but most modern historians ignore the important place of the jester in the court, writing books on the court of King So-and-So with hardly a mention of his omnipresent pal and adviser.

In Europe, primary material about him is found principally in letters, court account books, poems, and plays. In Britain especially, playwrights paid greater attention to the jester than historians did, and indeed the current understanding of the jester in English-speaking countries is based far more on Touchstone, Feste, and Lear's fool than on Will Somers or Archy Armstrong. In addition England had many jestbooks that featured well-known jesters. These could be compositions about jesters by jesters, such as Robert Armin's *Foole upon Foole* (1600) and *A Nest of Ninnies* (1608), or books containing anecdotes attributed to a specific jester, such as *Tarlton's Jests* (1611).[12] Works on the jesters of other cultures comprise collections of jester anecdotes occasionally mingled haphazardly with other witty stories and, like the European equivalents, lack much in the way of analysis.

Jokes were often attributed to famous jesters simply to lend them greater street credibility or market appeal, rather like asking everybody's favorite footballer to advertise instant coffee: if he drinks it, it must be good. This practice becomes clear when identical anecdotes are credited to jesters from Baghdad to London, perhaps indicating some humorous exchange of comic currency. There is even one instance of a Chinese jester anecdote's turning up in India about a thousand years after it was first recorded in China. Coincidence can reasonably account for many of the duplications, since the nature of jesters was so alike that it is not hard to see how they could arrive at the same response to a given situation. Nevertheless, sometimes the anecdotes are so similar as to arouse suspicions of having been recouched.

This leads to the problematic question of historicity. The difficulty lies not so much in ascertaining which jesters actually existed, but rather in determining which story was a story and which was history. This is where variants can give clues. In China there can be several versions of a particular anecdote—a nugget or more of truth wrapped in different, credible embellishments. In Europe there is often very little discrepancy in the actual story; it is just pegged to various jesters. In this case chronology can help us guess where it all started. With a combination of detective work, circumstantial evidence, and inspired guesswork it is possible to establish with reasonable if incomplete certainty the historical veracity of anecdotes about certain jesters. Many such anecdotes are perfectly convincing as history when taken in isolation. It is only the duplication that raises doubts.

Many jesters enjoy legendary status, both in the sense of being real men who have acquired reputations of mythological proportions, such as Birbal, jester to Akbar the Indian Mogul emperor (r. 1562–1605), and in the sense of perhaps having always been a figment of many imaginations, such as Tenali Rama, another Indian superjester. The distinction can be blurred, but if the historical veracity of some jester anecdotes is open to doubt, I believe they nonetheless reflect the way jesters were perceived and the high regard people had for them. If real occurrences were embellished, the embellishments themselves can tell us a great deal about how a jester was expected to be.

To the European jestbooks may be added the literature of folly (of which Germany seems to have been the fountainhead and greatest repository), flourishing from medieval times and reflecting the bewildering array of ideas about the nature of fools and folly. After the departure of the jester from court (to take on other guises), the Europeans started writing about him in earnest. The seminal work, which has yet to be surpassed, is

Karl Flögel's *Geschichte der Hofnarren* (1789), the source from which many subsequent works spring. It is as readable and relevant today as it was in the eighteenth century, lacking any old-fashioned quaintness. The only work to equal Flögel is Enid Welsford's *The Fool: His Social and Literary History,* published in 1935.[13]

Both works are superlative, and comprehensive as far as they go. But together with every other Western book on the court jester, they almost completely ignore China. The Chinese are partly to blame, since they have kept their jester-light hidden under a bushel, doing little to disabuse us of our insular misperceptions. Nevertheless, Western sinologists, with one or two notable exceptions, have also shown little interest in the Chinese court jesters. For these or other reasons, the West has been given to believe that Europe was the center of the jester's cosmos and that he was not equaled, let alone surpassed, anywhere else. In fact the Chinese jesters were easily on a par with their Western cousins, from whichever angle one cares to view them.

While this century has seen a plethora of European books about jesters, most of them well written and researched within the constraints referred to above, the same cannot be said for China. There are only two writers who have taken a serious interest in the court jester, Wang Guowei and Ren Erbei. The latter has built on the foundations of the former and has done an immense service to anybody wishing to write about Chinese jesters, by gathering a large number of anecdotes from diverse sources. His work is an invaluable starting point for finding primary sources, but it does not itself offer much analysis. This points to another difference between China and Europe, China is strong on primary sources and weak on secondary ones, while Europe has less accessible primary material and more secondary sources. Records of jesters' exploits were not necessarily recorded five minutes after the event by eyewitnesses and earnest historians, and even with the efforts of chroniclers, particularly impressive in China, it is likely that those skits lost to posterity in the ephemera of spontaneous wit are legion, so that we are left with the tip of an iceberg of incisive social and political commentary.

The crux of this work is that the jester was a universal phenomenon, not the product of a particular culture or era. In presenting my case I hope also to redress the balance in favor of the Chinese jester, who has been left out of the equation for too long. Even within Europe there is an unequal division of glory that I cannot pretend to have yet redressed, although it is my lifelong aim to do so. Any contributions from readers concerning neglected jesters or countries will be gratefully received (<beatrice@jester life.com>).

In this regard I have had more luck with Italy and Spain than with other countries still deserving greater attention. Although Italy is often included in books about court jesters, it usually is not given nearly as much detail as, for example, England and France, except by Italian writers, whose research is rarely quoted in the bibliographies of their northern counterparts, with the exception of Welsford. Yet they provide access to some marvelous and detailed primary sources, a few of which I have quoted, at least giving a glimpse of what awaits discovery. Spain has been neglected across the board except by art historians and the authors of some excellent studies on Spanish literary jesters.

Jesters in China, Europe, the Middle East, and India aimed their humorous arrows at the same targets—religion and its representatives, self-important scholars, venal officials and nobles, and erring, corrupt, or lazy rulers, together with anything deemed sacrosanct. There is a whole class of skits devoted to mocking Confucius (Kongzi), including the wittily presented argument by Li Keji of the court of Tang Yizong (r. 860–74) to prove that Confucius, the great man himself, was in fact a woman. The need, or desire, for such all-embracing irreverence is attested by the general tolerance of the jester's role in court.

Compared with his European golden age of some five hundred years from the twelfth century, the Chinese jester was of more enduring stock, flourishing during some two thousand years from the Spring and Autumn Period (770–476 B.C.). He was a distinctly recognizable character in the courts where he cavorted, and despite cultural chasms, the superstar jesters of the world were so similar in their functions and the way they fulfilled them that if Will Somers were airlifted from the court of Henry VIII (r. 1509–47) to the court of Caliph Harun al-Rashid (r. 786–809), he would not disgrace his profession. And if the Indian Tenali Rama, jester to King Krishnadevaraya (r. 1509–29), were called on to replace an indisposed Jester Meng (You Meng) at the court of King Zhuangwang of Chu (r. 613–591 B.C.), he would acquit himself honorably. If I manage to impress on my readers the universal nature and vitality of these quick-witted, colorful creatures, I shall have succeeded in my endeavors.

A maister swynhird swanky
And his cousing copyn cull
ffowll of bellis fulfull
led the dance and began.

Colkelbie Sow[1]

1

Facets of the Fool

"Who Is Not a Fool?"
["Qui non stultus?"]
Horace (65–8 B.C.), *Satires*, 2.3.158[2]

Then come jesters, musicians and trained dwarfs,
And singing girls from the land of Ti-ti,
To delight the ear and eye
And bring mirth to the mind.
Sima Xiangru (ca. 179–117 B.C.), *Rhapsody on the Shanglin Park*[3]

The jester is an elusive character. The European words used to denote him can now seem as nebulous as they are numerous, reflecting the mercurial man behind them: fool, buffoon, clown, *jongleur, jogleor, joculator, sot, stultor, scurra, fou, fol, truhan, mimus, histrio, morio.* He can be any of these, while the German word *Narr* is not so much a stem as the sturdy trunk of a tree efflorescent with fool vocabulary. The jester's quicksilver qualities are equally difficult to pin down, but nevertheless not beyond definition.

The Chinese terms used for "jester" now seem vaguer than the European, most of them having a wider meaning of "actor" or "entertainer." In Chinese there is no direct translation of the English "jester," no single word that to the present-day Chinese conjures an image as vividly as "court jester," *fou du roi,* or *Hofnarr* would to a Westerner. In Chinese the jester element often has to be singled out according to context, although the key character *you* does seem to have referred specifically to jesters, originally meaning somebody who would use humor to mock and joke, who could speak without causing offense, and who also had the ability to sing or dance: "The *you* was also allowed a certain privilege, that is, his 'words were without offence' . . . but the *you* could not offer his remonstrances in earnest, he had to make use of jokes, songs and dance."[4] The term is often combined with other characters giving differing shades to his jesterdom, an acting or a musical slant, for example: *paiyou, youren, youling, changyou, lingren, linglun.* All could include musical and other talents, *chang* suggesting music, *ling,* playing or fooling, and *pai* a humorous element to bring delight.[5] Several of these terms are too frequently translated as "actor" regardless of where they appear on the etymological chain of evolution and even though they were used long before the advent of Chinese drama.[6]

Perhaps the earliest antecedents of the European court jester were the comic actors of ancient Rome. Several Latin terms used in medieval references to jesters (including numerous church condemnations of them), such as *scurrae, mimi,* or *histriones,* originally referred either to amusing hangers-on or to the comic actors and entertainers of Rome. Just as there is now no clear distinction between the terms for "actor" and "jester" in Chinese, so the Latin terms could merge the two. If there was no formal professional jester in Rome, the comic actors fulfilled his functions, sometimes even bearing a striking physical resemblance to what is usually considered a medieval and Renaissance archetype. With periodic imperial purges against actors for their outspokenness, many of them took to the road and fanned out across the empire in search of new audiences and greater freedom. Successive waves of such wandering comics may well have laid the foundations for medieval and Renaissance jesterdom, possibly contributing to the rising tide of folly worship that swept across the Continent from the late Middle Ages.[7]

An individual court jester in Europe could emerge from a wide range of backgrounds: an erudite but nonconformist university dropout, a monk thrown out of a priory for nun frolics, a *jongleur* with exceptional verbal or physical dexterity, or the apprentice of a village blacksmith whose fooling amused a passing nobleman. Just as a modern-day television stand-up comedian might begin his career on the pub and club circuit, so a would-be jester could make it big time in court if he was lucky enough to be spotted. In addition, a poet, musician, or scholar could also become a court jester.

The recruiting of jesters was tremendously informal and meritocratic, perhaps indicating greater mobility and fluidity in past society than is often supposed. A man with the right qualifications might be found anywhere: in Russia "they were generally selected from among the older and uglier of the serf-servants, and the older the fool or she-fool was, the droller they were supposed and expected to be. The fool had the right to sit at table with his master, and say whatever came into his head."[8] Noblemen might keep an eye out for potential jesters, and a letter dated 26 January 1535/36 from Thomas Bedyll to Thomas Cromwell (ca. 1485–1540) recommends a possible replacement for the king's old jester:

> Ye know the Kinges grace hath one old fole: Sexten as good as myght be whiche because of aige is not like to cotinew. I haue spied one yong fole at Croland whiche in myne opinion shalbe muche mor pleasaunt than euer Sexten was . . . and he is not past xv yere old.[9]

Fuller's *History of the Worthies of England* (1662) gives an account of the recruiting of Tarlton, jester to Elizabeth I (r. 1558–1603), that further illustrates this informality:

> Here he was in the field, keeping his Father's Swine, when a Servant of Robert Earl of Leicester . . . was so highly pleased with his *happy unhappy* answers, that he brought him to Court, where he became the most famous *Jester* to Queen Elizabeth.[10]

A dwarf-jester called Nai Teh (Mr. Little) at the court of King Mongkut of Siam (r. 1851–68), described by Anna Leonowens in *Anna and the King of Siam,* was similarly recruited:

> He was discovered by one of the King's half-brothers on a hunting trip into the north and brought to Bangkok to be trained in athletic and gymnastic tricks. When he had learned these, he was presented to the king as a comedian and a buffoon.[11]

A German, Paul Wüst, declined an offer of a post as jester with the sort of brazen dismissiveness that explains why he was asked. When Duke Eberhard the Bearded of Würtemburg (1445–96) invited him to be his jester he replied, "My father sired his own fool; if you want one too, then go and sire one for yourself" ("Mein Vater hat einen Narren für sich gezeugt, willst du aber einen Narren haben, so zeuge dir auch einen").[12] The same story is attributed to Will Somers, who uses the joke to mock Henry's predilection for chalking up wives:

> His Majesty after some discourse growing into some good liking of him, said; fellow, wilt thou be my fool? who answered him again, that he had rather be his own father's still, then the king asking him why? he told him again, that his father had got him a fool for himself, (having but one wife) and no body could justly claim him from him: now you have had so many wives, and still living in hope to

have more, why, of some one of them, cannot you get a fool as he did? and so you shall be sure to have a fool of your own.[13]

The post of court jester might also appeal to somebody in need of a safe haven. The thirteenth-century French tale of *Robert le Diable* has him fleeing a populace baying for blood and forcing his way past the footmen to gain access to the emperor, who duly takes him under his wing as a jester, saying that nobody should be allowed to beat him.[14] Alfred de Musset's play *Fantasio* (1834) is about a dandy whose job as jester allows him to escape and evade creditors, and a Scottish miscellany tells us how one of the most roguish historical jesters found his vocation:

> Archie Armstrong . . . after having long distinguished himself as a most dexterous sheep-stealer, and when Eskdale at last became too hot for him, on account of his nefarious practices, he had the honour of being appointed *jester* to James I. of England, which office he held for several years.[15]

Tarlton tended pigs, Archy stole sheep, and Claus Hinße (d. 1599), jester to Duke Johann Friedrich of Pomerania (d. 1600), began his working life as a cowherd.[16] Wamba, "son of Witless," the jester in Sir Walter Scott's *Ivanhoe*, was, like Tarlton, a swineherd, and Claus Narr (Fool), one of Germany's most famous and long-serving jesters, was tending geese when he was recruited.[17] He was jester to four Saxon electors and one archbishop during the last quarter of the fifteenth century and first quarter of the sixteenth, and there are more than six hundred stories about him. One day when the first of his patrons, Elector Ernst (d. 1486), was traveling through Ranstadt with a lot of horses and wagons, Claus became curious about all the commotion and went to see what was happening. Worried that his geese would be stolen, he secured the goslings by putting their necks through his belt while he carried the older geese under his arms (fig. 2). When Ernst saw him he laughed at his simplicity and decided he was a born jester. He asked Claus's father's permission to take him to court:

> "That would be great, Sir! I'd be relieved of a great encumbrance thereby; the youth is no good to me—he makes nothing but trouble in my house and stirs up the whole village with his pranks."

> ["Sehr gern, Gnädiger Herr, ich würde dadurch eines grossen Verdrusses überhoben, denn der Junge ist mir nichts nütze, in meinem Hause macht er nichts als Unruh, und durch seine Possen wiegelt er daß ganze Dorf auf."][18]

Ernst then gave Claus's father twenty guilders as compensation for the strangled goslings and other gifts besides. The story is an insight into the charitable element often involved in the recruiting of "naturals." To a poor family, a natural might be a heavy burden, and it could clearly be a relief to have him taken in and looked after by a wealthy family. Generally speaking there is little to suggest that this was not done in a humane and kindly manner, although in England there was a law allowing the estates of a natural to be handed over to a person offering to care for him, which could lead to their being recruited under false pretenses.

A similar story is told of Jamie Fleeman (1713–78), the Scottish jester to the laird of Udny. He complemented his jesting duties with those of a cowherd and goose guardian, and when he one day grew irritated by the geese wandering willy-nilly, he twisted some straw rope around their necks and started walking home, unaware that they were being throttled one by one. By the time he realized it was too late, and since it was a rare breed of geese, he would have been in big trouble. So he dragged the corpses into

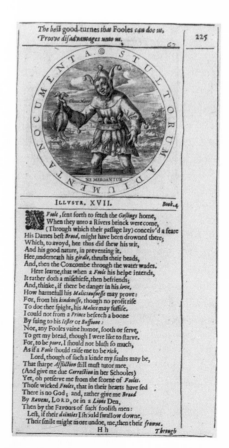

Figure 2 Claus the Fool throttles his goslings

the poultry yard and stuffed their throats with food. When asked whether
the geese were safe and sound, he replied cheerfully, "Safe! they're gobble,
gobble, gobblin' as if they had nae seen meat for a twalmonth! Safe! Ise
warran' they're safe aneuch, if they hae nae choked themsells."[19]

In India the same entrance requirements prevailed: make me laugh
and you're in. Tenali Rama, one of the three superstar jesters of India, is
said to have earned his position as jester by making King Krisnadevaraya
laugh. According to one story, he contrived for the king's guru to carry
him around on his shoulders within sight of the king. Outraged at the humiliation of his holy man, the king sent some guards out to beat the man
riding on the guru's shoulders. Tenali Rama, smelling impending danger,
jumped down and begged forgiveness of the guru, insisting that to make
amends he should carry him on his own shoulders. The guru agreed, and
when the guards arrived the guru was duly beaten. The king found the trick
amusing enough to appoint Tenali Rama his jester.[20] In China, despite the
abundance of anecdotes about jesters once they enter royal service, there
is very little background information available. Nevertheless the universal
jester skills displayed by the Chinese jesters suggest that their appointment
was as meritocratic as in Europe.

A description of Rabelais's Panurge encompasses many of the jester's
characteristics: "Irreverent, libertine, self-indulgent, witty, clever, roguish, he is the fool as court jester, the fool as companion, the fool as goad
to the wise and challenge to the virtuous, the fool as critic of the world."[21]
He could be juggler, confidant, scapegoat, prophet, and counselor all in
one. If we follow his family tree along its many branches we encounter
musicians and actors, acrobats and poets, dwarfs, hunchbacks, tricksters,
madmen, and mountebanks. This chapter will view him through a prism,
resolving him into his many facets.

A RIGHT SONG AND DANCE

Keep clear of learning sir, if so you may,
Lest you should lose your pittance for the day.
Play buffoon and learn the fiddler's skill:
On great and small you may then work your will!
ᶜObeyd-e Zakani, fourteenth-century Persian poet[22]

Zakani's poem underlines the musical dimension of the jester, perhaps the
most common connection between court jesters and other entertainers.

Music provided one of the pools jester talent could be drawn from in both Europe and China and elsewhere. A description of a Ugandan jester at the turn of this century emphasizes his singing role: "The 'tomfool'—for Uganda, like the old European monarchies, always keeps a jester—was made to sing in the gruff, hoarse, unnatural voice which he ever affects to maintain his character."[23]

The Persian Abu Bakr-e Robabi, "the rebec player," was a musician and jester said to have been the director of court singers at the court of Sultan Mahmud of Ghazna (r. 998-1030), although it seems likely that he lived a century before Mahmud.[24] Both Nasrudin and Birbal (1528-83), half-historical, half-legendary jesters, had musical talents. Tamerlane (1336–1405), the Turkic conqueror remembered both for his ferocity and for the azure, turquoise, and gold mosaics of Samarkand, asked his jester Nasrudin to play the theorbo (a kind of lute) for him, and Birbal was a singer and musician as well as a joker and storyteller.[25]

Even when jesters became distinct from musicians, there were still many who were musically proficient. In Chinese, *changyou* implies a jester with musical talents. Sima Qian describes the dwarf Jester Twisty Pole (You Zhan) of the Qin dynasty (221-207 B.C.) as a *chang,* and one of the earliest named jesters in Chinese history, Jester Meng, is referred to as a *yueren,* literally "music man."[26] *Linglun,* name of the ancient Chinese god of music and music master to the legendary Yellow Emperor, is also used to denote a court jester. The jester Gradually Stretching Taller (Shen Jiangao) is so termed and was probably a musician-jester. Similarly, an epitaph to a musical entertainer begins by waxing lyrical about his personal virtues and his musical virtuosity and ends by praising his ability as a jester: "His skill in jesting, oh, there was none to surpass him!"[27]

The musical foundations of jesterdom were perhaps more widely spread in Europe, where many entertainers were poet-singers, such as bards, skalds, and troubadours. The German jester-poet Friedrich Taubmann (1565–1613) was a lute player of such skill that he was flattered by a bishop and several chaplains who likened him to a "second Orpheus," to which the jester in him quipped, "It must be true, since I also have a lot of Roman beasts [sitting] around me" ("Muß wohl sein, denn auch ich habe einen Haufen römischer Bestien um mich her sitzen"). Simplex Simplicissimus, hero of Grimmelshausen's seventeenth-century novel of the same title, is trained in the lute once he has been appointed jester.[28] Petro Mira, or Pedrillo, was an Italian violinist who came to the Russian court of Anna Ivanovna (r. 1730–40). When he had the chance to perform a solo for her, he turned it into a joke by grimacing and clowning around and was instantly appointed court jester, from which he made a tidy enough pile of money to retire comfortably.²⁹

In China, jesters seem to have emerged from a more confined source of entertainers already working in the court and certainly appear to have had their roots in court musicianship, although court entertainment often commuted between palace and public.³⁰ Hsu suggests that musical court jesters derived their song and dance from the song and dance of court ceremony but were the first to dance in the court for pure entertainment.³¹ Many jester skits are attributed to members of the Pear Orchard (Liyuan) or the Court Entertainments Bureau (Jiaofang), both established by Emperor Xuanzong (r. 712–56), traditionally the patron god of the Chinese theater and also patron of some of the most silver-tongued and musically skilled Chinese jesters. The Pear Orchard, which did not survive him, trained hundreds of court musicians, acrobats, and other entertainers. Jesters are also often described as belonging to the Music Ministry (Yuebu).³²

The musicological work *Miscellaneous Notes on the Music Bureau (Yuefu zalu)* (ca. 894) devotes a section to court jesters and their short, mocking skits and begins with a specific reference to one of the most musically proficient Chinese jesters, In Full Streamer Huang (Huang Fanchuo). Since there were originally no written scores for clappers, the emperor asked him to write one. He answered with a joke, taking a piece of paper on which he drew a pair of ears: "If you have but ears to hear you won't lose the rhythm!"³³ He is also mentioned in another musicological work, the Tang dynasty *Jie Drum Record (Jiegu lu),* for having stunned Xuanzong with his ability to guess the emperor's mood from his musical playing. One day he was summoned but failed to turn up when expected. When he did arrive, he waited outside where he could hear the emperor playing a tune, entering only when the tune was finished and a new one begun. When Xuanzong discovered that In Full Streamer had loitered outside he asked for an explanation. The jester had been using his musical ear to assess when the emperor was in a rage and when it had subsided:

> Xuanzong was amazed at his accuracy and said sternly, "How can such a slave of a court attendant know my deepest feelings from my playing? Tell me, how do I feel now?" In Full Streamer rushed down some steps, faced north in deference and bowing low shouted, "I respectfully accept Your Majesty's royal pardon." The emperor laughed and dropped the matter.

上奇之，復屬聲謂曰：『我心脾肉骨下安有侍事官奴聞小鼓能料之耶？今且謂

我如何？』綽走下階，而北鞠躬大聲曰：『奉敕豎金難！』上大笑而止。[34]

The Song dynasty jester Immortal Revelation Ding (Ding Xianxian) was a grand commissioner of the Court Entertainments Bureau at the court of Emperor Huizong (r. 1101–25). His musical skill was sufficient for him to be chosen as arbiter in deciding whether the attempted re-creation of a defunct musical mode had been a success. Someone had the bright idea that the musicians of the Court Entertainments Bureau should try to re-create the *zhi* key. Immortal Revelation pointed out that the kind of music in question had long since ceased to exist and was not within the capacity of the musicians, so it could not be re-created on a whim without giving posterity something to laugh at. Duke Lu of Cai was not amused and forced the musicians to do it:

> The musicians were hastily gathered together, and the music was performed in the chancellery courtyard while Immortal Revelation was made to stand by listening to it. When it ended, the duke looked smug and asked Immortal Revelation what he thought of it. The jester walked slowly forward, turned to look at the seated throng, and said, "Nice lyrics, shame about the tune!" The audience could not help but burst out laughing.

> 丞召眾工，按試尚書少庭，使仙現在旁聽之。樂闋，有得色，問仙現如何。仙

> 現徐前環顧坐中曰：『曲甚好，只是落韻！』坐客不覺大笑。[35]

In 1626 in the reign of Emperor Xizong (r. 1621–27) there was a jester called Advance Court King (Wang Jinchao), nicknamed Cripple King (Wang Quezi) (deformity being everywhere considered an attractive attribute in a jester), who in addition to "putting on makeup and cracking jokes" also acted as a secretary to the Bells and Drum Office (Zhonggusi), the department for palace eunuchs providing musical accompaniment at court audiences and small palace entertainments.[36] Cripple King was a jester-actor who performed in short farcical plays and yet was under the aegis of an office that was principally concerned with court music.[37] Something similar to the Bells and Drum Office can be found in England. In 1469 Edward IV (r. 1461–83) founded a guild of minstrels that was directed by his own royal minstrels, although before this there had been a court of minstrelsy that issued licenses.

There was common ground in the duties of minstrels and jesters— both provided entertainment at banquets and festivals, and both could be called on at any time of day or night to offer solace or companionship (fig. 3).[38] The crossover between the jester and the minstrel is illustrated in the court accounts of Henry VII (r. 1485–1509). On 4 October 1504 a payment of 13s. 4d. was made as a reward to "Watt the luter that pleyed the fole." By the following month his ability to act the fool seems to have made him a jester rather than a luter: on 4 November there is a payment of 10s. to "Watt the fole."[39] The medieval minstrel may also have shared the jester's paradoxical privilege of being able to judge those he served, and many minstrels composed songs of derision about unpopular matters. Like the Scandinavian skalds, Anglo-Saxon bards, and any other itinerant entertainer, minstrels, and jesters were in a position to compare different courts and to convey news between them. This, together with the information they picked up on their travels, could give them an insight into society that their more settled masters might not have.

Ministrelli, a Latin term for minstrels used in England, would include music and singing but also covered reciting epics, jesting, juggling, tumbling (one of the most skilled performers, or *saltatrix,* had the lovely name

Figure 3 A musical jester (late fifteenth century)

Matilda Makejoy), puppet shows, buffoonery, magic tricks, archery, and knife throwing.[40] According to Southworth, *menestrel,* deriving from the Latin, referred simply to a minor court servant without necessarily any musical or other entertainment function. He describes how the fluidity of functions in early medieval courts meant that a waferer (confectioner) could double as a postprandial cabaret artiste.[41]

The term *joculatores* was described by Thomas Chobham in the thirteenth century as referring to those "who sing the deeds of princes and the lives of saints and give people comfort either when they are ill or when they are troubled" ("qui cantant gesta principium et vitas sanctorum et faciunt solatia hominibus vel in egritudinibus suis vel in angustiis suis").[42] However, in England it later became a high-sounding, perhaps mocking title for the court jester, *domini regis joculator,* and this humorous association has lived on in words such as "jocular," and "joke."

The French *jongleurs* covered the same wide range of talents as the *joculatores* and *ministrelli.* They chanted or sang tales of heroic exploits *(chansons de geste),* short, mocking verse narratives *(fabliaux),* and stories of the lives of saints.[43] They were generally considered slightly second-rate wandering entertainers who were more likely to perform in the marketplace than to be affiliated with a court, unlike their higher-class equivalents the *menestrels,* although they could also perform in court on a casual basis (fig. 4). Not all the *jongleurs* were second rate—some were knights and would accompany their lords into battle, such as Taillefer, who helped psych up the warriors for the Battle of Hastings (1066) with songs about Charlemagne and Roland.[44]

In Russia the *skomorokhi,* a term that like the European *ministrelli* or *jongleur* covers a wide range of entertainers including the court jester, also performed as magicians, animal trainers, and puppeteers and "were certainly part of the counterculture that existed beneath the surface of officialdom."[45] Their origins lie with the Byzantine mime entertainers and the *Spielmänner* who came from Europe in the tenth or eleventh century. They began as wandering entertainers but could also be found in the houses of nobles, and Czar Ivan IV (Ivan the Terrible) (r. 1533–84) was the first to keep them at court. The court jester *skomorokhi* became known as *Spielmen,* and they were loved for their uninhibited mockery of the church and other institutions. They were immensely popular, and their golden age coincides with that of the European jester from the fifteenth to the seventeenth century, although it was curtailed in 1649 by imperial ordinances that, together with persecution by the church, caused them to decline as a profession.[46]

Figure 4 Doré's Rabelasian minstrels

The origins of the European jester lie in all these variations on the theme of an entertainer—*ministrelli, joculatores,* and *jongleurs* who had inherited from both the northern bardic traditions and the southern *mimi* and *histriones* who ambled around the Roman world. A medieval jester could be referred to by any of these terms, with specific words for jester being variations on the theme of "fool," or *stultus,* and "jester" appearing more from the sixteenth century. From the fourteenth century there was a trend toward greater specialization, with minstrels becoming more distinct from jesters, although this did not preclude a jester's boasting any or all of the talents he might have had in earlier times. A similar move toward specialization occurred in China as early as the late Spring and Autumn Period (770–476 B.C.), so that the formal (as opposed to impromptu) musical, singing, and dancing elements of the jester were increasingly taken over by others.[47]

Despite much common ground between them, the court jester was distinct from musicians, actors, and other entertainers by being singled out of the multitude and closely identified with a king, emperor, or other person of high social or political standing, by having far greater privileges of free speech and ready access, and by virtue of his salient characteristics of humor and forthrightness. Given a quick and fearless tongue, a repertoire of jokes and anecdotes, and endless erumpent humor combined with either some physical feat or a deformity, a would-be royal merrymaker would just have to catch the monarch's eye and make him laugh to be assured of a job for life.

"Is It Not Said That Poets Are Fools?"

["Ne dit-on pas que les poètes sont fous?"]

Gabriel Antoine Joseph Hécart, *Stultitiana* (1823)[48]

> Well (quoth one of the jury), if we cannot finde the foole we looke for amongst these fooles before named, one of us will be the foole: for in my minde, there cannot be a verier foole in the world then is a poet; . . . therefore we thinke fit to have a parliament of poets, and to enact such lawes and statutes, as may proove beneficial to the commonwelth of Jacke of Dovers motly coated fooles.
>
> *Jacke of Dovers Quest of Inquirie* (1604)[49]

The jester is often associated with the poet. The Russian *skomorokhi* were influenced by the Kiev court poets *(gusliari),* and when written literature started to replace the oral tradition the poet's court function sometimes merged with that of the jester.[50] In Europe the connection may be due to the bardic origins of the jester, or it may be that both poet and jester are able to present a different angle or interpretation of reality—the position of court jester was on occasion filled by the court poet. There were men in the Italian Renaissance courts who were halfway between poet and jester.[51] The French court poet Andrelini inherited the post of jester from Seigni Johan. He was renowned for his ugliness and was the first *poeta regius,* an equivocal title brought to life under the popular monarch Louis XII (r. 1498–1515) and translated into French as *fou du roi.* He "appears also to have enjoyed somewhat of the license and privilege of the jester, for he uttered bitter satires against the theologians at a time when to attack them was to run the risk of death. And yet Andrelini shot his bolts with impunity."[52]

In Ireland the poet has always enjoyed high status, and in the past the power of his words meant he was as much feared as revered, descended as he was from the Celtic bards whose influence could "persuade armies poised for attack to cease hostilities."[53] Like the jester, the Irish court poets could be sent on missions for their master or could accompany him to war.[54] They are often linked with the *druith,* or jester. The poet, like the jester, could advise and admonish the chieftain. It was believed that words could cause not only shame but actual physical harm, almost like a magic spell, and often it was enough for the poet to threaten the chieftain with "the blisters of reproach or disgrace" to make him mend his ways.[55] In *A Vewe of the Present State of Irelande* (ca. 1596), Edmund Spenser describes their power:

> Theare is amongst the Irishe a certen kinde of people Called Bardes which are to them in steade of Poets whose profession is to sett fourthe the praises and dispraises of menne in their Poems or Rymes, the which are hadd in soe highe regard and estimation amongest them that none dare displease them for feare to runne into reproch throughe their offence.[56]

In the Irish story "The Death of Fergus Mac Leide" (ca. 1100), Esirt, the court poet of the leprechaun king Iubhdan, very much resembles a jester in his scoffing forthrightness. When the king asks his courtiers at a banquet to confirm that he is the greatest king, and that his horses and fighters are the best, they fawningly agree in unison, ignorant of the diminutive size of the leprechauns. Except Esirt, who sets out to show the king the folly of his arrogance:

> "Have you ever seen a king that was better than myself?" And they answered, "We have not." "Have you ever seen a strong man better than my strong man?" "We have not." "Horses or men of battle have you ever seen better than they which to-night are in this house?" "By our word," they made answer, "we never have". . . . All which when he had heard, the king's chief poet Esirt burst out laughing.[57]

He is arrested for his mockery but persuades the king to give him three days to prove he has good reason to question the flattery of the courtiers. He makes his way to the court of Fergus, king of Ulster, to whom he displays an equal lack of awe despite being the size of Fergus's finger. Fergus comments on what "a flippant and a mocking fellow" he is, also noting that like a jester he is "an approved man of veracity."[58]

The jesters of Scandinavia probably originated with the skalds, whose verses often had a double meaning. The skald was closer to the jester than the minstrel in that he shared the license to speak freely—one type in particular was very close, being a poet "skilled—or feared—as a maker of lampoons *(niovisur)*." Skalds flourished from about the ninth century to the fourteenth, and the names of some 250 are still known. In one saga we are told that one of the greatest Scandinavian warriors, Harald I of Norway (Harald Fairhair, r. ca. 870 – ca. 930), valued his skalds more than any of his other followers.[59] Skalds often had a close relationship with the king that very much resembles the tight-knit jester-king duo, and

> there frequently sprang up a relation of devotion and friendship—
> the prince on his part honoring and respecting the skald, often mak-
> ing him his confidential adviser and plenipotentiary; the poet in his
> turn aiding him with friendly and sincere counsel. He was hardly ever
> found among those who flattered and humored the king. In fact, it
> is characteristic of the skalds that they knew how to preserve their
> independence of opinion and maintain an attitude of frankness and
> self-possession which inspired respect.

He had the jester's right to criticize, apparently with the same fine balance between pleasing and displeasing the king with his honesty.[60] His determined independence and refusal to be cowed by power are also qualities of a jester. He seems to have had the same easy access to the king, although one poem complains that since the king has become more important, the skald cannot reach him through all the courtiers surrounding him. The king thereby ensures that room is made for him and gives him leave to speak:

> Thickly throng ye round the
> thane so young, ye good men—
> push me back from peerless
> prince, whose speech I need, though:
> easier access had I,
> Olaf, to you when through
> wet snow, weary both, we
> waded, on Dovre Mountain.[61]

The seventeenth-century Friedrich Taubmann was both a court poet and a jester to Duke Friedrich Wilhelm of Weimar, by whom he was well loved, and he was frequently invited to the table of Elector Christian II of Saxony. His poems showed great humor, and he had the jester's freedom to come and go. He also used his wit to make the duke behave more humanely and to expose corruption.[62] The Persian poet ʿObeyd-e Zakani (fl. fourteenth century) was known as a kind of jester because of his satirical criticism of Persian society. Hafez (d. 1390), a poet contemporary with Zakani, used his wit to attack the "extravagances of religious zealots and hypocritical divines," both plum targets for any jester.[63] The Indian poet

Tolan was "said to have been the jester and companion to King Kulasekharavarman (eleventh century?)." Birbal, close friend and jester to Akbar
the Great, in addition to being a gifted musician and storyteller, was also
given the title of Hindu poet laureate.[64] Siegel describes him as "a poor
brahmin writer of Hindi verse who, through the exuberance of his wit and
the tirelessness of his charm, became one of Akbar's favorite courtiers. In
folk legends, told aloud throughout north India, the courtier had become
a royal jester, a trickster in the court, a joker in the deck."[65]

The connection between the jester and the poet worked both ways, and
the qualifications of a good jester included the ability to extemporize verse
and trot out rhyming retorts or cringe-inspiring doggerel. Poetic skill was
a vital part of the jester's ragbag of tricks at all times and in all places. The
Elizabethan comic actor and jester Richard Tarlton was so renowned for
his ability to extemporize witty verse that he gave his name to a verb, "to
tarltonize," and William Kemp, another Shakespearian clown actor, was
also known for this ability. Actors such as Kemp, needing the actual skills
of the jester rather than the ability simply to play the part from a script,
came very close to being jesters in their own right.

A frequent pastime involving jesters was verse capping, in which one
person supplied the first line and the second would complete the couplet,
preferably with suitable rhymes and parallels. Jesters often used the second
line to offer a witty comment on the first, or simply a ridiculous match.
The poet-jester Camillo Querno, whose wine would be watered down if
he made an error in his versifying, engaged in bouts of verse capping with
Pope Leo X, the pope apparently being the wittier.[66] In Samuel Rowley's
play *When You See Me You Know Me* (1604) there are several examples of
verse capping between the jester Will Somers and Henry VIII, Cardinal
Wolsey (ca. 1475–1530), and the Holy Roman Emperor.[67] Henry begins
with "The bud is spread, the Rose is red, the leafe is green," which Somers
parries with "A wench 'tis sed, was found in your bed, besides / the Queene"
(lines 3044–46). The king tries again: "In yonder Tower, theres a flower,
that hath my heart"; Somers ripostes with "Within this houre, she pist full
sower, & let a fart" (lines 3054–55). When the emperor decides to have a
go, he is no more successful than Henry. Somers first bursts the bubble of
imperial pride before reverting to ribaldry:

> *Emperor.* An Emperour is greate, high is his seate, who is his foe?
> *Somers.* The wormes that shall eate, his carkas for meate, whether he
>   will or no.
> *Emperor.* A ruddy lip, with a cherry tip, is fit for a King.

Somers. I, so he may dip, about her hip, i'th tother thing.

(lines 3058–62)

A sixteenth-century Spanish miscellany describes how Gabriel la Mena, jester to Don Fadrique Enríque, admiral of Castille, used an impromptu poem to be rid of a bothersome noble. He was playing chess with the duke of Alba and was being pestered by the duke's brother, commander-in-chief of León. The commander refused to leave, and Gabriel became exasperated, saying, "Leave us, or I'll tell you six things that are wrong with you" ("Dejadnos, sino deciros he seis tachas que tenéis"). The commander promised not to say another word if Gabriel told him his six faults. The jester looked at him and promptly summarized his shortcomings in verse, for which he was rewarded six ducats:

> One, you never stop demanding;
> Two, you never give,
> Three, you're always reprimanding,
> Four, you always persist.
> Five, you happen to be wearing
> A doublet all greasy,
> Six, you now appear like
> A thief with concrete feet.
>
> [La primera que pedís;
> La segunda que no dais,
> La tercera que reñís,
> La quarta que porfiais.
> Y la quinta que traeis
> El jubón lleno de grasa,
> La sexta que pareceís
> Pisada de gato en masa.][68]

Hideyoshi (1536–98), Japan's greatest general, asked his jester Sorori to celebrate *in verse* his having tricked the man who unified Japan into giving him an exceptionally large reward for cheering him up.[69] The Chinese jester Upright Fellow Wish (Zhu Hanzhen)—later flogged and banished for accepting a bribe—served several emperors with his great humor and an ability to trip seven-character-line poems off the tongue at a moment's notice. When the emperor's attention was caught by something, he would "suddenly order him to come up with a poem about it which he would do quick as a flash, as though he already had one up his sleeve, which particularly delighted the emperor."[70]

Moving Bucket (Shi Dongtong), jester of Emperor Gaozu (r. 550–59) of the Northern Qi, was exceptionally gifted in oral wit and could run rings around scholars and clerics. The emperor was once reading from Xiao Tong's (501–31) great *Anthology of Literature (Wenxuan)* and sighed appreciatively over a poem titled "Wandering Immortal" ("You xian shi"), by Guo Pu (276–324). Moving Bucket reckoned he could easily improve on the poem:

> Moving Bucket stood up and said, "What's so great about this poem? If you ask me, I could compose one twice as good." Gaozu was displeased and said, "Just who d'you think you are? Telling us you can write a poem twice as good as Guo Pu's! You deserve the chop for that." Moving Bucket then said, "Right, Your Majesty just needs to ask me to compose a poem and if it isn't twice as good as Guo Pu's then I'll gladly agree to give you my head!" The emperor ordered him to do it. Moving Bucket said, "Guo Pu's poem about a wandering immortal says, 'Halfway along the clear stream, stretching for a thousand ells or more, there is a Daoist master.' Well, I say, 'Halfway along the clear stream, stretching for two thousand ells, there are two Daoist masters.' How can that not be twice as good?" Only then did Gaozu have a good laugh about it.

> 石動筩起曰：『此詩有何能？若令臣作即勝伊一倍。』高祖不悅，曰：『汝是何人？自言作詩能勝郭璞一倍，豈不合死？』動筩即云：『大家即令臣作，若不勝一倍，甘心合死。』即令作之，動筩曰：『郭璞游仙詩云：青溪千餘仞，中有一道士。臣作云：青溪二千仞，中有二道士。豈不勝伊一倍？』高祖始大笑。[71]

Newly Polished Mirror (Jing Xinmo) was also skilled in versifying. When the prince of Qin presented a poem he had composed, the emperor showed it to the jester, who praised it and then made the emperor laugh with a little joke about the prince's understandably being good at poetry since his "old man" had liked it all his life too.[72] He also presented a declamation at a banquet to celebrate the snow that had fallen outside, and when an allegedly six-eyed turtle was sent to the court as tribute, he made up a rhyme:

> Roll up, roll up, still your noise, hear this six-eyed turtle ditty!
> With my peepers half a dozen I'm worth three sleepers when a-dozin'.

不要鬧，不要鬧！

聽取龜兒口號：

六雙眼兒睡一覺，

抵別人三覺。[73]

The Tang dynasty musician-jester In Full Streamer was also able to produce short rhymes off the cuff. A mandarin called Liu Wenshu was renowned for his rhetoric and excelled at addressing memorials to the throne. He also had a long beard that made him look like a kind of ape, which, combined with his eagerness to admonish, made him a harangue-utang asking to be mocked, which the emperor ordered In Full Streamer to do. Wenshu hated being nicknamed an ape and secretly bribed the jester not to do it. In Full Streamer succeeded both in fulfilling the emperor's request and in honoring his bribe—just. The emperor knew about the bribe and burst out laughing to see how he circumvented it with a verse ending, "Not that I look like a chimpanzee, no, it's the chimpanzee looks just like me!"[74]

Emperor Zhuangzong of the Later Tang (r. 923–26) gave a little party at which fresh oranges were presented, and he commanded all his entertainers to compose poems about it. Tang Chaomei (whose name could sound like Best at Mocking) was the first to finish a verse with a pun using the oranges as a metaphor for the prime minister and his "eight or nine brothers," presumably hangers-on, daring the emperor to have the prime minister peeled—in other words, to have his followers and trappings of office removed. The emperor at least took the point, as he laughed loudly and rewarded the jester with the golden goblet he had been using:

> Golden and fragrant appears the great minister
> With his eight or nine little brothers,
> Rip off his pips, peel pith and kin,
> Will you be the man to do such a thing?

金香大丞相，

兄弟八九人。

剝皮去渾子，

若個是如人？[75]

When the poet Li Shen (772–846) occupied Guangling, Zheng Dan was his subordinate. In 844 Can gave a banquet for Li Shen. Entertainment was provided by an aging dancer. The jester Many Grandsons (Sunzi

Duo) thought up a rhyming jingle about this, giving Li Shen a good laugh. He used a pun on the name of a previous empress, A Wu Po, which with a twist and a shake of characters became A Po Wu, referring to the elderliness of the dancer:

> His Lordship is versed in the arts and in war,
> His faithful servant loves all things present and past,
> They've heard that in former days there was A Wu Po
> And now with their own eyes, they see Old Granny Prance.

> 相公經文復經武，
>
> 常侍好今又好古。
>
> 昔日曾聞阿武婆，
>
> 如今親眼阿婆舞！[76]

A musician-jester of the Southern Tang (a short-lived state lasting from 937 to 975), was aptly named Subtle Reformer King (Wang Ganhua). He was on the Music Census Register (Yueji) of Guangzhou, and he entered the Court Entertainments Bureau in the capital, Jinling. The *General Compendium of Poetry Critiques (Shihua zonggui)* by Ruan Yue (fl. ca. 1082), which has a section devoted to jesters, describes him as being "good with words, witty and nimble tongued, and endlessly humorous" and gives several of the impromptu poems he trotted out at banquets, either at royal command or on his own. One composition was at a farewell banquet for a regional commander who was being replaced, when Subtle Reformer King was the first to offer a short verse to wave him off and welcome the new incumbent:

> With your banners and flags you leave for Tiantai,
> Over streams and mountains a dawn colored sky,
> Ten thousand families in spirits low and high,
> To welcome one Buddha and to another. . . . "Bye-bye!"

> 旌旆赴天台，
>
> 溪山曉色開。
>
> 萬家悲更喜，
>
> 迎佛送如來！[77]

A more famous jester of the Southern Tang, Adding Clarity Li (Li Jiaming), who brought lucidity and laughter to the imperial household, used verse to a more serious end.[78] When Emperor Yuanzong (r. 943–61) moved to the southern capital, sailing along by the southern bank of the

Yangtze River (Changjiang), he had already lost fourteen provinces to the north of the river. When he reached Zhaotun he stopped the music and drinking of his entourage and gazed northward to the Duke Wan Mountains (Wangongshan), commenting to his jester how green and steep were the row upon row of mountains and wondering what they were called. Adding Clarity answered with an improvised poem reminding the emperor of the territories he had lost, so that he hung his head in shame as they passed.[79] On another occasion he used his poetic skills to cheer up the emperor, one of the vital functions of the jester. Yuanzong invited his close ministers to go fishing, and between them they caught dozens of huge fish. Only the emperor failed to catch anything, so Adding Clarity made up a ditty about it. "The emperor was delighted and rewarded them all with a banquet, and there was great merriment."[80]

The association of the jester with the poet can also be seen in his often acting as a mocking judge of other people's poetry. The Spanish jester Estebanillo González, who served Ottavio Piccolomini (1599–1656), duke of Amalfi and one of the most powerful people in Spain as well as a key player in the Thirty Years' War (1618–48), used poetry to mock the pretensions of others. He entered a poetry competition and deliberately wrote an incomprehensible sonnet that won first prize because since nobody could understand it they thought it must be good ("y celebrándolo por no entenderlo").[81]

In the Tiansheng reign-period (1023–32) of Emperor Renzong a banquet was held at which poems were to be presented, the rhyming scheme to follow the word *paihuai*, "dithering." Jesters put on a skit using the various meanings of the word. A group of them wandered about aimlessly and said they were "loitering" *(paihuai)*. Then they started looking behind them, and when asked what they were doing, they all said "hesitating" *(paihuai)*. Another one laughed and said, "That's all very well, but there's too much 'dithering' going on around here!" perhaps mocking the stilted versifying.[82] When an ornamental rock was presented to the palace, Renzong ordered that poems be composed to praise its beauty. Among those submitted there was a lot of shoddy drivel, prompting a skit. The jester acted

as though he were reciting a poem. He suddenly tripped over an edging stone and fell flat on his face and everybody rushed to help him up. Once he was standing he said, "For several days I've been trying to compose this nature poem in response to the imperial command, but I just keep being tripped up by this rock!" Everybody had a good laugh.

若吟詠狀。其一人忽仆於界石上，眾赴掖起之。即起曰：『數日來作一首賞花
釣魚詩，準備應制，卻被這石頭擦倒！』左右皆大笑。[83]

Su Dongpo (1036–1101), one of the greatest Chinese poets, saw fit to
ask Immortal Revelation for his opinion, the same jester we have seen act
as an arbiter in a musical context. Su and Liu Yong (fl. ca. 1045) were both
famous for writing *ci* poems (lyrics composed for existing tunes), and Su
asked Immortal Revelation how his compared with Liu's. The jester said
Liu's would lose any competition with Su's poem that had generals, bronze
lutes, and iron clappers while Liu's just had a load of women singing. Not
surprisingly, "Su clapped his hands—*the words of jesters always contain
sound judgment.*"[84]

There are other anecdotes relating to Su Dongpo and jesters. Su wore
a kind of hat that was named after him. Some jesters were boasting at a
feast about how well they wrote, but Immortal Revelation dismissed their
efforts: "'You lot can't even begin to write as well as I do!' The others all
asked why not. 'Two heads are better than one, can't you see I've got a Su
Dongpo on mine!' The emperor was amused."[85] On one occasion Su attended a banquet at which jesters were employing every kind of trick,
none of which made him laugh. The jesters adapted a line of Su's to cure
his po-face:

> A jester suddenly appeared brandishing a club with which he began
> cudgelling the performers while yelling at them, "The Hanlin Aca-
> demician [Su Dongpo] is not laughing, and you call yourselves fine
> jesters!" Another jester answered, "It's not that he's not *laughing*, it's
> that in *not laughing* he's *laughing* all the more!" Dongpo then burst
> out laughing.

一優突出，用棒痛打作技者曰：『內翰不笑，汝猶稱良優乎！』對曰：『非不
笑也，不笑者乃所以深笑之也！』坡遂大笑。[86]

"DWARFS AND HUNCHBACKS WERE ALWAYS JESTERS"
Discussions of the States (Guo yu)[87]

Gentlemen, a million dwarfs. Do you have any idea what kind of
strength there is in that? Do you understand the power that repre-
sents? It would be enough for one dwarf to hide under the table at
every government meeting in the world—and there's nothing easier
—and we'll have all the secrets of the world. Gentlemen, do you

understand what that means? Who will be able to thwart the plans of the next Hitler? We will, gentlemen, we dwarfs.

Avigdor Dagan, *The Court Jesters* [88]

Having dwarfs and hunchbacks in attendance at one's side is like keeping company with mischievous children.

Discussions of the States [89]

A quick-witted mind could be complemented by nimble-footed capering or set off by some appealing deformity. Dwarfs, with or without humps on their backs, have enjoyed universal popularity (fig. 5). Francis Bacon's (1561–1626) essay on deformity comments that such people "will, if they be of spirit, seek to free themselves from scorn . . . and therefore let it not be marvelled if sometimes they prove excellent persons." [90] This is borne out by many stories of dwarf and hunchback jesters. Could there be a connection between the hunch of the hunchback, and the almost prophetic insight or hunches occasionally attributed to jesters? Although less common, hunchbacks had a status similar to that of dwarfs, and like them were prime candidates for the position of court jester—a stock figure in Sanskrit

Figure 5 *Dwarf with Dog and Bird,* sketched from a painting by Eugène Dévéria (1805–65)

literature is the female hunchback servant who could be a confidante to a queen.[91]

The earliest reference to a court jester is in ancient Egypt during the Sixth Dynasty (ca. 2323–2150 B.C.) during the reign of Neferkere (Pepi II). An official wrote to tell him he had discovered a dancing dwarf, and it seems that "pygmies were welcomed at the courts of the pharaohs because, in their dancing, they celebrated the rising each day of the sun-god Re."[92] The pharaoh answered:

> Thou hast said in this thy letter that thou hast brought a dancing dwarf from the land of spirits, like the dwarf which the treasurer of the god Burded brought from Punt in the time of Isesi. . . . Come northward to the court immediately; thou shalt bring this dwarf with thee . . . for the dances of the god, to rejoice and gladden the heart of the king of Upper and Lower Egypt, Neferkere, who lives for ever.[93]

Egyptian grottoes at Beni Hassan also feature sculptures of dwarfs and deformed men in the entourages of the rich, suggesting that they were kept in courts as early as 3,500 years ago. The Egyptians carried small terra-cotta figures of a dwarf-god as amulets against evil, and in Rome people also carried good luck charms in the form of bronze dwarfs, a custom continued in Italy in the form of hunchback *gobbi,* since touching the hump is considered lucky.[94] When Priscus was sent as an envoy to Attila the Hun (d. 453) he was entertained by a dwarf, and in "the caves of Cannara, Ambola, and Elephanta, in the East Indies . . . were discovered many figures of deformed dwarfs."[95] Dwarfs were often the subjects of portraits by the court painter—Van Dyck painted the English queen, Henrietta Maria (1609–69), with her dwarf Sir Hudson (b. 1619), who was sent on missions on her behalf.[96] Velasquez painted several dwarfs at the Spanish court of Philip IV (r. 1621–65), and in Italy such paintings were also common.[97]

In modern times dwarfs have been immensely popular in circuses, usually as part of the clown troupe, and in Senegal a music video produced as part of an AIDS prevention campaign featured a dancing dwarf—wait for it—"dressed as an HIV particle."[98] And two of the best-loved Chinese jesters, Twisty Pole and Shi, were dwarfs *(zhuru),* as was Archy Armstrong, jester to James I (r. 1603–25), "a yard high and a nayle, no more, his stature" as Armin says of another Scottish jester.[99] The *shi* of Jester Shi's name is also part of the classical Chinese term for hunchback, and it is possible his name would have derived from such a deformity. In "The Death of Fergus Mac Leide," referred to above, the leprechaun court poet Esirt takes his newfound friend Aedh to meet his king. The king asks who this giant is and Esirt answers, "No giant is he, but Ulster's poet and man of science, and the king's dwarf."[100] In the French court accounts of 1319 there is listed the purchase of thirty-two pairs of shoes for "the queen's dwarf" ("le nain de la royne"), and in 1543 Catherine de' Medici (1519–89) gave a dress with taffeta and silver trimmings to the female dwarf of the visiting queen of Hungary.[101]

The great Aztec king Montezuma II (1466–1520) was an enthusiastic keeper of jesters, and every mention of them points to their having been deformed in some way, giving the impression that no man wholly sound of body could make it as an Aztec jester. Bernal Diaz de Castillo (1492–1591), who visited Montezuma's court, tells us that "sometimes some little humpbacked dwarfs would be present at his meals, whose bodies seemed almost to be broken in the middle. These were his jesters" (fig. 6).[102] Francisco Clavigero (1731–87) echoes and expands on this, confirming the charitable element also apparent in European courts:

> Montezuma who was not satisfied with having every sort of animal in his palace, also collected there all irregularly formed men, who either from the colour of their hair, or of their skin, or some other deformity in their persons, were oddities of their species. A humour this, however, not unattended with beneficial consequences, as it gave maintenance to a number of miserable objects, and delivered them from the inhuman insults of their other fellow-creatures.[103]

Figure 6 A Mayan hunchback

Similarly, at the court of Suleiman I (Suleiman the Magnificent, r. 1520–66), sultan of the Ottoman Empire at the time of its greatest glory, dwarfs were cherished but could earn even greater favor if their dwarfism were complemented by deafness and dumbness. A French travelogue by Tournefort, *Voyage du Levant* (1717), shows Turkish jesters in all their glorious grotesqueness:

> The dwarfs are real little monkeys pulling a thousand grimaces between them or together with the mutes to make the Sultan laugh, this prince often honoring them with a kick. And when a dwarf is found who was born deaf and is consequently mute, he is regarded like the phoenix of the palace, more admired than the most handsome man in the world, particularly if this ape is a eunuch. Yet these three flaws, which ought to render a man contemptible, instead combine, in the eyes and judgement of the Turks, to form the most perfect of creatures.

> [Les nains sont de vrais singes qui font mille grimaces entre eux, ou avec les muets pour faire rire le sultan, et ce Prince les honore souvent de quelques coups de pied. Lorsqu'il se trouve un nain qui est né sourd, et par conséquent muet, il est regardé comme le Phoenix du Palais: on l'admire plus qu'on ne ferait le plus bel homme du monde, surtout si ce magot est Eunuque: cependant ces trois défauts qui devraient rendre un homme très méprisable, forment la plus parfaite de toutes les créatures, aux yeux et au jugement des Turcs.][104]

However, perhaps the most misshapen dwarf-jester on record was Mr. Little, serving the king of Siam as capering, juggling jester. Anna Leonowens

> found him revolting. His head was covered with woolly hair, his forehead was low and receding, his eyes were set close like those of an ape, and were wild and rolling. From his enormous mouth two great teeth protruded. His ears were large, his chin sharp and pointed. He was only a few inches more than three feet tall, and his legs were so short that except for the immense flat feet they seemed hardly strong enough to support his huge head and square shoulders.

Nevertheless she did allow that even a hideous appearance can be matched with skill and delicacy:

> It was this creature who now approached the beautifully appointed table and picked up a tureen of soup which he began to juggle au-

daciously to the breathless amazement of the guests. . . . Nothing spilled![105]

Dwarfs were commonly part of a noble's retinue—William I (r. 1066–87) kept them as pages, as did many of his contemporaries, and they could also be used to hold the king's horse in a procession.[106] Philip II of Spain (r. 1556–98) was accompanied by a host of dwarfs when he visited England.[107] They could be kept simply for novelty value, and this may have been the case for the most part in the Roman courts, just as in eighteenth- and even early nineteenth-century European high society dwarfs enjoyed great popularity because of their diminutive size, though if they were witty or charming into the bargain then so much the better. A nineteenth-century travel writer described the immense popularity of dwarfs among Russian nobles, giving the impression they were doted on like spoiled pets.[108]

That dwarfs could be found in every environment that might have jesters is not to suggest they all were jesters. Many jesters were dwarfs, but not all dwarfs were jesters, although dwarfism would be an asset to an aspiring jester and the two do often overlap. Perhaps the dwarf is singled out for his distinctive appearance, and this may give him a perspective on the world, literally as well as figuratively, that is different from that of most people around him. The twelfth-century poet Geoffrey Gaimar records in his *Lestorie des Engles* the assassination of the English king Edward the Martyr (ca. 963–78), lured to his death by his dwarf, who clearly had the entertaining skills of the jester:

> He had a dwarf named Wolstanet
> Who could dance and play.
> He could leap and pipe,
> And play many other tricks.
> The king saw him, called him,
> And ordered him to play.
> The dwarf said he would not,
> He would not play at his order.
>
> (lines 3991–98)[109]

In China it often seems to have been taken for granted that "dwarf" *(zhuru)* could be synonymous with "jester" *(youren)* and that as such a dwarf was as likely to give humorously indirect advice as a jester. The Chinese Legalist philosopher Han Fei (280–233 B.C.) gives such an account:

> In the time of Duke Ling of Wei, Mi Zixia was the favorite. A dwarf had an audience with the duke and said, "My dream has come true."

The duke asked him about it. "I dreamed I saw a stove, which is why I sought an audience with Your Highness." The duke said angrily, "I heard that before someone has an audience with their ruler, they dream of the sun, so how can you be coming to see me because you dreamed of a stove?" The dwarf said, "The sun shines over everything under heaven, and there is nothing that can block its light; a ruler shines over the whole country, and no one person can block him. That is why people who have an audience with their ruler dream of the sun. As for the stove, if one man cooks in front of it, the people behind cannot see its light. Perhaps someone is cooking in front of Your Highness? Could that be why I dreamed of a stove, perhaps?" The duke said "Spot on!" and sent away [his favorite] Yong Chu, dismissed Mi Zixia, and employed [the virtuous and able] Si-kong Gou.

衛靈之時，彌子瑕有寵於衛國。侏儒有見公者，曰：『臣之夢踐矣。』公曰：『奚夢？』『夢見竈者爲見公也。』公怒，曰：『吾聞見人主者，夢見日，奚爲見寡人而夢見竈乎？』侏儒曰：『夫日兼照天下，一物不能當也，人君兼照一國，一人不能壅也，故將見人主，而夢日也，夫竈，一人燖焉，則後人無從見矣，或者一人燖君耶，則臣雖夢竈，不亦可乎？』公曰：『善！』　遂去壅鉏，退彌子瑕而用司空狗。。。則侏儒之未見也，君壅而不知其壅也，已見之後，而知其壅也。

Han Fei commented on the skill of the dwarf in waking the duke to the folly of favoritism, adding that "if the dwarf had not made him see, the ruler would have been blocked without knowing it; whereas no sooner had he opened his eyes than he realized he had been blocked and so dismissed the ministers who had stood between him and the rest of the country." [110] Suetonius (ca. 70–ca. 130) tells us of a dwarf who addressed Emperor Tiberius (r. 14–37) with all the brazen forthrightness of a jester. Tiberius was

> suddenly asked in a loud voice by one of the dwarfs that stood beside the table among the jesters why Paconius, who was charged with treason, remained so long alive; the emperor at the time chided him for his saucy tongue, but a few days later wrote to the senate to decide as soon as possible about the execution of Paconius.

> [interrogatum eum subito et clare a quodam nano astante mensae inter copreas, cur Paconius maiestatis reus tam diu viveret, statim

quidem petulantiam linguae obiurgasse, ceterum post paucos dies scripsisse senatui, ut de poena Paconi quam primum statueret.][111]

Many Tang dynasty clay figures show dwarfs in comic stances, as does a bronze figure of the second century B.C., and there is no reason these should not have been jesters.[112] Dwarfs were sent from a certain district as annual tribute to the court (fig. 7), and Knechtges suggests that the district or country referred to was probably Jiaoyao, where a tribe of the Man people lived, and says "the dwarfs were unquestionably foreigners."[113] Bai Juyi (772–846) wrote a poem titled "The People of Daozhou" ("Daozhou min"), drawing attention to the plight of the dwarfs, who were often coerced into serving at court.[114] This is not to suggest that Chinese court dwarfs were always treated as being "beneath beneath contempt."[115] Dongfang Shuo (154–93 B.C.), one of the greatest courtier-jesters of China and a great favorite of Wudi of the Han (r. 140–87 B.C.), was rebuked by the emperor for deliberately frightening the court dwarfs. In his defense he complained that they undeservedly received the same allowances as he. In addition, some of the most doted-on Chinese jesters were dwarfs, as we will see.

The popularity of dwarfs was so great that in Europe and South America the practice of artificially stunting children arose to keep up with demand, and it was already noted in Rome.[116] According to a miscellany of 1670, dwarfs could be created by anointing babies' spines with the grease of bats, moles, and dormice, while more palatable prescriptions used drugs such as the aptly named dwarf elder, knotgrass, and daisy juice and roots mixed with milk to stunt growth. Children were kidnapped or bought to be turned into artificial dwarfs, and it was in Italy and Spain that the practice was most common, its perpetrators in Spain being called *comprachicos,* or "child-buyers."[117] The practice was clearly known in England, as Lysander in *A Midsummer Night's Dream* (1600) testifies:

> Get you gone, you dwarf;
> You minimus, of hindering knot-grass made;
> You bead, you acorn!
>
> (3.2.327–29)[118]

In the time of Montezuma poor Aztecs would also stunt their children in the hope of improving their chances in life. Or death. It was believed that the existence of both dwarfs and hunchbacks was ordained by the sun— glorious except for the unfortunate repercussion that when the sun was in

Figure 7 Pygmies could be sent to the Chinese court as tribute

distress, his "children" would be sacrificed, the natural supply then having to be artificially supplemented.[119]

In India dwarfs had auspicious connotations and could be found in the court.[120] The *vidusaka,* principal comic character of Sanskrit drama and to all intents and purposes a court jester, was described in the second-century B.C. classic of dramaturgy the *Natyasastra* as preferably both dwarfish and hunchbacked. Just as a dwarf or hunchback was often believed to deflect evil, fools of mental deficiency could have been kept partly to protect the king, to ward off the evil eye.[121] This notion of averting the evil eye is raised by Shulman in his observations of Tamil village clowns of southern India, who could be used to provoke improvident forces, airing rather than averting them.[122]

In addition, deformity may have been a reminder to the ruler of his own not so apparent shortcomings. Siegel suggests that "corporeal disfiguration provides the comic metaphor for spiritual deformity, intellectual misproportion, psychological rigidity, or emotional awkwardness."[123] Perhaps because their experience of life gives them a different perspective, people of physical abnormality would also share the detachment vital to jesters. In addition they were often the most willing to tell a king what others dared not, and they could do so without threatening him, since a dwarf or hunchback could not physically look down on a king. Imperfection in a jester would enable him to jokingly point out imperfection in his master: "I know I'm not perfect, but have you looked at yourself recently?"

> Whosoever hath any thing fixed in his person that doth induce contempt, hath also a perpetual spur . . . to rescue and deliver himself from scorn. Therefore, all deformed persons are extreme bold. . . . Also, it stirreth in them industry, and especially of this kind, to watch and observe the weakness of others, that they may have somewhat to repay. Again, in their superiors, it quencheth jealousy towards them.[124]

"Everything Is Folly in This World Except to Play the Fool"
["Tutto è follia in questo mondo fuorchè il folleggiare"]
Giacomo Leopardi, *Zibaldone*[125]

> Everyone was dazed by him even though—and maybe because—no one was sure how seriously to take his words. Sometimes he sounded like a prophet and sometimes like a mocking chatterbox, like a real court jester who had everything but those little bells that clowns used to wear on their hats and sleeves in real courts centuries ago.
> Avigdor Dagan, *The Court Jesters*[126]

The principal factor that seems to set the European tradition apart from the Chinese (and Middle Eastern and Indian), is the obsession with fools and folly that permeated the length and breadth of European society during the Middle Ages and Renaissance. To simplify the phenomenon, the court jester in Europe seems to have developed from a view of the world that became intricately woven into the fabric of medieval and Renaissance being. The difference between medieval and Renaissance attitudes to folly may be summed up in the fact that Brant's *Ship of Fools (Das Narrenschiff)* (1494) places Wisdom in the pulpit, from which he admonishes the foolish audience.[127] In Erasmus's *Praise of Folly (Encomium moriae)* (1515), it is Folly herself who takes the floor and mocks an audience of supposedly wise and eminent men.[128] It seems that with the Renaissance some of the ambivalence toward the fool dissolved and judgment came down on his side. Erasmus's work may have marked the watershed in the transition, since it featured a fool praising folly.[129]

The interpretations of "folly" encompassed a vast spectrum, from the fool as sinner to the fool as the innocent closest to God. The medieval fool was also often identified with the devil, as a German proverb states: "Where there is dancing and capering, there is the devil" ("Wa man tanzt vnd springt, da ist der tufel"), and the ritual fools of the Mayo and Yaqui Indians could also be referred to as "devils."[130] In the Middle Ages the figure representing death was also often depicted wearing the cap and bells of the jester, perhaps to remind people that death has the last laugh over everybody and is the great equalizer.[131] Nowhere is this mocking aspect of death more eloquently expressed than in Shakespeare's history of *King Richard II*, (1597):

> . . . for within the hollow crown
> That rounds the mortal temples of a king
> Keeps Death his court, and *there the antic sits,*
> *Scoffing his state and grinning at his pomp.*
>
> (3.2.160 – 63)[132]

A fool could also be anyone who did not conform to a particular set of norms—a category not limited to medieval notions, having existed in some totalitarian state psychiatric wards. Folly could be attributed as much to those who refused to join in the fray of material and political gain as to those who did, who in God's eyes and the eyes of many jesters, were the greatest fools of all, as Foly puts it in *Ane Satyre of the Thrie Estaits* (1540):

> Sum seiks to warldlie dignities,
> And sum to sensuall vanities:
> Quhat vails all thir vaine honouris,
> Nocht being sure to leife twa houris?[133]

The fool as simpleton, the natural, was laughed at and whipped, but he was also held in awe as a potential mouthpiece for God. The church's attitude toward the fool ranged from condemning him as the man who thinks he does not need God to considering him the man closest to God. The Franciscans called themselves "fools for Christ's sake," Saint Francis himself being known as "God's jester," and both the Greek and Russian Orthodox churches canonized "holy fools," while madmen had an aura of holiness in the Muslim world.[134] The Coptic church in Egypt boasts its share of "fools of God" who wander the desert, and the Algerians respected naturals, whom they regarded as saintly.[135]

It is perhaps this perceived link with a higher authority that gave rise to the idea, in Europe and elsewhere, that "iesters do oft prove Prophets."[136] A Jewish proverb states that "a whole fool is half a prophet," and according to Rabelais, the Turks revered such fools as doctors and prophets ("les Turcs reverent tels folz comme musaphiz et prophetes").[137] There are many examples of prophecy among Irish jesters, and a jester of Philip II of Spain was said to have foreseen that three visiting cardinals would all become popes. The three, Ugo Buoncompagni, Felice Peretti, and Niccolò Sfondrato, subsequently became Gregory XIII, Sixtus V, and Gregory XIV.[138]

Although jesters elsewhere often shared the physical abnormalities of the European fool, they do not generally seem to have shared his mental deficiencies (fig. 8). The keeping of naturals may well have involved an element of charity—monasteries took in a number of people who nowadays would be "in care," but some would have been left to wander, and the charity of the rich could provide for them. Originally the wardship of the lands and person of those deemed mentally unsound went to the local lord. Under Henry III (r. 1216–72) this right was transferred to the king, and the law began to differentiate between an "idiot," the wardship of whose property could be used profitably, and a "lunatic," somebody who became insane and whose revenues the king could not use. In the latter case the king was obliged to return any property to the lunatic's heirs or to the lunatic himself should he regain his sanity.[139]

In Henry VIII's reign a law was passed that often led to abuse of the system. An inquiry into the sanity of a person could be made, "De idiota inquierendo," and if he was deemed insane the law entitled a family to take over the lunatic's property on condition they look after him.[140] Court jesters were occasionally procured this way, and some people were legally decreed insane under false pretenses. To apply to care for a person judged insane was "to beg him for a fool," often a profitable exercise, since the

Figure 8 Claus the Fool, sketched from a painting attributed to Hans Lautensack (1530)

revenue could far outweigh the expense. However, fools so procured were not necessarily so foolish as to be unaware of their worth:

> A rich landed foole wm. a Courtier had beggd & caryed about to waite on him, com.g w/ his Mr. to a gentlem.s house where the picture of a foole was wrought in a fayre suit of Arras, cutt the picture out w/ a penknife, & being chidde for so doing, You h. more cause, sd. he, to thanke me, for if my Mr. had seen yr. picture of the foole he wld h. beggd the hangings of yr. H.[ouse] as he did my lands.[141]

A Banquet of Jests (1640) describes another case where a young nobleman was begged for a fool but managed to muster sufficient wit to convince those questioning him that he deserved to keep his estate:

> A foolish young Gentleman, son to a wise and well-reputed Knight, after his fathers decease, was begg'd for a foole, and summoned to the *Court of Wards* for his answer. When question was made to him, what hee could say for himselfe, why his Lands should not be taken from him, hee answered, *Why may not I a foole, beget a wise man to*

inherit after me, as well as my Father being a wise man, begot me a foole?
His answere carried it, and the demeanes were confirmed to him and
his heires, who are possessed of them unto this day.[142]

The word "fool," used so interchangeably with "jester," is a vital aspect
of the jester's persona. This ambiguity was useful, since "the dignity of the
[king] . . . was preserved by a simple arrangement, namely, the ranking as
'fool' or of deranged wit, every one who ventured to utter to his superior
a disagreeable truth."[143] In English "court fool" is completely synonymous
with "court jester" and is the most common designation in European languages—*fou du roi* in French, *Hofnarr* in German and *hofnar* in Dutch,
bufón and *buffone* ("buffoon") in Spanish and Italian—and the Latin term
for fool *(stultor)* was often used in medieval references to jesters. In Chinese "fools of no offense" *(wu guo chi)* is a nickname for jesters, although
there seems little evidence of naturals in the Chinese court.

Medieval and Renaissance culture was suffused with the concept of
the "sage-fool," "foolosopher" or "*morosophe,*" an oxymoron that was by no
means alien to other cultures. Empson describes how he gave a text to a
Chinese class on the idea of the fool as sage and "a student wrote that he
had not supposed this good-natured paradox to be European at all; it was
more likely to be a translation from some oriental philosopher," while
Gentili points out that the word "oxymoron" is a combination of *oxus,*
"sharp" and *moros,* "fool."[144] The Zen master Sengai referred to the wisdom of the fool in stating that "there are things that even the wise fail to
do, while the fool hits the point."[145] In Russian comic folk tales the character Ivan the Fool (Ivan-durak) shows by his foolishness that he is sur-
rounded by even greater fools.[146]

Perhaps the greatest jester of the Arabic world was Buhlul the Madman (Buhlul al-Majnun, d. 807), also known as the Lunatic of Kufa, who
was considered the prototype for the "wise fool" *(al-ʿuqala al-majanin),* a
concept clearly understood not only in Arabic countries but also in Persia,
where he was known as Wise Buhlul (Buhlul-i dana, or Buhlul-i Da-
nanda). As with many jesters, Buhlul's foolishness seems to have been
a feint. According to Zakani, he used unabashed impudence to address
Harun al-Rashid, the caliph who presided over the Abbasid empire at
its zenith, a lavish patron of the arts who could also execute someone on
a whim.

Harun asked Buhlul, "Who is the man you most admire?" "The person who most fills my belly," he replied. "If I fill it, will you admire

me?" asked the Caliph. Buhlul replied, "Perhaps, but you cannot obtain admiration on credit."[147]

In Europe the license of the court jester to speak truthfully rested heavily on his foolishness. Such at least was the theory: in practice it was often sufficient for somebody to don the cloak of the fool to be granted the same privilege. The feigning of folly could be a profitable business, and in fifteenth-century Scotland there was such a proliferation of artificial fools that the Act for the Away-Putting of Feynet Fools was passed on 19 January 1449, meting out such gentle punishments as ear nailing and amputation to those who tried to pass themselves off in court as genuine fools. The act

> ordainit that sheriffs, baylyiss, and officials inquer at ilk court gif thair be ony that maks them foolis that are nocht; and gif ony sic be fundyn, that thai be put in the king's warde, or in his yrnis, for thair trespass, as lang as thai haf ony gudes of thair awin to leve upon; and fra thai haf nocht to leve upon, that thair eris be naylt to the trone, or to ane uther tre, and cuttit of, and bannysit the cuntre; and gif thairafter thai be fundyn again, that thai be hangyt.[148]

Liselotte, duchess of Orléans, wrote in 1710 of her acquaintance with the last French court jester, L'Angeli, giving us an unusual firsthand account of a jester's faking it:

> I knew Angeli. He was not a fool, but he acted like one. He knew German very well. When he saw me, he said, "I know, because I have been warned, that Your Royal Highness fears fools. Well, do not be afraid of me: I am not mad, I just feign it, but don't betray me."

> [J'ai connu Langelli. Ce n'était pas un fou, mais il simulait la folie. Il savait fort bien l'allemand. Quand il me vit: "Je sais, me dit-il—car on m'en a prévenu,—que votre Altesse Royale craint les fous. N'ayez pas peur de moi: je ne le suis pas, je feins de l'être, mais ne me trahissez pas."][149]

In China there was no such cloak for the jester, who was expected to rely on his humor and wit to speak the truth without suffering for it rather than drawing on the protection of borrowed foolishness with its notion of including a direct line to God. His license was based on the exercise of his wit and the emperor's affection for him combined with a desire to be addressed with candor from time to time. Despite the understanding outside Europe of the concept of wise folly, such as the dervish who accosted

Mahmud or the madman of Chu who told Confucius he was wasting his time, references elsewhere to madmen residing in the court, now and then enlightening the monarch with a flash of wisdom coming like a bolt from a clouded mind, remain elusive.[150]

The high proportion of naturals in European courts makes Europe the exception rather than the rule in this respect. Jesters elsewhere are in a sense much easier to define. As far as we know, there was not the variety of deformities trooping through other courts that we see in Europe. Certainly there were dwarfs, but jesters in China, India, and other places were in full command of their faculties, whereas some European court jesters, particularly before the seventeenth century, were assigned a guardian to take care of them. Although there were many European court jesters who were entirely sane, so-called artificial fools donning the apparel of the natural, many of them do seem to have been genuinely mad or simple, hence their license to speak the truth with impunity, a license usefully appropriated by men with their wits about them as well as by actors and playwrights speaking through the mouths of their stage fools.

The Rogue and the Trickster

> The Trickster myth is found in clearly recognizable form among the simplest aboriginal tribes and among the complex. We encounter it among the ancient Greeks, the Chinese, the Japanese and in the Semitic world. Many of the Trickster's traits were perpetuated in the figure of the mediaeval jester, and have survived right up to the present day in the Punch-and-Judy plays and in the clown.
>
> Paul Radin, *The Trickster*[151]

The trickster figure appears in numerous folktales and myths around the world. He often takes the form of an animal: a hare in some Winnebago North American Indian stories, a spider among the Dakota, Sioux, and Navajo Indians and in African trickster stories, a raven among the Indians of the Northwest Coast of North America, the Chinese fox spirit *(huli-jing),* and—my personal favorite—Reynard the Fox. Or he can be a godlike being. In Icelandic sagas it is Loki who plays the trickster part, and the Winnebago trickster stories are classified as *waiken* myths, those that are sacred as opposed to those that are merely recounted *(worak).*[152]

The similarities between the trickster and the jester are numerous. Tricksters can use their wit to extricate themselves from sticky situations or to show up the avarice, arrogance, or dishonesty of others. They often have a humorous element and possess the jester's paradoxical combination of cleverness and foolishness—the Winnebago trickster is called Wakdjunkaga, or Foolish One.[153] Tricksters can be the butt of pranks as well as the perpetrators. They also give the impression of being capering, nimble creatures. Like the jester, they have a certain license to behave contrary to the norms of society, share the same peripheral status, and are treated with a similar combination of affection and contempt. They stand outside society and thereby give people who live firmly within its confines a glimpse of what lies beyond, showing life from a different vantage point. They also share the jester's resilience and apparent indifference to physical harm.

Particularly in Europe and the Middle East, where trickster tales are generally linked to historical or at least human rather than mythical beings, the similarities are such that a collection of anecdotes about a trickster will regularly include instances of his serving as a court jester, or fulfilling the functions of the jester at least occasionally, and a common term for court jester in German and Dutch is "rogue-fool" *(Schalksnarr, schalksnar)*. Timpane's lively thesis on the rogue cites Eulenspiegel as a comic example, indistinguishable from other human forms of the trickster. Tricky Till Eulenspiegel (fig. 9) is seen pitting his wits against the jester of King Casimir III of Poland (known as Casimir the Great for the benevolence of his rule, 1333–70), and beating him. Casimir had heard a great deal about Eulenspiegel, and when he arrived at court he was given a warm welcome. The king also loved his own jester, and the two were brought together, affirming the proverb "Two fools under one roof will seldom do any good" ("Zwen Narren in einem Huß, die thun selten gut").[154]

Casimir set a competition for them: whoever could outdo the other in foolery would win a new outfit and twenty guilders. They went through a whole gamut of tricks and tales and matched each other at every turn, while the king and his knights laughed at the display. Finally Eulenspiegel decided the prize was so good that he calculated what it would take to win, a "gross roguery" ("grober Schalkheit"); and having won his guilders, he left the court showered with the king's praise:

> So Eulenspiegel went to the middle of the room and took his trousers down and did a pile of shit right there in the middle of the room and took a spoon and divided the pile exactly in two and shouted to the other one saying, "Fool, come here and make me a delicacy like I've made for you!" Then he took the spoon and stuck it in his half and

ate it up and offered the spoon to the jester and said, "See there, you eat the other half and then do me another pile and divide that so I can have it for dessert." Then said the king's fool, "No, no way! You take after the devil with your tricks. I would rather spend my whole life going naked than eat your shit, or even mine!"

[Also gieng Ulenspiegel mitten in den Sal und hub sich hinden uff und scheiß ein Huffen mitten in den Sal und nam ein Löffel und teilet den Treck recht mitten entzwei und rufft dem andern und sprach: "Narr, kum her und thu mir die Leckerei auch nach, als ich dir vor wil thun!" und nam den Löffel und faßte den halben Treck darein und ißt den uff unnd bote den Löffel dem Schlackßnarren [*sic*] unnd hin, iß du das ander halb Teil und darnach so mach du auch ein Hauffen und teil den auch voneinander, so wil ich dir auch

Figure 9 Till Owlglass (Eulenspiegel), by Rudolf Warnecke

nachessen." Da sprach der Künignar: "Nein, nit also! Daz thu dir der
Tüffel nach. Solt ich all mein Lebtag nacken gon, ich iß von dir oder
von mir nit also!"] [155]

In Spain the court jester Estebanillo González is an example of somebody who is officially a jester but who has something of the trickster too.
He has no qualms about tricking people for his own benefit, and though
he usually concentrates on those deserving to be unmasked, he can also
choose well-meaning innocents as his victims, lending him a trickster's
amoral mien.

In Rouen he scraped up some ashes, wrapped them in a piece of paper,
and showed them to a group of wealthy Jewish merchants, telling them
this was all that remained of his father since the Inquisition caught up
with him (alluding to the Inquisition's practice of digging up corpses to
see if they had been buried in a Jewish manner). He told them he carried
the ashes next to his heart. The merchants were so saddened and sympathetic that their tears welled up. They took him to the house of the richest merchant, who showed him great generosity, giving him twenty-five
ducats and a letter of introduction. Having been congratulated for being
such a worthy son of his father, he took his leave of them, happy to have
done so well out of people who always cheat others and are never themselves cheated ("Mi felicidad en haber merecido ser su hijo, me despedí
de ellos, alegre de haber salido tan bien de gente que siempre engañan y
jamás se dejan engañar"). [156]

Like the trickster, the rogue has much in common with the jester, being peripheral to society and irrepressible by it and enjoying a similar freedom of action and speech. Europe boasted jestbooks about rogues as about
jesters, and it was in these that in written literature "the rogue first became a fully-fledged comic character, one who could expose and desecrate
accepted values and get away with it." The rogue further resembles the
trickster and jester in that he generally lacks the purpose of a rebel or revolutionary, and while contravening the mores and laws of the world in
which he wanders, he will not set out to overthrow them. [157]

In other parts of the world the trickster often takes on superhuman aspects, and when his wit is insufficient he can resort to magic or shape-
shifting, appearing as a man, an animal, or a godlike figure. The Winnebago trickster is a curious mixture of man and beast, wiliness and naïveté.
He is frequently made a fool of, and some of the stories about him may
be warnings not to tamper with nature or taboos. In this respect he resembles the ritual clowns who violate taboos not to encourage anarchy,

but to manifest the chaos that might be unleashed if they are not respected, serving as "a reminder that the universe is oddly hinged." [158]

There is a magical story of a historical jester displaying supernatural roguery, including the shape-shifting of tricksters outside Europe. Zytho served Wenceslas IV, king of Bohemia and Holy Roman Emperor (r. 1376 – 1419), and the story was told by the bishop of Olmüß as "undoubted historical fact." Wenceslas was known for being extremely fond of jesters and jugglers, so when he married a Bavarian princess in 1389, his father-in-law, duke of Bavaria and Palatine prince of the Rhine, brought a whole wagonload of them to Prague. Since there was no lack of jesters already there, it was decided to have a competition between the two groups. The Bavarian jesters were winning until the master jester of the Bohemians, Zytho, walked up to the leading jester of the Bavarians, seized him by the collar, and ate him up. Since the Bavarian jester's shoes were covered in filth, Zytho quickly spat them out. The Bavarian duke was angry to have lost his favorite jester, so Wenceslas ordered Zytho to return the jester he had eaten, which he did by squatting over a bowl of water and excreting him naked.

The distinction between jester and trickster lies in the fact that the trickster is a completely free entity, not affiliated with any particular person in authority. In addition—and this may be the most significant difference—he is generally less discerning than the jester in choosing the victims of his pranks and wit. Jesters are often guided in their mockery by a certain kindliness that prevents their treating a friendly old farmer in the same way as an avaricious cardinal or a venal magistrate, and their mockery is often intended to show up a vice of some sort. The trickster, on the other hand, rarely has scruples about cheating anybody for fun or gain. The jester is usually aware of the effect he can have and frequently uses his talents to help others, cause merriment, give advice, or defuse a perilous situation. It is perhaps this more ethical input, together with his close connection to the king, that distinguishes him from the boundless trickster.

A Jester by Any Other Name

The clowns represent us in our misdeeds . . . the clowns show life as it should not be . . . the clowns show, mimic the "hidden immoralities" and bring them into the open so we can see where we have gone wrong. . . . This is a small village and people gossip. Women gossip about men and men gossip about women. . . . Only the clowns can

do it in public and get away with it. They can get away with anything. . . . When we came here to live with the Great Spirit, someone hollered and we looked back and there were the clowns . . . the
clowns show what is the essence of morality . . . clowning is a public confession for humanity.

A Hopi Indian [159]

And so the age-old, deep-rooted human need for clowns. As universal as
the jester was in court, there are many tribes in Africa, America, and elsewhere that have had such clowns, and may still have them. These often
played an important role in ritual, but they also had the jester's license to
offer comic criticism. The Ostyaks of western Siberia celebrated the killing of a bear with a night of song and dance during which some people
wore masks and adopted mock names, the masks affording them the latitude to mock even visiting Russian officials with complete liberty.[160] In
Sri Lanka there is an ancient masking tradition *(kolam)* that affords license for social satire, while the Pende tribe of Zaire had different masks
for various village characters, including the fool who would mock those
who did not fit in.[161] The Aztecs also had jesters outside the royal courts
as well as inside.[162]

In India the Tamil village clown *(komali)* encapsulates many qualities
of the jester. He wears a conical cap, has a row of cowrie shells draped in
front of his mouth in permanent grinning inanity, and wears small bells
on his legs; he capers, laughs, and sings songs about the beatings he en-
dures. On festival days a Tamil buffoon will comment on the performance
of dancers, taunting them and making crude comments.[163] In Tonga there
were no permanent official jesters, but they did exist ad hoc: "At times certain individuals, termed *fakaaluma,* or *fakatakataka,* who were considered
particularly witty, took it upon themselves to amuse the chiefs." [164] In the
middle of this century, the Wolof people living between the Senegal and
Gambia Rivers in Africa still had a special caste or outcaste of clowns who
could marry only each other. The profession was hereditary, and they were
also the only people permitted to become musicians. Like the court jester,
they were of lowly status while enjoying great informal power. Gorer described them as

> family *jesters and buffoons with unlimited licence,* whose duty it is to
> keep the company amused; they are the family bards, who learn and
> recite the family and national history . . . and the traditional stories
> and fables; they are family magicians, who must be present at all cere-

monies and *whose advice must be taken;* they are the first to hold the newborn baby and the last to touch the corpse; they are the actual recipients of most gifts given to their patrons; they are the spiritual mentors and guides of the young . . . *they console the mourner and comfort the downcast . . .* they are the family's official boasters . . . *they are lower than the meanest servant and often richer and more powerful than the master.*[165]

The Bougouni tribe of Sudan also had sacred clowns who retained their function of clown in daily life rather than being limited to specific ceremonies, as is often the case. Some would use a pause in a ritual dance to hurl abuse at the spectators, VIPs in particular, and they needed to be gifted in repartee in case any of the audience dared answer back.[166] Another tribe, the Chagga, used impromptu skits with mocking songs and a pointed denouement to correct behavior, as Chinese jesters did throughout their luxuriant history.[167]

Concerning the sacred clowns of the Mayo and Yaqui Indians, Parsons listed among their functions "personal satire; discipline for children or adults . . . social discipline," and among the Pueblo Indians they had "a punitive and policing function in ceremonial matters and through their license in speech and song a somewhat similar function in domestic matters."[168] The idea of choosing certain people to act as both clowns and censors was common among American Indians, for whom "the clown is the person par excellence who is *privileged to ridicule,* burlesque and defile the most sacred and important ceremonies, persons and customs. He is licensed to behave as no ordinary mortal would dream of behaving. *He is held accountable for nothing.* In his transgression of custom lies much of his comedy."[169]

Among the New Mexico Pueblo Indians there existed a brotherhood of "delight makers" *(koshare).* They had several duties, the foremost being to keep people merry, particularly during festivals. They had to be witty and to see the ludicrous in any situation; they would sing, tumble, caper, and dress in as hideous and outrageous a fashion as possible. They enjoyed special privileges on festive occasions, when they could ridicule without fear of retribution. In addition, they would assist the shamans in public ceremonials, acting as heralds and marshals during celebrations. But their merrymaking was combined with a more sinister aspect, since they had the right to investigate people suspected of breaking certain taboos and to execute them publicly and cruelly.[170]

Freese has shown the importance of the Pueblo clowns in interpreting for the tribe the incursions of foreign influences into their culture, a function they have fulfilled since the arrival of the first Spanish colonialists, whom they tried to resist through humor when they realized that open warfare would not work. They continue to fulfill this function: with the advent of the space age, they have used parody to mock moon landings, thereby expressing the fears of the elders that the Moon Mother would be disturbed. One Zuni said that the clowns were mimicking moon walks a year before they actually happened—the fool is ever a prophet.[171]

The Tübatulabal Indians of east-central California had a hereditary clown *(hili'idac)* who would turn the world on its head and "go around talking crazy . . . at fiestas; he danced backward, too," like Spike Milligan's song, "I'm Walking Backwards for Christmas."[172] The Tübatulabal clown "didn't care what he said, either to women or the chief; *if the chief was no good the clown walked around saying so; then all the old men would get together and choose a new chief.*" Most jesters can do no more than hope to reform an inept king rather than have him replaced.[173] The Sioux Indians have their "contrary" *(heyhoka),* a person permanently licensed to break traditional norms, to do things in reverse, such as pitching their tepees with the poles on the outside, or by sitting down with their feet in the air, or entering a tepee any way but by the door. They make people laugh, and nobody knows what to expect next. Like a jester sauntering around the court always on the lookout for the next joke or pratfall, they can keep people on their toes in anticipation.[174]

Among the Hopi Indians of northeastern Arizona, ritual clowns take part in a clowning ceremony *(tsukulalwa)* and also mediate with the spirit world on behalf of the Indians, much as the court jester would intercede with the king on the part of ordinary people. Most clown types among the Hopi are believed to have a spiritual clownterpart. They have colored markings on the face and body, or wear masks, and they perform ritual dancing and singing. In addition they have a strong ethical aspect, and like many ritual clowns they exercise it by showing "life as it should not be." The violation of taboos and social mores can be used to reassert their worth to society.

The jester also has this ethical element informing much of his humor, although he perhaps does this by showing life *as it is.* The Hopi clowns cause uproarious laughter, but their purpose is more than mere comic relief; their short skits emphasize the resolution of specific problems or inconsistencies rather than trying to put forward a whole system of ethics. The clowns also appear as "warning figures," another function of the court jester illustrated in an anonymous German print of 1543 titled *The Warn-*

ing Fool (Der wärner Narr), in which a jester stands facing the king while pointing to the bishops to whom he has his back turned.[175]

One difference between the clowns described above and the court jester is that the license of the jester was always attached to the man, whereas the license of ceremonial clowns is often attached to the occasion or ritual and is therefore of limited duration; in this it resembles the festive license of the medieval European Feast of Fools and of other Saturnalian liberties taken with established social structures. However, some ritual clowns remain clowns when the ceremony is over and further resemble jesters in being neither revolutionaries nor rebels. No matter how outrageous their behavior, or how many taboos they violate, their aim is not to overthrow the existing order even if they point out its faults. Usually the clowns serve the whole group, even if their mockery can be more strident when aimed at its upper echelons; jesters, on the other hand, are linked inextricably with the leader (or at least leading members) of the group. Ritual clowns are sometimes only distant cousins of the court jesters, but in other cases they are almost indistinguishable, principally by virtue of their license to say or do almost anything and to correct by mockery and humor:

> In Pueblo tradition, the clowns were created at the "time of the beginning" to entertain people and heal them through laughter. They were allowed everywhere and instructed not to consider anything sacred. Thus, the clowns have become ubiquitous and powerful beings by virtue of this license given by the gods. They cavort in the plazas of the Pueblo villages poking fun at everyone and everything. No one is immune from their penetrating humor.[176]

And yet I name you two shapes immediately
Which reign supreme in every one of you:
A little king and a great fool.

*[Und doch nenn ich sofort euch zwei Gestalten,
Die unbotmäßig in euch allen walten:
Ein kleiner König und ein grosser Tor.]*
                    Frank Wedekind, Prologue, *King Nicolo, or Such Is Life* [1]

In this way, say the mathematicians, kings and fools are born under
the same horoscope.

*[En ceste maniere disent les mathematiciens, un mesme horoscope estre à
la nativité des roys et des sots.]*
                    François Rabelais, *Tiers Livre* [2]

One ought to be born a king or a fool.

[Aut regem, aut fatuum nasci oportere.]
                    Desiderius Erasmus, *Adages* [3]

2

The Scepter and the Bauble

THE "ORIENTAL DESPOT" REVISITED

They are moreover the favourites of kings, so much so that many great rulers can't eat a mouthful or take a step or last an hour without them, and they value their fools a long way above the crabbed wiseacres they continue to maintain for the sake of appearance.

Desiderius Erasmus, *Praise of Folly*[4]

There was A grete lorde that had A Sage fole, the whyche he lovyd Marvaylous well, Be Cawse of hys pastyme. And the Fole in lyke wyse lovyd well hys lorde A-Bove All hother. And at lenthe the lorde desesyd, for the whyche the fole was in grete sorow. And the sonne of this lorde had All hys faders possessyons, & was lorde after hys fadyr, & he lovyd hys fole in lyke wyse as hys fadyr dyde.

"A Sage Fool's Testament" (ca. 1475)[5]

We are often presented with an image of the Chinese emperor as an unwavering symbol of magisterial aloofness, occasionally combined with exquisite cruelty. Resplendent in his cosmic significance, the emperor can seem an isolated figure, and the term he often used to denote himself, "orphan" *(gu),* reflects this. Yet the enduring image of "Oriental despot" begins to fade when seen in the light of the close relations between many emperors and their even more numerous jesters. Similarly, examining the proximity of king and jester in other parts of the world may give a greater insight into the more human aspects of the ruler not always apparent in history books. This chapter will concentrate on the closeness and informality of the jester's relationship with the monarch, giving instances of the ruler's protecting him, enjoying his impertinence and familiarity, indulging his requests, rewarding him, and even being kind to his family.

In Europe, letters and court account books testify volubly to the king's generosity and affection toward his jester. In addition the jester is often portrayed in art, either on his own or with the king, or in group or family portraits, and he is usually so honored by the court painter. In 1628 a French ambassador visiting the count-duke of Olivares, principal adviser to Philip IV for the first few decades of his reign, commented on "a small gallery full of all kinds of portraits of jesters" ("une petite gallerie toute pleine de portraits de fols de toute sorte de manière").[6] Although perhaps preeminent in this predilection for painting jesters and dwarfs, the Spanish were not alone. A fresco by Francesco Cossa in the Palazzo Schifanoia in Ferrara (ca. 1470) shows a group of noblemen surrounding the Italian jester Scocola, shorter by a head than everybody else, with his master Borso d'Este (r. 1450–71) smiling at him while presenting him with a gift, the two forming the focus of the work with the courtiers seeming little more than a colorful backdrop.[7]

Occasionally, access to the royal person was promoted by the jester, a further sign of the trust the monarch placed in him. As a contrast to the king, he could be a perpetual reminder of the human limits to regality, whether through forthrightness, earthiness, or physical and mental defects. Ministers and advisers sometimes seem to obstruct communication between the top (king) and bottom (people), so a jester who belongs nowhere and is at ease everywhere could help the monarch reach his subjects, often being a vital, unofficial link between them. Jesters tend to have relatively humble backgrounds, and certainly the best of them would be in touch with the feelings of ordinary people: "The fool begins socially, as the outcast, the parasite, the tramp, though he may in the course of this show prove himself more powerful than the king and in a fuller relation than the king is to the intelligence and vitality of the world that embraces the microcosmic kingdom in a larger whole."[8]

The demands of kingship can leave the king feeling isolated, despite the frequent lack of privacy in his life, as Marais, jester to Louis XIII (r. 1610–43), put it: "There are two things about your job I couldn't handle . . . eating alone and shitting in company" ("Il y a deux choses dans votre métier dont je ne me pourrais accommoder. . . . De manger tout seul et de chier en compagnie").[9] Although other people, whether mistresses, friends, or advisers, are able to see the man behind the monarch, they are more likely than a jester to be caught up in court politics and factions and so to constitute a potential threat to his power. The trust bestowed on a jester by his sovereign is perhaps due to a shared sense of isolation, the king's despite his being central to the court, and the jester's for being a figure peripheral to the establishment even while operating at its core.

"Mingling Kings and Clowns"
Sir Philip Sidney, *An Apologie for Poetrie* [10]

A banquet was held at the court of Henry VIII of England to celebrate his winning the title of Defender of the Faith. His jester shook his head with the words "Let thou and I defend one another, and let faith alone to defend itself."

Erika Tietze-Conrat, *Dwarfs and Jesters in Art* [11]

As foil or antithesis to the monarch, jesters could also be mock kings and were often given high-sounding mock titles as well as affectionate nicknames. Elizabeth I called an Italian jester "Monarcho," and the Russian czar Peter the Great (r. 1696–1725) named one Patriarch of Russia and King of Siberia, while his jester Lacosta, a Portuguese Jew who spoke several languages and was well versed in Scripture, became known as King of the Samoyeds after Peter gave him the island of Sommer in the Gulf of Finland.[12] Zuñiga, the most famous Spanish jester, called himself the Duke of Jerusalem, perhaps because he was a Jewish convert, and was also known as King of the Jesters (Rey de los bufones), while the French jester Angoulevent had the sobriquet Prince des sots.[13] The German word for the jester's bauble *(Narrenzepter)* implies his reflection of the king by equating the bauble to the king's scepter.

The interchangeable nature of the king and the jester is a recurrent theme. A medallion (ca. 1461–66) of the French jester Triboulet bears this inscription: "The regal vestments mock me [mockingly endow me], the king's fool, with the king's office and appearance; and they clothe me, the laughing-stock, with alluring charm" (fig. 10).[14] The puppet shows of Russian fairgrounds in the nineteenth century could feature a fool as king, and Longfellow's "King Robert of Sicily" has the king changing places with his fool.[15] The poem has a long history and ancient antecedents. The story of a king's being forced to become a jester to teach him humility was widely known in the Middle Ages in Latin, French, English, German, and Ital-

Figure 10 Triboulet I, sketched from a fifteenth-century medal

ian manuscripts, but its origins go back further.[16] A fifteenth-century manuscript describes Robert's demotion:

> Thou art a fole seyde the Aungell
> Thou shalt be shavyn over ylke a dele like a fole and a fole to bee
> Thy babull schall by thy dygnyte.[17]

In Wedekind's *King Nicolo* the inept and self-centered monarch is overthrown by a butcher, Pietro, who proves to be the better king. Nicolo roams as a tramp for a while with his daughter Alma as the Fool to Nicolo's Lear in the wilderness. With his world turned on its head, he comes to the half-serious conclusion that with a butcher as king, there is only one position in life open to a deposed monarch, that of court jester ("Denn wenn der *Schweineschlächter* auf den Thron erhoben wird, dann bleibt für den König schlechterdings keine andere Lebensstellung im Staate mehr übrig, als die eines—*Hofnarren*") (2:533). Nicolo becomes court jester to the new king, complete with cap and bauble, his daughter Alma acting as second fool or *Hanswurst*. As a jester offering advice to a king, Nicolo is more responsible for the sensible running of the country than when he held power formally. Like Robert of Sicily, "Nicolo is the king who is hurled from the heights to the depths and can begin his regeneration only when he becomes the fool." [18]

In *Escurial* (1929), by the Belgian Michel de Ghelderode, the king is not forced to become a jester but agrees to do so for a game. [19] As the queen lies dying the king orders the jester to think up a game, and Folial suggests the age-old jester-king exchange of roles, beginning by describing a carnival version: "In my land, during Lent, a nobody is chosen and provided with bright-coloured rags, a crown, and a scepter, and this nobody is made a king!" (5:171). He then snatches first the king's crown and then his scepter. Peculiarly, both the jester and the king are better able to tell the truth under the guise of each other than in their real roles. [20]

George Buchanan (1506–82), scholar-jester to James VI of Scotland (r. 1567–1625), engineered a role swap with the king to shock him into being more sensible. Determined to cure the king of happily signing unread documents, Buchanan presented him with a document that transferred regal authority to himself for fifteen days, which the king signed and returned:

> No sooner had he received it, but he goes to the king, and told him it was not time for him now to be sitting there; with that the king, greatly amazed, started up, and George, in great haste, set himself down in the king's chair, forthwith declaring himself king, saying, You, who was king, must be my fool, for I am now the wisest man. The king at this was greatly offended, until George shewed him his seal and signature. *From that day the king always knew what he signed.* [21]

In the seventeenth century, artists in the Spanish court commissioned to do portraits of past kings of Castile used the existing court jesters as their models, seated on thrones and dressed in full regalia. At a bullfight given in honor of the duke of Modena in 1638, the jester of Philip IV was seated at the foot of the throne sporting a crown and scepter. [22] What are the implications of this—that the real wearer of the crown is a fool? If Philip had been fearful that others perceived him as a fool, he might not have allowed his jester to advertise the fact. Allowing his kingly dignity to be mocked in a sense reinforced that dignity.

Buhlul, jester to Caliph Harun al-Rashid, is said to have clambered onto the caliph's throne before being beaten by the guards for his sacrilege, an incident recorded in a poem by Farid al-Din Attar (1136–1234).

Buhlul comments to Harun that if only five minutes on the throne has brought him such a beating, how much worse will it be for the caliph, who has been sitting there a lifetime?[23]

In his novel about Chicot, debonair courtier-jester to Henri IV, Dumas has him turn up at banquet dressed as the king, in the king's presence, thereby confusing some of the guests who are not sure to which king they should show deference.[24] In this case the jester was taking on the king's persona not to make a point or to mock him, but in collusion with the real king, for their exclusive amusement. The entertainment value lay in observing the discomfiture of courtiers not wishing to be seen bowing and scraping to the wrong king.[25]

Prince Morris of Orange was a renowned laughter lover. When putting his troops into battle order he once said lightheartedly to his jester, "What d'you think, wouldn't it be better if you commanded the army for a while, and I took your place as jester?" The jester answered, "That wouldn't work, you'd be as useless a jester as I'd be a field commander, so if we changed positions we'd both be dismissed!"[26] In a modern series of poems about a jester whose name is Latin for "king," the real king asks to change places with him, while Rex points out the complications this will engender:

> "Can you dare to play me?" said the King.—"How well?"
> Rex asked.—"Don't dare to play me badly!"—"If I
> did my best (and at acting, note, I excel),
> wouldn't your subjects all mistake me for you?"—
> "What an insult! They all would identify
> Rex, the mad jester! Easy to tell the true
> from the false!" "Dear old nunc, the furless monkey,
> strutting in ermine, that's the joke of tonight!
> You need genius to act me. You're a flunkey,
> nunc, in comparison. To copy you quite
> properly, you've set me a teaser, you see:
> I must act you acting a king acting me!"[27]

"In Chess the Fool Is Closest to the King"
["Les fous sont aux echets les plus proches des Roys"]
Regnier, *Satyre XIV: La folie est générale*[28]

I can assign no reason for these pieces of deformity, but the opinion all the absolute princes have, that 'tis below them to converse with

the rest of mankind, and, not to be quite alone, they are forced to
seek their companions amongst the refuse of human nature, these
creatures being the only part of their court privileged to talk freely
to them.

Letter from Lady Montague (1777)[29]

Now the hunchback, whom all this bother was about, was the Sultan's
jester, and the King could not abide him out of his sight for an hour.
The Book of the Thousand Nights and One Night[30]

Well, him and George got on after that like wildfire, they were the
best friends in the worl an George remaint wi the king ti the rest of
his days. An there's millions o stories tellt about George Buchanan
the King's Fool.

D. Williamson and L. Williamson,
"George Buchanan, the King's Fool"[31]

The jester, in view of his real and symbolic closeness to the monarch, could
be a kind of privileged partner. He would be with his master in both a
public and a private capacity, accompanying him on progresses, military
campaigns, and hunting trips. Nasrudin was once asked by Tamerlane to
accompany him on a hunt, as was Motke, the Hasidic Jewish fool whose
company the king is said to have enjoyed.[32] Zuñiga went with Emperor
Charles V on his campaign against the French in Navarre in 1523, and in
1524 he accompanied the princess to the border of Portugal to join her
new husband. He was also an eyewitness to a historic meeting of papal
legates and various potentates from Europe and elsewhere, held in Toledo
in October 1525.[33] In China, too, the jester would go with the emperor on
his travels: "Emperor Yuanzong liked to go on trips, and Adding Clarity
would always go with him."[34]

A jester could also follow the king into his private apartments: one
anecdote about Nasrudin has him chatting with Tamerlane in a Turkish
bath, and it is said that the favorite jester of Pope Leo X, perhaps the
keenest of pontifical jester-keepers, was by his bedside when he died.[35]
And jesters often addressed their masters in a tone of familiarity unlikely
to be tolerated in other members of the court. Will Somers (fig. 11), favorite jester of Henry VIII, called him Harry, or Uncle, the latter a name
also used by the Fool in King Lear, and Chicot would *tutoie* Henri IV, as
did the jester Brusquet when he spoke to Charles IX (r. 1560–74).[36]

Something of the tenderness that could exist between jesters and their

Figure 11 *Will Sommers, Kinge Heneryes Jester.* © The British Museum.

patrons is shown in a letter of 7 February 1505 from the priest-jester Fra Serafino, expressing his delight at having received a letter from Isabella d'Este, the marchioness of Mantua (1474 –1539), who had popes eating out of her hand. He leaped around the room with excitement until everybody thought he had gone mad, and the duchess of Urbino took him by the hair and asked what was the matter with him. He explained his exuberance by asking her to read the letter from Isabella ("et tanto saltai in quella Camera che tutte quelle donne credeuano che fusse impacito. La S. Duchessa me pigliò per i capelli et me disse: che hai tu? Io gie disse: legete queste litere").[37]

A painting done in the 1580s by a follower of Sanchez Coella shows the Spanish infanta Isabella Clara Eugenia (1566 –1633) in an affectionate pose with the dwarf natural Madalena Ruiz. Madalena served at court for forty years from 1565 and accompanied Princess Juana to Lisbon, where the princess wrote letters mentioning her with utmost tenderness and solicitude, giving us an unusually intimate insight into the affection bestowed on fools and jesters. On 26 June 1581 she mentions that Madalena was feeling very lonely since her daughter-in-law had left that day and that she was angry with herself for having scolded her for something she did in Belén ("Madalena anda hoy con gran soledad de su yerno, que partió hoy para ahí. . . . Y estuvo muy enojada conmigo porque le reñí algunas cosas que había hecho in Belén"). Madalena also seems to have had a problem with drink, which made her maudlin (15 and 29 January 1582). However, on 7 May she was very chirpy with Juana's sister, although Juana comments on her tatty taffeta dress, blaming herself for not having given her anything, even if it was also partly Madalena's fault for not reminding her: "Madalena anda muy alegre con mi hermana, aunque muy rota una ropa de tafetán que trae. Pero yo tengo la culpa, que no le he dado nada, aunque ella no ha dejado de acordármelo."[38]

Talhak, jester to Sultan Mahmud of Ghazna, would say whatever he felt like, and the Persian word for jester (dalqak) is derived from his name, which in turn may derive from the Persian word daghal, meaning "fraud, falsification, adulteration."[39] One day "Sultan Mahmud was lying down with his head on the knee of Talhak. Suddenly he asked, 'What is your relation to cuckolds?' He said, 'I am their pillow.'"[40] The Persian poet-satirist Zakani seems to have used Talhak as a cover for his own criticisms, and he resented "the immense power of jesters in despotic courts where nobody could venture to speak to the king while he was angry, except for the idiot jester."[41]

The German jester Steffen was so beloved by the Holy Roman Emperor Charles VI (r. 1711–40) that Prince Eugène of Savoy and other ministers would be kept waiting a long time when emperor and jester were together. The relationship between Henry VIII and Will Somers seems to have been one of the closest between monarch and fool that can be found anywhere. This kindly jester could enter the king's presence at will and was always welcomed. He once took his uncle in to meet the king, lending him his best fool's coat so he would not look too poor.

> And up they came, and to the king they goe, who, being with the lord
> treasurer alone, merry, seeing them two, how Will had got another
> foole, knew there was sport at hand. How now! sayes the king, What
> news with you? O, Harry! sayes he, this is my owne uncle; bid him
> welcome. Wel, said the king, he is welcome.[42]

A relationship of equal proximity existed between another Henry and William: Henri IV and Maître Guillaume. This jester followed his king everywhere, attending the swearing in of the new king in 1593, although he did not make himself too popular with the Ligueurs (adherents of the Holy League that formed in the 1570s to fight the Huguenots), since he kept sticking his tongue out at them. In October 1595 he accompanied Henri to Amiens, where the king was to meet various local dignitaries. A deputy from Brittany subjected Henri to a lengthy harangue, despite the king's twice asking him to speed it up. Exasperated, Henri stood up and left with the words, "You can tell the rest to Master William" ("Vous direz donc le reste à Maître Guillaume").[43] Guillaume was with the king even as he was dying.[44]

In his diary entry for "this month of April . . . dry, cold and windy" ("ce mois d'avril . . . sec, froid et venteus") in 1592, Pierre de l'Estoile, recording the death of Chicot, speaks of the great affection Henri felt for his jester: "The king loved this man, foolish as he was, and found no fault with anything he said, which is why he got away with a thousand follies" ("Le Roy aimoit cest homme, tout fol qu'il estoit, et ne trouvoit rien mauvais de tout ce qu'il disoit: qui estoit cause qu'il s'esgaroit en mille folies"). Chicot was not officially a jester, being a gentleman-cavalier with a military career, and "fou quand il vouloit," when the mood took him.[45] Before Henri IV he served Henri III (r. 1574–89), acting as portmanteau—a repository for news that could not safely be committed to paper. He accompanied the king on various nocturnal escapades, mocked his enemies and his friends, and imparted scandalous gossip. Although he did not formally hold the post of court jester, there is an entry in the account books of 1580 that lists a gift of taffeta for making an outfit for "Chicot, jester to His Majesty, for 23 pounds" ("Chicot, bouffon de S.M. pour 23 livres").[46] Chicot would even sign his letters "Superintendent of His Majesty's Buffoonery" ("Superintendant de la Bouffonerie de Sa Majesté").[47]

Perhaps the most startling examples of a jester's being impudent to the point of lèse-majesté can be found in anecdotes concerning Emperor Zhuangzong and Newly Polished Mirror. This brassy jester constantly pushed his luck and almost paid for it, but he always managed to talk his way out of trouble. This was the crux of his success: he made Zhuangzong laugh so that he could not bring himself to punish the jester. On one occasion the emperor was fooling with a group of entertainers, and

> looking all around him he said, "Son of Heaven Li! Where's Son of Heaven Li?"—referring to himself. Newly Polished Mirror rushed forward and slapped him across the face. Zhuangzong turned ashen, and the courtiers were all terrified. The crowd of entertainers, also panic-stricken, seized the jester and asked, "Just what d'you think you're playing at, slapping the Son of Heaven in the face?" Newly Polished Mirror, feigning innocence, explained, "But there is only one Son of Heaven Li, so who was asking for him?" Thereupon the courtiers all laughed. Zhuangzong was delighted and rewarded Newly Polished generously.
>
> 四顧而呼曰：『李天下！李天下何在？』新磨遽前以手批其頰。莊宗失色，左右皆恐，群伶亦大驚駭。共持新磨詰曰：『汝奈何批天子頰？』新磨對曰：『李天下者一人而已，復誰呼耶？』於是左右皆笑，莊宗大喜，賜與新磨甚厚。[48]

Queen Elizabeth II (r. 1952–) is known for a sense of humor, but it is hard to imagine anybody, even a favored comedian, slapping her face for a joke and being rewarded with a laugh and a gift. On another occasion the jester was presenting a memorial to the emperor. There were a lot of dogs running around, and one of them came after him. He shouted to the emperor, "Your Majesty shouldn't let your sons and daughters go round biting people!" Apart from calling the dogs children of the emperor, the jester also broke an imperial taboo: the word "dog" featured in the character of Zhuangzong's family name, Di, and was therefore forbidden. The emperor did not see the funny side and was about to fire an arrow at the jester until he used another pun to deflect it.[49]

After the jester Going Round in Circles (Zhou Za) was captured during a military campaign against Liang, Emperor Zhuangzong was always
longing for him. When they were finally reunited in 924 the emperor was
delighted, and Going Round in Circles, blubbering with emotion, explained how his life had been preserved only by the intercession of two
Liang officials. He asked the emperor to repay their kindness with a generous gift of land to the tune of two regions. Overjoyed at seeing his beloved jester again, he agreed.[50]

Another aspect of the jester's close relationship with the king is that he
stands by him in the face of peril, either warning him of impending danger
—hence the reputation of jesters for possessing the powers of prophecy—
or protecting him. The Russian jester Koshelioff was hardly ever apart
from his master, the Toushinsky pretender who tried to pass himself off
as the younger son of Ivan the Terrible, and as a result he shared his fate
when the pretender was found out.[51] In the twelfth century *Roman de rou*,
Goles, the jester of Duke William of Normandy, wakes him to warn of the
approaching enemy:

> "Open, open, open!" he cries,
> "Thou art but dead, arise! arise!
> Where art thou, William? Why sleepest thou?
> If seized thou wilt be slain, I trow;
> Thy foes are arming even now."
>
> ["Ovrez," dist il, "ovrez, ovrez!
> Ja morreiz tuit, levez, levez!
> Ou giés Guilliame? pour quei dorz?
> S'ateinz i es ja seras morz;
> ti enemi se vont armer."][52]

Mathurine, a dwarf and perhaps the most memorable jestress in history, risked her life to catch the assassin who tried to murder Henri IV.
When Jean Chastel tried to stab the king in the throat, Henri moved his
head, so that he was cut in the lip only. But in the tumult he looked around
him and wondered whether Mathurine had done it, while she ran to the
door of the chamber and blocked the exit of the young boy, endangering
her own life to do so.[53]

Kunz von der Rosen, the "straightforward, unselfish, and uncommonly
witty" lifelong jester of the Holy Roman Emperor Maximilian I (r. 1453–
1519), managed to gain entry to the prison where Maximilian was held, offering to take his place.[54] This selfless intercession seems particularly com-

mon among Irish jesters, many of whom were able to foresee the king's death. In the *Minor Annals* there is an account of a jester who in 626 chose to die with his king:

> Fiachra's jester was listening to the conversation with his ear against the house. He besought Comgall that he and his master should die together in the battle and that as he was beside his master here in this life he would be with him in heaven. Comgall said "God will do it thus."[55]

"The Battle of the Plain of Mucrama" ("Cath Maige Mucraime") in the late twelfth-century *Book of Leinster* describes how Do Dera, jester to Lugaid MacCon, took his master's place in battle when he had a premonition of his death:

> A month from that day the two armies met, and MacCon went to converse with his fool before the battle. The fool, Do Dera, foresaw defeat and death for Lugaid and offered to go into battle in Lugaid's place, for they were much alike. . . . Do Dera was slain.[56]

In "The Destruction of Da Derga's Hostel" ("Togail Bruidne Da Derga"), an Irish saga written no later than the eighth or ninth century, Taulchinne, juggler to Conaire, the high king of Ireland (ca. second century A.D.), combined the skills of a juggler with the jester's knack of forewarning the king. He also had the baldness often associated with fools and jesters in medieval Europe:

> "There," said Ingcel, "I beheld a great champion. . . . The shame of baldness is on him . . . Earrings of gold around his ears. A mantle speckled, colored, he wore. Nine swords in his hand, and nine silvern shields, and nine apples of gold. He throws each of them upwards, and none of them falls on the ground, and there is only one of them on his palm; each of them rising and falling past another is like the movement to and fro of bees on a day of beauty. When he was swiftest, I beheld him at the feat, and as I looked, the company uttered a cry about him and his implements were all on the house-floor. Then the prince . . . said to the juggler: 'We have been together since thou wast a little boy, and till tonight thy juggling never failed thee.' 'Alas, alas, fair master Conaire, good cause have I. A keen, angry eye looked at me. . . . Battles are fought with it,' said he. 'It should be known till doomsday that there is evil in front of the Hostel.'"[57]

Gradually Stretching Taller (Shen Jiangao) rescued Emperor Liezu (r. 961–76) of the Southern Tang from a brush with death. The emperor was unable to control the increasingly powerful Zhou Ben, so he invited him to a banquet and presented him with a goblet of poisoned wine. Ben suspected this and, pretending to be drunk, took the goblet intended for the emperor and poured half the poisoned wine into it, then knelt down and offered it, wishing him long life and suggesting that if he did not drink the same wine it would show there was no unity of heart and virtue between monarch and minister and so he could not think of acceding to the emperor's command. This put the emperor in a catch-22 situation:

> The emperor's face drained: a long silence ensued and he still did not speak. The courtiers did not know what to do and looked at each other, sweat pouring off them. The resourceful jester realized what was going on, and on the pretext of turning the whole thing into a joke, seized both cups and drank them, then whizzed out of the room. The emperor secretly sent a trusted courtier to him at his private residence, taking the finest medicines as an antidote, but to no avail—the jester's brain burst, and he died of a hemorrhage.
>
> 上色變，無言久之。左右皆相顧流汗，莫知所從。伶倫申漸高有機智者，竊諭其旨，乃乘詼諧，盡併兩盞以飲之，內杯於懷中，亟趨而出。上密使親信持良藥詣其私第，解之，已不及矣；漸高腦潰而卒。[58]

The name of Vidusaka, the jester of Sanskrit drama, originally meant "reviler." The jester's wit could be employed on behalf of the king if the king was not up to parrying a verbal attack himself. Wang Jian (r. 903–18), founder of the Former Shu dynasty, had once stolen a donkey. When he was besieging Dongchuan the city watchmen kept taunting him by shouting "donkey thief." To his jester Rajagriha (name of a holy city in India—could he have been Indian?) he said, "'Curse them for me!' The jester jabbed his finger at the men on the city wall, ordering them to listen quietly, then said, 'Oi! Did I go into the shed and pinch your ass?!' The guards all laughed." [59]

A jester might also accompany his ruler into exile as the Fool stood by King Lear through thick and thin. When the king of France, Jean II (r. 1350–64), was captured at the Battle of Poitiers in 1356 and taken to England as prisoner, his jester Jehan accompanied him. On Tuesday 21 April 1360 the accounts report that when the king departed for London, five coaches were procured for transport, including one for the jester.[60] At table he had his own silver goblet, which the king had reworked and gilded in England along with his own.[61]

The jester could also be used for delicate diplomatic missions. Jester Shi, who flourished during the reign of King Huiwang (r. 676–652 B.C.) and whose master was Duke Xian, recommended himself for a piece of intrigue with the words, "I am a jester, my words cannot give offense."[62] On one occasion when a Chinese jester interfered in diplomatic affairs, his joke backfired. In 1105, during Huizong's reign, the Liao attacked the Song and then sent Niu Wenshu to sue for peace. A large banquet was held for them, and a jester appeared dressed as a Daoist master. He asked for mud and a crucible, as though to mix a medicine, commenting that there was too little soil to mix it properly. The pun rested on *tu*, meaning both soil and territory, and *he*, meaning "mixed in" or "to reach a peace," suggesting that the Liao envoys were not offering to return enough territory to merit a peace accord. Wenshu responded in kind with a visual and verbal pun, threatening to break off negotiations.[63]

In England Archy Armstrong (fig. 12), jester to James I, accompanied Prince Charles, the duke of Buckingham, and others to Spain to negotiate the marriage between the prince and the infanta Maria, and he was said to have learned more through his wit than anybody else. On 28 April 1623 he dictated a letter to James to tell him he had free access to the king of Spain, who enjoyed his company, and that if James would send an interpreter, he could gather a great deal more information. The letter sounds boastful, but according to others present it was not exaggerated:

> To let your Majesty know, never was fool better accepted on by the King of Spain, except his own fool; and to tell your Majesty secretly, I am better accepted than he is. To let your Majesty know, I am sent for by this King when none of your own nor your son's men can come near him. . . . You will write to your son and Buckingham, and charge them to provide me a trunchman [interpreter], and then you shall know from your fool, by God's help and Christ's help, and the Virgin Mary's, more secret business than from all your wise men here.[64]

George Buchanan, poet and historian as well as tutor, private counselor, and allegedly jester to James VI of Scotland, accompanied the British ambassador to Italy. He also managed to defuse a difficult diplomatic situation. The French king sent a provocative letter with the words, "Will I come? Will I come? Will I come?" Parliament was indignant and wanted to accuse the French king of a breach of peace and to remind him of their

Archee, the *Kinges Iester.*

Archee by *king's,* and *princes* grac't of late
Iested him-selfe into a *fayer* estate
And in this *Booke,* doth to his *friends* Commend
His Ieeres, Taunts Tales, *which no man can offend.*

Figure 12 *Archee the King's Jester.* © The British Museum.

last treaty, but Buchanan sent the ball back into the French court with, "And ye come, and ye come, and ye come," which impressed the king with its dismissive neatness.[65]

Perhaps the most exciting story regarding the involvement of jesters in diplomacy concerns the lovable Matyas of Hungary (r. 1458–90) and his father-in-law, George of Bohemia (r. 1458–71). In 1461 there was a battle between them, although the two kings would meet for parleys in a tent set up between their armies. On one occasion they even had a meal together at which their jesters were present, trying to keep negotiations alive with their sallies. A Bohemian noble called Isdengo had other ideas and suggested that the two jesters be allowed to decide between Catholicism and Hussite Protestantism by having a punch-up. The kings agreed to the idea, telling their respective jesters to fight in a knightly manner. They set at each other with fists and feet, egged on by their masters. It was thought the Bohemian would win until the Hungarian picked up "the monstrous machine" and threw him, his fall being broken by another Bohemian. Isdengo was the referee, and when he saw the defeat of the Bohemian jester, he sprang up and gave him a hard slap across the mouth. At this there was such an uproar that it looked like a bloodbath until the kings intervened.[66]

Canel suggests that the jokes of a jester could be an essential diplomatic tool before the development of a full-fledged diplomatic corps, but even afterward they could still make a useful contribution at the negotiating table.[67] A meeting between the British prime minister John Major and the Reverend Ian Paisley from Northern Ireland was said by Downing Street to have been "frank and forthright," although Paisley described the prime minister, usually a man of sangfroid, as having shouted and slammed documents on the table. Might a jester not have eased tensions between the two men, smoothing their communication with his merry frankness?

GRACE AND FAVOR

At this the king laught hartely, and was exceeding merry, and bids Will aske any reasinable thing and he would graunt it. Thanks, Harry, saies he; now against I want, I know where to find it, for yet I neede nothing, but one day I shall.

Robert Armin, *A Nest of Ninnies*[68]

Newly Polished Mirror . . . enjoyed great favor with Zhuangzong.
Tao Yue, *Supplement to the History of the Five Dynasties*[69]

According to Armin, "there was in the time of Will Sommers another
artificiall foole, or jester, in the court, whose subtiltie heapt up wealth by
gifts given him," and Iñigo López de Mendoza (1398–1458) makes it clear
that even the naturals, whom so many writers like to believe were habit-
ually maltreated, were in fact cared for lavishly.[70] Largesse toward jesters
(and other entertainers) is a recurring theme. Francesillo Zuñiga, short, fat
jester to Charles V of Spain, about whom he wrote a burlesque chronicle,
dressed richly, particularly when paid for by the king, and we hear of him
"with a gorgeous gown of purple velvet lined with tawny damask . . . and
other such gowns and some even better" ("con vna rropa rrozagante de terciopelo morado aforrada en damasco leonado . . . [y] otras tales rropas y avn
mejores").[71] In 1522, when on progress, the emperor seems to have given
him his own outfit of crimson silk lined with white damask ("Este Don
Francisco, cuando el Emperador entró en Córdoba, su ropa carmesí aforrada en damasco blanco la dió á este coronista Don Frances") and later a
coat of violet velvet lined with orange damask, which causes him to express
the hope that he will be rewarded in like manner, or even more extrava-
gantly, in other towns they visit ("una ropa de terciopelo morada, aforrada
de damasco naranjado; y si su voto del autor se tomase, en todas las ciu-
dades ó villas que su Mag. entrase, le darian otra tal ropa, y aun mejor").[72]

The Spanish court accounts from 1563 to 1700, which Moreno Villa has
scoured for references to jesters and dwarfs, yield an endless yardage of silks
and damasks, shoes, and other gifts in addition to daily living expenses, as
well as providing a catalog of portraits, some now lost. Zuñiga was by no
means alone in wallowing in silken opulence. Calabacillas ("Little Pumpkins," pumpkins commonly referring to the hollow heads of fools), who
was immortalized by Velázquez (fig. 13), served Philip IV from 1632 until
his death in 1639. He was given an annual salary, which was supplemented
with allowances worth more than double the salary together with occasional gifts such as a carriage and a mule.[73]

The material generosity of monarchs toward jesters also occurs elsewhere. The Roman emperor Commodus (r. 180–92), said to have been deranged by power and strangled by an athlete for his depravity and cruelty,
nevertheless bestowed many gifts on his jesters, and Heliogabalus (r. 218–
22) gave money to his and even pledged credit for them.[74] Gorgeous clothing of damask, brocade, or taffeta was the most common gift in Europe.

Figure 13 Sketch of Velázquez's "Little Pumpkins" (ca. 1648)

It is said that "whenever Ivan [the Terrible] rode out, he was always accompanied by jesters in buffoons' costume, made of cloth of gold," and in China a large number of anecdotes testify that wit could be lucrative, since an exchange with the emperor often ends with a reward of silk:

> The emperor laughed and rewarded him with a hundred bolts of silk.

> Zhuangzong was delighted and rewarded Newly Polished Mirror generously.

> "Splendid!" said the emperor, and presented him with ten rolls of silk.

> 帝大笑，賜物百段。

> 莊宗大喜賜與新磨甚厚。

> 上曰：『善！』賜帛十匹。[75]

Pei Tan, a censor in the reign of Emperor Zhongzong (r. 684 and 705–10), had a shrewish wife who terrified him. The emperor's wife, similarly intimidating, was a commoner who modeled herself on the notoriously sadistic Empress Wu Zetian (r. 690–705), and the emperor came to fear her. At a palace banquet a jester sang a verse, saying that it was a great thing to fear one's wife, referring to Pei Tan but adding that within the palace nobody surpassed the emperor, whose family name was Li, for wife-induced quaking:

Oh, whirling waves and wicker wares,
Great if your wife gives you the scares!
Outside the court there is only Pei Tan,
But within, no one surpasses Li Old Man.

回波爾時栲栳，

怕婦也是大好！

外邊抵有裴談，

內裏無過李老。

The empress, far from being offended, looked very pleased and rewarded the jester with silks.[76] On 30 July 1667 Samuel Pepys recorded a similar instance when the jester Tom Killigrew showed Charles II to be under the thumb of his mistress, mocking the monarch's masculine pride with impunity. The indirect allusion to the king's subservience lies in the reference to Tom Otter, a henpecked husband in Ben Jonson's *Epicoene, or The Silent Woman* (1609).[77] He described

> how the King, once speaking of the Duke of Yorke's being maistered by his wife, said to some of the company by that he would go no more abroad with this Tom Otter (meaning the Duke of York) and his wife. Tom Killigrew, being by, answered, "Sir," says he, "pray, which is the best for a man to be, a Tom Otter to his wife or to his mistress?" —meaning the King's being so to my Lady Castlemayne. Thus he went on.[78]

In European courts gifts were very often in the form of sumptuous clothes rather than bolts of cloth—August II of Austria (fl. ca. 1728) is said to have had ninety-nine jester outfits *(Narrenkleider)* made for Merry Joseph (Joseph Fröhlich).[79] The French King Charles IX replaced the costumes of his jesters as often as he replaced his own.[80] Geffroy, jester to Philippe V (r. 1316–22), is mentioned repeatedly in the king's accounts from 12 July 1316 until 1 January the following year, while the accounts of Jean II are replete with references to his jester and that of the dauphin, later Charles V (Charles the Wise, r. 1364–80).[81] Velvet hats, one lined with squirrel fur, trimmed on the outside with ermine, and dripping with Cypriot silver buttons and another with a vermilion feather, were made for Jehan Quarrey and his valet. He is also given a regal ration of white lambskins, and on 7 October 1389 a length of gold damask for a robe.[82] The clothes were often made of material that was *marbré* or *royé*, that is,

of different colors or striped, pointing to the motley or particolored costumes we associate with European jesters.

> To Master Jehan, the king's fool, to line the gown of his Easter liv-
> ery with fur; for the two long tunics and the cloak, four strips of fine
> white lamb's fur at 40 sous each; and for the hood, two hoods of
> white Arragon at 20 sous each; and for two dozen trimmings for the
> said gown, at 8 sous each, totaling 19 pounds and 12 sous.

> [Maistre Jehan, le fol du Roy, pour fourrer sa robe de sa livrée de
> Pasques; pour les deux surcoz et la cloche, quatre pennes d'aigneaux
> blanches fines, pièce 40 s. p.; et pour le chaperon, deux chaperons
> d'Arragon blans, pièce 20 s. p.; et pour deux douzaines de létices a
> pourfiler ladicte robe, 8 s. p. pour létice, valent tout 19 l. 12 s. par.][83]

English monarchs also furnished their jesters with furs and fine gowns,
and their clothing seems on occasion to have been the product of considerable carnage. To give some idea of the value, a medieval minstrel's outfit
was allowed one lamb's fur for trimming and was considered costly, perhaps £300 in modern terms.[84] The accounts of Queen Mary (r. 1553–58)
refer both to her jestress Jane and to Will Somers, the favorite jester of her
father, Henry VIII:

> Item for furring a gowne (for William Sommer our foole) with
>   gray jennets tayles, with a peere of sleves and a caape of jennets
>   tailes to the same gowne, and fourtie white lambskynnes.
> Item for furring of a gowne of grene figured Vellat (for hym) with
>   sixtene white hare skynnes and fourtie and six white lamb
>   skynnes . . .
> Item, for furring of a gowne of the same Vellat with six white hare
>   skynnes for Jane our foole.[85]

Very little is known about Jane other than that the queen dressed her
gaily and provided her with more pairs of shoes than she could possibly
have worn out—almost every account reference to shoes for her reads
"Item, for 12 peire of shewes for the said Jane."[86] Elizabeth I continued to
look after Will Somers until his death in 1560, and there are also numerous references in the accounts of her reign to another jester, "William
Shenton our Foole," and to "Thomasina, our woman dwarf," who features
in accounts from 1578 to the death of Elizabeth in 1603.[87]

Court account books might put paid to the popular theory that jesters
always slept on straw with the spaniels. The Valois accounts for 3 January

1389 tell us that Franchequin, valet to the king's jester Jehan Quarrey, was reimbursed for a pair of sheets he had bought for Jehan, while sometime in 1351–52 a lined quilt was provided for the jester's bed.[88] In October 1565 La Jardinière, the French jestress that Mary Queen of Scots brought home with her, was provided with a bed, mattress, sheets, and a lined green plaid cover.[89]

Many of the gifts were on impulse if the king was feeling particularly amused by a jester. It need not even be his own jester or a person normally acting as a jester; in the accounts of Edward II (r. 1307–27) we find, "Item, when the King was at Woolmer, to Morris, then clerk of the kitchen, who, when the King was hunting, did ride before the King, and often fall down from his horse, whereat the King laughed greatly: 20s."[90] In 1538 François I (r. 1515–47) ordered the sum of "22 livres 10 sols" to be given to his *plaisant* Guillaume de Louviers simply for the delight he had brought him ("pour le plaisir qu'il luy donnoit").[91] In 1382–83 we have a payment to "Master Johan the fool . . . to have a horse"; during Henry VII's reign a horse was given to "Martyn the kinges fole"; and "an horse and sadell, bridell and spoures [were] bought for Dego, the Spanish fole."[92]

The accounts show Henry to have been rather more fun loving than many histories would have us believe, and they give a delightful insight into the accessibility and informality of the court, since apart from the numerous jesters who feature regularly, Henry was munificent in his rewards for impromptu performances: on 27 July 1495, "one that leped at Chester" was given 6s. 8d. for his pains, while by far the most generous of these spontaneous gifts was to "a litell mayden that daunceth," who was given £12. Other entries of this sort between 1494 and 1508 include:

Item to one that joculed before the King	x s.
Item to a Walsheman for making a ryme	x s.
Item to the women that songe before the King and Quene . . .	
	vj s. viij d.
Item to one that tumblet at Eltham	xx s.
Item to one that brought the king a Leopard	xiij li. vj s. viij d.
Item to iiij children that played afore the King	iij s. iiij d.
Item to John Redes marynors that rowed vpe and down syngyng	
afore the Kynges manor at Grenewyche	xx s.[93]

From these entries it can be seen that generosity toward jesters was not exceptional—anybody who could turn a somersault or exhibit a party trick could expect a handout—but the jesters were established members of the court, so payments to them were more frequent, combining regular wages with occasional gifts, and include jesters who were not the king's, perhaps accompanying a visiting dignitary. Between 1492 and 1506 we have, for example:

Item to my Lorde Privy Seall fole in rewarde	x s.
Item to a Spaynyarde that pleyed the fole	xl s.
Item to the King of Fraunce fole in rewarde	iiij li.
Item to my Lorde Cardynalles fole	xj s. viij d.
Item to my Lorde of Oxon. joculer	vj s. viij d.
Item to the King of Castilles fole in reward	xl s.[94]

An account of the French court's expenses for 1620 gives the sum of 1,800 livres for the jester Maître Guillaume and 1,200 for his female counterpart, Mathurine la Folle.[95] Another male-female pair were left equal bequests. On 22 December 1535 Isabella d'Este made her will, and having provided for her servants she went on to mention the dwarfs Morgantino and Madonna Delia:

> Item: this lady testamenter in good faith recommends Morgantino to the above-mentioned Illustrious Lord Duke, and when he cannot or does not wish to stay any longer with His Excellency, wishes that he will give him 50 scuti a year for as long as he lives, and similarly she very much recommends Delia to the Most Illustrious Lady Duchess her daughter-in-law, wishing that when she no longer wishes to, or cannot stay with Her Excellency, she will give her 50 scuti a year for as long as she lives.

> [Item essa signora Testatrice di buon cuore raccomanda Morgantino al prefato Ill.mo S. Duca, et quando non potesse o non volesse stare con sua Ex., vole che li dia scuti cinquanta per ogni anno fino che viva. Et similmente molto raccomanda la Delia all Ill.ma S.ra Duchessa sua nuora, volendo che quando non volesse o non potesse stare con sua Ex. che quella li dia scuti cinquanta ogni anno fino che viverà.][96]

The Spanish accounts inform us that jesters and dwarfs could be provided with a daily ration of ice to keep them cool in summer and of coal to keep them warm in winter, an impressive luxury for the time. In 1658 María Bárbara Asquin, a female dwarf of the queen who served in court for just under half a century (1651–1700), was given four pounds of snow every summer day, and in 1678 the queen ordered that a dwarf natural,

Bernada Blasco, who topped a quarter-century in her service, be given four pounds of snow a day in summer, and of coal in winter, in addition to rich clothing.[97]

Jesters occasionally used humorous means of deception to secure gifts or favors, frequently relying on the useful jester formula of adhering to the letter of language and ignoring the spirit. The second unifier of Japan, Hideyoshi, was tricked into giving more than he bargained for by Sorori (Sugimoto Shinzaemon), a scabbard maker whose great wit and humor enabled him to become "a kind of buffoon to Hideyoshi" and the only named Japanese court jester in the available records. Sorori was to be rewarded for comforting a melancholy Hideyoshi, and he couched his request in deceptively humble terms:

> Hideyoshi asked Sorori what recompense he wished. He replied, "A paper bag full of rice." Hideyoshi, pleased with his moderation, promised him what he desired. However, several days later Sorori arrived dragging after him an enormous paper bag, which he put over a great barn. Hideyoshi was much amused, and asked Sorori to celebrate the matter in a verse.[98]

Another instance of such mirthful trickery has the jester Adding Clarity Li con money out of the emperor to pay for his mother's funeral expenses. When the emperor had some time off from affairs of state, he sat in his leisure hall practicing calligraphy. Adding Clarity hoodwinked him by saying,

> "I'm always trying to imitate people's signatures, so that others can't tell the difference." . . . The emperor asked him, "Can you imitate mine?" and Adding Clarity said, "Although I'm a dull-witted fool, I'm willing to have a go at imitating your divine traces." The emperor took out some hemp paper and signed in big characters and asked him to try to copy it. The jester took it and wrote above the signature: "I order the Xuanzhou Imperial Treasury to pay Adding Clarity Li 200 strings of cash so his mother may rest in peace." The emperor saw it, laughed out loud, and agreed to it.
>
> 『臣每竊學人著字與之，不疑。』嗣主曰：『卿能學孤為乎？』家明
> 曰：『臣雖愚魯，願效神蹤。』嗣主乃於麻紙上大押字，命試學焉。
> 家明得之，輒於草字上書云：『宣州上供庫支錢二百緡付家明安厝母
> 親。』嗣主見之大笑，因而賜焉。[99]

Land was sometimes the reward. John Scogin, jester-scholar to Edward IV, was given a house at Cheapside and a mansion at Bury St. Edmunds.[100] Charles I (r. 1625–49) gave Archy Armstrong, hitherto jester to James I, an Irish estate of one thousand acres. Estates at Walworth belonging to Canterbury cathedral were bequeathed by Hitard (whose wit perhaps hit hard), jester to Edmund Ironside (r. 1016), who bestowed the town of Walworth on him in 1016 ("Predictam villam Walworth Edmundus Rex dedit cuidam joculatori suo, nomine Hitardo").[101] In about 1200 William Picol, jester to King John (r. 1199–1216), was given land at Fontaine-Osanne, which would pass to his descendants and which he was to be allowed to enjoy in peace and quiet for his services rendered as the king's fool *(follo nostro)* ("Piculfus et heredes sui habeant et teneant in perpetuum bene et in pace, libere et quiete predictam terram cum omnibus pertinenciis suis per predicta servicia").[102] Zuñiga was awarded land in the province of Avila by Charles V, and the jester Miguel de Antona received estates from Philip II.[103] The village of Hinßendorf was given to and named after Claus Hinße (d. 1599), jester to Duke Johann Friedrich of Pomerania (d. 1600), who also granted that the village be exempted from wolf hunts in perpetuity.[104]

Gifts were occasionally in the form of honors as well as being of material benefit. Archy Armstrong, that "most impudent and boisterous of fools," was granted a pension and in 1617 was given freedom of the city of Aberdeen. Scocola, a jester of the powerful Renaissance d'Este family, was granted the same freedom in Ferrara. Archy was also given a patent for making tobacco pipes in 1618, while the self-appointed jester to Charles II, Thomas Killigrew, managed to obtain a monopoly of all licenses issued to mountebanks and was also master of the revels.[105] Brusquet, jester to Henri II (r. 1547–59), was made a magistrate, carrying out his duties conscientiously.[106] Both Brusquet and Chicot held the lucrative office of *maître de poste,* Chicot also being ennobled in March 1584 by Henri III, despite official opposition: "These titles I bestow on many others who don't serve me anything like as well as he does or help me pass the time" ("Ces titres je les confère à beaucoup d'autres qui ne me font pas tant de services que lui qui me sert bien et me fait passer le temps").[107]

The chief fool *(capo di mati)* of Pope Leo X also held the post of affixer of seals to official documents *(offizio dei piombi),* and the Spanish dwarf El Primo (Don Diego de Acedo) painted by Velázquez, seems to have held a similar position in the Secretaría de la Cámara y Estampa o Estampilla.[108] The formal title Fou du roi en titre d'office, which some French jesters

sported, was instituted by Philippe V, who was so keen to keep his favorite jester Geffroy that he gave him an official post complete with payments
from the treasury.[109] In China something like a jester's title was bestowed
on Hu Zan (the *hu* character perhaps suggesting foreign origins) of the
Five Dynasties period (907–60), also called Ever Upright (Heng Zhi).
The title seems to be Grand Scribe of the Nine Jesters *(jiuyou taishi),* although its provenance and meaning are uncertain.[110] In addition Wang
Yan made an entertainer, Yan Chang, prefect of Fengzhou, an honor also
bestowed by Emperor Zhuangzong on the jester Chen Jun (Chen the
Outstanding or Handsome).[111]

Charles V of France buried his jester Thevenin, who died in 1374, in
a grand tomb.[112] His successor, Grant Johan le Fol, was buried at Saint-
Germain-l'Auxerrois, no mean honor, since it was the parish of the French
kings from the time when the Valois were installed at the Louvre, and Isabella's jester Bernadino the Madman ("Il Matello") was buried in the d'Este
family tomb.[113]

Affection for a jester was often demonstrated by helping his family in
some way. In the anecdote given above, Adding Clarity Li tricked his emperor into paying for his mother's funeral, and the French accounts for
11 July 1365 refer rather wistfully to Nicolas de Saint-Flarcy, the duke of
Burgundy's fool, who was sent home to his mother "without any hope
of his return" and given money for his journey and to clothe himself
("Mond.sr le renvoye chez sa mère, sans espérance de retours devers luy,
et luy fait donner, pour son voyage, dix deniers d'or frans et 4 pour se ve-
stir"). That "Nicolas le fol" appears in the accounts until 1371 suggests he
might have returned, however.[114] An account reference to the jester of Edward II, Robert Withastaf, states, "To Dulcian Withastaf, mother of Robert, the King's fool, coming to the King, at Baldock, of the King's gift, 10s,"
and Queen Mary's accounts provide "three yerdes of Russet Clothe to
make a gowne for William Sommers his sister."

The Spanish accounts show payments in 1565 and 1567 to the daughter and son-in-law, respectively, of Miguel de Antona ("the mad," *el loco*),
jester to Philip II, as well as to a servant of the jester's. When the jester
Antonio Bañules (served 1626–62) died, the queen ordered that the allowances paid to him during his life should continue to be paid to his
widow and children, and in 1643 a gift of clothing was made to the son of
the dwarf Claudito.[115] On 25 August 1637 the accounts state that

> to Manuel de Gante, courtly jester, His Majesty, God preserve him,
> had the mercy to grant permission for him to go to Italy for an un-

limited period, and that during his absence his wife, Floriana de Mercado, should enjoy the two allowances which were earmarked for him.

[a Manuel de Gante, gentil hombre de placer, su majestad, Dios le guarde, ha sido servido de hacerle merced de darle licencia para ir a Italia sin tiempo limitado, y que Floriana de Mercado, su mujer, goce el tiempo que él estuviere ausente las dos raciones que él tiene señaladas.]

Similarly, in 1693 Antonio Macareli, an Italian natural, was allowed to return home for two years and to continue to enjoy his allowances during that time. How many people nowadays can expect two years' paid holiday? [116] But generosity toward jesters does not seem to have been confined to Chinese emperors and European kings—caliphs and moguls could also be persuaded to favor their witty entertainers with gifts. Mu'tadid (r. 892–902), "one of the greatest Abbasid caliphs . . . known for his ruthless skill in dealing with competing provincial dynasties, sects, and factions," was nevertheless indulgent enough to pay "vast debts incurred by his entertainer Ibn Hamdun for fear of losing his society, if he were handed over to his creditors." [117] In India there is a magnificent house known as Raja Birbal's House, built by Akbar for his warm and witty jester as a sign of his affection (fig. 14).

The ability of the jester to intercede on behalf of others could make him a candidate for bribery. Borra, jester of King Martin of Aragon (r. 1396–1410), was said to have accumulated more than a barrel of gold and would often say that he had made more through his folly than scholars could earn with their wisdom. Since he was so much in the king's favor, people would try to win his goodwill with gifts. [118] Simplex Simplicissimus, fictitious protagonist of a seventeenth-century novel, was often given presents by people hoping to butter him up:

Thus I provided entertainment for my master. All the officers showed me their good will, the richest burghers honored me, the servants and soldiers wished me well because they saw how much my master liked me. I got presents here, there, and everywhere, for people knew that jesters and fools have more influence with their masters than straightforward people, and their gifts were meant that way; some gave them that I mightn't tell on them, others to have me do just that, and thus I picked up a pretty penny. [119]

The misnamed Upright Fellow, jester to Emperor Gaozu of the Northern Qi (r. 550–59), was known for his nimble tongue, and the em-

Figure 14 Birbal's House

peror favored him more than anybody. The court director Wang Qianyou
tried to win his friendship with gold and silks in the hope of gaining a pre-
fecture. The jester took all the bribes but had not yet thought fit to speak
up on his behalf when he was impeached by the censorate and flogged
twenty lashes before being deported to a garrison at Tiande.[120]

This is not the only instance of a jester's paying the price for taking a
bribe. When Holy Roman Emperor Frederick Barbarossa (r. 1152–90)
was in Italy the Milanese, having failed to be rid of him by force, decided
to apply a little cunning. They bribed his jester, who knew how to make
himself well loved by the emperor with his joking, to defenestrate Frederick. He almost succeeded, but Frederick was strong and grasped a pillar
while shouting for his servants. They came to his rescue and seized the
jester, hurling him from the window and breaking his neck.[121]

Love Me, Love My Fool

Than sayde the kinges xij. prouostes that is to wyte Neuthur, Bena-
dachar, Benesya, Bena, Benanides, Banthabar, Athurady, Bominia,
Josephus, Semes, and Samer. Wherto com[e]th this fole oure sov-
eraign lorde althus to trouble and mocke? Tho sayde salomon, not
so, but geue hym wele to ete and drinke, and lete hym than goo in
pease.

*The Dialogue or Communing between the
Wise King Salomon and Marcolphus* [122]

There was sometimes resentment at the closeness of the king and jester.
Andare, the legendary court jester of Sri Lanka who still enjoys the same
fame as Birbal and Tenali Rama in India, "being the court jester, always
had his way inside the palace as well as outside. The rest of the courtiers
being envious of this one day conspired to make him look a fool." Need-
less to say it was to no avail, since he countertricked them.[123] The Persian
poet ʿObeyd Zakani complained of the favoritism the king showed his
jester. In his *Biographies of the Poets (Tazkirat al-Shuʾara)* (1487) Dawlatshah describes ʿObeyd's annoyance:

> It has been related that he had composed a treatise on Rhetoric in
> the name of Shah Abu Ishaq that he desired to present to the king.
> But he was told that the king was busy with his jester (and had no
> time for him). ʿObeyd was astonished and wondered if the king's
> most intimate society could be accessible through jesting and rib-
> aldry, and the jesters become his favourites and courtiers, whereas
> the men of accomplishment and learning be deprived of his favors.[124]

Ariosto lamented that jesters were more welcome than the virtuous
and the good ("Più grati assai che 'l virtuoso e 'l buono"), and another
writer gives a lengthy description of all that might feature in a jester's repertoire, adding that jesters had become so highly prized that the tables of
nobles were more encumbered with them than with any kind of virtuous person ("Hor ne' moderni tempi la buffoneria è salita sì in pregio, che
le tavole signorili sono più ingombrate di buffoni, che d'alcuna specie di
virtuosi").[125]

In Europe, where many jesters were natural fools, they could be persecuted by courtiers or pages, and two such instances concerning French jesters are recorded. Caillette, a natural serving Louis XII, had his ear nailed

to a piece of wood by a group of pages and was released by a courtier. Efforts were made to catch the culprits, and the courtier, suspecting the pages, summoned them for questioning. One by one they claimed alibis, and hearing them all use the same words, Caillette also denied it was this or that page. By the time they had gone through all the pages he had forgotten what they were there for, and seeing himself the only one who had not yet been accused, he jumped in with, "I wasn't there either" ("Je n'y estois pas aussi").[126] Triboulet II was similarly treated by some pages and left outside with the nail in his (unusually long) ear. It was the king who rescued him and offered to punish the pages, although Triboulet asked him to forgive them.[127]

Such naturals were often assigned a guardian by the king, not just to protect them but to take care of them generally, just as artificial fools might have a valet. Morata, a natural who served Philip II from 1579 to 1587, and for whom Philip professed an extraordinary affection in his letters, had his own guardian, as did most Spanish naturals at court.[128] In France the accounts generally distinguish between "guardian" and "valet," although the Valois accounts of 11 July 1371 reimburse Jehannot Le Bourgoingnon, both guardian and valet to Nicolas the Fool.[129] Louis XII assigned a guardian, Michel Le Vernoy, to look after Triboulet, and in 1523 another guardian is mentioned for him:

> Gifts made by the king to François Bourcier, keeper of Triboulet, the sum of one hundred pounds given to him and ordered by the king our master . . . on the sixteenth day of February 1523, both for his wages for the current year . . . and for cleaning and taking care of the linen and paying for the lodgings of the said Triboulet.

> [Dons faits par le roi à François Bourcier, gouverneur de Triboulet, la somme de cent livres tournois à lui donnée et ordonnée par le roy nostre sire . . . le sixiesme jour de febvrier mil cinq cent vingt-trois, tant pour ses gages de cette présente année . . . que aussi pour blanchir et entretenir de linge blanc et payer le logis dudit Triboulet.][130]

La Jardinière was a jestress who seems to have had a doppelgänger. She probably began by serving Mary Queen of Scots (r. 1542–67) when she was still dauphine of France.[131] Once Mary returned to Scotland, two La Jardinières are mentioned, one with Mary and one serving Catherine de' Medici. Catherine's features repeatedly in court accounts, and there is one reference indicating that solicitude seems to have extended to her guardian. On 17 July 1560 we find:

To Charlotte Mariel, keeper of La Jardinière, jestress of the queen, the sum of thirteen pounds and sixteen sous to help her buy a gown.... To Charlotte Mariel ... to help her pay for the board and keep of her daughter whom she is maintaining as a nun.

[A Charlotte Mariel, gouvernante de La Jardinière, folle de la royne, la somme de 13 liv. 16 s. pour lui aider à achapter une robe. . . . A Charlotte Marielle ... pour lui aider à paier la pension et entretènement d'une sienne fille qu'elle tient en religion.] [132]

It was often the king himself who would protect the jester, rather than a guardian. The last recorded French court jester, L'Angeli, who features in Victor Hugo's *Marion de Lorme* (1829), was known for his biting wit and would hide behind Louis XIV (r. 1643–1715), using the Sun King as a shield when he launched his attacks. The *skomorokhi*, Russian entertainers including jesters, "were frequently under the protection of wealthy boyars, princes, and tsars." [133]

Robert Armin describes how Jemy Camber, a natural to James VI, was given medical treatment at the order of the king to help cure him of his obesity. The only remedy the physicians could suggest was a trip at sea, and so "to sea they put in a ship, at whose departure they discharged ordinance, as one that departed from the land with the king's favour." In addition, "the Earle Huntly was sent with him to sea to accompany him, so high he was esteemed with the king." One day Jemy was sweating profusely (being overweight) while trying to control a mule and was laughed at for his inability; later however, "the king caused him to be washed and perfumed." In a race between fat, unfit Jemy and a footman, the king saw how exhausted Jemy was becoming and so helped him out of his misery:

And the king, loath hee should have any harme with labour, caused him to have a mixed drincke to cast him into a sleepe; who, when he had drunck, as hee ran on his wager, he dropt downe in the streete, as heavy as if a leaden plummet.... There hee slept, and was carryed by commaund to the top of the hill, and laid downe againe: there hee slept halfe an houre, and when he wakt he remembered his journey ... up hee gets, away he jogs ... and seeing Cannegate so neare him, had not the wit to wonder how hee came there. [134]

While there is no sign of Chinese jesters' having needed the services of a guardian, there is one instance of an emperor's protecting a favorite jester, Immortal Revelation, from the wrath of the prime minister Wang Anshi (1021–86), who instituted a series of sweeping reforms, although he later fell into disfavor and his policies were reversed. Wang was reportedly frugal, unwashed, and obstinate.[135] It was his arrogance rather than his policies that made him the butt of jesters' skits and gibes. In the reign of the Song dynasty Emperor Shenzong (r. 1068–85) Wang wielded immense power, and even the emperor

> acceded to him in everything. Decrees poured forth, but the people felt disaffected. Old ministers and famous scholars voiced their disapproval, and many found themselves demoted or dismissed. Thereafter, new ones tied up their tongues and kept quiet. . . . One of Wang's laws had just been enacted, and the jester put it into a skit on stage at a banquet and gave free rein to his mockery. The joke was passed on to make people laugh, which Wang could not endure, although he could do nothing against his mocker. In a rage he determined to have Immortal Revelation executed, so the emperor secretly dispatched two favorite younger brothers to spirit the jester away and hide him in a royal residence. A saying was made up about the affair: "A top minister can't top a jester."

> 而神廟方然，一切委聽。號令驟出，但於人情適有所離合，於是故臣名士，
> 往往力陳其不可。且多被黜降，後來者乃寖結其舌矣。。。丁使過介甫法制
> 適一行，必因設燕于戲場中，方便作爲嘲譯，肆其情難，輒有爲人笑傳。介
> 甫巨擘，然無如之何也。因遂發怒必欲斬之；神廟乃密詔二王取丁仙現匿諸
> 王邸。二王者神廟之兩愛弟也。故一時諺語有『臺官不如伶官』。[136]

Indian jesters did not need guardians to defend them either, and judging by the failed attempts of jealous courtiers to be rid of Birbal, he did not even need the king to intervene on his behalf. On one occasion the courtiers arranged for Akbar's barber to persuade him that a magician could spirit people away to the hereafter with no injury to themselves. In this way Akbar could find out how his father was if he sent somebody to find him. The barber recommended Birbal as being wise enough to cope with whatever might confront him in heaven. Birbal smelled the skulduggery and dug a tunnel from the pyre to his house. As soon as the smoke rose, he escaped to hide for a few months. He then sauntered into the court and told Akbar how well his father was and how happy he had been to receive the gifts his son had sent. He also brought a message from Akbar's father saying that if there was one thing he missed in heaven it was a good shave. Akbar agreed to send his own barber to grant his wish, and the courtiers did not plot against Birbal for some time.[137]

It might be not the jester who needed to rely on the king or his own wits to protect himself, but rather the wretch who offended him. One cachinnating, frothing fool, whose vindictiveness was matched only by his stupidity, meted out dire retribution for a minor transgression:

> These sort of Fools are sometimes very malicious, and bloodily re-vengeful, for any Affronts they receive: As a poor Fellow, a Carpenter, once sadly experienced, who having anger'd a Nobleman's Fool, by throwing Water in his Face, he kept his Resentments to himself, but watched an Opportunity. The Man not thinking any harm, after Dinner, it being hot Weather, lay at his length, upon a Log, a-sleep, with his Axe by him; with which the Fool being a sturdy Fellow, with one strong blow struck off his Head, and hid it in the Saw-dust: Then running in a doors, he fell into a fit of laughter, till he drivel'd again: And being ask'd why he did so? Oh! said he, the bravest funn that ever you heard of. What is that Jack, said one of the Servants? Why, reply'd he, I laugh to think, when the Carpenter wakes, how like a Fool he'll look without his Head, and lose his Afternoon's work, to find it out where I have hid it.[138]

"HE WHO CANNOT BE SOFTENED INTO GAIETY CANNOT EASILY BE MELTED INTO KINDNESS"
Samuel Johnson[139]

> Her highest Favorites would, in some cases, go to Tarleton before they would go to the Queen, and he was their Usher to prepare their advantagious access unto Her.
>
> Thomas Fuller, *The History of the Worthies of England*[140]

> Well, to the Court he was brought, and had admittance into the presence of the King . . . and now who but Will Summers the King's fool? what had got such an Interest in him by reason of his quick and facetious Jests, that he could have admittance into his Majesties Chamber, and have his ear, when a great noble man, nay, a Privy Councellor could not be suffered to speak with him: and further, if the king were angry, or displeased with any thing, if no man else durst demand the cause of his discontent, then was Will Summers provided with one pleasant conceit or another, to take off the edge of his displeasure.
>
> *A Pleasant History of the Life and Death of Will Summers*[141]

In China "the emperor and the prime minister had no hangers-on and could only be approached by the [the jester] Immortal Revelation," and in India Birbal apparently used his influence "to act as a liaison between Akbar and his Hindu subjects, to protect them from Muslim prejudices."[142] Many jesters would profit from their closeness to the king to intercede on behalf of those who had little influence themselves. Armin tells of a poor woman who, seeing Will Somers asleep on a stile and likely to fall backward and hurt himself, fetched a cushion to make him more comfortable and a rope to tie him so that he could sleep safely. She then stood by and watched over him. When he woke and learned of her kindness, he rewarded her by pleading to the king on her behalf and obtaining the release of her son, who was due to be hanged for piracy.

Somers once interceded on behalf of his uncle and other villagers whose heath was enclosed by a local gentleman so that they had nowhere for their cattle. He promised the king that if he helped the villagers, it would "make thee rich, and my uncle shall be made rich by thee." The king asked how helping them would make him rich, to which Somers replied, "The poore will pray for thee; and thou shalt be rich in heaven, for on earth thou art rich already." The king assented.[143] And as Henry lay dying, Somers appealed to him on behalf of his first master, who had suffered from the voracity of the king:

> Will Summers was some time a servant in the family of Richard Farmor, esq. of Eston Neston, in Northamptonshire, ancestor to the earl of Pomfret. This gentleman was found guilty of a praemunire in the reign of Henry VIII. for sending eight pence, and a couple of shirts, to a priest, convicted of denying the king's supremacy, who was then a prisoner in the gaol at Buckingham. The rapacious monarch seized whatever he was possessed of, and reduced him to a state of miserable dependance. Will Summers, touched with compassion for his unhappy master, is said to have dropped some expressions in his last illness, which reached the conscience of that merciless prince, and to have caused the remains of his estate, which had been much dismembered, to be restored to him.[144]

Jester Meng one day bumped into a man carrying firewood, who turned out to be the son of the former chancellor, Sunshu Ao. Sunshu had "recognized in Jester Meng an extremely fine character and treated him with great favor," advising his son to turn to the jester if he ever needed help. The chancellor's integrity meant that he had not stashed away bribes, so within a few years of his death his son was reduced to poverty. Jester

Meng decided to help him; he dressed up as the deceased chancellor and appeared before the king, who was so astounded at the resemblance that he assumed it must be a reincarnation and invited him to become the new chancellor. He used a song to awaken the king to the plight of the Sunshu family, with the result that they were given a fief of four hundred households:

> Sure, it is a hard life,
> and the living's rough and rude
> in your hovel in the mountains,
> ploughing for your food.
> And if you get yourself a government post
> by methods however vile,
> and are meaner and greedier than most,
> you can loot yourself a tidy pile,
> caring not for fame or face,
> indifferent to all disgrace,
> living, dying, with no sniff for moral health
> you can leave with your kith and kin just rolling in the wealth.
>
> All very nice and jolly,
> but I fear there's something more:
> if you pocket filthy bribes
> and bend the honest law,
> with the flood of all your crimes unabated
> when you die, your kith and kin
> may all be liquidated.
> So for all the loot and lucre
> one can stack by being sinister,
> what's the good of ever being
> a greedy-gutted minister?
>
> And yet, and yet, on the other hand,
> if you should make a moral stand
> and respecting the laws of lord and land
> aspire to be a just official
> incorrupt and loyal all day long,
> tenacious ever of integrity to the very last,
> guiltless of all greed or wrong—
> why, who's the mug would fall for that?
> Just tell me, if you can,

what minister is daft enough
to be an honest man?
For Sunshu Ao, the Premier,
was a righteous man all his livelong days:
now his wife and son hawk firewood—
who says that virtue pays?

山居耕田苦，

難以得食。

起而為吏，

身貪鄙者餘財，

不顧恥辱。

身死家室富，

又恐受賕枉法，

為姦觸大罪，

身死而家滅。

貪吏安可為也！

念為廉吏，

奉法守職，

竟死不敢為非。

廉吏安可為也！

楚相孫叔敖持廉至死，

方今妻子窮困負薪而食，

不足為也！[145]

One day during a feast given by the First Emperor of the Qin (Qin
Shi Huangdi, r. 246–210 B.C.), the dwarf Jester Twisty Pole noticed that
the palace guards who were on duty outside were shivering in the pouring
rain, and he decided to help them. He told them how to respond when he
gave the sign. During the official toasts

> Jester Twisty Pole leant over the balustrade overlooking the steps and
> yelled, "Gentlemen of the guard!" "Present and reporting for duty,
> sir!" responded the guards. "Huh, look at you," he said, "great tall,
> lanky fellows! And what good does it do you? There you are, left out
> in the rain. While I'm just a short-arsed runt, and here I am taking it
> easy indoors with the Emperor." Hearing this, the Emperor arranged
> for guard duty to be taken in shifts.

優旃臨檻大呼曰：『陛楯郎！』郎曰：『諾！』優旃曰：『汝雖長，何益？辛雨
立。我雖短也，辛休居。』於是始皇使陛楯者得半相代。[146]

Guo Sheren was a favorite jester of Emperor Wudi of the Han. When
Wudi was a baby the mother of Marquis Dongwu had acted as his wet
nurse. When he grew up he always listened to everything she said, and as
a result her younger relations ran rampant, believing themselves unassail-
able. However, marshals requested that she and her whole family be removed to the frontiers, and the emperor agreed to this. When the wet
nurse was due for an audience, she first went to see Guo Sheren and asked
him what she should do. He told her that when she was refused, she
should walk away quickly, then turn her head back for a last look. Guo was
present at the audience, which went as he anticipated, the wet nurse being refused to her face. She did as he had advised:

> Guo Sheren cursed her fiercely and said, "Ugh! You old woman!
> Why don't you get lost! His Majesty is a grown-up now, d'you think
> he still needs your milk to keep him alive? What are you looking
> back for?" Thereupon the emperor felt pity for her, and regretted
> [his decision]. He then issued an edict preventing his wet nurse from
> being exiled and punishing the people who had slandered her.
>
> 郭舍人疾言罵之曰：『咄！老女子！何不疾行！陛下已壯矣，寧尚須汝乳而活
> 邪？尚何還顧！』於是人主憐焉悲之，乃下詔止無徙乳母，罰譖讒之者。[147]

The German jester-poet Friedrich Taubmann spoke up for a soldier
who had shot his colonel from behind and was to have his right hand
hacked off as punishment. The duke spoke of the matter at table, and
Taubmann said it was too late, they should have cut his hand off before
he shot the officer. The duke laughed and pardoned the soldier.[148] There
is a similar anecdote attributed to a number of French jesters, including
Triboulet in the reign of François I, although the intercession was strictly
on behalf of himself. When a nobleman threatened to kill Triboulet for
having offended him, the jester ran for protection to the king, who reassured him that if the threat were carried out, the murderer would be
hanged within a quarter of an hour. The jester begged the king to hang
him a quarter of an hour before he was killed, not after.[149] And when
Tamerlane was getting carried away doling out thrashings, Nasrudin
talked him out of imposing his punishments:

> One day Nasreddin Hodja was with the King when they brought
> some criminals before him to be sentenced. The Sultan roared: "Give

this man 800 lashes, and this one 1200, and this one 1500 lashes!"
Nasreddin Hodja interrupted the King by asking: "O King, do you
know everything?" "Of course I do!" he snapped back. "Then how
could you inflict such a punishment? Either you don't know the meaning of the number 1500 or you don't know the sting of a whip!"[150]

Emperor Akbar kept trampling crops in his hunting ardor, and the
farmers complained to Birbal about it. When they next went hunting they
rested a while under a tree in which some owls were twittering, and Akbar
asked Birbal what they were saying. He listened carefully and explained
that one of them refused to give his daughter away in marriage unless he
be given twenty-five trampled fields as bride price, while the boy's father
was saying that if he could only wait a few months he would be able to
have thirty such fields. Akbar was puzzled and asked how the boy's father
could have thirty ruined fields in a few months if he did not have even
twenty-five now:

> Birbal pretended to listen again. "Quite simple, my Lord," he replied.
> "The boy's father says that the king loves hunting very much. He
> rides through the fields. He has already damaged many crops. If he
> does not stop hunting, he will soon ruin many more." Akbar was very
> sad when he heard this. "I have not thought of the damage I have been
> causing, Birbal," he said. "I have only thought about my own plea-
> sure. I shall never go hunting in the fields again."[151]

Tenali Rama was summoned urgently by the queen, since the king
had stopped visiting her because she had yawned while he was reading her
a play he had written. She had apologized but to no avail, so she asked
Tenali to help. He visited the king as he was discussing with his ministers
how to increase the rice crop and produced a single rice seedling that he
said could yield three times more than any other if it were planted by
somebody who had never yawned and never would:

> "Fool!" said the king. "Can there be a single person in the whole world
> who has never yawned?" "I forgot that. How silly of me!" said the
> jester. "It is a good thing that your Majesty has remembered it. I
> must go and tell Queen Tirumaladevi about this folly of mine." "No.
> I shall go and tell her myself," said the king. Everybody laughed. The
> king went, after the durbar, and made up with the queen and gave
> the jester a bag of gold. So did the grateful queen.[152]

On another occasion a wrestling champion turned up looking for
people to beat. The local wrestlers were terrified, and Tenali Rama volun-

teered to save them from a certain thrashing. He borrowed all their badges and said he would take on the champion if he could recognize certain secret symbols familiar only to first-class wrestlers. Tenali Rama then proceeded to demonstrate a lot of esoteric sign language of Masonic intricacy. The champion was stumped and had to leave without a fight. The king asked his jester to explain all the mysterious signs. He acted them all out again, this time with a running commentary: "Atisura! If I approach you, you will pierce me with your dagger in my chest and kill me. I shall then drop down stretched on the ground with my face upward. Then who will protect my wife and child?" The king (and no doubt the relieved wrestlers) had a good laugh at the ingenuity of the jester.[153]

Sometimes the jester's intercession went only as far as sounding out the mood of the monarch, or engineering access to the royal person, perhaps in return for a "gift." Mathurine, dwarf-jestress to Henri IV, managed to introduce the wife of a condemned man to the king's presence, where she was able to plead successfully for her husband's life. Everyone at court knew that the king could refuse his diminutive jestress nothing and that it was therefore worthwhile to enlist her aid in obtaining favors.[154] And there is one instance of a jester's asking another jester to speak up for him by pleading directly with God rather than any mere earthly authority. As Don Francesillo de Zuñiga lay dying, his close friend Perico de Ayala, jester to the marquis of Villena, visited him and said:

> "Brother Don Francés, for the sake of the great amity we have always had, I make this request: that when you are in heaven—which I am sure will be the case since you have led such a good life—you ask God to have mercy upon my soul." He answered, "Tie a thread to my little finger so that I won't forget." And those were his last words before he died.
>
> [Hermano Don Francés, ruégote por la grande amistad que siempre hemos tenido, que cuando estés en el cielo, lo qual yo creo será así, según ha sido tu buena vida, ruegues a Dios que aya merced de mi ánima. Respondió: Átame un hilo a este dedo meñique, no se me olvide. Y ésta fué la postrera palabra, y luego murió.][155]

A FRIED PANCAKE, OR RISIBLE RIDDLES

Emperor Gaozu held a banquet for his close ministers at which they amused themselves with entertainments. Gaozu said, "I'm going to give you all a riddle, and you lot solve it: 'Cu lu ge da.'" None of the courtiers could work it out. Someone asked if it was a kind of eolian arrow. "Wrong," said the emperor. Moving Bucket piped up, "I've got it!" "What is it then?" asked the emperor. "It's a fried pancake!" The emperor laughed and said, "That's it, Moving Bucket's cracked it. Now you lot ask me one and I'll solve it for you." Before anybody else had thought of one, Moving Bucket again asked: "Cu lu ge da." The emperor couldn't figure it out and asked, "So what is it then?" "A fried pancake." "But I asked that one first, why are you asking it again?" Moving Bucket explained, "Well, I thought I'd strike while the griddle's hot and make another one." The emperor laughed heartily.

"Shi Dongtong"[156]

The exchange of riddles was a very popular pastime in Chinese courts. Usually for simple amusement, it could also be used by the jester to straighten out an erring emperor. The jesters most gifted in riddle solving were Moving Bucket and Dongfang Shuo (154–93 B.C.), who was at the court of Emperor Wudi of the Han. In addition to being a scholar who had several works attributed to him, he was also one of China's greatest and most popular jesters and later became known as a Daoist immortal. When the emperor made his jesters play a game of "guess what's under it," hiding something under an upturned cup, Shuo was the only one who guessed it, after making a show of consulting the classic of divination, the *Book of Changes:*

> "I would take it for a dragon but it has no horns. I'd say it was a snake except that it has legs. Creeping, crawling, peering here and there, good at moving along the wall—if it's not a gecko, it's bound to be a skink!" "Splendid!" said the emperor, and presented him with ten rolls of silk. Then he ordered him to guess some other objects. Again and again Shuo guessed correctly and was immediately presented with more silk.

> 『臣以爲龍又無角，謂之爲蛇又有足，七七脈脈善緣壁，是非守宮即蜥一。』

> 上曰：『善！』賜帛十匹。復使射他物，連中，輒賜帛。[157]

Another jester, Guo Sheren, peeved at Shuo's repeated successes, decided to challenge him to some riddles. There are several examples of their bantering exchanges in Ban Gu's (32–92) biography of Dongfang

Shuo in the *History of the Former Han (Hanshu)*, and although Ban Gu says that Guo "enjoyed great favor with the emperor for his never-ending fund of waggery and was constantly in attendance at the ruler's side," he nevertheless was unable to best Shuo.[158] He gave him a "guess what's under it" challenge, and so confident was he of his certain victory that he even offered himself for a beating if he lost. He lost.

The emperor ordered him to be beaten, and when he cried out at the pain, Shuo laughed and said, "Ugh! Mouth with no hair—voice all ablare—rear end in the air!" which incensed the other jester and caused the emperor to ask why he was trying to humiliate Guo. With the jester's feigned disingenuousness, a favorite technique for avoiding trouble, he explained that he was only making up more riddles for his fellow court fool. The "mouth with no hair" referred to a canine equivalent of a cat door, "voice all ablare" meant baby birds chirping for more food, while "rear end in the air" was simply a crane with its head down pecking the ground.[159] In another exchange between the two, Guo again offered to submit himself to a beating:

> Guo said, "I want to ask Shuo something, and if he gets it, I'll willingly submit myself to a hundred strokes of a cane; if he doesn't, then Your Majesty must give me silk: 'A guest comes from the east, singing as he goes; doesn't enter by the door but leaps over the wall; plays in the middle court then moves to the great hall. You hit him with a slap, slap, but the dying one still resists and dies fighting, although the master is also wounded'—what is it?" Shuo said, "A long beak and a thin body, it hides in the daytime and walks at night, loves meat, hates smoke, and is often swatted; I, Shuo, in my foolishness say it's a mosquito. Guo has lost, so he should pull down his trousers again."

> 郭曰：『臣願問朔一事，朔得，臣願榜百；朔窮，臣當賜帛。曰：客來東方，歌謳且行，不從門入，踰我垣牆。遊戲中庭，上入殿堂。擊之拍拍，死者攘攘。格鬥而死，主人被創。是何物冶？』朔曰：『長喙細身，晝匿夜行。嗜肉惡煙，常所拍捫。臣朔愚戇，名之曰蟲。舍人辭窮，當復脫褌！』[160]

More recently, the dowager empress Cixi (1835–1908), something of a murderous megalomaniac and de facto ruler of China for over half a century, displayed an oddly enlightened quirk in encouraging her jester-actors to invest their spare time in reading, painting, and calligraphy, and some of them became quite skilled. She also enjoyed exchanging riddles with them and would reward them generously if they managed to solve them.[161]

The Indian King Krsnadevaraya made up a riddle for his courtiers, asking them what was the source of the quality of sweetness in the poems of Dhurjati. Some put it down to fate, some to the poet's own purity, and others to the grace of a goddess. The jester Tenali Rama felt he could do better, and he succeeded in revealing the seamy side of the sensitive poet while he was about it; he followed Dhurjati, who spent the night with a prostitute. Tenali Rama's answer to the riddle was a tongue-twisting one-liner that makes the mouthful of the famous Welsh village, Llanfairpwll-gwyngyllgogerychwyrndrobwllllantysiliogogogoch, look pathetic:

> "Aha! I have discovered [the secret]—[the sweetness comes from] sipping the streams of nectar issuing from the sweet lips which remove great distress, the lips of delicate but aggressive women who delude the whole world."

> ["ha telisen bhuvanaikamohanoddhatasukumaravaravanitajanata-ghanatapaharisantatamadhuradharoditasudharasadharala grolutam jumi!"][162]

Riddles could also be put to serious purpose. King Weiwang of Qi neglected his duties as king to indulge in booze and women. The state was in chaos, and adjacent countries were encroaching on its borders. "None of his courtiers dared suggest he should mend his ways. But Baldy Chunyu attempted to reason with him by means of a riddle." The king solved the riddle and accepted the reproof, subsequently applying himself conscientiously to the running of the country:

> "There's a big bird in this land who has settled on the royal palace and for three years it hasn't flapped its wings or uttered a single peep. Does Your Majesty know what sort of a bird it is?" "As long as that bird doesn't spread its wings and fly," countered the King, "all well and good. But once it does, it will smash its way through Heaven itself. As long as it stays silent, that's all there is to it. But once it opens its beak and sings, it will give people one hell of a fright."

> 『國中有大鳥，止王之庭，三年不蜚又不鳴，王知此鳥何也？』王曰：『此鳥不飛則已，一飛沖天；不鳴則已，一鳴驚人』。[163]

In *Throne of Straw* (1972), a play set in the Jewish ghetto of Lodz, Yankele fulfills all the functions of the court jester to Rumkowski, head of

Figure 15 Rupert and the riddler. © Express Newspapers PLC.

the Judenrat (the Jewish Council with which the Nazi authorities "coop-
erated"), and he is one of the most jesterlike of fool characters in modern
drama. Other Jews in the ghetto try to reassure themselves that something
will happen, that the Allies will come to their rescue. Yankele sings a riddle
to show how much faith he places in the imminent rescue operation:

> A riddle without a middle
> Is a question that's lost its mind
> Here's one with which you can fiddle
> A knot at the edge of the wind
>
> I ask you—why is a blindman
> And our allies alike as two peas?
> The man with no eyes sees no one
> And their armies none of us sees.

(182)[164]

A riddle can be a lighthearted form of amusement (fig. 15) or a useful method of indirectly uttering painful truths without causing offense.

According to the early sixth-century Chinese classic on literary theory by Liu Xie (ca. 465–ca. 522), *The Literary Mind and the Carving of Dragons (Wenxin diaolong)*, "from the Wei dynasty [220–65] on, there were no jesters who did not exchange riddles with their rulers," although Baldy Chunyu's riddle with Weiwang suggests that the practice predates the Wei by a long chalk.[165]

"NONE BUT THE FOOL, WHO LABOURS TO OUT-JEST / HIS HEART-STROOK INJURIES"
Shakespeare, *King Lear* (3.1.16–17)

> Our Tarlton was the master of his Faculty. When Queen Elizabeth was serious (I dare not say sullen) and out of good humour, he could un-dumpish her at his pleasure . . . and cured her melancholy better than all of her Physicians.
> Thomas Fuller, *The History of the Worthies of England*[166]

> "Rocmid, the king's fool. There was never trouble or tiredness on any man of Ulster that he would not forget if he saw Rocmid."
> "The Awakening of Ulster"[167]

Tarlton's Jests describes his cheering up a despondent Elizabeth I: "The Queene being discontented, which Tarlton perceiving, took upon him to delight her with some quaint jest. . . . Whereat Her Majestie laughed heartily."[168] Will Somers could "undumpish" Henry VIII, and Armin gives an account that he says was in living memory of some still at Greenwich, of how he succeeded in making a solemn Henry first smile and then laugh enough to forget his bad mood, all with a riddle:

> The king being on a time extreame melancholy, and full of passion, all that Will could doe will not make him merry. Ah! sayes hee, this must have a good showre to clense it; and with that goes behinde the arras. Harry, saies hee, Ile goe behind the arras, and study three questions, and come againe; see, therefore, you lay aside this melancholy muse, and study to answere me. I quoth the king: they will be wise ones, no doubt. . . . I promise thee, Will, saies the king, thou hast a pretty foolish wit. I, Harry, saies he, it will serve to make a wiser man than you a foole, methinks. At this the king laught, and demaunds the third question. Now, tell me, saies Will, if you can, what it is

that, being borne without life, head, lippe, or eye, yet doth runne roaring through the world till it dye. This is a wonder, quoth the king, and no question; I know it not. Why, quoth Will, it is a fart.[169]

Giles Fletcher was appointed English ambassador to Czar Fedor I (r. 1584–98) on 6 June 1588. His account of his stay in Moscow was one of the most widely read travel books in Elizabethan England and provides perhaps the only firsthand Western account of jesters in the Russian court, illustrating also their vital function in relaxing the czar with their fooling:

> After his sleep he goeth to evensong, called *vechernia* and, thence returning, for the most part recreateth himself with the Empress till suppertime with jesters and dwarfs, men and women that tumble before him and sing many songs after the Rus manner. This is his common recreation betwixt meals that he most delights in.[170]

The Italian jester Fra Mariano Fetti would run along tables at banquets to liven up the proceedings, since the court jester's main raison d'être was to get people laughing.[171] Jokes could even be simple pratfalls; Emperor Gaozu (r. 936–41) of the Later Jin (936–46) had a jester who would pretend to fall down in a drunken stupor, lying there until somebody important came along, and then leap to his feet in feigned terror.[172] And Sima Qian tells us that the "favorite jester, Guo Sheren, although not deeply philosophical, nevertheless brought pleasure and delight to the emperor" (fig. 16).[173]

During the reign of Emperor Gaozong (r. 1127–62) of the Southern Song dynasty (1127–1279), a banquet was held in the palace and a jester pretended to be good at astrology, saying that there was some correlation between officials and their stars and that he could easily spy them out. He explained that normally he would of course use an armillary sphere and jade transverse sight, but since this could not be set up on the spur of the moment, he would make do with a copper coin instead. This comic shamming is reminiscent of the astrologer-jester Sky Colour (Himmelfarb), who entertains guests of a Nazi concentration camp commander by reading their stars through a cardboard telescope.[174] Gaozong's jester began by pointing at the emperor and then the prime minister, and finally a man known for his wealth, commenting on what he saw through the eye of the coin—Chinese coins came from the mint with a hole—that related the star to the person. Beginning with the emperor, he said:

> "This is the imperial star!" At Qin Shiyuan, he said "This is the prime minister's star!" To Prince Zhang Xun he said, "I can't see his

star." Everybody was shocked and asked him to try again. He said, "I still can't see a star, all I see is Prince Zhang Jun sitting in the eye of the coin." The emperor burst out laughing. Jun had a lot of money, which was why he was mocked.

『帝星也！』秦師垣，曰：『相星也！』張循王，曰：『不見其星。』眾駭，復令窺之，曰：『中不見星，只見張郡王在錢眼內坐！』殿上大笑。張最多資，故譏之。[175]

At the court of Emperor Jingzong (r. 825–27) of the Tang, the jester Tall Towering Mountain (Gao Cuiwei) excelled in acting the fool. For a joke the emperor ordered that his head be pushed under water. He was held for quite a while, and when he came up for air he was laughing about it. The emperor was amazed and asked him what was so funny. Towering Mountain explained that he had seen Qu Yuan, the famous ancient minister who drowned himself in the Miluo River because his king was ruling badly and refused to heed his good counsel. The jester claimed Qu Yuan had said to him:

> "I was landed with King Huai of Chu [r. 328–299 B.C.], who lacked virtue, so I drowned myself in the Miluo River. You're lucky enough

Figure 16
The merrymaker

to have met with a sage emperor, so what are you doing here?" The emperor laughed and rewarded him with a hundred bolts of silk.

『我逢楚懷王，無道！乃沉汩落水；汝逢聖明主，何為來？』帝大笑，賜物百段。[176]

The jester-mulla Nasrudin in his centuries-spanning Orlandoesque career was said to have been the jester to Tamerlane. According to one anecdote, Tamerlane wept when he saw his cyclopic ugliness in a mirror, and his courtiers wept in sympathy before attempting to cheer him up. Only Nasrudin continued sobbing, and when asked why, he answered, "If you, my lord, wept for two hours after seeing yourself in the mirror for but an instant, is it not natural that I, who see you all day long, should weep longer than you?" Tamerlane had a laugh.[177] Talhak, jester to Sultan Mahmud of Ghazna, enjoyed a close and easy relationship with him. Like jesters in Europe and China he could use his sense of humor to cajole the sultan into a better temper:

> One day Sultan Mahmud was very angry, and Talhak wanted to change his mood. He asked, "O Sultan, what was your father's name?" The Sultan was annoyed and turned away from him. Talhak walked around him and once more asked the question. The Sultan said, "Cuckold! what do you want my father's name for?" Talhak retorted, "Now we know what your father's name was. What about your grandfather's name?" Thus the Sultan was made to laugh.[178]

Akbar grieved so much over the death of his jester Birbal that he was unable to function for days. A verse said to have been composed by Akbar when his jester died conveys his sadness, and Birbal's capacity to cheer him in his moments of gloom:

> When I was melancholy
> Birbal gave me everything
> Except more sorrow to bear.[179]

In Europe jesters were occasionally sent by their masters to another court, either as a mark of friendship or if somebody was ill or sorrowful and needed cheering up. A noble of Brittany sent his favorite jester from Paris to Lyons to delight a cousin of his who was ill ("pour aller réjouir un sien cousin qui estoit malade").[180] Frederico, eldest son of Isabella d'Este, lent the priest-jester Fra Stephano to a Duke Alfonso, who wrote a letter on 14 November 1525 to

cordially thank you for the great service rendered to me by such a
servant as yours, truly worthy of serving any great prince, for besides
his pleasantries, which suffice to provide ample entertainment at any
great court and to keep the company merry and in good cheer, he has
also the quick wittedness to be of worth in other circumstances. In
short I am most satisfied with him and feel obliged to your most se-
rene and illustrious self whom I pray will pardon me if I have so long
kept you without your Father Stephano.

[la ringratio cordialmente de la comodità ch'ella mi ha fatto de un tal
suo servitore, degno veramente di servire ad ogni gran Principe, per-
chè oltra le sue piacevolezze che bastano per dar spasso add ogni gran
corte et per tener festante et in piacer una compagnia, esso ha ancho
ingegno da possersene valere in altre occorrentie. In summa io resto
optimamente satisfatto di lui, et ne sento obligo a V. S. Ill.ma, la qual
priego che mi perdoni se così longamente l'ho tenuta senza esso Pre'
Stephano.][181]

There is one instance of a jester's doing such a good job of cheering
up a sickly king that he killed him with laughter. When Martin of Aragon
(r. 1396–1410) was suffering a high fever, having eaten some aphrodisiac-
enriched goose, his jester Borra went to see him in his room. The jester
told a joke that seems to allude to the king's having fallen ill from the aph-
rodisiacs before he was able to profit from them. At this the king laughed
so heartily that he died without even the blessing of a priest.[182]

The duty of the jester to defuse anger or ease melancholy or sickness
could have a serious bearing on the king's ability to rule in a just and impartial manner. A bad mood could cloud the judgment of a man whose
decisions might have widespread effect, as the king in Ludwig Tieck's *Puss
in Boots (Der gestiefelte Kater)* (1797) acknowledges:

> One cannot work hard enough, my friends, to keep in good humour
> a king about whose neck hangs the welfare of an entire country and
> countless subjects. For if he gets into a bad mood, then he very easily
> becomes a tyrant, a monster; for good humour promotes cheerful-
> ness, and cheerfulness according to the observations of all philoso-
> phers makes men good. For this reason, in contrast, melancholy is to
> be scorned as a vice because it promotes all vices.

> [Man kann nicht genug dahin arbeiten, meine Freunde, daß ein
> König, dem das Wohl eines ganzen Landes und unzähliger Unter-
> tanen auf dem Halse liegt, immer bei guter Laune bleibe. Denn wenn

er in eine üble Laune gerät, so wird er gar leicht ein Tyrann, ein Un-
mensch, denn gute Laune befördert die Fröhlichkeit, und Fröhlichkeit macht nach den Beobachtungen aller Philosophen den Men-
schen gut, dahingegen die Melancholie deswegen für ein Laster zu
achten ist, weil sie alle Laster befördert.] (78–79)[183]

Indications of the jester's closeness to the monarch far outweigh the
occasions when his mockery was considered offensive. He was not merely
tolerated, he was cherished, trusted, protected, and indulged. His proximity to the throne allowed him to intercede on behalf of those who may
not have had the necessary contacts or *guanxi,* or when the ruler was not
in the mood to listen to serious appeals. Rulers often showed tremendous generosity toward their jesters, and if they failed to provide what was
wanted, the wily fools could usually find some way of laughing them into
coming up with the goodies. The jester's mockery was clearly not always
a pointed attack, often being just a gentle teasing of people's foibles or else
straightforward mirth: "A gentleman meeting the King's jester, asked
what news? Why, Sir, replied he, there are forty thousand men risen today. I pray, to what end, said the other, and what do they intend? Why,
to lay down again at night."[184] In addition, he had the vital function of
cheering up an unhappy or anxious monarch and of dispelling his anger,
thereby saving the court and other subjects from having to deal with an
all-powerful man in a bad mood.

And, let me tell you, fools have another gift which is not to be despised. They're the only ones who speak frankly and tell the truth, and what is more praiseworthy than truth?

Desiderius Erasmus, *Praise of Folly*[1]

The Antichrist can be born from piety itself, from excessive love of God or of the truth, as the heretic is born from the saint and the possessed from the seer. Fear prophets, Adso, and those prepared to die for the truth, for as a rule they make many others die with them, often before them, at times instead of them . . . Perhaps the mission of those who love mankind is to make people laugh at the truth, to make truth laugh.

Umberto Eco, *The Name of the Rose*[2]

3

In Risu Veritas, or Many
a True Word Spoken in Jest

A Man of Many Disguises

But one day he was on the road, he wis only aboot fifteen or sixteen at the time an he sees this knight come a-ridin on this horse. But he didna ken hit wis a king, he thought it wis a knight. (This is away back when the king used tae travel roond his subjects unknown tae see what like the folk really was, way back in the ninth an tenth century a king wad dress hissel as a knight an set sail through the country tae see how the people wis gettin treatit. They didna ken who he was, but he wis their king aa the time.)

D. Williamson and L. Williamson,
"George Buchanan, the King's Fool"[3]

It was not uncommon for a monarch to go out in disguise, either to sound out the real feelings of the people or simply to escape from the pomp and circumstance of kingship, and the jester might accompany him on these escapades. Caliph Harun al-Rashid would wander through Baghdad in disguise at night in the company of his jester-poet Abu Nuwas; Chicot abetted Henri III on his incognito jaunts; and Akbar also liked to go out in disguise either on his own or with Birbal. Once when he ventured out alone, he was attacked and the royal seal stolen from him, so that when he tried to convince people who he was they ignored him while the thief brandished the seal. When he returned to the palace he found a parcel waiting for him that contained the seal and a note saying, "Never go into the city alone," with Birbal's signature.[4] During the Xuanhe reign-period (1119–25), Emperor Huizong decided to go out incognito and had to scale a wall—his jester jumped down first so the emperor could stand on his shoulders.

Matyas Corvinus I of Hungary (r. 1458–90) was something of a jester-king in addition to being fond of keeping jesters, even being said to resemble a jester, with his long nose and accentuated features. This well-loved and merry monarch could learn more through his disguises than he might otherwise have done and be amused into the bargain—there are tales of corruption and cruelty being exposed, and kindness rewarded, by the tricks of the king. In one story the manager of a silver mine in Transylvania was known for cheating and stealing. Matyas appeared in disguise, and when he saw four porters placing golden dishes before the manager as an opulent footstool, the king arranged for a trusted man to give the manager a piece of parchment. When the manager read it he fainted and died of fear:

> King Matyas was here
> He saw the golden dishes
> Beneath the feet of the manager.[5]

Matyas was one of that rare breed of kings who could act as his own jester. He certainly kept jesters, but he could have supplied his own entertainment and indirect means of uncovering the truth about the way his people felt. For the most part, however, the ruler had to rely on indirect sources of information, memorials from ministers, and hearsay. If the ministers were conscientious and themselves in touch with the public, and if the courtiers were reliable in their accounts, this would probably be enough. Nevertheless, the frequency with which the jester stepped in to give the king an insight into popular needs and sentiments suggests that the formal sources of counsel did not always function as efficiently as they should, either because the king was being insulated from the truth by his ministers and courtiers or because he was simply deaf to all conventional counsel. In this case the jester was called in.

The Infanterie Dijonnaise was one of the most prominent medieval French fool societies, and its motto, that anyone who did not wish to see a fool should smash his mirror, was a reflection of a widely held perception of the mirror as truth revealer, a quality shared with jesters: Holbein's marginal illustrations to Erasmus's *Praise of Folly* show a jester looking in a mirror.[6] A mirror shows us as we really are first thing in the morning; similarly, a jester can hold up a mirror to the king, making him see himself clearly and perhaps encouraging him to polish his image. In China one of the all-time jester greats was called Newly Polished Mirror, and a jester-actor was known as Mirrorlike Lu (Lu Ruojing). In a pack of fifteenth-

Figure 17 The topsy-turvy motley.
© Express Newspapers PLC.

century Austrian playing cards, the female joker holds up a mirror and
grins at herself. The name of Eulenspiegel, archetypal jester-trickster,
combines "owl," an association with wisdom, and "mirror" because he
shows things as they really are.

"I am upside down in this life," says Nasrudin, the jester who crosses
more national and temporal boundaries than any other.[7] Another facet of
the mirror image is its reversal of reality. The jester can turn the world on
its head (fig. 17), making people see the ultimate insignificance of many of
the things they hold dear, perhaps showing them their priorities from a
different angle or a wider perspective. This topsy-turvy aspect of the jester
can be seen everywhere, and much of his humor is based on upsetting and
inverting accepted logic: "O! saies Jemy, how cold the wether is. . . . No,
says the king, it is hot; looke how I sweat. No, says Jemy, the sunne
blowes very cold. No, says the king, the winde shines very hot."[8] A former chaplain of the clowns' church of Holy Trinity in London put it suc-
cinctly: "The clown stands on his head and sees the world the right way
up."[9] There was even a European genre of art devoted to turning the world
on its head, and for about three hundred years from the mid-sixteenth

century, broadsheets with the title "World Upside Down" enjoyed wide-spread popularity. Sebastian Brant used the mirror metaphor in his *Ship of Fools*, with its list of over a hundred types of fool not to be emulated:

> For fools a mirror shall it be,
> Where each his counterfeit may see.
> The glass of fools the truth may show.
>
> [In diesen Spiegel sollen schauen
> Die Menschen alle, Männer, Frauen;
> Die einen mit den andern ich mein'.] [10]

The liminal quality of the jester allows him to perceive reality perhaps more clearly than those who are less peripheral to society. "The fool knows the truth because he is a social outcast, and spectators see most of the game," an idea expressed in a Chinese four-character proverb, *pang guan zhe qing*. [11]

"SPEAK WHAT YOU THINK"
["Fare quae sentias"] [12]

> Then came lunch and I did a lot of talking again, for I had decided to discuss all foolishness and punish all vanity, and my job at that time gave me an excellent excuse for it. No one at table was too great to escape my tongue. And if there was one who wouldn't stand for it he was either laughed at by the others or he was told by my master that no wise man would ever get angry at a fool.
> Johan Grimmelshausen, *Simplex Simplicissimus* [13]

If there is no clear Chinese term for "court jester," there is a very clear term for the kind of indirect humorous advice he gave: *fengjian* (indirect, mock-ing, or satirical remonstrance) and also, occasionally, *youjian*, "jester's re-monstrance." Although no other language seems to have such clear terms, the concept was far from being unique to China. The common ground of the jester everywhere lies in his duty to entertain and his license to speak freely, even if this earns the ire of his master. Jesters are rarely recorded in fawning mode (fig. 18). It is this privilege that distinguishes him from the armies of acrobats and actors employed to enliven a court, a distinc-tion that is blurred in the nomenclature of the entertainer-actor continuum in China and its entertainer-fool equivalent in Europe. It is attested by

Samuel Pepys as late as 1668, when the Chinese court jester had long declined and the European one was certainly past his heyday. He writes of

> Mr. Brisbanke, who tells me in discourse that Tom Killigrew hath a fee out of the wardrobe for cap and bells, under the title of the King's foole or Jester, and may with privilege revile or jeere anybody, the greatest person, without offence, by the privilege of his place.[14]

This is perhaps their most sensitive and dangerous as well as most widely recognized function. It is the right to present indirect and even

Figure 18 Fools be not flatterers, Niklaus Türing (1500)

forthright mockery of universal human foibles and more precisely aimed critical advice, sharp edges softened with colorful and witty wrapping, that prevents the jester from being relegated to the general ranks of court entertainers. A work published in 1682, *L'enfant sans soucy,* after the name of one of the most famous French *sociétés joyeuses,* or fools' societies, states that "jesters have a privilege which the wisest have not — that they are able to say and do what the Socrates, the Scipios and the Catos of the world dare not" ("les bouffons ont un privilège que les plus sages n'ont pas, qui est qu'ils peuvent faire et dire ce que les Socrates, les Scipions et les Catons n'oseroient entreprendre").[15] A common designation for the court jester in German is "merry counselor" *(lustiger Rath),* and in Dutch the fool of the chambers of rhetoric was called a "reasoning fool" or "fool rhetorician" *(rederijkersnar),* perhaps pointing to the verbal skills usually employed in this role.

Pußmann, jester of Friedrich I of Prussia (r. 1701–13), was refused a church burial by the clergy, perhaps because he had once addressed harsh words to Bishop Ursinus von Bähr ("Bear of Bear"). When the king heard this he ordered that the jester be buried in the main church close to the altar, among the clerics, and that nobody should object. The reasons he gave stress the importance of the jester's tendency to speak honestly: "Puß-mann was a preacher of truth and didn't even spare me. Consequently he deserves to be buried in the center of the church, a place where nothing but the pure truth should be preached" ("Pußmann war ein Prediger der Wahrheit, und hat meiner selbst nicht geschont, verdient folglich mitten in der Kirche zu liegen, wo nichts als lauter Wahrheit gepredigt werden soll").[16]

European jesters are distinguished from jesters in other parts of the world in that their license was often due to their offering two types of *fengjian.* In addition to the satirical, mocking *jian,* they could also claim to be proffering *jian* combined with the *feng* that means madness. "Truth can be tolerated only under the guise of folly" ("La verité ne se fait tolérer que sous le masque de la folie"), says Dumas. Touchstone in *As You Like It* "uses his folly like a stalking-horse, and / under the presentation of that he shoots his wit" (5.4.105–6), and Olivia in *Twelfth Night* confirms that "there is no slander in an allowed fool" (1.5.76).[17] However, the excuse of folly, feigned or otherwise, was rarely invoked explicitly and seems to have been taken for granted, since the jester was almost invariably allowed to have his say.

When Charles IX of France was suggested as a possible match for Elizabeth I, her jester told her not to marry the fourteen-year-old, who was "but a boy and a babe"; instead she would do better to marry the Hapsburg archduke who was also on offer, so that "she would have a baby boy." Elizabeth translated his opinion for the imperial envoy, who commented that "babes and fools speak the truth." This statement is echoed in many proverbs, such as the Greek "If you want to know the truth, ask a child or a fool" and the German "Narren und Kindern reden die Wahrheit."[18] For this reason it was commonly appreciated that great men need jesters, and not just to amuse them. In 1701, when jesters were perhaps still thriving only in the courts of Germany, Russia, and Spain, Johann Balthasar Schupps wrote that

> a great lord should either read the histories or keep fools. For what a Chancellor meanwhile does not wish to say and what a Court Chaplain should not or dare not say will be said by a fool and the histories. Histories tell us what has happened. A fool speaks what is still to happen. It is said that children and fools speak the truth. Since neither Chancellors nor counsellors, nor any other grandees, Court Chaplains or governors wish to be seen as fools, so it comes about that great lords so seldom hear the truth.

> [ein großer Herr solle entweder Historicus lesen oder Narren halten. Dann was unterweilens ein Cantzlar nicht will sagen / und was ein Hoffprediger nicht darff oder nicht erkühnt zu sagen / das sagt ein Narr und ein Historicus. Ein Historicus sagt / es sey geschehen. Ein Narr sagt / es geschehe noch. Man sagt / Kinder und Narren sagen die Warheit. Weil nun Cantzlar und Räthe oder andere Grandes, Hofprediger und Superintendenten / nicht wollen für Kinder oder Narren angesehen werden / daher kommt es / daß große Herren so selten die Warheit hören.][19]

There is a plethora of proverbs and quotations testifying to the belief that a fool (and by extension a feigned fool) could be relied on to expose the folly of those purporting to be sane. Burton expresses the idea that "fools and madmen tell commonly the truth," and a German saying states that the wise would do well to learn from fools ("Der wys mag von dem torechen leeren!"). Brantome suggests that we speak of fools as sages ("Il faut parler aussi bien des fols comme des sages").[20] In Russia, naturals enjoyed the favor of czars who would take heed of their advice.[21]

Chicot was by profession a soldier who nevertheless employed his jester qualities to envelop his wise counsel in witty wrapping, encouraging the king to adopt a policy of tolerant benevolence. He would chat with the king on an intimate footing, now and then casually slipping in some sound advice that might have been ill received from any other quarter. Fuller tells us that the jester-actor Tarlton "told the Queen more of her faults than most of her chaplains," and Sima Qian describes Jester Meng as having had "a fund of witty repartee at his disposal . . . always offering his ruler useful advice in the guise of a good joke."[22]

In France during the sixteenth and seventeenth centuries it seemed common to appropriate the license of a known jester by publishing satirical pamphlets in his name. The most frequent instances of this practice occurred in the name of Chicot and his contemporary jester Maître Guillaume. There is a long satirical poem called "Le songe de Chicot," dated 1586, that lambastes members of the courts and the Ligueurs (adherents of the Holy League that formed in the 1570s to fight the Huguenots), and a pamphlet titled *The Parables of Chicot in the Form of Advice concerning the State of the King of Navarre in Paris (Les paraboles de Cicquot en forme d'advis, sur l'estat du roy de Navarre à Paris)*, which addresses the following quatrain to readers:[23]

> Formerly Chicot like a fool would prate
> But a Doctor of Law he has become of late
> *Mocking the vices of the head of state*
> A sign his head is screwed on straight.

> [Chicot au temps jadis faisoit toujours la beste
> Mais changé maintenant en Docteur de la loy
> *Reprend en gaudissant les vices de son roy,*
> C'est signe que Cicqvot est bien tourné de teste.][24]

Persians often used the jokes or stories of Ash'ab, the eighth-century jester from Medina, as a cover for their own opinions, and Zakani, the Persian poet-satirist, would use Sultan Mahmud's jester Talhak as a mouthpiece for his criticisms.[25] The Indian jesters were fearless truth tellers, merrily exposing greed and hypocrisy and helping those who had no other recourse to appeal, and the Aztec jesters also mingled truth with jest. Montezuma II, the greatest of their kings, was an avid jester keeper:

> He frequently heard music, during the time of his meal, and was entertained with the humorous sayings of some deformed men whom he kept out of mere state. He showed much satisfaction in hearing them, *and observed that amongst their jests, they frequently pronounced some important truth.*[26]

For all this supporting evidence of the jester's vital truth-telling function, however, it is the Chinese records that provide us with by far the greatest number of specific anecdotes, although qualitatively they do not differ from those found elsewhere. In most cases the jester's words were heeded, and very frequently they were rewarded and acted on.

"He Who Restrains His Prince Loves His Prince"
Mencius (Mengzi) (372–289 b.c.)[27]

> Though Shuo was given to jests and buffoonery, he would on occasion observe the emperor's mood and, if he found it right, would speak out boldly in severe reprimand. The emperor always listened to what he had to say.
> Ban Gu, *Biography of Dongfang Shuo [Dongfang Shuo zhuan]*[28]

The jester was perhaps the supreme untitled "remonstrating official" *(jianguan)* and the place where the buck stopped. One is often given the impression that the difficult and even dangerous duty of telling the emperor where he was going wrong could fall to the jester as a last resort, when nobody else dared, and he complemented the official *jianguan*, providing an "extralegal dynamic."[29] Sima Qian commented that "even a joke or witty turn of phrase can do a good job solving some of the world's knotty problems and tricky situations."[30] The first part of this quotation is still in circulation as a four-character phrase meaning to hit the mark by indirect means *(tan yan wei zhong)*. Hong Mai (1123–1202) described how jesters, despite their formally low status, were able to reform government with their jokes and sallies: "Jesters and dwarfs were the lowest of the Zhou dynasty entertainers, but by jests and humorous indirect advice, even they could prod their government to reform."[31] Mao Qiling (1623–1716) tells us that "they would crack jokes about current affairs in order to offer indirect advice."[32] And Immortal Revelation Ding, in addition to being solicited for his opinions on music and poetry, also used his position to offer advice: "Every time he put on a skit before the emperor, he would try to correct contemporary matters with his counsel."[33]

In the fourth century b.c. the state of Chu launched an attack on Qi, and the king of Qi sent his jester Baldy Chunyu to ask for relief forces from another state, Zhao, showing the trust that could be invested in a jester. The gifts he was sending with Baldy were rather paltry, and the jester laughed his head off. The king asked if he thought the gifts insufficient. The jester denied this, explaining that he was amused because he had seen a man who was performing sacrifices in hope of a bumper harvest; his offerings comprised a pig's trotter and a cup of wine, yet he was asking that heaven "Grant cartloads from the low ground and full hampers from the high, / grain in ripe abundance and sheaves piled to the sky."[34] It was just the huge disparity between the man's measly investment and his expectation of high returns that made Baldy laugh. The king understood the analogy and sent Baldy off with a splendid supply of gifts. Zhao responded with sufficient reinforcements to persuade Chu to withdraw the same night.

A jester wanted to draw the attention of Sultan Mahmud of Ghazna to the fact that his people were hungry. He did this by making a fool of himself for the amusement of Mahmud, only obliquely alluding to the people's hunger. Appearing oblivious to the assembled guests, he began to search the banqueting hall, complaining that he could not find a single sheep's tail. The sultan ordered a servant to give him a vegetable shaped like a sheep's tail, which the jester began to eat, asking Mahmud if it reminded him of anything:

> "What would a sheep's tail in your mouth remind me of, except the proverb that 'Extremes meet'?" the sultan said, then asking him what he thought of his "sheep's tail." The jester answered, "It's not bad, but it's not as fat or tasty as they used to be when your predecessor was on the throne, but maybe that's neither here nor there, since people are so much leaner now too."

The sultan realized his jester was not as foolish as he made out, and since another jester had told him how grateful the owls were to him for all the ruined villages, he took steps to improve the lot of his subjects.[35] When the sultan was walking in his garden one day, he tripped over a blind and sleeping dervish. These eccentric holy men of the Islamic world, peripheral to the mainstream of their colleagues, had a certain license to speak plainly. The dervish was awakened by the royal kick and abused the sultan for his clumsiness. A courtier shouted at him, saying he was stupid as well as blind and should take care whom he abused when he could not see him. The dervish shocked Mahmud by telling the courtier he was shallow if he thought a sultan should not be criticized. The sultan was so impressed that he quietly asked the dervish why a monarch should have to listen to the vituperation of a blind dervish:

"Precisely," said the dervish, "because it is the shielding of people of any category from criticism appropriate to them which is responsible for their downfall. It is the burnished metal which shines most brightly, the knife struck with the whetstone which cuts best, and the exercised arm which can lift the weight." [36]

The court jester is a skilled burnisher of the king's mettle, a constant whetstone to prevent his becoming blunt with flattery and complacency, and a perfect counterweight to his majesty. Louis XIII allowed jesters to sit in council with him, and one of his councillors asked that they withdraw: "Sire, when the king your father, of glorious memory, did me the honour of consulting me on the affairs of his kingdom, he began by withdrawing the jesters and the buffoons" ("Sire, lorsque le roi votre père, de glorieuse mémoire, me faisait l'honneur de me consulter sur les affaires de son royaume, il commençait par faire retirer les bouffons et les baladins"). [37]

Tom Killigrew took a sartorial step to discourage Charles II from accepting bribes. The king ordered a new suit of clothes at a time when memorials and appeals were coming to him from all over the kingdom. Killigrew ordered the king's tailor to make an outfit with a very large pocket on one side and on the other side one so small that the king could hardly fit his hand inside. The king questioned the tailor, who said he had done it at Killigrew's request. Killigrew was summoned to explain himself, and he said that the big pocket was to put all the appeals in and the small one to keep the money they would try to give him. [38]

A monarch would often ask his jester for an opinion—Emperor Charles V frequently asked Zuñiga what he thought of someone, and we have two examples of Henry VIII's asking Will Somers for advice. The lease on a piece of land had expired and was in the king's gift. Three contenders appeared before the king to make their appeals: a servant of the Pantry and two lawyers. Henry asked Somers whom he considered the most deserving. The jester took a walnut, broke it in half, and gave half a shell to each of the lawyers and the nutmeat (land) to the servant, saying that lawyers always charge a lot of money and leave people with nothing but empty shells. On another occasion Henry was selecting men to be his guards and, seeming pleased with the ones before him, asked what Somers thought. The jester pointed out the various scars they bore and suggested Henry find the men who had inflicted them, since these would make better guards. [39]

One method of admonishing a king is to offer him the title of fool, a verbal equivalent of making him change places with his jester. A list of fools was drawn up by a man from Damascus with the sultan's name at the top. The sultan summoned him and asked why he was at the top of the list. He explained it was because he had been taken in by a charlatan. The sultan insisted that the man was doing an errand for him and would soon return. "'If he returns,' was the retort, 'I promise to erase your name from my list and substitute his.'"[40] This fool's register of fools is a common trick, and similar anecdotes exist concerning, among others, Will Somers when Henry VIII gave a Spaniard £1,000 to buy Spanish horses for him and the jester of Alfonso, king of Naples, who sent a slave on the same mission.[41] A variation of the theme is told of Archy Armstrong, jester to both James I and Charles I:

> When Prince Charles took that unaccountable journey into Spain, the king being in one of his pensive moods, Archee addressed him with a request, that his Majesty would change caps with him. Why? says the king. Why, who (replied Archee) sent the Prince into Spain? But what (answered the king) wilt thou say when the Prince comes back again? Mary, said Archee, I will then take my cap from thy head, and send it to the King of Spain.[42]

Triboulet once registered François I in his book of fools for overpaying a man for a mission he could not possibly complete in the time he promised. The king reassured Triboulet that the man had promised to reimburse him if he did not succeed, and Triboulet responded that, if so, the man would deserve to be registered alongside the king.[43] This may have been a regular trick of Triboulet's, and with it he succeeded in unnerving the Holy Roman Emperor Charles V, who in 1540 visited François in Paris. He wanted to leave, but François kept inviting him to attend more hunts and outings. Despite the generous hospitality, Charles felt uneasy for reasons recorded in the memoirs of Martin du Bellay (1569):

> He did not ignore the joke that had a short while before slipped from Triboulet, François's fool, making a great impression on the courtiers. This joker, who was not lacking in spirit, had publicly written on his slate that the emperor was more of a fool than he since he dared to cross France. Questioned by the king as to what he would say if this prince passed freely, Triboulet answered, "Well, Sire, I would erase his name and replace it with yours." This retort, which made François laugh heartily, seemed to Charles to have great significance, and he could not grasp how his rival failed to consider it as a piece of very sound advice.

[Il n'ignorait pas la plaisanterie échappée peu de temps auparavant à Triboulet, fou de François, et qui avoit fait une grande impression sur les courtisans. Ce baladin, qui ne manquoit pas d'esprit, avoit écrit publiquement sur ses tablettes que l'Empereur étoit plus fou que lui, puisqu'il osoit traverser la France. Interrogé par le Roi sur ce qu'il diroit si ce prince passoit librement: "Alors, Sire," avoit répondu Triboulet, "j'effacerai son nom et je mettrai le vôtre à la place." Cette répartie, qui avoit fait beaucoup rire François, paroissoit à Charles d'un grand sens, et il ne concevoit pas comment son rival ne la consideroit pas comme un conseil fort sensé.] [44]

Chicot frequently used a light and bantering tone to deliver serious advice, and instances of this were recorded in the memoirs of Pierre de l'Estoile, where we see the ease and informality with which a jester could address the king. On one occasion he warned of the perils the king faced from the Ligueurs. They opposed Henri III and supported a rebellion against him that continued under Henri IV, both of whom Chicot served. The mocking tone that introduces the warning leads to the punch line, which suggests the Ligueurs would gladly string the king up, and it ends on a note of flippant understatement:

"I'm not surprised . . . if there are so many people dying to be king, and if there are crowds queuing up for it: it's a desirable thing; it's nice to be called King of France, and the job is an honest one: for in working one hour a day at some little exercise, you have the means to live for the rest of the week while overtaking your neighbours. But for the sake of God, my dear Sir, beware of falling into the hands of the Ligueurs, for you will be falling into the clutches of those who would string you up like a sausage and then write on your gallows. . . . That's rather dangerous for the living."

["Je ne m'esbahis pas . . . s'il y a tant de gens qui abbayent à estre rois, et s'il y a de la presse à l'estre: c'est chose desirable; c'est un beau mot que roi de France, et le mestier d'estre tel en est honneste: car en travaillant une heure de jour à quelque petit exercice, il y a moiien de vivre le reste de la semaine, et se passer de ses voisins. Mais pour Dieu, monsieur mon ami, gardés vous de tumber entre les mains des ligueus: car vous pourriez tumber entre les mains de tel qui vous pendroit comme un andouille, et puis feroit escrire sur vostre potence. . . . Cela est dangereux pour le passage des vivres."] [45]

His jocular comments about what a great job it is to be king, with an hour's work lasting for a week, is echoed by the jester of Duke Huan of Qi (b. 643 B.C.). The duke and his minister Guan Zhong were known as an ideal example of the powerful ruler and capable minister, and the duke relied on him heavily. The jester laughed about it and said, "It's dead easy being a ruler; all you have to say is Father Zhong this, Father Zhong that." But the duke had a ready answer:

> "I have heard that the work of the ruler is in finding good people, and his loss is in not using them. It was hard enough for me to get hold of Father Zhong, and so having got hold of him, why shouldn't I have it easy!"

『易哉爲君！一曰仲父，二曰仲父』。。。『吾聞君人者勞於索人，佚於使

人。吾得仲父，亦已難矣！得仲父之後，何爲不易乎哉！』[46]

The advice of a jester was not always heeded, and occasionally this led to disaster for the ruler. Hans Kuony warned Duke Leopold I of Austria not to engage in an attack. The duke ignored him and suffered a disastrous defeat in 1315. This story was so well known that the jester was being portrayed in pictures half a century later.[47] In 1386 a later duke of Austria, Leopold the Pious, who wanted to launch an attack on the Swiss, held council to discuss the matter. He asked the opinion of his jester, Jenny von Stockach, which was delivered bluntly: "You fools, you're all debating how to get into the country, but none of you have thought how you're going to get out again" ("Ihr Narren, ihr rathet alle, wie ihr ins Land hineinziehen wollt, aber keiner denkt darauf, wie ihr wieder herauskommen wollt"). They failed to listen, and the army suffered a rout with the knights in armor passing out from heat and thirst before they had even engaged in battle and at least two thousand killed (including the duke) when the Swiss rolled rocks down the mountains.[48]

Another example of unheeded warning is given in the early Chinese work *Discussions of the States*, in which a king insisted on having a huge bell cast despite the enormous financial cost and the suffering it would cause the people. A duke tried to dissuade him, to no avail, and when the king consulted his jester, Prefectural Turtledove (Zhou Jiu), he was told that to indulge such an excessive whim would disaffect the people and anger the gods. The king ignored the advice and went ahead with the casting of the bell. The jester's dire prediction that the king would be overthrown was met with contempt: "You old fool! What do you know?" But the king was toppled the following year.[49]

In 1264 a German jester managed to warn his master's opponent of impending attack. The jester served Grave Ulrich of Regensberg, who had a dispute with Grave Rudolph of Hapsburg (later Holy Roman Emperor, r. 1272–92) and started to build up an army in secret. When it was assembled, he commented that there were enough men to "knock the big nose off the Hapsburg" ("von Hapsburg seine große Nase zu klopfen"). The jester overheard this and supposed that Rudolph's nose must be a mile long to need an entire army to storm it. He ran to see it and was allowed in to see Rudolph. He stood for a long time looking and then said: "As far as I can see, your nose isn't as big as my master says to need so many people to knock it off. I think I'm strong enough to wallop it off myself, lock, stock and barrel" ("Wie ich sehe, so ist die Nase so groß nicht, daß mein Herr so viel Volk ausgebothen hat, dieselbe zu klopfen; ich meine, ich willte allein stark genug seyn, diese Nase dergstalt zu dreschen, daß weder Stumpf noch Stiel sollte übrig bleiben"). Rudolph realized what Ulrich was planning and managed to beat him down to the extent that a few years later he was reduced to the status of a commoner.[50]

The ubiquitous Nasrudin was said to have offered advice to a king. He told him that laws in themselves did not make people better, they needed also to have a kind of guiding "inner truth." The king disagreed and felt that he could force people to be truthful. Guards were posted at the city gate, and everybody entering was questioned. If they told the truth they could pass; if not, they were hanged. Nasrudin approached and was asked where he was going. "To be hanged." The guards said they did not believe him. "Very well, if I have told a lie, hang me!" "But if we hang you for lying, we will have made what you said come true!" "That's right: now you know what truth is—*your* truth!"[51]

The Indian jester Tenali Rama exposed the greed of his king by telling him that an astrologer had predicted he would soon die and he feared he had made no provision for his family. The king assured him he would take care of them. A while later Tenali Rama allowed people to think he was dying, hid his gold and jewels, and climbed into his money chest. As soon as the king heard he had died, he sent servants to fetch the chest. They pried open the lock, and Rama climbed out. "'What, you are not dead?' cried the embarrassed king. 'With someone like you as my family's guardian, how can I afford to die?' the jester replied."[52]

An enemy of the king bribed his astrologer to dissuade him from a military campaign by predicting defeat. Tenali Rama unmasked the charlatan by asking if he was sure his predictions were correct. The astrologer insisted they always were. The jester then asked how long he thought his own life would be. The astrologer confidently predicted another thirty years, saying he would die at seventy-four. At this a general, at Rama's behest, took a sword and decapitated him, proving the fallibility of his forecasts.[53] This is not the only instance of Tenali Rama's using decapitation as a means of exposing someone. In one story he stepped in some excrement while out walking with the king. The king told him he would have to amputate the offending toe. Tenali Rama built a shit pit, covered it with turf and beautiful rose bushes, and invited the king to view the fragrant flowers. In leaning forward to sniff them, he landed up to his neck in warm, malodorous feces:

> "Wait a minute. I shall bring a sword, and cut off the polluted portion, neatly, at the neck," said Rama. "What! Cut my head off?" asked the king, in surprise. "What else can be done unless Your Majesty revises your opinion. . . . " "I revise the opinion. Pull me up quick, before others see me," said the king frantically, and Rama pulled him out.[54]

The Indian jester Gopal also offered his king a taste of his own medicine. Rama offered a reward to anybody who could spend the whole night immersed to the neck in a cold pond. Gopal did so, but Rama told him that the distant light of an oil lamp must have kept him warm and refused to give him the reward. Gopal invited Rama to dinner and lit a fire with a pot of food suspended over it from a high branch of a tree. Rama commented that the distance between the pot and the fire meant the food would never cook, to which Gopal retorted that if the distant light of an oil lamp could keep him warm, the food would cook. Rama gave in and paid up.[55]

Birbal was often able to laugh Akbar into seeing his own folly. We see this in a precursor of Monty Python's parrot sketch. Akbar had a prize parrot that he valued above all his other pets. He warned his servants that they must look after it well, for whoever brought him the news of the parrot's death would himself have to die. Despite their best efforts the parrot died, and they were too frightened to tell Akbar, so they appealed to Birbal. Birbal went to him to tell him how amazing the bird was, since it had reached a state of perfect *samadhi* and was a real yogi. The king wanted to see this for himself and was enraged when he saw the dead parrot:

> "The bird isn't in *samadhi*, you fool! He's dead." The royal trickster smiled, "Your Highness must die, according to your own decree, for telling you that the parrot is dead." The king had no choice but to admit his folly—"I sometimes say foolish things"—and to laugh the

humorous laughter which is directed at oneself, and in that laughter forgive his servants, his jester, and himself as well.[56]

This underlines another facet of the jester's truth-imparting function. He might be the only one capable of breaking bad news to the king. When Edward III of England (r. 1327–77) routed the French army nobody dared tell the king, Philippe VI (r. 1328–50), until the jester took it upon himself. He went to the king and repeatedly shouted, "The English cowards! The lily-livered English!" The king asked him why he was saying this, and he answered, "Because they don't even have the guts to jump into the water like our brave French!" The king realized he had lost the battle.[57]

After the quelling of the An Lushan rebellion, Emperor Xuanzong was returning from exile. There was a camel loaded with his expensive trinkets, and the emperor noticed its bells tinkling. He commented to In Full Streamer that they made a sound like a human voice. The jester took the opportunity to comment on the way the country had been run, combining a name for the emperor (Sanlang) with "dissolute" or "sloppy" *(langdang)* to make an onomatopoeic imitation of the bells: "They sound like someone saying *'san lang lang dang, san lang lang dang!'*" ["『似言「三郎郎當！三郎郎當！」』明皇笑且愧之。"]. The emperor laughed and felt ashamed.[58]

During the Chongning reign-period (1102–6) another skit exposed the inconvenience of the new high-value coin minted in 1103. Cai Yuanzhang proposed that it be devalued by 10 percent, although among the people this was not considered sufficient. At a palace banquet a jester played the part of a wine seller. Someone gave him one of the new big coins, drank a cup of wine, and asked for the change. The vendor said that he had just come out and did not have enough small change (the coins that were in the process of being called in), although the customer was welcome to keep drinking wine in order to have his money's worth:

> After he had drunk five or six cups in a row, he rubbed his stomach and said, "Just think what a difference it would make if the prime minister debased the coinage a hundredfold!" *The Emperor was moved by this, and the law was changed.*
>
> 乃連飲至於五六，其人鼓腹曰：『使相公改作折百錢，奈何！』上爲之動，法由是改。[59]

Two musicians of Louis XIII had angered the king, and he halved their pay as punishment. His jester Marais arranged for the musicians to appear in a masque before the king. They were only half clothed, and the king asked the meaning of this. They answered that people who were on half pay only half dressed themselves. The king laughed, and they were in favor again.[60] A strikingly similar technique is used by a Chinese jester at the court of Emperor Huizong: there were agricultural shortages, and it was suggested that the part of the mandarins' salary that was paid in grain should be halved. Visual and verbal puns on the character *xing* meaning both "to walk" and "to carry out" or "put into practice" were used to quash this idea:

> A jester dressed up as a mandarin and started removing his hat, his belt and the skirt of his robe until he was only half dressed. The other jesters wondered at this and asked him what he was doing. "Cutting down by half!" He put both his legs into one trouser leg and hopped forward. He was again questioned about it, and again he answered, "Cutting down by half!" The jester who asked gave a long sigh and said, "Although you've got cutting down by half to a T, you just don't realize how crippling it'll be!" *This story was passed around the palace and the suggestion [to halve the grain pay] was abandoned.*
>
> 優人乃為衣冠之士，自冠帶衣裾被身之物輒除其半。眾怪而問之，則曰：『減半！』已而兩足共穿半褲，躄而來前。復問之，則又曰：『減半！』問者乃長歎曰：『但知減半，豈料難行！』語傳禁中亦遂罷議。[61]

A play on the word "half" was also used by Groucho Marx to counter an anti-Semitic regulation. In classic jester style he did not overtly challenge the rule itself, let alone make any direct accusations of injustice. He simply asked a straightforward question that combined the apparent innocence, flawless logic, and razor wit of a jester to expose folly: he wanted to become a member of an exclusive beach club but was politely told by the management that Jews were not allowed to swim from the beach: "What about my son? He's only half-Jewish. Would it be all right if he went into the water up to his knees?"[62]

There is an anecdote attributed to three giants of jesterdom, two from India—Gopal ("So exquisite was Gopal's wit that he violated the laws of the domain and defied the Rama's pride with impunity") and Birbal—and the Middle Eastern Nasrudin, in which the jester's master has to find a way to count how many stars there are in the sky. In the Gopal version the jester promises to take over the onerous task and asks for a lot of money and a year in which to do it. He spends both the year and the money in riotous licentious delight (in one version then asking for another year and another million rupees to complete his "research") and finally turns up with some sheep, claiming there are as many stars as the sheep have hairs. Since the emperor asked how many without demanding a specific number, he cannot argue.[63]

Sometimes a jester would use shock therapy to cure a king of misguided policy. No witty puns or jokes, just plain speech. A pardon arrived for James I to sign for a murderer who had already been pardoned for two murders. When the king told George Buchanan that it was for a man who had killed three men, Buchanan retorted that in fact the murderer had killed only the first one, and the king had killed the other two because he failed to give justice after the first murder. The king was taken aback by this and thereafter refused to pardon murderers.[64]

There is an Arabic tale of a jesterlike hunchback who helps the king see the stupidity of his superstitiousness by making him laugh. A hunchback was supposedly a bad omen, a malign being who should be avoided. One day when the king was out hunting, the first person he met was a hunchback, whom he ordered beaten and imprisoned. He then continued with the hunt and caught a good deal of game. When he returned, unharmed despite the hunchback's having crossed his path, he ordered that the prisoner be brought to him and given some money to compensate him for his incarceration. The hunchback refused the money but asked permission to have his say, which was granted:

> "Prince, you met me, you beat me, you imprisoned me; I met you, you caught a lot of game and you returned safe and sound. So which of us was the bad omen for the other?" The king began to laugh and gave him a present.[65]

A similar tale is told of Birbal. A merchant in Delhi was known for having a face so ugly it would put someone off his food for a day. Akbar was curious and asked to see him. He was immediately gripped by stomach cramps, so he decided to execute the merchant for making him suffer. The man begged for mercy but was dragged away from Akbar by the guard who, feeling sorry for him, called Birbal to find a solution. Birbal briefed the merchant, who then asked to see Akbar and told him that although seeing his face had meant the mogul could not eat for a day, this was nothing compared with the bad luck the mogul's face had brought the merchant, who was to be executed as a result. Akbar knew Birbal was behind this and sent the merchant away with gifts, saying, "Birbal has saved me from executing an innocent man."[66]

Let it not be imagined that only the ruler was subjected to the mocking correctives of the jester. Other members of the court were just as readily upbraided. The jester Adding Clarity once mocked Wang Yanzheng, the prefect of Jianzhou who had tried to found his own dynasty only to surrender three years later to Emperor Yuanzong, ruler of the Southern Tang. He was known to be miserly, so Yuanzong's jester asked him for a gift, addressing him with sarcastic humility:

> "This lowly craftsman of no skill begs you to bestow a rich reward upon him. I beg you great prince to give me just one thing." "What is it?" asked Yanzheng. Adding Clarity said, "Well, since you won't be needing it, I was wondering whether I could have the imperial crown so I could use it for my jester's outfit?" Yanzheng was silent and was greatly ashamed, and because of this he died of depression.
>
> 『賤工無伎，優賜巨富。然告大王，乞取一物。』延政曰：『汝何求？』家明曰：『大殿平天冠，今已無用，家明敢取爲優服。』延政默然，慚恨而罷。自是快快病卒。[67]

Sometimes the jester was in collusion with the monarch, who either requested or approved of the mockery. Peter the Great encouraged his many jesters to make "game of the old-fashioned prejudices and customs so firmly rooted in society, and under cover of a jester conveyed many a plain truth to the nobles. When the latter used to complain to him of the too unceremonious behaviour of the jesters, he would answer, 'What can I do with them? They are fools, you know!'"[68]

The Hungarian king Matyas decided to cure his nobles of gift grabbing and favor foraging. He had a plow made of gold and shown to them, promising that if they could tell him how much it was worth he would grant their wishes. The nobles spent a long time looking at the plow and measuring it, but since none of them could work out its value, they gave up and kept quiet:

> So Matyas *kiraly* [king] said to them, "Don't worry too much, my special friend will tell you." His special friend was the court fool. But he wasn't foolish, only he had lived for twenty years in exile from Hungary, that is why he pretended to be half-witted. "Come in, old boy," said Matyas *kiraly*, "Come and tell these gentlemen how much this plough is worth." The fellow came in, looked rather disparagingly at the plough, and scratched his head. "Well, go on, these men are waiting." "All right, I'll tell you. If it rains then it will be priceless.

But if it doesn't rain then it won't be worth a brass farthing." And that was the end of that. The nobles slunk away, and they got nothing because the only one who had guessed was the Fool.[69]

In 1483 Zhu Yong, duke of Baoguo, ran twelve military camps and used conscripted soldiers to repair his vast residence. The jester Brother Clown (A Chou) used a historical allusion to expose his corruption. Pretending to be a scholar reciting poems, he referred to Liu Bang (r. 206–195 B.C.), who when fighting Xiang Yu of Chu, ordered his men to sing songs of Chu, thereby lowering the morale of the Chu army enough to make it disperse. The jester intoned:

> "Six thousand soldiers scattered by the songs of Chu." Another jester said, "But it was eight thousand who were scattered," and they had an endless argument about it. Then Brother Clown said slowly, "Didn't you know? Two thousand were at Duke Baoguo's house building a roof." Thereupon the emperor secretly sent the eunuch Shang Ming to investigate. Baoguo quickly dispersed the workers and bribed the eunuch, so the matter was dropped.

> 『六千兵散楚歌聲。』一人曰：『八千兵散』爭之不已。徐曰：『爾不知耶？
> 二千在保國公家蓋房。』於是憲廟密遣太監尚明察之。保國即撤工，賂尚明，
> 得止。[70]

In 1499 Cheng Minzheng, chief examiner of the civil service examinations, accepted bribes from candidates who wanted to sneak to the top of their year by getting the questions in advance. Some jesters put on a skit before the emperor, using a pun on "cooked" and "uncooked trotters" *(shu ti* and *sheng ti)*, homophones for "seen" and "unseen questions." A jester walked in with a tray of seven cooked pigs' trotters, crying his wares:

> "Buy my trotters!" Somebody went to buy one and asked the price. The vendor told him, "A thousand taels each!" The customer asked why they were so expensive, and the vendor explained, "These are all cooked trotters *[shu ti]*, not raw trotters *[sheng ti]*." The whole hall burst into an uproar, *and the emperor woke up to what was going on.*

> 『賣蹄呵！』一人就買，問價幾何。賣者曰：『一千兩一個！』買者曰：『何
> 貴若是？』賣者曰：『此俱熟蹄，非生蹄也。』闔堂而罷，孝皇頃悟。[71]

During the Xining reign-period (1068–77), Prime Minister Wang Anshi implemented his New Reform Laws. Wanting to make use of people's talents, he sometimes bypassed the formal channels to appoint as his circuit supervisors people who had not passed the requisite exams.[72] Zhao Ji and Liu Yi were both promoted in this manner as defense judges for Xiongzhou, and they in turn recommended people under them for other posts. A bold-faced jester

> put on a skit before the emperor. He straddled an ass and rode up the hall to the royal dais; when the courtiers tried to stop him he said, "But I heard that anyone with legs could climb to the top!" *The numbers of those selected informally decreased.*
>
> 伶人對上作俳,跨驢直登軒陛,左右或止之,其人曰:『將謂有腳者盡上
>
> 得!』薦者少沮。[73]

During the Baoyou reign-period (1253–58) of Emperor Lizong (r. 1224–64), Prime Minister Ding Daquan (d. 1263), who was later drowned, was in cahoots with Dong Songchen, and between them they monopolized power with the backing of the emperor. During a banquet a jester started banging on some gongs and drums until another jester scolded him:

> "The emperor wants some peace and quiet, so why d'you keep up this dreadful ding-dong ding-dong din?" He answered, "Well, since the whole country is run by Ding and Dong these days, why can't I make my own ding-dong?"
>
> 『聖上要寧靜,汝丁丁董董不已,何也?』答曰:『於今國事皆丁,董,安得
>
> 不丁董?』[74]

One day at a palace banquet in the reign of Emperor Xianzong (r. 1465–87), the Bells and Drum Office put on a skit at a command performance, suggesting that grain collection for tax was causing hardship to the people while the boats transporting grain to the capital for the government were bursting at the seams. The emperor seems to have been pleased by the message, since "the heavenly countenance slightly cleared, as sunshine after the rain."[75]

There is an example, also in Xianzong's reign, of a senior official's using jesters to criticize the behavior of a subordinate. Magistrate Lin of Jiashan County ordered a family of thirteen flogged to death. The harshness of this was brought to the attention of Si Zhong, his superior, who planned to deal with him severely. Lin therefore lavishly bribed another official to lay on a banquet for Si to soften him up, but Si forestalled this by ordering jesters to mock the magistrate. One of them pretended to be an official who loved snow and who had a snow lion built, which he ordered hidden in a shady place so he could enjoy it later. There was a discussion as to the shadiest place for the lion to be stored, the sun being an image for justice:

> "How about in Mountain Shade?" "That's no good." "How about Rivershade then?" "No, that won't work . . . but you could hide it in Jiashan County." "But that place has no shade, why hide it there?" "Haven't you seen how Magistrate Lin of Jiashan got away with murder by beating a family of thirteen people to death without their having committed a capital crime? Wouldn't you call that a shady place where the sun doesn't shine?"
>
> 『山陰可乎？』曰：『不可。』卒又曰：『江陰可乎？』曰：『不可。』其官高聲曰：『但藏在嘉善縣可也。』卒曰：『此地無陰，何以藏之？』官曰：『汝不見嘉善林知縣打殺一家非死罪十三人，不償命，豈非有天無日頭處？』[76]

KEEP IT IN THE FAMILY

Another favorite target of the jester's biting humor is royal and ministerial nepotism. Emperor Yuanzong's younger brothers all had titles bestowed on them, but not the ministers beneath them. During a banquet, Adding Clarity put on a skit with an old man and woman sitting side by side and their daughters-in-law performing a lot of ceremonies before them. They said, "Your own father- and mother-in-law, why d'you stand on ceremony so much?"—an indirect way of asking why so many titles were being given to relatives of the emperor. "The emperor laughed and said, 'I am the sovereign, I don't spread my favors beyond my family!'" Nevertheless the officials were promoted, so he did heed the advice.[77]

During the reign of Emperor Xuanzong his favorite concubine, Yang Guifei—the most famous concubine in Chinese history—showed great favoritism toward her "adopted" son, An Lushan, the man who later instigated a rebellion that brought down the dynasty. While An Lushan received Yang Guifei's "maternal" favor, the son of the emperor, the future Emperor Suzong (r. 756–63), was being pitifully neglected. When the emperor asked his jester, "What sort of sons earn one's sympathy?" He answered, "Your own." *When the Emperor heard In Full Streamer's words, he bowed his head [in shame] for a long time.*[78]

"Although at that time jesters of the Liao court were numerous, there was only Light Coat Luo who could use humor to offer indirect advice, thereby dispelling disorder before it had chance to happen."[79] Emperor Xingzong of the Liao spoiled his younger brother Zhongyuan, drunkenly promising him he could inherit the throne. Zhongyuan became so arrogant he thought he was above the law, and while playing backgammon he "won" several cities from the emperor, but none of the courtiers dared to say anything.

> One day, when they were gambling again, Light Coat Luo said to the board, "Backgammon! What stupidity, we'll lose everything because of you!" *The emperor suddenly realized what he had been doing, and didn't gamble anymore.*
>
> 一日，復博，羅衣輕指其局曰：『雙陸！休癡，和你都輸去也！』帝始悟，不復戲。[80]

Under Emperor Xiaozong (r. 1488–1505) a relative of the empress was enfiefed as a marquis, and a wine party was given in the palace. After three cups he almost felt as if he were "a creature like the sun," on a par with the emperor. A jester mocked him with a pun on *hou* (meaning "marquis" and "monkey"), by acting like a monkey jumping up high while pointing at him saying, "'As for monkeys, the higher they climb, the harder they fall!' There was silence as the emperor grasped the meaning of this; his face fell, and he ordered the banquet to end."[81]

There is one instance where it was the monarch who decided to act against nepotist aspirations and had to be restrained by the jester. Furious over the incessant demands of his numerous brothers-in-law, Akbar decreed that all brothers-in-law in the court should be executed. Birbal arranged for a golden gallows to be built, and when Akbar asked for whom it was intended he replied, "The golden gallows are for you. You too are a brother-in-law."[82]

Nepotism was not always confined to members of the royal family, and high-ranking officials were often guilty of it. Qin Gui (1090–1155) was a minister during the Song dynasty who was part of the appeasement party that preferred to cede territory to the invading northern Jin rather than fight them. In 1134 he secured a peace with the Jin that served their interests, yet his influence over the emperor was still immense, and he had honors heaped on him. In 1145 his son and two nephews all "passed" the provincial exams. People were very perturbed by this, but nobody dared to speak out. Jesters acted as members of the gentry on their way to the capital, discussing who would be promoted from the provincial exams and sent to court. The leading jester said Peng Yue would be sent. The jester based his joke on Peng Yue (fl. ca. 200 B.C.) and Han Xin (fl. ca. 200 B.C.), two of the generals involved in carving up the Qin empire into the "Three Qins," a pun on the three relatives of Qin Gui. The joke, obscure in translation, nevertheless cut close to the bone, since "the surrounding courtiers did not dare show their comprehension, so they all charged out and *Qin Gui did not dare punish the jesters.*"[83]

THE STATE VERSUS WINE, WOMEN, AND SONG

There is a good honest able man that I could name, that if your Majesty would imploy and command to see all things well executed, all things would soon be mended; and this is one Charles Stuart—who now spends his time in imploying his lips and his prick about the Court, and hath no other imployment. But if you would give him this imployment, he were the fittest man in the world to perform it.

Samuel Pepys, Tom Killigrew to Charles II, *Diary*[84]

The emperor loved carousing, and no one dared criticize him for it.

Wang Qi (fl. ca. 1565–1614)[85]

The courtier-jester Tom Killigrew "imploys" a combination of indirection and humor to tell the king he is neglecting affairs of state—another delicate task of the jester. Killigrew could persuade the king to attend to his duties more willingly than he might otherwise have done. When a council urgently assembled could not proceed without the king's presence, the duke of Lauderdale (1616–82), a chief minister, failed to make him turn up. Killigrew bet £100 that he would do so in half an hour, and knowing of the king's antipathy to Lauderdale, he promised Charles he could now be rid of him forever: "'If I win my wager, the Duke will rather hang himself than pay the money.' 'Well then,' said Charles, 'if that be the case, I positively will go.'"[86]

It seems Charles was given to relapses and had to be frequently reminded of his royal duties. When he once spent the best part of the night carousing with Lord Rochester and other nobles, Killigrew walked in, and the king braced himself for a rocket: "Now we shall hear of our faults." But Killigrew denied him the satisfaction, "No, faith! I don't care to trouble myself with that which all the town talks of."[87] On another occasion Killigrew adopted a more direct tone to make Charles sit up and heed advice, suggesting that Charles's republican predecessor would have done more for the country than he:

> In the reign of king Charles the second, the Dutch, who had been but a little before raised from obscurity by the generosity of England, began to infest our trade, and insult our fleets; frequent memorials, and humble remonstrances had been presented to his majesty to no effect. And when it was thought useless, and even unsafe to trouble him any farther, Killigrew the jester made use of the liberty his office intitled him to, to tell his majesty the sentiments of the nation. He came into the king's presence booted and spurred, as if for a journey: Where are you going to-day, Killigrew? said the king; To hell, Sir, answered he, to bring back Oliver Cromwell, to chastise the insolence of the Dutch. Which sarcastical answer had more weight with that witty monarch, than all the grave applications that had been made to him.[88]

On another occasion he warned Charles of the dangers of frittering away the nation's resources. He wrote the word "all" on five slips of paper and placed them, partially visible, beneath a candlestick. At dinner, Charles spotted and read them, asking Killigrew what they meant. The jester explained, "The Country hath sent All, the City hath lent All, the Court hath spent All; so if we don't mend All, it will be the worse for All."[89]

Baldy Chunyu used a riddle to cure Weiwang of Qi of his excessive carousing. On another occasion the king invited Baldy to a private wine party and asked how much it took to make him drunk. On formal occasions he only needed a gallon, but the more relaxed the atmosphere, the more he could quaff:

> "Then I'm really on top of the world and I can put away up to ten gallons. But, yes, that's where the old proverb comes in: When you go too far with wine, you lose control; a surfeit of pleasure brings a host of sorrows. It's the same with everything, mind you. You can't go too far with what you say, either. If you do, it spells ruination. *That's why some people couch good advice in humour.*"
>
> 『當此之時，髡心最歡，能飲一石。故曰酒極則亂，樂極則悲；萬事盡然，
>
> 言不可極，極之而衰。以諷諫焉。』

This persuaded the king to give up his unrestrained boozing and to make Baldy his "chamberlain in charge of receptions for visiting foreign princes and ambassadors, and whenever he attended parties given by royal clans-men and nobility, Baldy was always at his side."[90] Xiangzi, ruler of Zhao (r. 457–425 B.C.), once managed to drink uninterruptedly for five days, and he boasted about it, pointing to the ubiquity of booze bragging. Jester Don't (You Mo) simply likened him to Zhou and alluded to Jie, two prime ty-rants whose dissolute ways contributed to the collapse of their dynasties:

> "Look at me, I'm champ of the land—I've been knocking it back for five days and nights, and I'm not the slightest bit ill!" Jester Don't said, "You just keep at it Sire, you're only two days short of Zhou: he drank for seven days and seven nights, and today you're up to five." The viscount was terrified and said to him, "Does that mean I'm done for?" "No, you aren't." The viscount asked, "But if I'm only two days short of being like Zhou, how can I not be doomed like him?" Jester Don't quipped, "The destruction of Jie and Zhou came about because they had to confront the good rulers Tang and Wu. But nowadays the world is full of rotten kings like Jie, and you're a rotten king like Zhou, and when Jie and Zhou exist side by side, they aren't going to destroy each other, are they? Still, you're pushing your luck."

> 『我誠邦士也。夫飲酒五日五夜矣，而殊不病！』優莫曰：『君勉之，不及紂二日耳。紂七日七夜，今君五日。』襄子懼，謂優莫曰：『然則吾亡乎？』優莫曰：『不亡。』襄子曰：『不及紂二日耳，不亡何待？』優莫曰：『桀紂之亡也遇湯武，今天下盡桀也，而君紂也，桀紂並世，焉能相亡，然亦殆矣。』[91]

Another instance of an emperor's being cured of his crapulence is given in the Song dynasty *History of the Southern Tang (Nan Tang shu)* by Ma Ling. Emperor Yuanzong succeeded to the throne and gave himself up to feasting, favoritism, and playing polo:

> Once he was really drunk and ordered [the jester] Subtle Reformer King to play *The Water Melody*. Subtle Reformer simply sang, "In the southern court the Son of Heaven loves the dashing life," over and over again. *Yuanzong came to his senses, knocked over his cup,* and said, "If the two rulers Sun and Chen had heard that line they would not have had the humiliation of holding their jade in their mouths [as vassals to other rulers]." Through this Subtle Reformer became a favorite.

> 嘗乘醉，命感化奏水調詞。感化唯歌『南朝天子愛風流』一句，如是者數四。元宗輒悟，覆盃歎曰：『使孫，陳二主得此一句，不當有銜璧之辱也！』感化由是有寵。[92]

A similar situation is described in the *History of the Jin (Jinshu)*, the jester Wang Luo persuading the emperor to adopt a more sedentary lifestyle by referring to historical precedents. Fu Jian (r. 357–85), the foreign invader who nearly conquered the whole of China and had an army of a million men, loved hunting in the west mountains and would do so until he was "so happy he forgot to go home" *(le er wang fan)*. Nevertheless, the jester's corrective was well received, "'*Splendid! Duke Wen was awakened to his errors by a man of Yu, and we hear of our faults from Wang Luo. I have been at fault!*' From then on he ceased his hunting."⁹³ A similar story is told of In Full Streamer persuading Xuanzong to give up sporting dangers.⁹⁴ Peter Bearskin (Peter Bärenhaut), jester to Landgrave Philipp the Magnanimous of Hesse (1509–67), cured his ruler's boozing by encouraging him to take a hair of the dog for his hangover:

"But then I'll feel even worse tomorrow than today."
"So drink even more tomorrow."
"And what will become of me in the end?"
"A fool, like me."
"In that case, I'd rather suffer my headache than be a fool like you."

["So werde ich morgen kränker seyn, als heute."
"So trink dich alsdenn wieder woll."
"Was wird aber endlich daraus werden?"
"Ein Narr, wie ich."
"So will ich lieber meinen Kopfschmerz erdulden, als ein Narr
        werden wie du."]⁹⁵

An anecdote about Emperor Xizong not only shows how amenable a monarch could be to the mocking good sense of the jester but also gives a refreshing picture of the emperor's human aspect, since few people would think an august ruler of ancient China would also be a soccer addict. His jester used a pun on *luo*, which could mean to fall over or trip up, or to fail an exam:

Emperor Xizong loved both cock fighting and football, and he reckoned he was a dab foot at dribbling. He told his jester Wild Pig [Yezhu], "If I sat an exam in dribbling, I'd come top of the class." Wild Pig answered, "But if [the great kings] Yao, Shun, Yu, and Tang were in charge of the Ministry of Rites Examining Board, Your Majesty would certainly trip up and land at the bottom of the league!" *The emperor laughed and gave up his idea.*

僖宗皇帝好蹴毬、鬥雞爲樂。自以能於步打，謂俳優石野豬曰：『朕若作步打

進士，亦合得一狀元。』野豬對曰：『或遇堯，舜，與，湯作禮部侍郎，陛下

不勉且落第！』帝笑而已。[96]

TAX ATTACKS

One of the kings of Persia . . . wished his people to enjoy the benefits
of instruction. Schools were established, and amongst others, the
court fool commenced to learn spelling. But . . . at the very com-
mencement of his progress . . . he opened the Koran, and pointed
out to his sovereign the passage in which Mahomet forbids the payment of impost to the kings of the earth.

John Doran, *The History of Court Fools*[97]

It was not uncommon for a jester to seek to remind the monarch that
"kings and government ought to shear, not skin, their sheep," as Robert
Herrick put it.[98] Unfair or ludicrous taxation is a favorite target of the court
jester. The success of the jester Gradually Stretching Taller in changing
the emperor's thinking, thereby easing the lot of the overtaxed, was considered at the time to be on a par with two of the most famous Chinese
jester anecdotes given in the "Biographies of Jesters" by Sima Qian, Jester
Meng's "Horse Burial" and Jester Twisty Pole's "Lacquering the Great
Wall." At the time there was a multiplicity of taxes, and merchants suffered by it. In the fields around the capital there was a severe drought, and
the Southern Tang Emperor Liezu asked his courtiers why rain was falling on the land beyond the capital but not in the vicinity, suggesting that
the will of heaven had been contravened within the city. Stretching Taller
got his wise-cracking oar in with, "The rain is terrified of being taxed, so
it daren't enter the city." Not only did *the emperor laugh heartily and give
orders to get rid of all excessive taxes,*" but overnight the drought was drowned
in heavy rain.[99]

In the last few years of the Liang dynasty (502–57), the prince of Wei
was commander of Xuanzhou and a rapacious tax collector, making the
people wretched. He went to the capital for a routine court audience and
found himself attending a banquet. A jester made a visual pun on the expression "stripping the topsoil," a euphemism for excessive taxation. He
wore green clothes and a mask that made him look like a demon, and another jester asked what he was supposed to be. He answered, "I am the

earth god of Xuanzhou. The prince came for an audience, and he stripped the topsoil to bring me with him, so that's why I'm here."[100]

A Chinese miscellany tells of a magistrate so greedy for tax revenue that he would do anything to raise taxes. Three jesters thought up a skit to humiliate him, also using a pun on topsoil stripping. Someone gave him a farewell feast even though he had been dismissed from office for his corruption. When he arrived he mingled with the guests, noticing in their midst three people dressed in ancient costume. The magistrate looked surprised and asked why they were dressed so. The three announced their names: Cao Cao (155–220), Qin Gui, and Yan Song (1480–1567), three of the most notorious villains in Chinese history, and explained their presence:

> "In our last life we committed grievous sins, so after we died God punished us by sending us down to the Nine Springs of Hell so that our spirits could never be free to ascend to Paradise. Now your greed is so great that you have scraped off the topsoil, thus enabling a thousand ghosts from Hell to see the light of day again. How can we ever repay you?" When the magistrate heard this his face took on a deathly pallor, and he left before the banquet ended.[101]

> 『吾輩生前，罪孽深重。死後上帝罰墮九泉之下，永不超生。今蒙父臺將地皮刮去數層，使千載幽魂重覩天日，此恩何以答報？』令聞之，面無人色，不終席而去。

For all the success of jesters in reforming rulers and policies, some people were immune to their correctives. Zhang Chong was commander of Luzhou and enjoyed flouting the law and making everyone miserable, gentry and ordinary people alike. When Chong went for a routine audience with his superiors, people were delighted, and thinking he would be transferred to a new post they said to each other,

> "That chap won't be back again!" Chong returned and, hearing this, imposed a "That Chap Tax" on every household. The following year he went for another routine audience, but this time the people did not dare say anything, so when they met in the street they would look at each other and stroke their whiskers to celebrate his departure. Chong returned and imposed a "Stroking Whiskers Tax."

> 『莫伊不復來矣！』崇歸，聞之，計口徵『莫伊錢』。明年，再入覲，盛有罷府之耗。人不敢指實，皆道路相目，捋鬚相慶。歸，又徵『捋鬚錢』。[102]

Jesters put on a skit about it, suggesting that in his next life he would be made an otter, a lowly water animal, but to no avail. He was unrepentant. Win some, lose some—if the records are to be believed, the jesters won far more often than they lost.

REDUCTIO AD ABSURDUM

> On one occasion, Bajazet had condemned many scores of his officers to death, for some trifling offence. "Ay, indeed," exclaimed the fool, "hang the knaves! hang them, what use are they? kill them for small offences, and rogues will fear to commit greater! excellent wisdom! Timour is at hand; away with them before he comes! The army can do without leaders. You take the standard; I will beat the drum; and we will thus meet that troublesome individual at the head of the forces. We will see how we can handle the Tartars, without such knaves as these to help us!" Bajazet comprehended the implied reproof, and spared the well-proved and lightly-offending leaders of his host.
>
> John Doran, *The History of Court Fools* [103]

"Truth is restored by reducing the lie to an absurdity": the enthusiastic endorsement of folly is a common technique used by the jester to enlighten the king or emperor. [104] By pushing an idea to its extreme the king is made to see the possible consequences of his actions without the jester's appearing to have criticized him. Sima Qian's "Biographies of the Jesters," written between 104 and 91 B.C., is the richest source of such examples, and a parallel to the Ottoman Bayezid I (Bajazet, r. 1389–1402) can be found in one of the most tyrannical emperors of China. The jester Twisty Pole was "a first class funster, but behind his every joke was a grasp of universal principles." [105] When the infamous Emperor Qin Shi decided to establish a huge game park, Twisty Pole agreed wholeheartedly:

> "What a marvellous idea!" said Jester Twisty Pole. "You could keep a whole mass of wild birds and beasts in it. And then, if there's an invasion, you can just let the gazelles and deer butt the invaders with their horns. That'll send them packing!" *That was enough to make the First Emperor drop his scheme.*

優旃曰：『善！多縱禽獸於其中，寇從東方來，令麋鹿觸之足矣。』始皇以故
輟止。[106]

When Er Shi (r. 209–207 B.C.), the second (and last) emperor of the Qin dynasty, came to the throne, he decided he wanted to lacquer the Great Wall. The jester used the same method to dissuade him:

> "That's a splendid idea," said Jester Twisty Pole. "If you hadn't mentioned it, Your Majesty, I'd certainly have suggested it myself. It might mean an awful lot of toil and trouble for the ordinary people, but all the same it's a magnificent project. Lacquer the Great Wall all smooth and shiny, then it'll be too slippery for any invaders to climb over. Now, let's get down to the practical side of the job. The lacquering's easy enough, but building the drying room may present a problem or two." *The second emperor burst out laughing and shelved his project.*
>
> 優旃曰：『善！主上雖無言，臣固將請之。漆城雖於百姓愁費，然佳哉！漆城蕩蕩，寇來不能上。即欲就之，易為漆耳，顧難為陰室。』於是二世笑之，以其故止。[107]

Jester Meng was so overzealous in agreeing with the king that he made him change his mind. The king had a favorite horse that he cosseted until it died of overweight. He arranged for the horse to be buried with all the ceremony due to a dignitary, and when some of his courtiers tried to suggest that this was a little excessive he issued a decree stating that "whoever dares to submit contrary advice to me about my horse will be committing a crime to be punished by death."[108] Jester Meng entered the king's presence crying his eyes out. The king was shocked and asked what was the matter:

> "It's that horse of yours, Your Majesty," sobbed Meng. "You loved him so much. With a great powerful nation like Chu at your disposal anything you want is yours for the asking. Yet all you're giving him is a minister's burial. That's a bit shabby. I beg you to bury him with the rites customarily accorded a monarch."
>
> 優孟曰：『馬者王之所愛也，以楚國堂堂之大，何求不得，而以大夫禮葬之，薄，請以人君禮葬之』[109]

He then listed all the sumptuous arrangements necessary to give the beloved horse a suitably impressive burial, including bestowing on his descendants a fief of ten thousand households, before ending innocently with the words, "Then, when the rulers of the other states in the world hear of this, they will all know that Your Majesty prizes horses above mere men!"[110] The king realized his folly and asked the jester how to make good his error, then he followed Meng's advice to

> "let a clay oven serve as his outer coffin, and a bronze tripod cauldron as his inner coffin. Shower him reverently with ginger and dates, strew offerings of magnolia upon him, and sacrifice the purest white rice around him. Enshroud him with the light of a fire, and lay him to rest in the bellies of men."

『。。。以壟灶爲槨，銅歷爲棺，齊以薑棗，薦以木蘭，祭以糧稻，衣以火光，葬之於人腹腸。』[111]

Emperor Zhuangzong was fond of hunting, and on one occasion he trampled the fields of the peasants. The local magistrate approached him and entreated him on their behalf to desist. The emperor was furious and ready to kill him until Newly Polished Mirror joined in the fray:

> "You're a magistrate," Newly Polished Mirror shouted accusingly at the magistrate, "And yet you're actually unaware that our Son of Heaven is fond of hunting, are you? Instead of indulging your peasants' whims here, letting them plant and harvest grain to provide government taxes, why on earth don't you let the peasants in this county starve, so that the area is empty of people and available for our Son of Heaven to gallop around hunting in! Your crime merits death!" Then he went up to the emperor and begged that the magistrate might be put to death without delay, and all the other jesters chorused their applause for this suggestion. *Emperor Zhuangzong burst out laughing, and the magistrate was able to get away, pardoned.*

責之曰：『汝爲縣令，獨不知吾天子好獵邪？奈何縱民稼穡，以供稅賦？何不飢汝縣民，而空此地，以備吾天子之馳聘？汝罪當死！』因前，請亟行刑。諸伶共倡和之。莊宗大笑，縣令乃得勉去。[112]

During the reign of Emperor Zhaozong (r. 889–904), a jester managed to criticize an unfair tax using reductio ad absurdum. Li Maozhen (856–924) occupied Qi. He was tolerant and generous, and the people were tranquil under him, but it was a poor area that did not raise much in tax revenue, and he established an oil monopoly to raise money. He forbade people to bring firewood into the city for torches so that more profit could be made from the sale of oil. A jester recommended that moonlight be prohibited so that more oil would be needed for light. Li laughed and did not become angry.[113]

The license and the inclination to speak freely are among the salient characteristics of the court jester everywhere, an irrepressible tendency even when the king has a bout of bad temper or stubbornness. The jester can voice his disagreement by agreeing with the king so profusely that he sees the absurdity of his ideas for himself. He can tell a funny story that apparently bears no relation to the issue at hand but that will make his point clear indirectly without causing any loss of face for the king. Occasionally he dispenses with subtlety and opts for bluntness, a change of tack that can have quite an impact on a ruler perhaps more used to hearing people's words cushioned with courtly unction.

In China, Europe, India, the Middle East, and elsewhere there is weighty testimony to the license of the court jester to speak the truth and to use that license on behalf of others or to reform behavior or policy. Yet the recorded instances of such reformist humor among non-Chinese jesters seem massively outnumbered by the detailed accounts given by Chinese writers. If Chinese records of the jester's corrective wit were confined to the official dynastic histories, we might assume that it was simply a matter of policy to preserve them. But there are numerous unofficial accounts of jesters, suggesting that they were preserved on impulse rather than by policy. Elsewhere the jester's activities were recorded in an altogether more haphazard fashion, and perhaps without a Sima Qian to make the subject respectable to scholars, some historians may have felt it unsuited to the writing of serious history. Has Herodotus failed us? Modern historians in particular will write a whole book about a king or his court with little and often no reference to the jesters who cavorted within, spending many hours of the day with him in a high-profile and influential position usually founded on trust and intimacy.

Whatever the reasons for the imbalance, the predominance of China in this chapter of lively truth telling does give the impression that this vital function had a more important place in his duties in China than elsewhere, even though in Europe the jester's license to speak was reinforced by the protective coating of assumed or genuine "foolishness." The Chinese jester had no such excuse to fall back on should his words cut too close to the bone and cause offense, yet he was apparently expected to offer *fengjian* more frequently than his counterparts in other countries, for whom the license to speak may have been less of an obligation.

It may also be that in Europe other court entertainments would have provided a channel for at least some dissent, entertainments in which the jester would often have played a part. Certainly in the court of Elizabeth I pageants and masques could be an outlet to express discontent, desires, and even anger with the ruler: "Elizabeth's entertainments were meant to be a dialogue, commissioned by others and presented to the queen. The queen could choose either to respond to or to ignore the presenters' message; in most cases, she responded."[114] In China such court entertainments were the almost exclusive province of jesters with their impromptu skits.

There is a European medieval medallion featuring a jester with the Latin inscription for "Truth" *(veritas),* an enduring testimony to the association of the two.[115] Many proverbs express the idea that a fool, whether natural or feigned, would readily tell the truth without being prompted. This trait set him apart from the hordes of court entertainers with whom he had much in common and is perhaps one of the main reasons he so frequently enjoyed an intimate and trusting relationship with his monarch. Jesters were generally by their nature straightforward and honest and did not tend to have vested interests or belong to formal power structures or informal cliques. The only person they were dependent on was the king, although this does not seem to have curbed their independent stance, a fact that a ruler accustomed to varying degrees of sycophancy and intrigue no doubt often welcomed. As Rabelais says:

> I have often heard it said in a vulgar proverb, the wise may be instructed by a fool. Seeing the answers and responses of sage and judicious men have in no manner of way satisfied you, take advice of some fool, and possibly by so doing you may come to get that counsel which will be agreeable to your own heart's desire and contentment. You know how by the advice and counsel and prediction of fools, many kings, princes, states, and commonwealths have been preserved, several battles gained, and divers doubts of a most perplexed intricacy resolved.

> [J'ay souvent ouy en proverbe vulguaire qu'un fol enseigne bien un saige. Puys que par les responses des saiges n'estez à plain satisfaict, conseillez vous à quelque fol. Pourra estre que, ce faisant, plus à vostre gré serez satisfaict et content. Par l'advis, conseil et praediction des folz vous scavez quants princes, roys et republicques ont esté conservez, quantes batailles guaignées, quantes perplexitez dissolues.][116]

It's mostly for saying the truth
That you get the harshest censure.

[Am ddweud y gwir rhan amla
Y ceir y cerydd garwa.]
        Anonymous fool, *Judgement on the Ideals of Government* (1785) [1]

A Notorious Rogue being brought to the Bar, and knowing his case to be desperate, instead of pleading, he took himself the liberty of jesting, and thus said, I charge you in the Kings name to seise and take away that man (meaning the Judge) in the red Gown, for I go in danger of my life because of him.
        John Ashton, *Humour, Wit and Satire of the Seventeenth Century* [2]

Overstepping the Mark:
The Limits of His License

Beatings, Banishment, and Beheading

Do you know why Jesus was crucified? I'll tell you: because he hadn't learned how to laugh, yes, Mary, I'm telling you, it's the truth. If on the cross, instead of imploring his father who had abandoned him he had started to laugh, he would have triumphed over everyone including himself.

[Sais-tu pourquoi Jesus a été crucifié? Je vais te le dire: parce qu'il n'avait pas appris à rire, oui, Maria, je te l'affirme. C'est la vérité. Si sur la croix, au lieu d'implorer son père qui l'avait abandonné, il s'était mis à rire, il aurait remporté sa victoire sur tous et sur lui-même.]

Elie Wiesel, *Les portes de la fôret* [3]

The power of laughter is immeasurable and brings with it a kind of conquest. The physical defeat of an oppressed being can still be a certain moral victory if he is able to laugh at his persecutors, forcing them to see that there is a part of their victim's battered armor that apparently is impenetrable, since "only the gallant . . . remain light-hearted in adversity." [4] An ability to grin and bear it is more frustrating to an attacker than stolid stoicism. A person who laughs at you as you hurt him defies logical expectations, which makes him seem slightly mad and thus an unknown quantity. Much anti-Nazi sentiment in Britain during the war was expressed in belittling mockery: "Whistle while you work, / 'itler is a twerp; / 'e is barmy, / so's 'is army, / whistle while you work," or "'itler 'as only got one ball, / ve uvver is in ve Albert 'all." Laugh at your enemy and you reduce him.

This ability to prevail with humor is characteristic of the court jester, who often seems coated in an inviolable layer of laughter (fig. 19), regard-

Figure 19 The irrepressible funster

less of the suffering that may be hidden beneath the surface. This stands him in good stead when he goes beyond his mirthful mandate and upsets his audience. Jesters did not always avoid retribution for their jocularity: among the Azande tribe of Africa, an actor-jester who offends somebody with his mockery is made to pay a token fine of spears, irrespective of how much everyone else enjoyed the joke.[5] However, the instances where the jester suffers for his effrontery are a distinct minority. Yet it is a curious paradox that for all the jester's independent stance and his flagrant disregard of authority, he was ultimately dependent on the good-willed tolerance of that authority. He was, after all, dealing with a man who, for all his regalia, was human; on a day when matters of state were weighing particularly heavily on him or his gouty leg was playing up, there was perhaps only so much ribbing a monarch could take. Overstepping the limits of his license was an occupational hazard.

If the European court jester could use his folly like a stalking-horse, the license of the Chinese jester was based more on the emperor's desire to be told the truth from time to time than on the jester's possessing or assuming a crazed aspect, and he was indeed held responsible for his words. Perhaps because he lacked such a readily acknowledged protective veil of madness, the limits of his license seem to have been more frequently breached. The jester's urge to make a point regardless of the consequences occasionally drove him to perilous brinkmanship and beyond. In *The Court*

Jesters, a novel about four jesters in a Nazi prison camp who together cover several aspects of the jester—juggler, dwarf, hunchback, and truth teller —the juggler takes this look-'em-in-the-eye obstinacy to its extreme. His master, Major Kohl, boasts of the juggler's breathtaking dexterity, claiming that nothing can distract him. One of the guests takes up the challenge and, in an attempt to stop the fine-fingered performance, has the juggler's wife brought in from another part of the camp. The juggler, faced with his wife, continues with single-minded impassivity even when the guest puts a revolver to her head. He shoots her, and still the juggler continues, stopping only when all the guests have gone and the other three jesters take him away. He has beaten the Nazi on the Nazi's terms, but the cost to him is immeasurable.[6]

However, it should not be assumed that a jester risked his neck only when he wanted to prove a point or do a good deed. If this were the case he would have been no more than a witty "remonstrating official." He did not always speak simply from an earnest desire to be truthful: jesters were not martyrs, even if they were occasionally crucified for their candor. Sometimes they quite simply pushed their luck for the sake of some aweless levity, and they paid for it. The kind of person who might become a jester was unlikely to use wit only as a tactical weapon, aiming at a specific target while calculating just how impudent he could be before the opposition struck back. His ebullient irreverence was visceral and unfettered. According to Tivadar Farkashazy, editor of the Hungarian humor magazine *Hocipo (Wellington Boot),* the risk of punishment may even add to the fun of mockery, as when he described one of the downsides of democratic freedom: "Telling a joke is more interesting when you can be put in jail for it."[7]

There is in the jester a quality of resilience that means that even when he is beaten it does not seem to injure him. It is a resilience of the spirit that might either complement the physical litheness often associated with the jester or offer a contrast to a deformity. He never seems particularly perturbed by a whip descending on him, never inveighing against the injustice or cruelty of his punishment or begging for mercy: "Like the comic characters in the film cartoons who may be cut in shreds, smashed flat, riddled with holes, or stretched into a thin line, yet which suddenly spring back into their original form or are miraculously put back together, the clown always seems to survive."[8]

There is nothing of the tragic about him, and the notion that the mask of the merrymaker hides a deep sadness is a modern myth—the jester sees all sorrow but does not necessarily embody it. A symbol of joie de vivre, his happy-go-luckiness allows him to face the prospect of pain or death with an equanimity sometimes bordering on gay abandon. Perhaps it was courage or foolhardiness, or a belief that freedom from constraint was worth incurring regal ire, or supreme confidence in their ability to talk their way out of trouble (until proved wrong), or none of these. On a level beyond the concerns of the individual man behind the jester, this devil-may-care attitude "reveals the clown's irrepressible resistance to punishment, the vitality of an eternal victim who can never truly be overcome, disciplined, or confined. The beatings merely underscore his basic immunity and capacity to survive, even as they contribute to the violent reordering and revitalization that the clown engenders."[9]

The jester's audacious dealings with the king fall into two categories: those where his impudence is tolerated—the majority of known cases—and those where it is not, some of which lead to the jester's being beaten, banished, or beheaded. Jesters everywhere were occasionally subjected to thrashings when there was a failure of the royal sense of humor. This chapter will deal first with the beatings and banishments, then with the beheadings, and will include, refreshingly, examples of jesters' talking their way out of the chop with verve and irresistible logic. As the jester Giraff says in Hugo's *Cromwell* (1827), the jester can always save his skin, and in order to reach old age in a world full of uncertainty, there is no wiser guise:

> Toujours de tout désastre un bouffon se sauva.
> Pour vieillir sur la terre, où tout est de passage,
> Il faut se faire fou: c'est encore le plus sage.[10]

"TRUTH EVER BEGETS HATRED, AND BLOWS AS WELL!"
Gelasimus, jester to Herod, in Nicholas Grimald, *Archipropheta* (1547)[11]

> And he gaue me such a box on the eare, that stroke me cleane through three chambers, downe foure paire of staires, fell ore fiue barrels, into the bottome of the seller, and if I had not well lickard my selfe there, I had neuer liu'd after it.
>
> Will Summers, in Samuel Rowley,
> *When You See Me You Know Me* (lines 621–24)

William Philips, a mountebank, that quick-talking quack cousin of the court jester, was publicly flogged at St. Bartholomew's Fair for speaking out against the government.[12] The comic mantle worn by jesters did not always succeed in cloaking them adequately. During the Shaosheng reign-period (1094–98) in Chengdu, the official who supervised the trading of tea for horses with the border countries of China was admired for his taxing and was rewarded with an insignia of high rank. A banquet was given in the prefectural court, and a jester came up with a jingle mocking the excess of the reward for the achievement. Although he was caned for his wanton words, the chronicler comments, "When low-born people have a sardonic eye they are the hardest to hoodwink."[13]

In the Xuanhe period (1119–25) of Emperor Huizong, Prime Minister Cai Jing was retired from government and given some nearby land where he built the Western Park, flattening several hundred ordinary dwellings to make room. One day Cai asked the jester Scorching Virtue (Jiao De) what he thought of the layout of the Eastern and Western Parks. Virtue said:

> "The Eastern Park of the Grand Receptor has a beautiful wood with luxuriant shade, and seeing it is like looking at a bank of clouds; in the Western Park people were scattered and their tears fell like the rain: so we could say, 'The Eastern Park is like clouds, the Western Park like rain!'" This got around, and he was punished. Someone said, "How dare a jester criticize a counsellor duke's injustices to his face?"

> 『太師公相東園嘉木繁陰，望之如雲；西園人民起離，淚下如雨；可謂：「東園如雲，西園如雨」也！』語聞抵罪。或云：『一伶人何敢面詆公相之非？』[14]

One of the worst beatings administered to a jester is described in vivid detail in a letter written in Rome on 10 April 1507 from Ludevico de Campo Sampiero to his most illustrious patron the marquis of Mantua. Fra Sarafino was a friar-jester known for his unrestrained mockery of religion and its prelates. During a dinner at the home of Monsignor di Nerbona he joked about various lords and cardinals, and even the pope and the Madonna, before fooling around putting a pancake on his head. He was returning home with Augustin Gisi and five men with swords when they were assaulted by some youths who insisted they were only after Sarafino.

The five swordsmen vanished, and while Augustin went for help, Sarafino was attacked so violently that it was not certain he would live, and he was left only with his big finger, the rest being severed at the knuckle of the right hand ("solo voleva fra Sarafino, e così se mise in cercha al pater e li dete due gran cortelate su la testa et un altra suso una man, credo sia la destra, e li butò via quatro deti neti e solo li restò el gamaut cioè el dito grosso"). Several of the attackers were caught, and one of them was killed, and the monk's wounds healed, but Luzio comments that to publicly mock "cardinals, the Madonna, and the pope" in sixteenth-century Rome was not particularly clever ("molto prudente"), and he should have stuck to innocuous tricks with a pancake.[15]

There is a letter written in dialect in 1495 from the dwarf jester Antonio da Trento to the marquis of Mantua. Another letter dated 24 July 1512, from the marquis to the dwarf, addresses him as "Little Dwarf" (Nanino) and graphically explains why he should rein himself in:

> Little Dwarf, we have heard of your bad behavior and of how much presumption and temerity you showed in striking the company and addressing villainous words to them, from which it appears you are no better than that Schips is. However, may we remind you that we have irons, manacles, and muzzles for your needs, and shortly, if God wills that we find ourselves together, we will find a remedy for your insolence. Master Christopher will say other things at greater length to your face on our behalf, and so we won't write them to you, but you will take heed of them as if they come directly from us.

> [Nanino, havemo inteso li mali portamenti toi lì et quanta prosumptione et temerità usi in battere li compagni et dirgli di villane parole, onde ni pare che tu non sei niente megliore li di quello che è Schips quà. Però ti recordamo che havemo ferri, manette et musarole per il bisogno tuo et di brevi se Dio vorà ni trovaremo insieme et ni sforzaremo trovare remedio all insolentia tua. Altre cose più diffusamente a bocca ti dirà maestro Christophoro da parte nostra, che non ti serivemo, al quale prestarai fede quanto a noi medesimo.][16]

Samuel Pepys recorded an incident in which Tom Killigrew, jester to Charles II, was struck in front of the king by a courtier his humor had offended. The court seemed less outraged by this than by the king's appearing to let the attacker go unpunished after what was considered a direct affront to the king's dignity. To strike a man in royal company was unseemly, and the insult to the king was perhaps compounded because it was his jester:

> And among the rest of the King's company, there was that worthy fellow my Lord of Rochester and Tom Killigrew, whose mirth and raillery offended the former so much, that he did give Tom Killigrew a box on the ear in the King's presence; which doth much give offence to the people here at Court, to see how cheap the King makes himself, and the more for that the King hath not only passed by the

thing and pardoned it to Rochester already, but this very morning
the King did publicly walk up and down, and Rochester I saw with
him, as free as ever, to the King's everlasting shame to have so idle a
rogue his companion. How Tom Killigrew takes it, I do not hear.[17]

In *As You Like It*, Celia threatens Touchstone with a whipping: "You'll
be whipped for / taxation one of these days" (1.2.78–79). Lear's fool is similarly threatened when his truths slice too sharply, "Take heed, sirrah; the
whip" (1.4.108), although he is not expected to stop telling them. When
the Fool asks Lear to "keep a schoolmaster that can / teach thy Fool to lie:
I would fain learn to lie," Lear responds, "And you lie, sirrah, we'll have you
whipp'd." The jester was caught between the devil and the deep blue sea:

> I marvel what kin thou and thy daughters are:
> they'll have me whipp'd for speaking true, thou'lt
> have me whipp'd for lying; and sometimes I am
> whipp'd for holding my peace.
>
> (1.4.175–81).

GET THEE HENCE!

"Get out of my court," ordered the Rama; "if you were not a clown I
would have had you hanged. Such impertinence!"

Rajani Bannerji, *Gopal the Jester*[18]

Gopal was only just saved from hanging, but not from exile, by his jester's
license, and even Chicot, beloved courtier-jester of Henri III, was sent
away, though soon forgiven and recalled.[19] Louis XIII amused himself
with shaving Marais, and when he had finished the jester gave him some
money. The royal barber joked that it was not enough, and Marais promised to give him more "when you are master" ("quand vous serez maître"),
implying that Cardinal Richelieu (1585–1642) held the reins of power.[20]
In 1459 the jester of a French duke was given a sum of money by the
duke's treasurer to leave and not come back ("pour s'en aller et ne revenir
plus"), although no reason is given for this redundancy pay.[21] In July 1535
Eustace Chapuys, imperial ambassador to London, wrote in describing
Henry VIII's harsh treatment of his daughter Princess Mary:

> He the other day nearly murdered his own fool, a simple and inno-
> cent man, because he happened to speak well in his presence of the

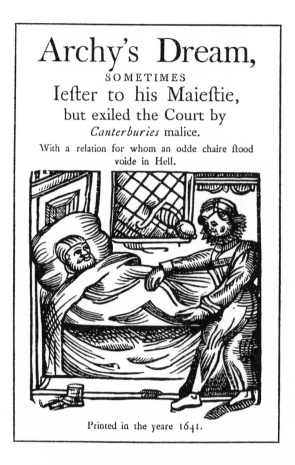

Figure 20 Archy exiled

Queen and Princess [Catherine of Aragon and Mary], and called the concubine [Anne Boleyn] "ribaude" and her daughter [Elizabeth] "bastard." He has now been banished from Court, and has gone to the Grand Esquire [Sir Nicholas Carew, master of the horse] who has sheltered and hidden him.[22]

The most detailed account of a jester's banishment relates to Archy Armstrong, whose outright insolence to the archbishop of Canterbury led to his dismissal (fig. 20). When the *Book of Common Prayer* was badly received in Scotland, Archy suggested the archbishop was a better candidate for the position of fool than he, taunting him with "Whea's feule now?"[23] A document from Whitehall, dated 11 March 1637, states:

It is this day ordered bij his Majesty, with the advice of the board, that Archibald Armstrong the King's fool, for certain scandalous words of a high nature, spoken by him against the Lord Archbishop of Canterbury, his Grace, and proved to be uttered by him, by two witnesses, shall have his coat pulled over his head, and be discharged of the King's service, and banished the court, for which the Lord Chamberlain of the King's household is prayed and required to give order to be executed. And immediately the same was put in execution.[24]

Greater men than the archbishop have been the target of a jester who then paid for his insolence. At a banquet given during the Taihe reign-period (827–35) by Emperor Wenzong, a jester mocked Confucius in a variety show. The emperor was angered by his irreverence and ordered him thrown out of court.[25] In the early ninth century some Chinese jesters were beaten and banished to a frontier garrison for offering to put on a skit mocking a disgraced minister. They were told that although the minister had rebelled he was not a lowly thief, and since the law had its own punishments there was no need for jesters' mockery—a rare denial of their right to make fun of people.[26]

During the Baoqing reign-period (1225–55) of Emperor Lizong, Prime Minister Shi Miyuan (1164–1233) gave a banquet at his residence at which variety skits were performed. The jesters alluded to the nepotism of the prime minister by referring to his place of origin, Siming. One jester dressed as a scholar, chanting a poem:

"All the nobles of the court in their robes of scarlet and vermilion are men of learning." Another "scholar" next to him said, "No they aren't! 'All the nobles of the court in their robes of scarlet and vermilion are men of Siming.'" After this there were no more variety skits performed during banquets at the prime minister's residence for the next twenty years.

『滿朝朱紫貴，盡是讀書人。』旁一士人曰：『非也！「滿朝朱紫貴，盡是四明人！」』自後相府有宴，二十年不用雜劇。[27]

John Scogin, one of those jesters who hover between fact and fiction, was said to be jester to Edward IV (1442–83), and there were several jest-books printed in his name. The first, in 1565–66, was *Geystes of Skoggon*, and the most famous was *The Merry Jests, and Witty Shifts of Scogin*, supposedly compiled by Andrew Boorde.[28] Scogin is alleged to have had the dubious honor of being exiled from two courts, first from England to France and then back again. The French king took him to his toilet to show him a picture of the English king on the wall. Scogin commented on the likeness, and the French king explained how it showed his contempt for the king of England. Scogin responded, "Jesu Christ! here is a wonderfull thing! What would you doe, if you did see the King of England in the face as he is, when that for fear you doe beshit yourselfe, when that you looke but upon a picture of him?" He was shown the door and deported.[29] The *Banquet of Jests* has a primly sanitized version ending, "I observe it well Sir, and withall, that you never looke upon it, but at the sight thereof, you are ready to bewray your Breeches."[30]

An almost identical response is told of the Scottish George Buchanan when an Englishman scorned the Scottish hero William Wallace, saying that "for honour of the Scots, we have his effigy in our shite houses to this very day."[31] Since Scogin lived in the century preceding Buchanan's, and the first Scogin jestbook was published in 1565–66 when Buchanan was flourishing, it is possible he would have read it. Alternatively, this story could have been borrowed on his behalf by the anonymous compiler of the book about him. Jokes enjoy no copyright.

OFF WITH HIS HEAD! THE KILLJOY KING

> It may happen that a companion of his majesty the sultan receives gold and it is possible that he loses his head. Philosophers have said that it is necessary to be on guard of the fickle temper of padshahs because sometimes they are displeased with politeness and at others they bestow robes of honour for rudeness. It is also said that much jocularity is an accomplishment in courtiers.
>
> Sa'di Shirazi, *The Rose Garden of Sa'di* (1258)[32]

> Terence asserts that truth can breed
> Deep hate, and he is right indeed
>
> [Wiewohl Terentius saget, daß
> Wer Wahrheit ausspricht, erntet Haß]
>
> Sebastian Brant, *Ship of Fools*[33]

In China the offering of either *fengjian* or gratuitous mockery went hand in hand with the risk of being literally axed if the jester's words were too unpalatable, witty seasoning notwithstanding. This is perhaps where there is some scope for the cliché of "Oriental despot" to come into play, although this is due less to the greater despotism of the Chinese ruler over his Western counterparts than to the more bold-faced determination of

Chinese jesters together with their lesser ability to hide behind a cloak of folly. If there are only rare instances of European jesters' being executed for excessive zeal in the business of telling home truths, it is also harder to find evidence of their having offered *fengjian* regardless of the personal consequences.

One such case, however, involves a tale of the Irish jester Lomna, who could not be silenced even by death, piping up with a posthumous prediction. When his master Finn went hunting with the Fianna, Lomna stayed at home and saw Coirpre, a man of the Luigne, the same clan as Finn's wife, making love to her. She begged Lomna to keep quiet, which he at first agreed to, until he could no longer bear to betray Finn. So he informed him indirectly by means of a riddle written on a rod: "An alder stake in a paling of silver; deadly nightshade in a bunch of cresses; a husband of a lewd woman; a fool among the well-taught Fianna; heather on bare Ualann of Luigne." Finn understood, and when his wife knew she sent her lover to lop off Lomna's head. Finn found the body, and the Fianna asked him whose it was. Finn did a divination by rhymes and told them it was Lomna and that the Luigne would know how he died.

Coirpre, the jester-slaying lover, was in his house cooking fish on a spit for his men, with Lomna's head on a stake by the fire. Coirpre divided the fish among his men in a way that was against the laws of the Fianna. The dead jester spoke of this and warned Coirpre, "You have shared a share that is not right; the Fianna will avenge it upon you, Coirpre." Coirpre ordered the head to be put outside, but it continued to prophesy: "It is in many pieces you will be; it is great fires will be lighted by Finn in Luigne." Finn then arrived, razing the house and wreaking revenge.[34]

The Liao dynasty jester Light Coat Luo had a great talent for impromptu wit and often offered humorously indirect advice *(guifeng)*. Emperor Xingzong was defeated by Li Yuanhao (1003–48) and made a dash for freedom on his own, barely escaping capture. Before this, Yuanhao had caught some men of Liao and punished them by cutting off their noses. Light Coat shamed the emperor for his spirit of *sauve qui peut*, innocently saying, "Let's see whether your nose is still there or not." The emperor was enraged and took a cord to have him killed behind a tent.[35] In 938 Emperor Meng Chang of the Later Shu (r. 934–65) took a trip to Great Compassion Monastery. He provided a banquet for his retinue in Jade Brook Temple, and people presented poems. A jester made a skit and was executed for it, although it is not clear why.[36] Another jester was beheaded for a subversive skit: when Sun Wu became governor of Guangzhou, he was given special funds for military supplies, but the goods were of poor quality, the prices were high, and soldiers griped about it. The skit drew attention to this, and Wu ordered the jester's death.[37]

In 1534 there was a great deal of debate about court rituals, the temple of Confucius, and the division of sacrifices. Some household actors of Guo Dingwu performed a skit before the court nobility in which a scholar announced that there was a famine. He appealed to Confucius for succor but was refused on the grounds that reforms to sacrifices meant reducing his own rations, and he was told to ask the ancestral emperor. The emperor, hungry himself, sent him away to ask God. But God said he had fallen on hard times and had nothing to spare for people below. The actors continued to mock contemporary affairs in this way to such a degree that the guests became nervous and fled in alarm. Guo Dingwu had been involved in the question of rituals and was furious when he heard about the actors' levity, and several of them died as a result.[38]

It is not always the jester's master who has him executed. In 1532 Zuñiga—short, fat favorite jester to Emperor Charles V—was killed by a noble he offended. He was brought home wounded, and when his wife asked about the commotion, he replied with gallant nonchalance, "Oh, it's nothing Madame, except that they have murdered your husband" ("No es nada, señora, sino que han muerto á vuestro marido").[39] Chicot was similarly killed, having captured a traitor and brought him before the king. When the noble discovered he had been arrested by a mere jester, albeit one who was also a professional soldier, his dignity was so outraged that he attacked him, inflicting mortal wounds.[40] These are rare instances of European jesters' being killed, and neither execution was ordered by the king.

When the fearsome Pang Xun rebelled in 868, he reached Sizhou, where the governor entertained him by a polo pitch. A jester presented a prologue to a play, and Pang Xun thought he was being mocked, so he seized the jester to chop his head off, while the other guests panicked and fled.[41] In 1145 other jesters "were sent to prison and died."[42]

On one occasion the jester was saved from the wrath of his joke victim by his master—only fair since it was he who instigated the mockery in the first place. Wu Zhi (177–230), a general under Cao Cao, was host to some other senior generals sent by Cao Cao. There was a great feast, and he wanted to be as merry as possible. Two of his guests were of Laurel and Hardy proportions, Zhu Shuo being thin and Cao Zhen fat. Wu Zhi ordered a jester to discourse on obesity and skinniness. Cao Zhen, very proud and also very sensitive about his adiposity, felt humiliated and angrily asked Wu Zhi if he was trying to treat him like a subordinate. Two other generals, apparently amused by the joke, cajoled him:

"What's your problem? If you want Zhu Shuo to be the loser in the matter, then go on a diet!" Cao Zhen became all the more enraged, seized his sword and glowering threatened, "A jester dares to treat me with such levity, I'll hack him in half!" Then he sat down cursing all and sundry. Zhi brought out his sword and said, "How dare you throw your weight around with such arrogance?" The thin general rose to his feet and said, "Now, now, His Majesty sent us here to have a good time, how has it come to this?" and so the matter was dropped.

『將軍必欲使上將軍服肥，即自宜爲瘦。』眞愈恚，拔刀瞋目言：『俳敢輕脫，吾斬爾！』遂罵坐。質案劍曰：『曹子丹！。。。何敢恃勢驕邪？』鑠因起曰：『陛下使吾等來樂卿耳，乃至此邪？』遂便罷也。[43]

In some cases the jester is executed in a fit of pique, or under the influence of officials or nobles, and the ruler can later deeply regret his violent reaction because he misses the lively jester and realizes how much he needs his open-hearted candor. Li Shi, governor of the capital, was extremely harsh, but since he had made a great effort to collect taxes he was looked on with favor and nobody took any notice of the complaints of ordinary people. In 804 there was a severe drought and famine, and the emperor asked about the people's suffering. Li Shi reassured him that despite the drought, crops were very good. As a result there was no tax exemption, and with no recourse to appeal the peasants could pay their taxes only by tearing off the tiles and timbers of their roofs to sell along with their corn seedlings. The jester Truly Assisting Uprightness (Cheng Fuduan) made a skit about it, dressing up like a man of Qin, an extremely poor province:

Shi heard about it and was angry. He said Assisting Uprightness had slandered the government, so Dezong had him tried and sentenced to death. Somebody at the time commented, "Blind people's recitation and admonishments *take their material from funny things so as to provide indirect advice, that's the ancient business of jesters.* Culling the rough-hewn opinions of lowborn people gets to the heart of things and incorporates oblique advice. Assisting Uprightness committed no crime." *Dezong heard this and felt profound regret,* while people in the capital clenched their teeth in anger at Shi!

實聞之怒，言輔端誹謗國政，德宗遽令決殺。當時言者曰：『瞽誦箴諫，取其詼諧以託諷諫，優伶舊事也。設謗木，採芻蕘，本欲達下情，存諷議，輔端不可加罪。』德宗亦深悔，京師無不切齒以怒實。[44]

There was a jester-musician of the Hebei region called Mule (Shi Luoer)—incidentally also the name of the megalomaniac jester, with a beaked nose and "long, lean limbs . . . with just a suggestion of having been thrown together at random," who tries to take over the universe in Isaac Asimov's *Foundation and Empire*. [45] Mule Shi was a gifted lute player much favored by Emperor Yingzong (r. 1321–23).

> One day the emperor was boozing in the Scarlet Sandalwood Hall, and the jester-musician sang the opening words "Wine immortal," to the tune "Merry in Front of the Hall." *The emperor blew up and bellowed at the attendants to kill him.* Afterward he regretted it and said, "Mule mentioned wine to indirectly correct me!"
>
> 一旦，御紫檀飲，驃兒歌殿前歡曲，有『酒神仙』之句。帝怒，叱左右殺之。
>
> 後悔曰：『驃以酒諷我也！』[46]

The king could come to regret the execution of a jester in other ways. The Roman emperor Gallienus (r. 253–68) was murdered by his bodyguard partly because "he appears to have enraged his soldiery by his atrocious treatment of certain scurrae whom he burnt alive for their indiscreet wit." [47] A sixth-century Irish king, Muircheartach Mac Erca, was banished to Scotland "for killing the *crosans*," cross-bearer jesters who sang satirical poems against anybody who misbehaved. [48] A story is told of the death in 1599 of Claus Hinße, jester to Duke Johann Friedrich of Pomerania. The duke had a fever that he could not shake off, and the jester, seeking an unorthodox cure, pushed him into a pond. The sudden change in temperature had the desired effect, but it was felt that for appearance' sake the duke should go through the motions of subjecting the jester to a trial. He was condemned to death, but the duke arranged for the sword to be replaced with a sausage. Nobody thought to tell the jester of this meaty reprieve, and he died of fright when the sausage hit his neck. [49]

HOLD YOUR FIRE! GALLOWS HUMOR

> Zhuangzong was enraged, so he drew his bow, aimed his arrow, and was about to shoot him. Newly Polished Mirror shouted urgently, "Don't kill me, Your Majesty, we are of the same mettle, you and I, and it would be unpropitious for you to kill me!" The emperor was astonished and asked him what he meant, so he answered, "When you founded your dynasty, you changed the reign-period title to

Unifying Splendor [Tong Guang] and all under heaven called Your Majesty the Emperor of Unifying Splendor. "Unifying" *[tong]* equals "bronze mirror" *[tong]*. If you kill Newly Polished Mirror, the bronze mirror *[tong]* will lose its shine *[guang]!*" The emperor burst out laughing and forgave him.

Ouyang Xiu, *"Biographies of Jesters" ("Lingguan zhuan")* [50]

Newly Polished Mirror managed to use a pun to laugh his way out of immediate dispatch. Not all Chinese jesters were as quick-witted or as fortunate, and a number of them were summarily executed. Although Estebanillo González, the jester-hero of a seventeenth-century Spanish picaresque autobiographical novel, was spared the death sentence because of his amusing jokes, it seems that execution, or even the threat of it, was rare for European jesters, and Chinese jesters were banished less often than their Western counterparts.[51] Moving Bucket had been asked by Emperor Gaozu (r. 550 –59) to recount his dreams, and he said he dreamed that the emperor fell into a honey pot. Gaozu tried to humiliate him by saying that Moving Bucket must have then licked it all off, but the jester was not to be bested; having made the emperor promise to forgive him his answer, he parried:

"Last night I dreamed I was walking with Your Majesty, and I fell into an open sewer. I got out [and you licked me clean], isn't that right?" The emperor was enraged and ordered the officers in charge to kill him. He said, "I'd just like to say one thing before I die." The emperor asked, "What's that?" "If Your Majesty takes my head, it will be absolutely useless to you. If I lose my head, [it'll be extremely painful to me]." *The emperor laughed and had him released.*

『臣昨夜夢隨陛下行，落一廁中，出來口口口口〔陛下爲臣〕舐之。』帝大
怒，賦所司殺？。曰：『臣請一言而死。』帝曰：『口口〔何言？〕』曰：
『陛下得臣頭，極無用，口口口〔極有痛〕』」笑而捨之。[52]

Cross-fertilization may account for the fact that an identical story is told of the Indian jester Tenali Rama and his king; or "is it by chance that Tenali Rama triumphs by means of a honeyed tongue?"[53] The two stories are so similar that it is tempting to wonder whether jester stories were included in the cultural exchanges between India and China. Tenali Rama supposedly flourished almost a thousand years after Moving Bucket— plenty of time for the honey-licking story to make its way from China and digest its origins.

During the An Lushan rebellion the emperor had to flee so precipi-
tously that none of his ministers or servants knew about it. In Full
Streamer fell into the hands of the rebels and was allowed freedom of
movement around An Lushan. In 757 when the rebellion was quelled, the
jester was arrested and taken to the emperor who, having always liked his
nimble wit, released him. However, somebody accused the jester of interpreting dreams flatteringly for Lushan and generally collaborating. The
jester explained his actions as mere sensible expediency in view of the real
meaning of the rebel's dreams:

> "I honestly did not know that Your Majesty had fled in a cloud of
> dust to Shu, and when I fell among the rebels, how could I not keep
> him entertained if that would prolong my life? Today I have been
> able to see your heavenly countenance again, and when I was inter-
> preting dreams for the Great Rebel, I knew he would get nowhere."
> The emperor asked how he knew and he answered, "When the rebel
> dreamed of long sleeves it meant he couldn't stretch out his hands
> and grasp his desires; when he dreamed of the falling casement, it
> meant he could not fix things to suit him, so you see, I could foresee
> that I'd be with you again." The emperor burst out laughing and let
> the matter drop.

『臣實不知陛下大駕蒙塵赴蜀。即陷在賊中，寧不苟悅其心，以脫一時之命？
今日得再見天顏，以與大逆圓夢，必知其不可也。』上曰：『何以知之？』對
曰：『逆賊夢衣袖長，是出手不得也；又夢隔子倒者，是胡不得也。以此臣故
先知之。』上大笑而止。[54]

In 901 Li Maozhen, governor of Fengyao, went to court for a regular
audience, and the next day he made his way to a banquet. It was said that
there was nobody who could be as violent as he, and at some time in the
past he had razed the whole capital. At the banquet the jester Fitting New
Bridle (An Peixin) alluded to this with unbridled gall by calling him a "fire
dragon" *(huo longzi)*. Li felt deeply humiliated, and after the banquet
someone commented that "one of these days he'll chop that jester's head
off." When New Bridle heard this, he asked for leave from court and went
to obtain a pardon from Li. Li saw him from a distance and cursed him:

> "That jester's had it! How dare he come here?" He casually answered,
> "I just came on a visit, I haven't come to ask for mercy or anything."
> [Li said to him, "Somebody as wretched and lowly as you, how can
> you not be begging for mercy?"] New Bridle quipped, "Well, [since

you burned the capital], the city's full of charcoal that I can sell, [so why would I need to beg?]" *Li burst out laughing, rewarded him richly, and forgave him.*

『此優窮也！胡爲敢來？』嚮新對曰：『只要起居，不爲求救。』〔茂貞曰：

『貧賤如斯，胡不求乞？』安曰：〕『近日京中且賣麩炭，可以取濟，〔何在

求乞？〕』茂貞大笑，而厚賜赦之也。[55]

Another Chinese jester managed to joke his way out of penal amputation. When the Jurcheds were invading China, Wang Kang accompanied an envoy to Hedong. Some villagers thought they had caught a prisoner of war and were about to cut off his arm. He asked them to cut off the left one, and when they asked why, he said, "If you cut the right one off, I won't be able to scratch an itch." They all laughed and said, "This one's a jester!"[56]

Caliph Harun al-Rashid asked the jester-poet Abu Nuwas (756–811) to produce an excuse that was worse than what it sought to exonerate. In one version Abu bided his time until he saw the caliph standing up, then crept up behind him and seized him by the shoe. The caliph asked him furiously what he thought he was doing, and Abu claimed he thought it was the caliph's wife he was manhandling. Only when Abu reminded the caliph of the task he had set did he see the funny side of it, laughing loudly and presenting him with a reward.[57] A funnier and more dramatic version has the jester pinch the caliph's backside, being threatened with execution for the assault. Abu extricates himself by saying he thought it was the backside of the caliph's wife.[58]

One situation that recurs with rich variants and great frequency concerns the exile of the jester and his trickery to circumvent it. Although no such examples have been found in China, they do seem to occur in both Europe and the Middle East, and they could be due either to the traffic of king-defying skills or to the individual ingenuity of jesters. When jesters were banished they were often ordered either never again to show their faces or never again to set foot in the area, and these two commands, both open to literal interpretation, were commonly obeyed to the letter and flouted in spirit. When Tenali Rama was ordered by the king never to show his face in court again, he simply covered his head with a pot and reappeared.[59]

George Buchanan was charged by the king "never to let him see his face on English ground."[60] So he went to Scotland to fill his boots with earth, returning to a place where he knew the king would be passing by, and from there he exposed his rear end out of a window. James VI, at whom Buchanan's prank was aimed, had himself once threatened to pull down his trousers and show an irritatingly adoring crowd what for.[61] On this occasion, however, he asked that the prankster be brought to him, and on seeing it was Buchanan, reminded him of his exile. Buchanan responded that he had not shown his face, and furthermore he was not standing on English soil. He showed the king his boots and was forgiven.[62]

The legendary Marcolphus, on account of his wit, was invited to dispute with King Solomon. Most of their debates entail a wise platitude from Solomon parried by a witty riposte or popular proverb from Marcolphus. Their dialogues may have been known as early as the fifth century in a work titled *Contradictio Salomonis*, although the first mention of Marcolphus by name is in the eleventh century: "Who is this so-called Marcolph who contests the sayings of Solomon?" ("Quid est enim, quum dicunt Marcolphum contra proverbia Salomonis certasse?")[63] By the twelfth century he has become a coarse but clever fool, and in his juxtaposition to the king he resembles a jester.

The story, with Marcolphus "right rude and great of body . . . but right subtyll and wyse of wyt, and full of understanding . . . of vysage greatly mishapen and fowle, nevyrthelesse he was right talkatyf elloquend and wyse," was most popular in Germany, where there were at least two versions circulating, one prose and one poetry. But there were also translations in half a dozen other languages, with the English *Dialogue [of] Salomon and Marcolphus* appearing in about 1492.[64] Marcolphus was banished from Solomon's court and told never to show his face again. The anecdote that follows shows him evading both exile and hanging, quite a feat even for a jester. The king finds him tucked inside an oven:

> The king Salomon discended from hys hors and began to loke into the oven. Marcolphus laye all crokyd, hys vysage from hym wardes; had put downe hys breche into hys hammes that he myght se hys ars hole and all hys othre fowle gere. As the kyng Salomon that seyng demawnded what laye there. Mar. answeryd, I am here: Sal. Wherefore lyest thou thus. Marcolf. For ye haue commaunded me that ye shulde no more se me betwyxt myn yes; now and ye woll not se me betwyxt myn yes, ye may se me betwene by buttockys in the myddes of myn arsehole. Than was the king sore meovyd [and] commaunded his seruauntys to take hym and hange hym upon a tre.

He manages to wriggle out of this one by asking that he may choose on which tree he will be hanged, a seemingly simple request:

Than the kinges seruauntes token and leddyn marcolph wythoute
the citie, and through the vale of iosaphath and ovyr the hyghte of
the hylle of olyvete from thens to iericho and cowde fynde no tre that
marcolf wolde chese to be hangyd on. From thens wente they ovyr the
flome iordane and alle arabye through, and so forth all the great wyl-
dernesse unto the rede see. And nevyrmore cowde marcolph fynde a
tre that he wolde chese to hange on. And thus he askapyd out of the
dawnger and handes of king salomon, and turnyd agen unto hys
howse, and levyd in pease and ioye.[65]

Both these tricks were attributed to Scogin, and since stories of Marcolphus had been circulating for centuries, it is not hard to imagine the compiler stealing the idea to add to Scogin's stature. Scogin tells his would-be
hangmen to "goe to your King and have me commended to him; and tell
him that I will never chuse a tree to bee hanged on: and so fare you well.
Hee is a mad man that may save his owne life, and will kill himselfe."[66]
The jester's face-saving moony prank is also ascribed to the trickster-jester
Nasrudin Afanti in tales told of his exploits among the Moslem people
of northwestern China, though who influenced whom in these globe-
trotting stories is anybody's guess.[67]

Tenali Rama evades execution with consummate ease. He asked for a
purifying bath before dying, requesting that the executioners stand on either side of the bath and chop his head off when he gave the signal. He
then signaled, at the same time diving into the water so that the two succeeded only in removing each other's heads.[68] Another time he was charged
with harboring a spy and was sentenced to death. When the king allowed
him to choose how he wanted to die, he replied, "I choose death by old
age." The king was amused and forgave him.[69]

A rather more gruesome death sentence had him buried to the neck,
exposing just his head, which was then to be trampled by an elephant.
While an elephant was being found for the job, a hunchback walked by,
and Tenali Rama persuaded him that he too had been a hunchback until
he tried this cure. The hunchback dug him out and, seeing his straight
back, decided to try it for himself. Since it was dark by the time the elephant was brought, the hunchback was trampled. Tenali Rama merely
commented that the man's wife would be relieved to have lost her deformed
husband—a rare sign of brutality from the more usually compassionate
jester. The king was delighted that his jester had not died after all, although he did order a generous pension to be paid to the hunchback's
widow.[70]

On a rare occasion when Akbar was angered by Birbal, he told him to leave the court and never return. Birbal reminded him of a promise he had once made that would allow Birbal to choose his own punishment should he ever offend the mogul. Akbar was annoyed but stood by his word. Birbal summoned the five poorest men in the city and asked them to decide his fate. They fined him fifty rupees—a fortune to them, but peanuts to the jester.[71]

When George Buchanan offended the queen, she demanded that the king allow her to punish him. Sure of his jester's Houdini-like ability to evade harm, he agreed, "well knowing that George would rescue himself by some intrigue or other."[72] An anecdote about Buchanan is still circulating in a Scottish folktale that has the wily jester seek a pardon for a crime before admitting to it. While walking into town he met a knight on a bridge who drew his sword and would not let him pass. Buchanan explains the situation to the king in somewhat oblique terms:

> "Well," he said, "Ir Majesty, I drew my sword tae, an we hed a fight."
> "Well," said the king . . . king get excited noo, ye ken! "Did yese hae a guid fight?" "Ay." "I'm glad ye enjoyed yirsel!" "Oh, A enjoyed masel," he said, "Ir Majesty." "But," he said, "what did ye dae ye want me tae pardon ye fir?" "Well," he said, "A *knockit his hat o'er the brig*." "Tut, tut," said the king, "that's nothing—what dae ye—" He said, "I want ye tae pardon me fir *knockin his hat o'er the brig*." "Of course, George," he said, "ye're pardoned, ye're pardoned as pardoned cuid be!" "Well, Ir Majesty," he said, "his heid wis in the hat!" Well, the wonst he pardoned him fir knockin his hat o'er the brig, he cuidna dae naethin aboot hit.[73]

The other of the two most famous Scottish jesters, Archy, is said to have become a jester by talking himself out of the death sentence, winning not only a reprieve but also a new and lucrative career as James's jester:

> Condemned to die for his crime, Archie Armstrong—for it was he —pleaded with the King that he was a poor and ignorant man, who had but recently heard of the Bible, and who was desirous, for his soul's sake, of reading through the precious volume: would his Majesty's grace be pleased to respite him until he had done this? The good-natured monarch easily acceded to the petition, on which Archie immediately rejoined, with a sly look, "Then de'il tak' me an' I ever read a word o't as lang as my een are open!" [In other words,

never.] The King was so pleased with the fellow's ready wit, that he forthwith employed him in his service.[74]

A German jester who was called Wolf Scherer until his name was changed to Peter Wrong-in-the-Head (Letzkopf) put small pieces of wood in all the keyholes to teach a lesson to the courtiers who were cruel to him. The count was annoyed by this and banished him from Mösskirch. He set off but returned the same day, and when the count questioned him, he replied that he had been sitting on a big stone, and looking all around he decided nowhere on earth pleased him like Mösskirch ("were er uf ain großen stain gesessen und hett in alle welt rings herum gesehen, so hett im aber kein ort an der welt mehr gefallen, dann Mösskirch").[75] The count was touched and took him in again.

In *The Court Jesters,* the astrologer-jester Sky Colour (Himmelfarb) is rescued from probable execution by the quick thinking of the dwarf-jester, who turns his blunt outburst into a big joke. At a party given by Major Kohl, Sky Colour begins by looking through a tube at the sky and telling the guests their horoscopes with enough canny accuracy and sexy insinuation to delight them. Suddenly however, he

> broke the rules of the game and went beyond the limit. . . . "How can you read the stars?" we heard him shout as he looked out the window again at the dark sky. "How can you read the stars when you can't tell the difference between the stars and the sparks from the ovens burning day and night? When you don't know what's rain and what's blood falling down from heaven?"[76]

The dwarf manages to make the whole thing look like part of a rehearsed routine by jumping on Sky Colour's shoulders and riding around shouting and cracking jokes, while muzzling the man's mouth until he has reined himself in and can continue with his horoscopes.

Usually the jester oversteps the mark after becoming a court jester. In the case of Nasrudin, legend has it that he did so *before* becoming jester. One day he was in a mosque preaching against the ferocious Tamerlane, who came in disguised as a dervish. When Nasrudin assured his congregation that God would strike the Tartars, the "dervish" told him his prayer would not be granted. Nasrudin asked who he was, and when his identity was revealed the mirthful mulla addressed the terrified congregation, gaining forgiveness for them all and a place for himself at court:

"Who are you, and what is your name?"
"I am a dervish, and my name is Timur."
"Does your name end in 'Lame' by any chance?"
"It does."
"Brethren, we have performed a congregational prayer. Now we shall
start the congregational funeral service."[77]

In theory, there were no limits to the license of the jester. In reality,
he was dealing with a person just as subject to moods and sensibilities as
any other, regardless of his regal standing, and with more power than
most to punish somebody whose usually welcome wit could also smack of
goading insolence. Yet considering that the license jesters enjoyed was established by custom and not by law, and that they were entirely dependent on their masters' good humor, it is surprising how far they *were* allowed to go.

Often the monarch's condemnation came in a moment of anger and
soon passed, particularly if the jester was given a chance to extricate himself with a wisecrack. It is even possible that he would be given the chance
without having to ask for it—in the Royal Navy, an institution in which
humor is rife and often used to soften rebukes, a sailor was given the clear
option to joke his way out of trouble. The punishment was to wade
through a stagnant pond unless he could tell a joke which would make
everyone laugh. Since this occurred at the Royal Naval School of Leader-
ship and Management, it seems that the use of humor both to criticize
people and to evade punishment is still not only tolerated but actively encouraged by authority. The spirit of the jester lives on.[78]

What a joke I find that old Li Tan—Laozi's—five-thousand-word *Way and Its Power* classic of Daoism, and that Sakyamuni's five thousand volumes of written words. All the one served to do was pointlessly stir up Daoist priests, sending them round bashing their cloud gongs, and the other just got the Buddhist bonzes going about rattling their wooden fish begging clappers—down-and-out jobs for urchin choirboys! And when in heaven's name was there ever such a creature as the green cow that Laozi's supposed to have ridden? Or ever the sniff of anything vaguely like the white elephant said to have been Buddha's dad? And Buddha's to blame for rousing that stinking old barbarian Boddhidharma and sending him here too, with his endless rechewing and rewashing of the crumbs of those same old dried turds! And what a laugh you are, old gaffer Confucius, with all your long-winded blabber about orthodox ethics and edifying writings or what-have-you, and you made a lot of living people into dead ones for no good reason as well!

Feng Menglong,
preface to the *Expanded Treasury of Laughter (Guang xiaofu)* [1]

5

Religion, Erudition,
and Irreverence

THE CLERIC, THE SCHOLAR, AND THE JESTER

With shauen heades as ideotes, in theire hoodes
made with eares & beset with belles much like to fooles.

Henry Cornelius Agrippa,
Of the Vanitie and Uncertaintie of Artes and Sciences (1569)[2]

For my laughter is cataclysmic: it upheaveth and it destroyeth. De-
moniac and heathenish is my laughter which maketh the bishops
frown and their ministers scowl.

Lin Yutang, "Zarathustra and the Jester"[3]

Agrippa was describing not court jesters but hypocritical monks, and
two Renaissance Italian jesters had the holy sounding names of Crucifix
(Crocifisso) and God-given (Diodato), perhaps reflecting something of
the complexities of examining the jester's relationship to religion, which
provides the starkest divergence between the European court jester and
his colleagues elsewhere.[4] Perhaps because religious representatives were
so much more bound up with the affairs of court and state in Europe, and
because the church wielded such hefty political power, the European
jester came up against clerics far more frequently (fig. 21).

The court jester's relationship to scholars and clerics was multifaceted.
They could be targets for his irreverence—the pompous, pedantic scholar,
the money-grubbing monk, the absurdity of many religious or ideological tenets—and the jester would rarely resist the temptation to laugh at
them. The other side of the coin had scholars, officials, and clerics in the
guise of jester, either ad hoc, if they perceived that the only way of gaining

Figure 21 The monk-mocking Eulenspiegel

the ear of the monarch was by making him laugh, or if their character naturally lent itself to playing the fool.

In China jesters' sacrilege usually goes no further than the deliberate distortion of scripture for the sake of a joke. This misquoting of religious canon occurred also in Europe and the Middle East and was not intended to attack religion per se, simply stemming from a discrepancy between religious ideals and realities or from a healthy disregard for all creeds and dogmas. Even the most vitriolic attacks of European jesters were not aimed at religion so much as at its representatives, and medieval and Renaissance Europe saw a staggering degree of irreverence toward the church from both clergy and laity in a society of widespread religious conviction.

Elsewhere religious mockery is altogether gentler, lacking the sometimes bitter edge found in Europe. The distinction may be due to the generally more relaxed attitude of Buddhism, Daoism, and Confucianism toward humor and consequently jesters. The antipathy between the European jester and the cleric is often mutual, and there are numerous condemnations by the church of entertainers who lead people from the righteous road. In China there was some fierce condemnation of the influence of entertainers and "lascivious" music, but the laughter-making jesters do not seem to have been singled out or necessarily included.[5]

Perhaps also because cardinals and bishops involved themselves in state and court politics far more than their Buddhist or Daoist brothers, they placed themselves directly in the line of fire of a jester's sharp arrows, causing the European jesters to reserve their strongest venom for ecclesiastics, whereas the sharpest attacks of the Chinese jesters are aimed at secular corruption. We know of Will Somers's legendary dislike for Cardinal Wolsey, how much Archy Armstrong detested Archbishop Laud, and the sparring that went on between Maître Guillaume and Cardinal Perron.[6] In China this is matched perhaps only by jesters' recurrent mockery of Qin Gui or Wang Anshi, both acting in the political rather than religious arena: there do not appear to be any instances of a Chinese jester's lashing an individual cleric with his acerbic tongue. This is not to suggest that European jesters stood only in fierce opposition to clergymen—the relationship is often far more complex, and sometimes the humor can be innocent and kindly. The Scottish Jamie Fleeman once picked up a horse's shoe and showed it to his minister, asking him what it was.

> "That! you fool, that's a horse-shoe!" "Ah!" said Fleeman with a sigh;
> "ae! sic a blessing as it is to be weel learned! I couldna tell whether it
> was a horse's shoe or a mare's shoe!" Mr. Craigie, who delighted

much in a joke himself, used to tell this anecdote with great glee, and remarked that wise men ought never to meddle with fools.[7]

"ALL PRAISE BE TO GOD,
AND LITTLE LAUD TO THE DEVIL!"
Archy Armstrong

Take care of Truth awhile yet, and dress her decently, even with a veil of gaiety, for Truth naked is not a sight for the eye of the bishops! Thus spake Zarathustra.

Lin Yutang, "Zarathustra and the Jester"[8]

The subheading above is a well-known grace said by Archy Armstrong, the pun resting on "Laud," archbishop of Canterbury. He was not punished for it, although it is hard to imagine that a present-day comedian invited to dinner at Buckingham Palace could tell the archbishop of Canterbury, quite literally, to go to hell. In 1637 Laud persuaded the king to have Archy banished from court for laughing at him once too often, but Archy had the last laugh, the archbishop ultimately being sent to the Tower:

> You which the dreame of Archy now have read,
> Will surely talke of him when he is dead:
> He knowes his foe in prison whilst that hee
> By no man interrupted but goes free.
> His fooles coate now is far in better case,
> Then he which yesterday had so much Grace:
> *Changes of Times surely cannot be small,*
> *When Jesters rise and Archbishops fall.*[9]

The two jesters who stand out for their clerical attacks are Will Somers, jester to Henry VIII, whose traditional archfoe was Cardinal Wolsey, and Archy Armstrong. Somers was a more kindly and refined character than Archy, who was known for being foul-mouthed and roguish, but they shared a distaste for two of the highest ecclesiastics in the country. Somers's dislike of Wolsey is well documented, in Armin's *A Nest of Ninnies* and in Rowley's *When You See Me You Know Me,* where Somers has one of the leading roles. Both works were published in the first decade of the seventeenth century, close enough to Somers's time for the anecdotes to be credible; yet according to Southworth, Wolsey's death predates Somers's arrival at court by five years, which would bring into question the historical accuracy of Armin's work, however true to life the accounts.[10]

Armin tells how Somers one day asked the king to lend him some money to pay the cardinal's creditors. Wolsey insisted he owed no money, saying the king could have his head if any man could claim he owed him money. The king obliged the cardinal to cough up, and Somers promptly distributed the sum among the poor. When he returned the king asked who the creditors were:

> Who received? sayes the king; the brewer or the baker? Neyther (Harry), saies Will Sommers. But, cardinall, answere me one thing: to whom dost thou owe thy soule? To God, quoth hee. To whom thy wealth? To the poore, sayes hee. Take thy forfeit (Harry) sayes the foole; open confession, open penance: his head is thine, for to the poore at the gate I paid his debt, which hee yeelds is due: or if thy stony heart will not yeeld it so, saue thy head by denying thy word, and lend it mee. . . . The king laught at the jest, and so did the cardinall for a shew, but it grieved him to jest away ten pound so: yet worse tricks then this Will Sommers serued him after, for indeede hee could neuer abide him, and the forfeiture of his head had liked to haue beene payed, had hee not poysoned himselfe.[11]

Another attack has the cardinal's natural, Patch, carousing with Somers in the cardinal's cellar (though Somers was said to have been brought to court to replace an aging and subsequently banished Patch), where they find that half the containers are full of gold rather than wine. Somers has no qualms about letting the king know, in Wolsey's presence:

> *Henry.* Is his wine turned into gold, *Wil?*
> *Wolsey.* The foole mistakes, my gratious Soveraigne.
> *Somers.* I, I my Lord, ne're set your wit to the fooles, *Wil Summers*
>   will be secret now, and say nothing, if I would be a blabbe of
>   my tongue, I could tell the King how many barrells full of gold
>   and silver there was six times filled with plate and jewells, twen-
>   tie great truncks with Crosses, Crosiers, Copes, Miters, Maces,
>   golden Crucifixes, besides the foure hundreth and twelve thou-
>   sand pound that poore Chimneys paid for Peeter pence. But
>   this is nothing, for when you are Pope, you may pardon your
>   selfe for more knavery than this comes to. (lines 2816–27)

Of the Chinese jesters it is Moving Bucket who wins the prize for impiety. He did not focus on a particular priest, as Archy and Somers did, nor was he trying to expose vaulting ambition or corruption. He simply punctured the aura of holy solemnity surrounding a venerable monk by asking disingenuous questions, then refuting the responses with literal or punning interpretations. The emperor would occasionally arrange Buddhist seminars at which a Master of Great Virtue would preside. Moving Bucket innocently asked the master what day it was:

> The monk answered, "Today is the Buddha's birthday [*ri* = both 'day' and 'sun']." Moving Bucket, pretending to misunderstand, said, "So the sun *[ri]* is the Buddha's son [also pronounced *ri* at the time]?" The monk reinterpreted for him, "On this day Buddha was born." Moving Bucket persisted, "So the Buddha is the son of the sun?" Everybody had a good laugh over this.

> 僧答云：『是佛生日。』動觛即云：『日是佛兒。』僧卻變云：『今日佛
> 生。』動觛又云：『佛是日兒。』眾皆大笑。

The discussions finally reached an impasse, and everybody was challenging each other. Moving Bucket put his oar in, addressing the Master of Great Virtue nonchalantly, lulling him. Moving Bucket's joke rests on a pun on the Buddha's extraordinary nature:

> "I'd just like to ask the Dharma Master one small thing: what creature did the Buddha ride?" The Dharma Master answered, "Sometimes he sat on a lotus flower of a thousand leaves, sometimes he was borne on a white elephant of six tusks." Moving Bucket said, "The Dharma Master has not read the sutras at all, since he does not know what the Buddha rode." The Dharma Master asked him, "Since Kindly Benefactor has read the sutras, what did the Buddha ride?" Moving Bucket retorted, "The Buddha rode an ox!" The Dharma Master asked how he knew, and Moving Bucket replied, "The sutras say, 'The World's Honoured One [the Buddha] was extraordinary' [*qi te, qi* is a homonym for 'ride,' and *te* has 'ox' in it and originally meant 'calf']. How can this not be 'riding an ox'?" All present burst out laughing.

> 『且問法師一個小義，佛常騎何物？』動觛云：『法師全不讀經，不知佛所乘騎物。』法師又即問云：『檀
> 越讀經，佛騎物何？』動觛答云：『佛騎牛。』法師曰：『何以知之？』動觛
> 曰：『經云：「世曾甚奇特」，豈非騎牛？』坐皆大笑。

When the Great Virtue Dharma Master began to expound on the doctrine of "There is neither one nor two, there is neither right nor wrong," the secular scoffer again turned the whole thing into a joke, at first mocking him lightheartedly. Moving Bucket asked Gaozu's permission to argue, promising he could tie him in knots. The emperor, perhaps bored by all the intricate wisdom being thrown at him, was delighted. The jester approached the pulpit, raised his robe, and stood squarely, asking the monk:

> "How many feet does your disciple have?" The monk said, "Two feet." Moving Bucket then raised a foot behind and stood on one leg, asking, "Now how many feet does your disciple have?" "One foot." Moving Bucket said, "Before I had two feet, now I have one foot, is this what you mean by 'neither one nor two'?" The monk replied, "If it is true that there are two, there can't be just one, and if there is one, it's clear that there can't be two."

『看弟子有幾個腳？』僧曰：『兩腳。』動甬又翹一腳向後，一腳獨立，問僧
曰：『更看弟子有幾個腳？』僧曰：『一腳。』動甬云：『向有兩腳，今有一
腳，若爲得無一無二。』

The jester could see that the monk was full of endless argument, so he tried a more heavy-handed approach, putting the monk in the awkward position of having to give in or appear to be insulting the emperor, running rings around him so that in the end *the monk had nothing to say and Gaozu clapped his hands and burst out laughing.*[12]

In Islam the misinterpretation or misquoting of Koranic scripture was a common source of jokes, although one caliph drew the line at the Koran, beyond which his court jester was not allowed to trample.[13] There is one long-winded anecdote about a fool who entered the presence of a governor of Baghdad and, seeing a dish full of nougat, found a way to earn himself more and more pieces of the delicacy. He asked the governor what was on the dish, and when a piece was thrown to him he then quoted a phrase from the Koran that contained the number two and was consequently thrown a second piece. He followed this with random Koranic quotations containing three, four, and so on, each time receiving an extra piece, up to twenty, then two hundred, causing the governor to hand him the whole plate.[14]

Nasrudin, mulla and part-time jester, was sent by the king to find out about mystical religious lore. He was told of the miracles, founders, teachers, and sayings of various sects. His report to the king was a perfect example of the jester's debunking: "Carrots." The king asked him to explain this enigmatic brief, which he did. "The best part is buried . . . if you don't work for it, it will deteriorate; there are a great many donkeys associated with it."[15]

In India it is Tenali Rama who succeeded in exposing the greed of his own class, the Brahmans. The king's mother had requested a mango on her deathbed but had died before one could be brought. He asked the Brahmans how he might appease her spirit, and they assured him that by giving gold mangoes to 108 priests, he could make amends. The king followed their advice, and the priests went away delighted. When Tenali Rama's own mother died he invited the priests to his house, and they arrived in expectation of extravagant gifts, since the jester was known for his wealth and generosity. Having locked the doors, he had them all branded with hot irons. The king heard of this and came to the house to release the priests, angrily asking Tenali Rama to explain himself:

> "May it please Your Majesty! My mother died of acute rheumatism. Her last wish to me was to brand her, and relieve her pain. But, before the irons could be heated and brought, she died. As these reverend men told Your Majesty, the other day, that whatever a dying person wanted but could not be given in time could be given to them, and that this would be sure to satisfy the departed soul, I gave them the brandings I could not give my mother in time." The king laughed and left. The Brahmans hung their heads and slunk away.[16]

George Buchanan was capable of outarguing everyone, and much of his wit is anticlerical. One story has him decapitating a bishop on a bridge and gaining the king's pardon for merely knocking the bishop's hat over the bridge, only then admitting that his head was in it at the time, although the modern folktale version has a knight's head.[17] The French king is said to have shown Buchanan a painting of Jesus Christ with himself and the pope on either side. Buchanan thanked him, saying, "For though I have often heard that our Saviour was crucified betwixt two thieves, yet I never knew who they were before."[18] When an English bishop offered an insulting pun on "Scot" and "sot," Buchanan turned the tables on him:

> What, says the bishop, are you a Scot? Yes, says George, I am a Scot; Well, says the bishop, and what is the difference between a Scot and a sot. Nothing at present, says George, but the breadth of the table, there being a table betwixt the bishop and George; so the bishop went

off in a high passion, while the whole multitude were like to split
their jaws with laughter.[19]

Two Scottish jesters following Buchanan maintained the tradition.
Archy, who could resist no jibe at Archbishop Laud, was once asked by
the king for his opinion of a set of coach horses. He answered that they
should be ecclesiastics, since they were so fat and pampered as to be too
unwieldy for service. Laud was incensed and so

> caused search to be made for him, to cause him to be punished; but
> he could not be found till some of his Friends prevailed with the
> King to make his Peace: And where then, said he, do you think all
> this while I have hid my self? We know not, reply'd they; Why, said
> Archee, I'll tell you; even in the Chappel-Pulpit, for I knew his Grace
> never would come there to look for me.[20]

The gentler Jamie, who served a Scottish laird in Aberdeenshire, was
once in church during a soporific sermon. The minister, seeing his words
of wisdom wasted on the snoring congregation, told them to take a leaf out
of Jamie's good book. But Jamie would not take credit for attentive piety:

> "My brethren, you should take an example by that fool there" (point-
> ing to Jamie); "fool though he may be, *he* keeps awake, while you
> —think shame of yourselves—are nodding and sleeping." "Ay, ay,
> minister," muttered Fleeman to himself, "gin I had nae been a feel I
> had been asleep tee."[21]

Theodora, wife of the Byzantine emperor Theophilus (r. 829–42), hid
the religious idols she used in prayer for fear that the jester Danderi would
find out about them and mock her idolatry.[22] The jester to Borso d'Este,
Scocola, preached mock sermons in the streets of Ferrara, and another
d'Este fool, Bernadino "Madman" ("Matello"—his nickname became a
generic term for jesters), acted as a friar to parody a religious service.[23]

Akbar's jester, the Hindu Birbal (fig. 22), whom Siegel describes as a
"playful brahmin gadfly," frequently upset Muslim courtiers, in particular the earnest chronicler Bada'uni, who hated the influence the infidel
Birbal had over the emperor, often calling him "that bastard." When Birbal died, Bada'uni duly recorded his death in his chronicle, apparently
delighted that "Birbal . . . was slain and entered the row of dogs in hell
and thus got something for the abominable deeds he had done during his
lifetime."[24]

Mulla Nasrudin converted three Christian monks to Islam with his bold-faced bluffing. The monks came with three questions for the Muslims, promising to convert if given the correct answers. The sultan's wise men were unable to solve the riddles, so Nasrudin was sent for. The first monk asked the location of the middle of the earth, the second the number of stars in the sky, and the third the number of hairs in his beard. Nasrudin's answers were "Between the legs of my donkey standing over there," "As many as there are hairs on my donkey," and "As many as there are hairs in the tail of my donkey." When the monks asked how he arrived at such answers, he told them they could always check for themselves if they disbelieved him. They gave in, and Rome lost three souls to Mecca.[25]

Figure 22 Akbar's beloved Birbal

There are several anecdotes concerning German jesters that show anticlerical humor. Squire Peter (Junker Peter), jester to Duke Wolfgang Wilhelm zu Neuburg, was asked to drink to the health of three ecclesiastics—a Catholic, a Lutheran, and a Reformist—so he feigned a stomachache, saying that since such people caused so much discord in the church it was hardly surprising they should disagree with his stomach ("Es ist kein Wunder, daß sich die Leute im Magen nicht vertragen, die in der Kirche so viel Unruh erregen").[26] Another jester, Lips, who served Duke Philipp of Baden, was asked whether Jews should be allowed into the country. He replied, "Yes, for then we should have *all* religions in the land except the Christian religion, which is still lacking to us."[27]

A very long-serving and popular court jester was Claus Fool, who entertained a series of Saxon electors and an archbishop. When his master Elector Friedrich the Wise (d. 1525) was invited to a banquet in Leipzig, guests at the end of the meal recounted various wonders they had witnessed. Claus announced that he too would like to describe some wonders, the first being that supposedly penniless monks could build splendid residences, the second that monastic orders reaped great wealth from the huge amount of corn they acquired without ever working on the land, and the third that some local monks who had vowed celibacy seemed to have children, which must have been grown in the garden or been borne by the monks themselves.[28]

The modern American clown, Bill Irwin, created a clerical character called the Reverend Nelson, a preacher "whose long-winded sermons were peppered with malapropisms," an act that proved immensely popular at fairs, and the Scottish comic Ricky Fulton often acts as a church minister.[29] From the Brahman-bashing tricks of Tenali Rama to the mock sermons of a Renaissance jester, a modern American clown, and a Scottish comedian, jokers can rarely resist desanctifying the sacred with their laughter.

HOLY FOOLS AND FOOLISH FEASTS

Go crazy tonight—just tonight, and God on his throne will envy you your luster.

[Devenez-fou ce soir—ce soir seulement et Dieu sur son trône vous enviera votre lumière.]

Elie Wiesel, *Zalmen, ou La folie de Dieu*[30]

There is greater convergence around the world in the holy man's bearing the imprint of a fool than in the jester's mockery of the holy man. The Franciscan "fool for Christ's sake" is echoed in the Indian Cuntarar, a "fool for Siva's sake."[31] There are holy fools in the Russian church, dervishes in the Middle East, the humorous wisdom of a Zen master in the East, and the aura of sanctity surrounding the lunatic in many parts of the world. Sufis advocate folly as a means to enlightenment: recognizing that this might itself be seen as folly, they call themselves "the Idiots" and use humor in their teaching, illustrated by tales of Nasrudin, to shock people and jolt them out of conventional patterns.[32]

The Imitation of Christ (Imitatio Christi) (1441) by Thomas à Kempis dealt with the concept of folly as the path to God.[33] This kind of folly worship interprets "folly" as that which is considered folly by the world, a rejection of ambition and comfort for humility or ascetic harshness, the folly of the martyr; it is radically different from Erasmus's brand, that of the warm and laugh-loving jester. Like the court jester who did not seek to overthrow the institutions he mocked, the holy fool did not hope to replace his religion, even if he appeared to turn his back on it: "Folly for Christ's sake . . . is the development of an apparently wild and unrestrained spirituality *firmly and loyally* within the limits of what to some seem monolithic, authoritarian, ecclesiastical organisations."[34]

The Middle Eastern dervishes were holy men who could say prayers on behalf of others; they were in a sense peripheral to society and could be madmen. They often wore patched clothes and a cap, sometimes of leaves, or had a shaven head like many fools and monks in medieval Europe.[35] It was believed their prayers were heard, and they enjoyed immense respect, not only on this account but also because they were feared for their imprecations, which they could express with jovial impudence. Stories about them abound, many in the Persian classic by Sa'di Shirazi, *The Rose Garden (Gulistan)* (1258), in which the dervishes display fearless cheek in addressing kings, often bluntly reminding them of their limits.[36] One story even crops up in an eighteenth-century English jestbook: a sultan came across a dervish intently studying a skull in his lap and asked what he was doing:

> "Sire, (said the Dervise,) this skull was presented to me this morning, and I have from that moment been endeavouring, in vain, to discover whether it is the skull of a powerful monarch, like your Majesty, or of a poor Dervise, like myself."[37]

References to the holy fools (*yurodivye, yurod* meaning "crazy") of medieval Russia are most common between the fourteenth and seventeenth

centuries, and some were canonized.[38] One of the most venerated was
Saint Basil the Blessed (d. 1552), a naked vagabond who "unmasked the
devil wherever he tried to hide himself, even when it meant *challenging the
authority of princes.*"[39]

> The *yurodivy* has the gift to see and hear what others know nothing
> about. . . . He plays the fool, while actually being a persistent exposer
> of evil and injustice . . . who in his public role breaks the commonly
> held "moral" laws of behaviour and flouts conventions . . . the yuro-
> divy could expose injustice and remain in relative safety. The au-
> thorities recognized the right of the yurodivye to criticize and be ec-
> centric. . . . Their influence was immense. Their confused prophetic
> words were heeded by tsars and peasants alike.[40]

In Ireland the holy fool was known as a "wild man" *(geilt),* and monks
were often associated with fools, lepers, and others marginal to society.
One Mac-da-Cherda went mad as a result of a druid's curse and would
suffer alternating fits of foolishness and wisdom, a paradox that embod-
ies the ambivalent medieval attitude to madmen—laughable creatures on
the one hand, possibly possessed, but watch out, God could be on their
side and as such they might see things we do not.[41]

Holy fools were not limited to individuals who chose an unorthodox
path to enlightenment. Whole monastic orders could take on elements
of this marginality, the Cistercians and Franciscans in particular.[42] Saint
Francis takes us from the holy fools who are often joyless martyrs to the
holy fool who is moving toward the court jester. He was not without mirth,
and he believed that preachers should be God's jesters *(joculatores Domini).*[43] A prior of Montaudon was also a troubadour and was concerned
that the two professions might not be compatible until reassured by a message from God:

> Keep to your singing, and let Montaudon prosper,
> I delight in your songs, I delight in your laughter,
> They're a boon to the world, and will be hereafter.
>
> [Ans am ieu lo chant e.l ris,
> e.l segles en es plus pros
> e Montaudos y guazanha.[44]

By far the most jesterlike of all saints is Saint Philip Neri (1515–95),
whose humor grew with his holiness. He was always cracking jokes and
playing tricks on people and would mock himself and the pomposity of

others. He cavorted in front of cardinals, wore his clothes inside out, believed that gloominess would harm the soul, and "took special delight in the joke-book of Piovano Arlotto, the remarkable fifteenth century priest buffoon."[45]

In China and Japan, the "holy fools" of Buddhism and Daoism were far closer to being jesters than martyrs. Daoist and Zen monks could display a joyously cavalier approach to the sanctity of their teachings, embodying a jesterlike "anarchism which laughs at all that is systematic and unpoetical."[46] In China during the late eighth and early ninth centuries Cold Mountain (Han Shan) was a Zen Buddhist monk who wrote some three hundred colloquial poems, including satires on the world's follies.[47] He and Shi De were the "two Marx brothers of Buddhism, who laughed and danced through the solemnities of Buddhism and Confucianism."[48] About a thousand years later the Japanese Zen monk-poet Ryokan, or Goodly Tolerance, admired and imitated Han Shan's poems, in particular the satires.[49] Ryokan had the odd appearance becoming a jester, being a "lanky, beak-nosed cleric," and his second religious name was Taigu, or Great Fool.[50]

The Chinese Buddhist monk Cloth Bag (Budai Heshang) (d. 917) would feign madness. Fat and jolly, he was said to be an incarnation of the laughing Buddha Maitreya, who will help anyone who asks find the way to heaven. There are other examples of mad monks in China: one living in Changzhou in the Qing dynasty refused to speak but would laugh a great deal, and the Qing dynasty fictitious Ji Gong is a monk driven insane with sorrow who becomes a laughing, happy simpleton capable of performing magic tricks to rescue people in need, a lovable combination of jester, holy fool, and Robin Hood.[51]

God is great, but you can have too much of a good thing—hence the Feast of Fools *(festum stultorum* or *fête des fous)*, allowing "an ebullition of the natural lout beneath the cassock."[52] The feast took place between Christmas and Epiphany and was a literal interpretation of Luke's statement that those of low degree could be exalted and the mighty lowered for a while. They would give mock sermons or *sermons joyeux,* interlarding pious scriptural passages with ribaldry. During the feast clerics might wear glasses with orange peel for lenses or play dice, eat, drink, dance, or burn things in the censer such as shoes or sausages and puddings.[53]

An etching from the *Illustrated London News* shows a jester at the front of a carnival procession. Carnivals continue to take place around the world, and although in many places they have lost their religious underpinnings, they still embody the symbolic inversion of power and the license to mock and cavort that are normally the province of jesters. The modern Chinese term for carnival is "crazy delight festival" *(kuanghuanjie).*[54] Since 1882 the annual carnival in the French city of Nice has had a king of the carnival in the form of a huge mannequin of Triboulet, court jester to François I.[55] If there were many jesters in the name of God, the Indian pantheon boasts the Pramathas Ganas, who are

> the Harassers or Shaker-Uppers. They are the cosmic clowns and jesters, mythic pranksters and fools, the zanies of heaven. Their laughter, given or found, borrowed or stolen, resounded once through the royal meeting hall, filled the lamplit theater, echoed even through the temple, suffused structures that have turned to dust and dream.[56]

The same may be said of their mortal counterparts, holy or unholy.

CLERICAL JESTERS

> A jest touching these letters, S.P.Q.R. Senatus, Populus-que Romanus. It so happened, that a new Pope being elected, meerely for his devotion, and austeritie of life, as using an extraordinary spare dyet, and seldome seene so much as to smile; yet after his Inauguration, comming to sit in Pontificalibus, he used to feede high, to laugh heartily, and to countenance Jesters, and Buffoones to make him merry at his Table, which being observed, one sets up these foure words, being correspondent to the foure former letters, Sancte Pater Quare Rides? Holy father why doe you laugh? Under which next day was written, Rideo quia Papa sum, I laugh because I am Pope.
>
> T. H. Jamieson, ed., *A Banquet of Jests*[57]

In Europe many cardinals, bishops, and pontiffs kept jesters, and of these Pope Leo X was best known for his jestermania. His jester Serapica "had authority to introduce at any hour, madmen, jesters, and other pleasing people," and somebody who wanted to gain access to the pope pretended to be a jester.[58] Nicoletto da Orvieto managed to win lifelong pontifical favor after a single instance of making the pope laugh.[59] When Hernán Cortés went to the court of the Aztec king Montezuma he was so impressed with the jesters and jugglers that he sent two of them as a gift to Pope Clement VII (r. 1523–34). It is said that George Buchanan, always ready to insult a cleric, was nevertheless sought by them: "Many of the clergymen in England desired greatly to be in company with him, because of his comical and witty expressions."[60] Cardinals Richelieu and Wolsey each had his own jesters (Boisrobert and Raconis, and Patch) in addition to being targets for royal jesters' witty barbs. A bishop of Bamberg had a fool who thought he was Jesus, and even the austere Jesuits had a jester-king in the sixteenth century.[61]

The material generosity of kings and emperors toward their jesters could be matched by prelates. A letter of 24 July 1524 describes in detail a sumptuous costume given to the jester Ambrosio by Clement VII:

> Ambrosio . . . is in greatest favor with the pope, who has had made for him a beautiful robe of golden brocade and morello red velvet in the French style, and a fine cloak of the same. Also a tunic and fine hose adorned with the same brocade and deep black velvet shoes with a beret of crimson velvet with a big plume and no lack of shirts of cambric worked with gold, velvet shoes, perfumed gloves, and kerchiefs edged with gold.

> [Ambrogio . . . sta in grandissimo favore del Papa, il quale gli ha fatto fare una bella roba di broccato d'oro e velluto morello alla francese, ed un bel saglio pur del medesimo, e giuppone pur così, e belle calze abigarate del medesimo broccato e velluto morello con una berretta di velluto cremosi con dentro suo gran pennacchio; poi camiscie di cortina lavorate d'oro non gli mancano, scarpe di velluto, guanti profumati, e fazzoletti orlati d'oro.][62]

Several Italian Renaissance jesters were members of the clergy, including Fra Sarafino, mentioned in chapter 4 for the serious drubbing he suffered, and Fra Mariano Fetti, who would run along tables at banquets as jester to Pope Leo X.[63] In 1519 Raphael designed a stage backdrop for a performance of a comedy by Ariosto on which a jolly monk was cavorting with devils—the monk is supposed to be Fra Mariano.[64]

One of the most popular medieval jestbooks was *Der Pfarrer von Kalenberg*, first appearing in German in the fifteenth century, with at least four editions before 1620. It contains stories about a jester-priest known for mocking his parishioners, his bishop, and his patron, Otto der Fröhliche ("the Merry"), duke of Austria (fl. ca. 1339). Kalenberg became curate to the village of Kalenbergersdorf, but he used all the tricks and techniques of a full-time court jester.[65] When the duke told him he could keep whatever was put on his plate, he found a huge dish and made the duke's horse stand on it.[66]

Nasrudin was the imam of Aqshehir (where there is a marble mausoleum in his memory) about 550 years ago, and he is said to have spent part

of his long and checkered career as Tamerlane's jester.[67] His jubilant au-
dacity was irrepressible, and he had no qualms about lying and no em-
barrassment when caught. He once started telling people he was a saint,
and when a man asked to see some miracles, he said:

> "I can order any tree to come to me and it will obey." "Tell that palm
> tree to come to you then." "Come here!" said Djoh'a, but the tree
> would not budge even though he called it three times. So he got up
> and walked over to the tree. "Where are you going, Djoh'a?" he was
> asked. "The saints and the prophets of God are neither proud nor
> blind; since the palm won't come to me, I'll go to the palm."[68]

One day he entered the mosque to preach. He stood before the wor-
shipers and asked them if they knew what he was going to say to them.
They said they did not, to which he replied, "What shall I say to you until
you do know?" and left. On another occasion he asked the same question,
and they all responded affirmatively, causing Nasrudin to remark that in
that case there was nothing he could say to them. When he asked the same
question a third time, some of the congregation said they knew what he
was going to say and some said they did not. The unbeatable mulla-jester
told them that those who knew could tell those who did not.[69] Strikingly
similar in exultant spirit is the Chinese monk Yang Qi (d. 1049): "He
climbed into the pulpit, and said 'Ha! ha! What's all this about? Let's go
and have some tea!' He then got down."[70]

There are several surviving European medieval medallions that feature a jester figure with a bishop. In one they are next to each other; another has the bishop on one side with three fools on the other; a third
shows an outsize jester next to a diminutive bishop, and the last has the
fool next to a woman, with the inscription "Veritas" and the bishop on the
reverse.[71] Probably coined by a "pope of fools" to be used as currency during the Feast of Fools, they convey something of the complex relationship
between the jester and the cleric.[72]

"IF WE BE NOT MADE OF CANNON PROOFE, WEE ARE IN DANGER OF EPISCOPALL CENSURE"
Archibald Armstrong, "Archy's Dream"[73]

> Let bishops beware that monasteries do not become repositories of
> the frivolous arts—that is of minstrels, cytharistae, musicians, and
> buffoons [scurrorum].
>
> Eighth-century canon[74]

In 1212 the Council of Paris forbade abbots and bishops to keep jesters, and monasteries were subjected to a ban on "hunting dogs, falcons, and jesters."[75] John of Salisbury said that actors, jesters, and other entertainers could not receive the Sacrament ("Histriones et mimi non possunt recipere sacram Communionem").[76] The Russian *skomorokhi* were energetically persecuted by the church, perhaps because of their pagan origins, and the *Primary Chronicle* (1068) likens them to the devil, just as fools in medieval Europe could be seen in this sinister light.[77] Similarly, the Irish jesters *(crosans)* used the cross in their anticlerical mockery, both appropriating the magic of the cross and showing their disrespect for it.[78] The second Council of Chalons in 813 expressed the church's antipathy in the clearest terms: "Churchmen should not only despise actors and buffoons and the improper custom of vile and obscene jests, but they should consider them despicable for religious laymen as well" ("histrionum sive scurrarum, et turpium seu obscoenorum jocorum insolentiam, non solum [clerici] ipse respuant, verum etiam fidelibus respuenda percenseant").[79]

In 1291 the Council of Salzburg attacked clerics for acting as jesters rather than merely enjoying their entertainments—among the multitude of itinerant entertainers who wandered about medieval Europe were the roguish, adventurous dropout monks who found the confines of the monastery too constricting. They were the *vagi* or *goliardi* immortalized in Carl Orff's *Carmina Burana,* and the church attempted to ostracize them: "We order that the clergy must not be jesters, goliards or buffoons; if they pursue such disgraceful accomplishments for a whole year, they are to be stripped of all ecclesiastical privileges" ("praecipimus quod clerici non sint ioculatores, goliardi seu bofones, declarantes quod, si per annum illam artem diffamatorium exercuerint, omni privilegio ecclesiastico sint nudati").[80]

The medieval church was suspicious of laughter and not generally tolerant of mockery. It was (and is) often considered that to be taken seriously one has to be earnest, that humor is frivolous and not suited to weighty matters. Yet earnestness implies rigidity while humor tends toward fluidity and as such is surely a better means of dealing with serious matters, since it is well equipped to take the complexities and contradictions of life in its stride. This is amply illustrated in Umberto Eco's *The Name of the Rose,* an intricate medieval whodunit that deals at length with the conflict between the earnest and the mirthful. Earnestness is not just generally less appealing, it can be also dangerous, since it allows for extremes of self-righteousness. Humor admits the doubts of self-mockery, a gentle moderating mechanism of the mind:

"You are the Devil," William said then.

Jorge seemed not to understand. If he had been able to see, I would say he stared at his interlocutor with a dazed look. "I?" he said.

"Yes. They lied to you. The Devil is not the Prince of Matter; the Devil is the *arrogance of the spirit, faith without smile, truth that is never seized by doubt.*"[81]

The frequent vehemence of ecclesiastic disapprobation of the jester is possibly due to the threat he posed. Jesters did not set out to overthrow a religious institution, and they generally mock those who corrupt religion, not religion itself. Nevertheless the jester is an affirmation of all that is uncertain in the universe, the random and unknown factors of existence, which makes him too hot to handle for the priest who wants to believe it has all been laid down and settled. Only a religious mind of great magnitude can encompass both faith and doubt, and many ecclesiastics took the easy option of accepting their dogmas and then defending them lock, stock, and barrel. To them the spanner-in-the-works jester would seem anathema.[82]

"Episcopall censure" was not the only source of condemnation of the jester; there were secular varieties too, starting with Seneca. In a letter to Lucilius he comments:

> You know Harpasté, my wife's female clown; she has remained in my house, a burden incurred from a legacy. I particularly disapprove of these freaks; whenever I wish to enjoy the quips of a clown, I am not compelled to hunt far; I can laugh at myself.

> [Harpasten, uxoris meae fatuam, scis hereditarium onus in domo mea remanscisse. Ipse enim aversissimus ab istis prodigiis sum; si quando fatuo delectari volo, non est mihi longe quaerendus; me rideo.][83]

Francisco Núñez de Velasco, an early seventeenth-century Spanish writer whose mission it was to offer advice on governance, harked back to a virtuous golden age of Rome when rulers' minds were not contaminated by the presence of jesters, a view that is belied by Seneca but that shows he believed merrymakers stand between a king and true greatness.[84] However, the award for the most eloquently visceral (and secular) disapprobation of the jester goes to another Spaniard, Cristóval Suárez de Figueroa, although even he grudgingly admitted that court jesters did have some uses:

All my life I have been an archenemy of jesters, considering them
to be utterly base scum of the earth, none of whom are any good except for trying out the various types of torture that exist in the world,
[although] I used to tolerate some of them, whose wit amused
and cheered princes, such that they owed to their jokes and sallies
some titbits of food, rather like the discarded bones flung at the
greyhounds.

[Toda mi vida he sido enemigo capital de bufones, juzgándolos vi-
lísimas inmundicias de la tierra, ya que por ningún caso son buenos,
sino es para ejercer en ellos cuantos géneros de martirios tiene el
mundo. Solía admitir el uso algunos de éstos, cuya graciosidad en-
tretenía y alegraba a los principes, de modo que era debida a sus agu-
dezas y a sus burlas alguna porción de cualquer mesa, bien como se
suele arrojar al lebrel el hueso desechado.] [85]

The Italian priest-jester Fra Sarafino was severely beaten up for his
mirthful raillery against cardinals, the Madonna, and the pope. [86] An Italian jester with the attractive name of Gentle Good (Dolcibene) came from
Florence but served the Holy Roman Emperor Charles IV of Bohemia
(r. 1347–78). He was not irreligious, even composing poetry to the Madonna, but he cracked many jokes about holy matters and was excommu-
nicated as a result. [87] Another Italian jester, the dwarf Nanino, was threatened with irons and manacles if he did not control his mockery, and his
offenses included the caricature of a priest. In 1515, three years after this dire
threat, he is described as having dressed up as a bishop and delivered mass,
to the great amusement of the marquis and marchioness watching him. [88]

By the sixteenth century the complex attitudes of the church toward
fools had simplified. The natural fool could still be seen as having an almost holy innocence, although possibly not to the same degree. The artificial and professional fool was no longer anathema to ecclesiastics, and
it became perfectly respectable for cardinals or popes to keep jesters. Nor
were jesters so much associated with the devil or death. Thomas More and
Erasmus advocated tolerance of fools, artificial or natural—there was no
longer a big ideological ax to grind with regard to the jester. Not for a
while, at least. An anonymous article in a Russian magazine in the 1880s
demanded that the censorship applied to theaters be extended to clowns
to curb their unlicensed tongues:

How, we venture to ask, do clowns amuse their public? With words,
of course. And do they speak in public? They do. And so why does

no one [in authority] take account of what they say and do? Who has given them the right to speak like this? There is only one answer: they have given it to themselves.[89]

In China there seems little indication that anybody, religious or secular, disapproved of court jesters as such, although people did occasionally voice strong criticism when they felt the jester had gone too far in his mockery. The most explicit and prim appraisal of the jester's role is in Liu Xie's (ca. 465–522) piece "On Humor and Enigma" ("Xie yin"), in *The Literary Mind and the Carving of Dragons*. Jesters' mockery was acceptable as long as it served a corrective function, and he approved of both Jester Meng and Baldy Chunyu "because in spite of their wandering and devious speeches they always aim toward the right principle," unlike Dongfang Shuo, who he suggests only "indulged in raillery and took indecent personal liberties."[90]

SCHOLARLY FOOLS AND FOOLISH SCHOLARS, OR CONFUCIUS WAS A WOMAN

> This rule is certain,
> "He that pursues his safety from the school
> Of state must learn to be madman or fool"
> John Ford, *The Lover's Melancholy* (1628)[91]

In Java there are jesterlike clowns who are also called "teachers" *(kijai)* because they are considered to have a wider view of reality than people who swim with the mainstream, and as such they are identified with a class of scholars whose teaching tradition involved "mystical and radical perspectives threatening the ruling hierarchies."[92] Charles Louis, an elector of the Rhine, did not feel the need to keep a court jester, for when he wanted to laugh he would summon two professors from the university, set them debating, then sit back and enjoy the folly of the scene.[93] This is a rare instance of a scholar's being unwittingly appointed court jester, although Ludwig Tieck's play *Puss-in-Boots* features a court scholar who in the king's eyes has the same status and function as the jester, as he hurls his scepter at the scholar's head:

> Sir Brazenbold of Scholarship! What presumption is this? The fool
> pleases *me, me,* his King, and if I find taste in him, how can you dare

say that the man is absurd. The one is Court Scholar and the other
Court Fool; you stand in the same employment . . . both are merely
to help me pass the time and make my meal tasty. Now, where then
is the great difference?

[Herr Naseweis von Gelehrter! was untersteht er sich denn? Der Narr
gefällt *mir, mir,* seinem Könige, und wenn ich Geschmack an ihm
finde, wie kann Er sich unterstehen zu sagen, daß der Mann abge-
schmackt wäre? Er ist Hofgelehrter, und der andre Hofnarr, Ihr
steht in einem Gehalte . . . beides soll mir nur die Zeit vertreiben und
machen, daß mir das Essen schmeckt: wo ist denn nun der grosse
Unterschied?][94]

More commonly, scholars, officials, and monks would act the fool con-
sciously, either temporarily as an expedient or permanently because it was
in their nature to do so. The jester's techniques, particularly in the realm
of advice giving, were occasionally adopted by scholars or officials trying
to find a more ingenious and attractive method of appealing to reason than
by reason alone. The humanist writer and entertainer John Heywood used
the padding of a jester's folly to soften his strong political views. He spoke
in a direct manner to Henry VIII but with sufficient wit and humorous
self-deprecation to be considered a jester-scholar.[95] Heywood had a parallel in Wan Xiao, a Chinese official of the Liao dynasty. His biography
in the official Liao dynastic history describes him as loving a laugh. At
banquets there was no limit to his humor, and people thought of him as
a jester. He commented on this as he was dying:

> When I was young, I tried to put my ideals forward to my ruler but
> I couldn't succeed by direct means, so I started joking, hoping that
> one in ten thousand times I might say something edifying, so is it
> any wonder I was called a jester?
>
> 『吾少有致君志，不能直遂，故以諧進，翼萬有一補，俳優名何避？』[96]

The foremost jester-scholar in England was Sir Thomas More (1478–
1535). As a young man serving in the household of Cardinal Morton he
was known for his great talent as a joker. A poem by the Victorian poet
Francis Thompson, "To the English Martyrs," describes More as a "Dear
Jester in the Courts of God."[97] Edward Hall's *Chronicle* speaks reverently
of More's many qualities that helped him become Lord Chancellor, but it
strongly disapproves of his propensity to jest and mock:

> A manne well learned in the toungues, and also in the Common
> Lawe, whose witte was fyne, and full of imaginacions, by reason
> wherof, he was to muche geuen to mockyng, whiche was to his
> grauitie a great blemishe.[98]

More even made sardonic remarks to his daughter the last time he saw
her before his execution, and on his way to the block he made a few dry
comments, first to the sheriff, whom he asked to help him up onto the
scaffold, adding that "when I come doune againe, let me shift for my selfe
as well as I can," and then to the executioner, and "thus with a mocke he
ended his life." Hall seems to have been mildly exasperated by More's
humor:

> I cannot tell whether I should call him a foolishe wyseman, or a wyse
> foolishman, for vndoubtedly he beside his learnyng, had a great witte,
> but it was so mingled with tauntyng and mockyng, that it semed to
> them that best knew him, that he thought nothing to be wel spoken
> except he had ministered some mocke in the communicacion.[99]

In addition, he himself kept a jester, William Patteson, who can be
seen in Holbein's portrait of the More family. Very little is known about
him except that he is said to have implored More's daughter to persuade
More not to provoke the queen for fear he pay for it with his head: "Bid
thy father e'en take a fool's advice, and eat humble-pie betimes; for
doubt not this proud madame to be as vindictive as Herodias, and one
that, unless he appease her full early, will have his head set before her in
a charger."[100]

One who combined scholar-jester, poet-jester, and clerical-jester was
John Skelton (1460–1529), educated at both Oxford and Cambridge and
like George Buchanan tutor to a king before becoming known as a jester.
He taught Henry VIII as a boy and became a poet laureate known for
his satire, forthright speech, and buffoonery, mocking many of the things
he stood for, including erudition and religion. He became a preacher in
Norfolk, and the jestbook about him describes many instances in which
he humbled his congregation with his wit and plain speech. He also attacked Cardinal Wolsey and was occasionally rapped on the knuckles by
his bishop for his loose living and loose tongue.[101] Similarly, Holinshed's
Chronicles (1587) tell us of Scogin's alleged transition from scholar to jester:

> Scogan, a learned gentleman and student, for a time in Oxford, of a
> pleasant wit, and bent to merrie deuises, in respect whereof he was

called into the court where, giving himselfe to his naturall inclination of mirth and plesant pastime, he plaied manie sporting parts, although not in such uncivil manner as hath been of him reported.[102]

In one anecdote he showed the queen to be open to the temptations of
money, which offended her so much that she asked the king to have him
punished, "wherefore it doth appeare, that it is not good jesting with lords
or ladies: for if a man be plaine, or doe tell the truth, hee shall be shent for
his labour."[103] Scogin is another one of those tricky characters who seems
to have jests pegged to him willy-nilly; many of them are standard quips,
thus begging the question whether he was a real jester.

George Buchanan is perhaps the most problematic of scholar-jesters.
The historical Buchanan was tutor to James I as a boy and later became a
courtier and counselor to him. He traveled widely, spending time at both
the French and Spanish courts, and served Mary Queen of Scots as a kind
of tutor and translator. He also had a flourishing academic career as a pro-
lific poet and writer and was known for his humanistic openness.[104] These
achievements pale beside his popular reputation as the king's jester. A folktale still circulating about him tells us that "there's millions o stories tellt
about George Buchanan the King's Fool."[105] Many were published during
the first quarter of the nineteenth century, with no introduction or provenance, probably collected from Scottish storytellers.

Two works about George Buchanan make no reference either to his
having been a jester or to any such legends about him. However, the truth
may lie somewhere between the legends and the history, and the link between the two may be that the history describes how Buchanan provided
poems for court entertainments and had an offhand manner when dealing with royalty.[106] His contributions to entertainments give the impression that he was no dour bookworm, and the offhand manner is a perfect
attribute of a jester. With these clues many of the anecdotes told about
how he tricked and cajoled the king out of folly become credible, and from
there it is not hard to see how the jester legend arose. The disparity between the historical courtier-poet and the legendary court jester is perhaps
not so great after all.

So much for the scholarly fool, the man who chooses to adopt certain
characteristics of the court jester. The other side of the coin is the foolish
scholar, the butt of the jester's deflating jokes. In their attitudes to scholars there is a much greater convergence of European and other jesters.
They tend to aim at the temptation for scholars to be self-serious, scoffing at stuffiness and pedantry. Tenali Rama attended a debate on the re-

ality of objective phenomena at which an eminent scholar argued that the whole world was an illusion and it was only thought that made us believe we were eating or smelling. Tenali Rama innocently asked him:

> "Sir, is there really no difference in our eating a thing, and thinking about its eating?" "None at all," was the reply. "In that case," said the Rama, to the assembled people, "it will be easy to test this learned man's theory. Let us all eat the rich feast, provided by this generous monarch, and let our friend think of it and fill his belly!" Everybody laughed at the discomfited Pundit. The King was so pleased at the joke that he gave Rama a purse of gold and made him his court jester on the spot, amidst universal approval.[107]

Confucius is a favorite subject of Chinese court jesters' exuberant impiety—their mockery aimed principally at the worshipful cult surrounding him—and being so revered, he was an irresistible theme for skits or puns. In the Song dynasty a descendent of Confucius, Kong Daofu, was sent on an embassy to the Khitan court. A feast was given for the envoys, and entertainers put on a skit about Confucius. Kong Daofu became angry and walked out. The master of ceremonies asked him to return, and he was even ordered to apologize, but he defended his action by saying:

> "The relations between China and the Khitan are good and we share the same patterns of court ceremony and the same culture. Today jesters have insulted Confucius and have not been suppressed; the fault is with the northern court! Why should I apologize?"

> 『中國與北朝通好，以禮文相接。今俳優之徒慢侮先聖，而不之禁，北朝之過也！道輔何謝？』[108]

These are not isolated cases of jesters' being in trouble for using Confucius and other worthies as material for their jokes. When Emperor Zhezong (r. 1086–1100) of the Northern Song visited Welcoming Good Luck Pond (Ying Xiang Chi), he gave a banquet for his ministers. Again the members of the Court Entertainments Bureau performed a skit with Confucius as the theme. The secretary of the Board of Punishments, Kong Zonghan, presented a memorial to the emperor complaining of this:

> "In the time of Emperor Wenzong of the Tang this [theme] was once used for a skit, and [the emperor] had them bellowed out of court. Today Your Sage Majesty has provided a banquet to reward your ministers, how can it be right to countenance this?"

> 『唐文宗時嘗有為此戲者，詔斥去之。今聖君宴犒群臣，豈宜尚容此？』[109]

Wang Shipeng of the Song dynasty was appalled by jesters' using Zhuangzi's story of the blood-lusting cannibalistic bandit Robber Zhi as a stick to beat Confucius. Confucius ventured into Zhi's lair confident that he could reform him; Zhi was tucking into a dish of diced human liver at the time and threatened to make mincemeat of Confucius if he lingered. In the event he only chopped up the sage with his words, and Confucius skulked from the interview, shaken but not stir-fried. Wang felt it was intolerable to watch a skit alluding to this humiliation of the great man, so he wrote a quatrain to vent his spleen.[110]

Another anecdote mocking Confucius was much appreciated and went unpunished. Erudites from the national university could be seen debating a difficult point, during which the number of Confucius's enlightened disciples was given as seventy-two. Moving Bucket made a joke of this, asking how many of the enlightened disciples were adults and how many were not, to which the scholar replied that the classics did not say. Moving Bucket was not convinced:

> "Since you have studied, can there be anything you would not understand? Thirty of his disciples were adults and those who were not numbered forty-two." The scholar said, "On what writings do you base your argument?" Moving Bucket explained, "The *Analects* say 'There are five [or] six adults,' five sixes are thirty; 'There are six [or] seven children,' six sevens are forty-two. How can that not add up to seventy-two?" All the guests were delighted, and the scholar had no answer.
>
> 『先生讀書，豈合不解孔子弟子着冠有三十人，未着冠者有四十二人？』博士曰：『據何文以知之？』動筩曰：『論語云：「冠者五六人」，五六三十也，「童子六七人」，六七四十二也，豈非七十二人？』坐中大悦，博士無以應對。[111]

Sometimes jesters brought Confucius into a skit not to mock him but as an indirect means of mocking or criticizing somebody else. Under Emperor Lizong a skit involved Confucius, his favorite disciple, and a pun on the name of Prime Minister Shi Miyuan to allude to nepotism.[112] Not all scholastic mockery in China used Confucius. During one of Emperor Gaozu's erudite gatherings Moving Bucket punned one of the scholars into a tight corner by using the homophone *xing,* which means both "nature" and "surname":

"Master! What is the surname of heaven?" The erudite said, "Heaven's surname is Gao." Moving Bucket said, "Since the Son of Heaven's surname is Gao, heaven's surname must also be Gao. You learned it from the Shu minister Qin Mi; it's not a new argument. On all Thirteen Classics there is the surname for heaven; the master can quote from classical texts and shouldn't just borrow old statements." The scholar admitted, "I don't know which classic has heaven's surname." The jester mockingly chided, "The master really hasn't read his classics, has he? It seems he hasn't even read the Classic of Filial Piety. The surname of heaven is Ye. Hasn't the master read 'the principles governing the relationship of father and son are in the nature of heaven' [*tian xing ye*, which also puns as 'heaven's surname is Ye']? So how can this not be heaven's surname?" *The emperor burst out laughing.*

『先生！天有何姓？』博士曰：『天姓高。』動箕曰：『天子姓高，天必姓高，此乃學他蜀臣秦宓，本非新義。正經之上，自有天姓，先生可引正文，不須假託舊事。』博士云：『不知何經之上得有天姓。』動箕云：『先生全不讀書，孝經亦似不見。天本姓也，先生可不見孝經云：「父子之道，天性也。」此豈不是天姓？』高祖大笑。[113]

During the Tianxi reign-period (1017–21) of Emperor Zhenzong (998–1022), Yang Danian, Qian Wenxi, Yan Yuanxian, and Liu Ziyi all won places at court by virtue of their literary achievements. Their poetry belonged to the school of Li Shangyin (813–58), and their later poems stole lines from his poetry. There was a palace banquet at which a jester played the part of the plagiarized poet, wearing shabby torn clothes and accusing his imitators: "I've been pulled to pieces like this by all these officials of the Assembled Noble Minds Academy." Everybody who heard had a good laugh.[114]

The irrepressibly bumptious Dongfang Shuo told the emperor what he thought of scholars, in terms of brazen self-praise. The emperor gave Dongfang Shuo a long list of some of the most renowned literary names in Chinese history,

"all of great wisdom and understanding, with superlative talent in letters and learning. Looking at yourself, how do you think you compare?" Shuo replied, "When I see them clacking teeth and fangs, puffing out jowls, spluttering from the mouth, craning necks and chins, lining up flank by thigh, pairing off buttock bones, snaking their way along, mincing side by side in crook-backed ranks, then I say to myself, Shuo, you may not be much, but you're still equal to all these gentlemen put together!"

『。。。皆辯知閩達，溢於文辭，先生自視，何與比哉？』朔對曰：『臣觀其

臿齒牙，樹頰胲，吐脣吻，擢項頤，結股腳，連雅尻，遺蛇其跡，行步偶旅，

臣朔雖不肖，尚兼此數子者！』[115]

The jester-trickster Till Eulenspiegel once posted a notice on the gates of the university in Greifswald claiming that he knew every language except Spanish. The rector decided to submit him to an examination by all the great linguists of the university, each speaking to him in turn in a different language. By a show of sham piety he managed to convince the scholars that each language resembled Spanish in some way such that he refused to speak it. The scholars were so impressed with his wisdom and erudition that they sent him away in a flurry of honor.[116] Eulenspiegel, having spent his life mocking learned scholars and greedy monks, was said to have become a pious monk, and posthumously a saint:

> And of a verity is Saint Owlglass, of all the saints that be in the calendar, that one which hath the government of the greatest number of devout folks here on earth. For fools be there many; and upon the first day of . . . April . . . do all men honour him, and indeed every day; for in that hour in the which they accomplish any idle vain work, do they increase his glory.[117]

This sermon began with Feng Menglong laughing at Daoism, Buddhism, and Confucianism. Chinese religious mockery was anything but partisan, and Chinese jesters were exceptionally even-handed in their scoffing. A jester to the Tang dynasty emperor Yizong, Attainable Li (Li Keji), reaffirms this. It was said of him that though not very good at using humor for corrective purposes, he was unsurpassable when it came to quick wit and jocularity. By means of apposite quotation and deft misinterpretation he managed to prove that Sakyamuni, Laozi, and Confucius were all women:

> Someone asked: "Since you reckon you're so familiar with the Three Teachings, what kind of person was the Buddha?" [Attainable Li] answered, "A woman." The man who had asked was astonished and said, "How can that be?" He answered, "The *Diamond Sutra* says, Buddha *"fu zuo er zuo"* [laid out a seat and then sat on it]. If Buddha wasn't a woman why would it mention her husband and then her son

sitting down *[fu zuo . . . er zuo]?*" The emperor smiled. He was then asked, "And what kind of person was Laozi?" He replied, "Also a woman." The person asking was even more baffled, so Attainable Li explained, "The *Way and Its Power* says, "My one big worry is that I *you shen* [have a body], if I had no body, I would have no worries." If Laozi wasn't a woman why would she worry about being pregnant *[you shen]?*" The emperor was very pleased. He was then asked what kind of person Confucius was, and again he said, "A woman." His interlocutor said, "How d'you figure that out?" and he answered, "The *Analects* say "Who will buy? I'm *dai jia* [waiting for a buyer]!" If Confucius wasn't a woman why would she be about to take a husband *[dai jia]?*" The emperor was absolutely delighted and rewarded him generously.

偶坐者問曰：『即言博通三教，釋迦如來是何人？』對曰：『婦人。』問者驚曰：『何也？』曰：『金剛經云：「敷坐而坐。」非婦人，何煩夫坐而後兒坐也？』上爲之啓齒。又曰：『太上老君何人？』曰：『亦婦人也。』問者益所不喻，乃曰：『道得經云：「吾有大患，爲吾有身，及吾無身，吾有何患。」倘非婦人，何患于有身乎？』上大悦。又問曰：『文宣王何人也？』曰：『婦人也。』問者曰：『何以知之？』『論語曰：「沽之哉，待賈者也。」向非婦人，奚待嫁爲？』上意極歡，賜予頗厚。[118]

At Supper she would also divert her self with her Friends and Attendance. . . . She would then also admit *Tarleton,* a famous Comedian, and a pleasant Talker, and other such like men, to divert her with Stories of the Town, and the common Jests, or Accidents.

Edmund Bohun, *The Character of Queen Elizabeth*[1]

6

All the World's a Stage

It's a well-known saying
That no play, no matter how short,
Must be without its fool.

[Es ist ein Spruchwort allgemein
Das kein spil jenen sig so klein
Inn dem nitt ein Narr musse syn.]

Martyr Christianus (sixteenth century)[2]

The court jester is not as universal a figure on stage as he is in court life, but his presence is widespread, and where he does not feature as a clearly recognizable character in a play, many of his functions are taken over by others: by fools or vices in Europe, slaves or parasites in Rome, clowns everywhere (including puppet shows), comic maidservants in China and Europe, and the actors themselves in China, Greece, and Rome. The theatrical court jester and his impersonators generally serve the same purpose as the court jester in real life. They amuse and entertain, stand on the sidelines and observe, and act as a control against which to measure the folly of others.

The stage fool could claim the license of the jester in another respect —to improvise some of his lines, an important distinction in deciding to what extent he is the actor's or the playwright's creation. The Chinese actors who took upon themselves the function of a jester did so without encouragement from playwrights, and in Rome the nature of the comic mime actors with their impromptu irreverence toward anything sacred and anyone in authority makes it safe to suggest they *were* the court jesters.

Tarlton seems to have had no qualms about embellishing his scripted lines and would even ad lib with the audience. In some early English plays the clown figure would wander onto the stage when he felt like it:

> Why, what an ass art thou! Dost thou not knowe a
> playe cannot be without a clowne? Clownes haue bene
> thrust into playes by head & shoulders, euer since Kempe
> could make a scuruey face, and therfore reason thou
> shouldst be drawne in with a cart rope.
>
> (5.664–68)[3]

In China, with the decline of the court jester more or less complete by the Ming dynasty (1368–1644), skits change from small improvised sketches put on for the court, or one-to-one bantering between the emperor and his jester, to impromptu lines inserted by the actor into scripted plays performed on stage. Anecdotes about these jester-actors continue well into the Republican era (1911–49) but seem to disappear without trace with the Communists. In contrast to these self-appointed jesters, and despite a rich tradition of clown roles, court jesters only rarely feature in the dramatis personae of a scripted play, but when they do the whole play revolves around them. There are references to a nonextant Yuan dynasty (1280–1368) play about Newly Polished Mirror, one of the greatest jesters of all, and there are several plays about the courtier-jester Dongfang Shuo.

The court jester of the English stage did not really appear until the late sixteenth century, although he was preceded by a long procession of "fooles" in medieval drama. He was rarely used to provide such sharply focused attacks on contemporary corruption and vice as the fools of the French *sotties*, his mockery aiming more at general human folly and foibles. Nowadays the widespread understanding in the English-speaking world of what constitutes a court jester owes more to a handful of Shakespeare's fools than to several centuries' worth of historical jesters. His characterizations may be added to historical evidence, since he was writing when jesters were still luxuriating in their golden age. Richard Tarlton, who acted as a real court jester to Elizabeth in addition to his stage clowning, straddles the wide spectrum of this chapter better than anybody.

In France critical comments were for a time put in the mouths of jesters on stage, with the most direct mockery being acted out by French amateur dramatic groups of lawyers and law clerks in the *sociétés joyeuses* of the fourteenth and fifteenth centuries. In a genre of play known as the *sottie*, four or five characters wearing the traditional jester's garb could attack profligacy and injustice. *Sotties* flourished under Louis XII, who subsidized the plays in the belief that they helped him uncover knavery, with the sole condition that the actors divert their verbal arrows from his wife.

The German *Fastnachtspiele* were perhaps a parallel of the French *sotties*. They were performed by citizens and dealt with social, political, and religious themes. Some were dramatizations of *Schwänke*, humorous narratives with popular fools such as Till Eulenspiegel or the Priest of Kalenberg besting their superiors with wit and impudence. Both genres flourished from the Middle Ages into the sixteenth century. The *fass* of *Fastnacht* may derive from *faseln*, to "blather or talk nonsense," and the fools of the plays could wear the cap and bells as they merrily exposed folly.[4]

In Sanskrit drama the *vidusaka* provides a depiction of the court jester that matches perfectly the international fact and fiction concerning this capering companion of kings and that, together with partly historical, partly legendary court jesters, gives very solid grounds for a conviction that real ones could be found in India as elsewhere. There is curiously strong resistance to this idea among some Sanskrit scholars, a resistance that the *vidusaka* will venture to quash.

In modern times there has been a swelling resurgence of the theme of the fool in Western theater, including a staggering variety of jesters, some modeled on historical figures, others conjured by playwrights who have brought a sparkling creativity to the task. The trend began in the early nineteenth century and still continues, with perhaps its least known but punchiest examples being the jesters of Holocaust drama.

While examining the court jester in relation to the stage, it is worth peeking at some of his dramatic relatives. The Italian Commedia dell'Arte has a few characters who at first glance resemble their court antecedents: Harlequin, one of the stock comic servants of the Commedia, had many traits resembling a jester, although he was more partisan and what he gained in terms of action he perhaps lost in existential importance. In addition, he tended to be a less sympathetic character, more scheming and scurrilous, closer to a witty rogue. But he could comment mockingly on current events, and his costume bore a resemblance to the jester's motley, with irregular multicolored patches later becoming the regular lozenge pattern still associated with him.

Harlequin is a clever servant, which leads to the worldwide tradition of the inverted servant-master relationship in which the servant has the upper hand in terms of wit, truth, and intelligence while the master must content himself with the trappings of superiority. It is a relationship that has much in common with that of king and jester, and it is hard to think of a dramatic tradition that does not have some manifestation of this duo, the hapless master and his canny servant, from the slaves of Plautus to the comic *kyogen* interludes of Japanese theater.

> *Crichton.* There must always be a master and servants in all civilised
> communities, for it is natural, and whatever is natural is right.
> *Lord Loam* (wincing). It is very unnatural for me to stand here and
> allow you to talk such nonsense.
> *Crichton* (eagerly). Yes, my lord, it is. That is what I have been
> striving to point out to your lordship.[5]

Seventeenth-century French drama was replete with clever servants who insisted on mocking the pomposity and stupidity of their so-called superiors.[6] These jester-soubrettes are found also in such classics of Chinese drama as the *The Story of the Western Wing* with Crimson Maid (Hong Niang), and Spring Fragrance (Chun Xiang) in Tang Xianzu's *The Peony Pavilion (Mudan ting)* (1598): Fragrance is both feisty and funny, chipping in with her sensible good humor.

Perhaps the nearest thing to a court jester on stage in the Japanese theater is the *kyogen,* a word combining "crazy, mad" and "words or language" but also implying "comic or humorous language" in a dialogue between servant and master, with the former often using techniques of the jester to outwit the latter: puns, riddles, double entendres, and verse-capping contests in which he invariably triumphs. The humor of *kyogen* includes the mockery of authority and of universal human situations, and the short plays, lasting about half an hour, are performed between serious *no* plays.[7]

Superior servants are, like jesters, in a formally inferior position to their masters while often being morally and intellectually their betters. They tend to speak their minds, claiming for themselves the jester's license never granted, and no threats of authority can subdue them—they are as fearless as the licensed fool. They mock their masters' faults and stupidity and offer them advice not always solicited. They speak with wit and humor, cracking jokes as they see fit, often at the master's expense. Here the similarities, striking as they are, end. The principal difference between the court jester and the superior servant is that it is not the latter's primary function to be entertaining; furthermore, when he is, it is the audience that is amused and rarely the master, whereas the jester would make both laugh at one time or another.

Rome does not seem to have had court jesters as a profession in their own right, and it seems likely that the jester's functions of confidant, foil, adviser, and joker were fulfilled ad hoc by comic actors and domestic slaves who became close to their masters and had the right traits: no-nonsense truth telling, dry asides, fearlessness in the face of threatened beatings. In Plautus's *The Weevil (Curculio)*, the slave is impudent and clever, cracks jokes, gives advice, and makes unsolicited comments. Like the *vidusaka*, he mocks his master's melodramatic swooning for love. He does pipe down when thrashed, but not for long: "It's scandalous, sir . . . to punch a man that gives you good advice" ("Flagitium probrumque magnum . . . bene monstrantem pugnis caedis") (1.3.198–99).

Two other slaves who show the jester's determination to speak out and be damned are Messenio in *The Two Menaechmuses (Menaechmi)*, and Stasimus in *Three Bob Day (Trinummus)* (ca. 194 B.C.). Messenio is cleverer than his master, and when he has told him one truth too many he is tersely put in his place, although the rebuke rolls off him like water off a duck's back. Stasimus, who serves both Lesbonicus and his father Charmides, is even harder to intimidate and wins the prize for the jester's defiance of impending torture:

> *Lesbonicus.* You add another word, and I'll gouge an eye out for you!
> *Stasimus.* By gad, I'll have my say, anyhow. If I can't with two eyes,
>   I'll have it with one!
>
> [*Lesbonicus.* Oculum ego ecfodiam tibi si verbum addideris.
> *Stasimus.* Hercle qui dicam tamen; nam si sic non licebit, luscus
>   dixero.] (2.4.463–65)[8]

In many parts of the world, puppet theater and shadow theater have some Punchlike characters who perhaps drew inspiration for both costume and behavior from court jesters. In Russia there is Petrushka, in Turkey Bebe Ruhi of the *karagoz* shadow theater, which spread to Greece and North Africa, and in Java there are also shadow theater clowns. In the religious puppet theater of Taiwan three of the marionette gods are described by Schipper as jesters. They are known as the Three Brothers (San xiongdi) and display several important attributes of court jesters, making people laugh and cheering them up, and using humor to lure the demons of an epidemic so that they can be captured.[9]

In the Commedia dell'Arte there is one character who can be associated with the jester: Pulcinella, who later developed into the English Punch and Russian Petrushka, hunchbacked with a beaked nose and pointed hat. He resembled a court jester in his kindliness, a quality he did not pass on to Punch or Petrushka. Petrushka shows would be performed from a tent structure that was carried by the puppeteer, like the Punch and Judy shows but less solid or stable, and he wore a red, sometimes striped, costume with bells on, very like the jester's motley.[10]

The Turkish shadow theater *(karagoz)* used improvised dialogues to provide harsh criticism of anybody in authority except the sultan, although even he could be included occasionally. The humorous attacks on authority within the plays were hard to censure because they were not scripted, although a blanket ban on all political references was made in 1911.[11] *Karagoz* dates from the Middle Ages and spread farther afield, to Greece, Syria, Egypt, Tunisia, and Algeria, where it was also used to criticize the authorities, whether foreign or domestic. One of the principal characters was Bebe Ruhi, a dwarf resembling Punch and by extension a court jester even down to the jester cap. He was often portrayed with a speech impediment or a hunchback and was very talkative and boastful.[12]

Clowns were also central to all forms of Javanese theater, including puppet shows.[13] They fulfilled a function very similar to that of the court jester, being affiliated with a master to whom they give wise advice. And although they themselves were gods, albeit fat and grotesque, they still interject contemporary or crude jokes into classical legends. Some of the servant characters in the shadow puppet theater of Java also have some qualities of the jester. Bagong clowns around, sings songs, and "speaks in a way that makes him sound dull-witted but [he] often speaks the truth."[14]

This chapter offers a brief survey of the stage jester. It does not attempt to be comprehensive—that would be impossible without dedicating the whole book to the subject. However, numerous detailed studies of the fool or jester of this or that dramatic tradition already exist—Shakespeare's fools in particular have been done to death—but there is very little that endeavors to place them in a global context. I therefore hope this overview will start pulling the strands together.

ACT I: THE ACTOR, THE ADJUTANT, AND THE ARTFUL DODGER

> The Chinese theatre may be said to begin with the court jesters of [the] late Chou [Zhou] dynasty. These jesters were personal companions to the dukes and princes they served, as shown by the various references to their witty contributions to ordinary conversation.
> Hsü Tao-Ching, *The Chinese Conception of the Theatre*[15]

If the Chinese stage is not as littered with historical and fictitious jesters as the English, the actors themselves went a long way to replacing court jesters, and from the Yuan dynasty (1271–1368) onward there was something of an overlap between the two until the court jester transmuted into stage actor. The overlap is reflected in the terms used for "jester," all of which began by meaning "jester" or "entertainer," including a musical or humorous element, and later came to include "actor." Until recently, *paiyou*, classically meaning a jester, was used in Taiwanese dialect to refer to a theater or film actor, having coming from the Japanese *haiyu*. The links are hardly surprising, since the origins of Chinese drama lie in the short, unscripted playlets of court jesters.[16]

There are numerous instances of a Chinese actor's choosing to improvise a joke to criticize some aspect of government or society. Such jester-actors are distinct from both the actor who took on a scripted role of court jester and jesters working within the confines of the court performing short improvised skits, since they performed scripted plays in public theaters, taking on the jester's role only spontaneously. The distinction can be hazy, however, since theater actors could be commissioned to perform a skit in order to mock somebody or to provide entertainment at a banquet, in the same way as habitual court jesters.[17] In this respect they perhaps resemble European actors such as Richard Tarlton, who was as much at home in the court as in the public theater. Previously jesters would have made up their own playlet in order to make their point, but by the Ming dynasty they were more likely to choose an apposite scripted play.

When the Qing emperor Shizong (r. 1723–35) watched the play *The Embroidered Jacket (Xiu ru)*, he was delighted with the performance and the excellent music and professional dancers, and he rewarded all the performers. An actor then asked, "So who's the governor of Changzhou these days?" and the emperor furiously replied, "You're just a lowly actor, how can you be qualified to ask about the governorship of a place?" Whatever the allusion, the actor hit an imperial nerve raw enough that he was beaten to death.[18]

Perhaps the Chinese equivalent to Tarlton in being a widely loved and acclaimed comic actor and a self-appointed ad hoc court jester was Liu Gansan (Qing), who had all the outspokenness of a jester and "left behind him the reputation of a wit who did not scruple to crack at those in high places." He and Tan Xinpei (1847–1917), the greatest Beijing Opera actor of the nineteenth century, were "both able to improvise indirect advice and there was nobody to match them."[19] In 1894 when Liu was acting the

part of a bawd, he managed to crack a joke at the expense of three imperial princes who were in the audience. At the time, prostitutes were called
by their number in the "family" hierarchy, and the three princes were fifth,
sixth, and seventh in their own families. Liu bellowed to summon three
harlots:

> "Old Five, Old Six, Old Seven, come out and take care of your
> guests!" . . . Prince Gong, who was easygoing, burst out laughing;
> Prince Chun, who was more restrained, was not pleased but did not
> dare say anything since the Empress Dowager was present; while
> Prince Dun, who was fierce and foul-tempered, flew into a rage,
> "Who is this crazy slave? How dare he be so discourteous!" and he
> stood up cursing and gave him forty blows before the matter was laid
> to rest.

> 『老五、老六、老七，出來見客呀！』。。。恭邸故脫落，喜詼諧，聞之大
> 噱；醇邸故恭謹，雖不悅，然以太后在座，未敢言；惇邸凤性嚴厲，則大怒
> 曰：『何物狂奴？乃敢無禮？』立叱侍者擒之下，重杖四十，事始寢。[20]

Hundred Year Old Luo (Luo Baisui) (Qing) was an actor skilled at
comic roles, with a gaunt face that was funny before he even opened his
mouth. Although he could rely on his own wit to draw attention to a corrupt official, he chose to make use of his role in a play. He acted the part
of a scribe called Mr. Mao in *Paired Bells (Shuangling ji)*. At the time there
was an infantry commander in disgrace who had been in collusion with a
clerk of the Ministry of Punishments known to have stashed away a tidy
pile by dubious means. Luo inserted some lines that alluded to this, and
the clerk "slightly drew in his claws" and reined in his corruption for a
while.[21]

Feng Jiazhen was an actor at the end of the Ming dynasty who excelled at composing songs, belonging to a Song Society. At the time there
was a man called Chen Mo who swaggered about threatening the locals,
so Feng inserted some extemporized wit to mock him. The blusterer was
furious and found a pretext to have the actor thrown into prison.[22] An actor who showed all the signs of being a jester was What Family Reputation (He Jiasheng). In 1898 he used an improvised pun to comment on the
lack of reform in government. He acted the role of Monkey, a part usually requiring the actor to amaze the audience with magical tricks and
changes and to chase evil demons. Instead he simply shook his body three
or four times then stood stock still. Somebody said,

"Everybody wants to see you perform your magic tricks *[bian fa],* so why don't you get on with it?" What Family Reputation pointed to the audience and said, "Look! Of all those great people, not one of them is even thinking of changing the law *[bian fa]!* So how can you expect me alone to start changing?"

『人人皆要看汝變法，汝何以竟變不出來？』何指座中諸人曰：『你看！諸位

大人沒有一個想變法的。如何你單叫我變起來？』[23]

A newspaper article of May 1911 described how one actor, Zhang Hei, drew attention to the perils of national debt while performing in a warrior play.[24] The actor Gu Wuwei acted in a play, *Dream of the Emperor (Huangdi meng),* in which he cursed the emperor, a cover for attacking Yuan Shikai (1858–1918), president of the new republic who later tried to found an imperial dynasty. Applauded by the audience, Gu was later arrested by the Shanghai police.[25] Another actor, Wang Xiaonong (1858–1918), whose name means Wang Laughed at Me, would also make biting comments from the stage that were aimed at both characters in the plays and people in the audience, whom he was able to shame with his tongue.[26]

Canjun or "adjutant" plays, popular during the Tang and into the Song dynasty, came from the license of court jesters to mock a disgraced official as part of his punishment. From this a slapstick comedy evolved in which the official was now the clown, feigning stupidity and being constantly beaten by his assistant wielding a *kegua,* a hollow gourd used as a comic cudgel like the European inflated bladder and almost certainly originating as a Chinese version of the jester's bauble, or *marotte.* Adjutant plays could be put on to provide the same kind of humorous criticism as the even more impromptu jester skits, and they seem to have been a stepping stone between these and the first full-blown structured drama.[27]

In addition to the adjutant role, Chinese drama has a highly developed range of clown characters *(chou),* although the clown "is not necessarily a fool and may portray a serious or evil character as against a mere ribald one." He does nevertheless resemble a jester in that "he is at liberty to improvise as the mood strikes him, the spontaneous quip and local jest are both part of his technique and he takes the audience into his confidence."[28] Moreover, the various clown types included the dwarf and hunchback, the simulation of both abnormalities requiring careful makeup and a demanding technique, and in the case of the dwarf role, physical stamina. And even if an individual character did not always fulfil the functions of a jester, the *qualities* befitting the *chou* role types could well be ascribed to a court jester: "There is a freedom and exaggeration in everything the comic actor says and does and not infrequently an earthiness springing from the very nature of his role, in which a nimble wit, a sense of satire, and a predilection for pure tomfoolery are important qualities for cultivation." [29]

In China the court jester rarely featured as a character in a play, and the few plays starring a jester deal with the historical Newly Polished Mirror and Dongfang Shuo. A Yuan dynasty variety play attributed to Zhou Wenzhi (d. 1334) was aptly titled *Newly Polished Mirror Uses a Skit to Advise Emperor Zhuangzong of the Tang (Jing Xinmo xijian Tang Zhuangzong)*.[30] Its theme was the story of the jester's dissuading the emperor from executing a magistrate who tried to prevent him from trampling farmland in pursuit of the hunt. Another variety play, *Nao zhong yi*, written in the Ming dynasty by Xu Fuzuo (1560–after 1630), dealt with the same story. Neither play is extant.[31]

There are several plays with Dongfang Shuo as a jester, mostly variations on one theme. Apart from an anonymous and nonextant Ming dynasty variety play called simply *Dongfang Shuo*, there is also a twenty-act *chuanqi* play by Wu Dexiu (fl. ca. 1692) titled *The Newly Cut and Annotated Woodblock Print of "Dongfang Shuo Stealing a Peach" (Xinke chuxiang yinshi dianban "Dongfang Shuo toutao ji")* and a one-act Qing dynasty sketch by Yang Chaoguan (1712–91) called *Dongfang Shuo Caught Stealing a Peach (Toutao zhuozhu Dongfang Shuo)* (fig. 23).[32]

Yang Chaoguan's sketch takes an anecdote from the *History of the Han Dynasty (Hanshu)* biography of Dongfang Shuo, and in this play he points out to the emperor that court dwarfs receive the same stipend as he does despite being a third his height, complaining that he is starving while they have plenty.[33] In Yang's play, he steals a peach of immortality and is caught and beaten for it. He tries to steal again and is caught a second time, using the jester's quick-witted humor to talk his way out of trouble. Dongfang Shuo opens the play by asking who can compare with him in humor, somersaults, and tricky talk and suggesting that anybody who wants to learn to steal should first learn to run (173). He ends with a poem asserting that immortality is nothing compared with the immortality of his witty "three-inch tongue" *(san cun she)* (178). The stage directions also give the jester the same license to improvise humor as the real court jester and the stage clown of English drama.

Wu Dexiu's is by far the longest and most complex Dongfang Shuo play. At the end of act 6 the emperor decides to make Dongfang Shuo his jester, and this gives us the Chinese phrase "to keep a jester" *(xu paiyou)* (14a). Although the play has a few inconsistencies—Dongfang Shuo starts

as a young, handsome scholar and is suddenly portrayed as being old—
it is a very accurate depiction of the jester and his relationship with the
emperor.

A third play about Dongfang Shuo takes another story from the *History of the Han Dynasty* in which the emperor ordered a gift of meat to be
given to his attendants. When nobody appeared to distribute the meat,
Dongfang Shuo took his sword and cut some to take home for his "little
lady," disregarding court etiquette. The emperor scolded him for his bad
manners and ordered him to criticize himself, which he did in terms of
bold-faced self-praise, making the emperor laugh and forgive. The play,
Dongfang Shuo Cuts Meat to Give to Xi Jun (Dongfang Shuo gerou yi Xi Jun),
has been attributed to Yang Shen (1488–1559), and the incident also appears in act 8 of Wu Dexiu's play.[34]

While Chinese drama has a few extant plays featuring historical court
jesters, I have not yet stumbled on evidence of a Chinese playwright's having created a Chinese Touchstone or Feste—perhaps this remains to be
unearthed, or perhaps the apparent willingness of Chinese actors to take
on aspects of the jester in their own ad lib comments and asides precluded
the need to create such characters.

Figure 23 Dongfang Shuo, immortal
peach thief

Act 2: Athens, Atella, and Archmimes

> These mimic actors set out with no moral purpose, but they were de-
> cidedly eager to take advantage of anything in life which, because of
> its baseness, its meanness, or its triviality, provided that laughter-
> provoking contrast between man's mind and the fettering restrictions
> of his body, and, moreover, they were ever ready to stand forward,
> like the mimes of old, as the secular exponents of popular feeling.
> Emperors might flatter and feed them, but they never lost sight of
> the follies to be found in a royal Court. Royally welcomed, they re-
> tained to the end their sense of humour.
>
> Allardyce Nicoll, *Masks, Mimes and Miracles* [35]

The origins of the European court jester may well lie in the comic mime
actors of ancient Greece and particularly Rome. The term "mime" is not
used in the modern sense to refer to the silent actor or his wordless art—
the Greek and Roman mimes were masters of the tongue—but indicates
that they imitated life. They were in all likelihood the principal source of
entertainers fulfilling some of the functions of the court jester in Rome,
and a cursory glance at some of the stock comic roles of the Greek and
Roman farces and the costumes they wore suggest that their later disper-
sal across the Roman Empire may well have sown the seeds of the medieval and Renaissance jester archetype (fig. 24).

There were writers of mimic plays, such as the Greek Epicharmus (ca.
530 – ca. 440 B.C.) and the Roman Decimus Laberius (ca. 105 – 43 B.C.), but

Figure 24 Roman mimic fool

essentially they relied on the comic improvisational skills of the mimes, who were unbound by scripts even when they existed—one name for a mimic actor was *autokabdalos,* meaning "unprepared" or "improvised." Improvisation gave the mimes a jester's freedom to mock, and throughout their history irreverence toward anything blindly revered was the cornerstone of their entertainment.

Mimes had sung and spoken parts and could include acrobatic skills in their repertoire. As in China, the line between actors and jesters was blurred—one entertainer called Agathocles was said to be both a "laughter maker" *(gelatopoios)* and a mime. With the mimes, "their acrobatic agility guaranteed that [they] should never be dull, never be fettered by religious prejudice or ceremonial. These professional entertainers, above all things, *stood for secularism and the right to laugh.*"[36] Just like jesters. In addition they further resembled their successors in using puns, verse, riddles, and songs and in frequently having an oddly comic appearance. The shaven head associated with medieval fools was a common feature, and statuettes of them often show Bardolphine noses, huge heads, and occasionally hunchbacks.

Another type of mime was the phallus bearer *(phallophoros),* who would undergo a strapadichtomy, a costume enhancement giving him a comically large penis, like medieval depictions of the fool with superschlong— a recurring joke perhaps alluding to the outsize place this relatively small part of the body occupies in the life of man. The phallus bearers would mount the stage and "ridicule certain members of the audience. There is certainly not much here that seems dramatic," and the actors seem to have been just cheeky jesters operating in a theatrical environment, mocking anyone and anything, living or legendary.[37]

In the theatrical tradition that flourished in Atella, the stock character Cicirrus seems the most jesterlike and often wore a coxcomb cap. When Virgil and Horace were guests at a friend's villa, two jesters, Sarmentus and Messius Cicirrus cracked jokes about each other to entertain the diners.[38] Mime actors were frequently invited to perform in the homes of nobles and emperors, and there are numerous references to the fondness of emperors for mimes and of mimes mocking emperors, usually with impunity, sometimes not. Both Augustus and Hadrian (r. 117–38) liked to have them in the court, and the only instance of Augustus's rebuking a mime was when he praised the emperor from the stage to the applause of the audience. Augustus hated flattery but was full of jokes and loved mimic humor.[39] The overlap between stage and court jester can be seen in Hadrian's having Atellan mimes attend his banquets.[40]

Suetonius describes an instance when Emperor Tiberius, old and lascivious, tried to seduce an unwilling woman. He subsequently had her tried for refusing him, and the humiliation causing her to stab herself. The mimes did not let this pass without comment: "Hence a stigma put upon him at the next play in an Atellan farce was received with great applause and became current, that 'the old goat was licking the does' [genitals]'" ("Unde nota in Atellanico exhodio proximis ludis adsensu maximo excepta percrebruit, 'hircum vetulum capreis naturam ligurire'").⁴¹ This won the applause of the public and the forbearance of the emperor, but when mimes alluded to an emperor's adulterous wife, the public criticized his tolerance of their effrontery. The wife of Antoninus Pius (r. 138–61) was having an affair with Tertullus, and despite catching them having breakfast together the cuckold promoted the lover. A group of mimes used a pun to make a skit:

> In regard to this man the following dialogue was spoken on the stage in the presence of Antoninus himself. The Fool asked the Slave the name of his wife's lover and the Slave answered "Tullus" three times; and when the Fool kept on asking, the Slave replied, "I have already told you thrice, Tullus [ter, Tullus] is his name." But the city populace and others besides talked a great deal about this incident and found fault with Antoninus for his forbearance.

> [De quo mimus in scaena praesente Antonino dixit, cum stupidus nomen adulteri uxoris a servo quaereret, et ille diceret ter "Tullus," et adhuc stupidus quaereret, respondit ille "iam tibi dixi ter, Tullus dicitur." et de hoc quidem multa populus, multa etiam alii dixerunt patientiam Antonini incusantes.]⁴²

Even Nero (r. 54–68), not noted for his niceness, allowed a certain latitude to his mocking critics, and these were probably mimes. Despite his renowned cruelty and all the disasters and abuses that befell the empire under his rule, Suetonius informs us that

> it is surprising and of special note that all this time he bore nothing with more patience than the curses and abuse of the people, *and was particularly lenient towards those who assailed him with gibes and lampoons.*

> [Mirum et vel praecipue notabile inter haec fuerit nihil eum patientius quam maledicta et convicia hominum tulisse, neque in ullos leniorem quam qui se dictis aut carminibus lacessissent exstitisse.]⁴³

When Emperor Verus (r. 161–69) went to Syria, supposedly on campaign, "he brought actors out of Syria as proudly as though he were leading kings to a triumph" ("his accessit, quod, quasi reges aliquos ad triumphum adduceret, sic histriones eduxit e Syria").[44] Verus perhaps surpasses most other emperors in his enthusiasm for entertainers of all sorts, and the comment in the *Scriptores historiae Augustae*, wry in its description of his delight in them, recognizes jesters as mimes:

> He had brought with him, too, players of the harp and the flute, actors and jesters from the mimes, jugglers, and any kind of slave whose entertainment had amused him in Syria and Alexandria, and in such numbers, indeed, that he seemed to have concluded a war, not against Parthians, but against actors.

> [Adduxerat secum et fidicinas et tibicines et histriones scurrasque mimarios et praestigiatores et omnia mancipiorum genera quorum Syria et Alexandria pascitur voluptate, prorsus ut videretur bellum non Parthicum sed histrionicum confecisse.][45]

However, despite the partiality of some Roman emperors to jesters or jester types, they were no different from Chinese and European rulers in occasional irritation at mimic mockery. Nero, despite his "surprising" tolerance, did banish an Atellan mime for singing references to the deaths of Claudius and Agrippa.[46] Commodus himself was "adept in certain arts that are not becoming in an emperor, for he could . . . dance and sing and whistle, and he could play the buffoon . . . to perfection" ("iam in his artifex, quae stationis imperatoriae non erant . . . saltaret, cantaret, sibilaret, scurram denique . . . perfectum ostenderet"); yet he could nevertheless be angered by jesters: "He was alluded to by actors as a man of depraved life, and he thereupon banished them so promptly that they did not again appear upon the stage" ("appellatus est a mimis quasi obstupratus easdemque ita ut non apparerent subito deportavit").[47]

The resemblance of the mimes to jesters is not limited to the type and techniques of humor they employed or to their fearlessness in the face of emperors who sometimes indulged, sometimes banished them. Their appearance could also bear a striking similarity to that of medieval and Renaissance jesters and fools. Apart from the bald-headed *stupidus*, the secondary fool to the archmime, there were mimes who wore the coxcomb or other headdress identical to the European jester's eared or coned cap (fig. 24). The *stupidus* could cover his bald head with a pointed hat like

Figure 25 Roman mime in cone-capped caper

that shown on a painted relief at Corneto, "divided vertically by strips of material." The relief also features a multicolored costume similar to the jester's motley. One painting shows a mime wearing a bicolored costume, and there is a reference to a *mimi centunculus*, "a cloak or other garment, either of patchwork or of mixed colourings."[48]

Appearance aside, the mimes bore strongest resemblance to the jesters of China with their short impromptu skits intended to entertain or to criticize, but always humorously. They had many qualities of the universal jester, an odd physique or great agility—a mime on a Roman lamp (fig. 25) is capering naked—quick extempore wit, a desire to make people laugh at serious as well as amusing aspects of life, and a determination to expose human folly through laughter. They shared too the willingness to risk royal rancor if they cut too close to the bone despite enjoying the jester's license: Choricius (sixth century) informs us that "the mimes were in the position to ridicule injustice with impunity."[49] They were in spirit and style as close to professional court jesters as we could hope to find.

ACT 3: TARLTON, TOUCHSTONE, AND TOM KILLIGREW

> *Tarleton,* who was then the best Comedian in *England,* had made a
> pleasant Play, and when it was acting before the Queen, he pointed
> at Sir *Walter Rawleigh,* and said: "*See, the knave commands the Queen*";
> for which he was corrected by a frown from the Queen; yet he had
> the confidence to add, that he was of too much, and too intolerable
> a power; and going on with the same liberty, he reflected on the over-
> great Power and Riches of the Earl of *Leicester,* which was so univer-
> sally applauded by all that were present, that she thought fit for the
> present to bear these Reflections with a seeming unconcernedness.
> But yet she was so offended, that she forbad *Tarleton,* and all her Jest-
> ers, from coming near her Table, being inwardly displeased with this
> impudent and unseasonable Liberty.
>
> Edmund Bohun, *The Character of Queen Elizabeth*[50]

Richard Tarlton (fig. 26), favorite jester of Elizabeth I, criticized the excessive attentions lavished by the queen on the maritime adventurer Walter Raleigh, for which he was punished with a regal sulk. In addition to
providing the queen with clear advice in his capacity as a court jester, he
was also able to advise her under the guise of the actor at court, since she
did not tolerate publicly performed plays criticizing her.[51] "The popularity of the fool was one of the most striking features of the English stage
at the time of its greatest glory," and Tarlton's popularity was easily on a
par with any top television comedian nowadays.[52] He was a household
name in taverns, theaters and the court, welcomed at the palace, recognized in the street, and renowned "for a wondrous plentifull pleasant ex-
temporall wit, hee was the wonder of his time."[53] In 1583 he became one
of the queen's players until his death in 1588, and he "enjoyed so much
celebrity that 'the year of Tarleton's death' was as common a phrase as 'the
year of the Armada.'"[54]

Considering that Tarlton himself was a court jester and was given to
adding improvisations to the lines scripted for him, it is reasonable to assume that nobody could have had a better idea than he of what it takes to
be a jester. His stage roles tended to be of more rustic clowns, the monu-
mental court jester roles not yet having been written, but he undoubtedly
drew on his own character and experience as a court jester and could observe other jesters at first hand. He spent a great deal of time at court banquets, wearing his jester's costume, singing ballads and capping rhymes as

Figure 26 Richard Tarlton. © The British Museum.

well as performing in plays.[55] The line between his theatrical and real-life personae must have been barely discernible.

If Tarlton was the prime example of the actor doubling as court jester, the influence was by no means in one direction only—court jesters were very much involved in court revels and plays. The scholars who insist that the traditional court jester costume of cap and bells was a literary device are perhaps ignoring this very close connection between jesters and actors.[56] It is inconceivable that the literary and stage fool would not be influenced by the historical jester, or exert influence on him, like two circles, one historical and one literary, that would never overlap. There was undoubtedly a great deal of osmosis between the two: history and literature are not enclosed in impermeable membranes.

Many anecdotes about Tarlton are told in *Tarlton's News out of Purgatory* (1590), attributed to Robert Armin (ca. 1568–1615), who is said to have been trained by him in jestership.[57] The first known edition was published in 1611, but it is likely there were earlier editions, since Tarlton died in 1588.[58] However, many of the entries are probably stock jokes that would sell better under Tarlton's name, and the jestbook has been described as "a more or less fraudulent catchpenny in which only the faintest glimmerings of his real qualities appear."[59]

Perhaps the first signs of a jester in English drama were in some of the Vice characters, such as Fancy and Folly in John Skelton's *Magnificence* (1515). Folly carries a jester's bauble and can be dressed in motley and mistaken for the fool of the play, whereas in fact it is he who makes fools of others.[60] Like the stage jester, the Vice character was a favorite with the audience, and the part was often played by the best actor in the troupe, who was free to improvise and to exchange banter and jokes with the audience. He also often wore multicolored bright patchwork clothes with bells, but he would not necessarily have been partnered with a king or noble in the way a court jester would.[61]

The Vice or fool could comment on the play as a comic chorus and could be used to convey bad news in a way that would soften the blow—another function of the real jester. The same could be said of the fool in the French *sotties*, which also provided a jester's protective mask to shield an actor or playwright from retribution. In England, however, the fool "enjoyed not only a far longer life but also a far wider range and licence than in other European countries, where he had no such recognized entrée into serious and even tragic drama."[62]

Robert Armin, who joined Shakespeare's Company in 1599 or 1600, influenced Shakespeare in his creation of Touchstone, one of the greatest stage jesters, in *As You Like It* (1599).[63] He was also the actor of Feste in *Twelfth Night* (1600) and the Fool in *King Lear* (1605). Unlike Tarlton and Kemp, he tended to keep to his lines, but if Tarlton was the greatest comic actor to take on the real role of a court jester, then Armin was the one who played the part of three of the greatest theatrical court jesters found anywhere.[64]

Touchstone (fig. 27) provides a healthy combination of the jester's percipient persiflage and witty bawdiness. His name points to one who could distinguish pure gold from mere alloys and "test or try the genuineness or

Figure 27 Thomas King as Touchstone

value of anything."[65] Jaques, who seems something of a jester manqué—
"O that I were a fool! / I am ambitious for a motley coat" (2.7.42–43)—
is constantly commenting on Touchstone's ability and freedom to reveal
folly: "The wiseman's folly is anatomiz'd / Even by the squand'ring glances
of the fool" (2.7.56–57).

There are no flies on Feste in *Twelfth Night,* or as he puts it, he wears
no motley in his brain (1.5.54–55). He is jester to Olivia and speaks to her
with unabashed cheek. Like many court jesters he plays the pipe and ta-
bor, and the play ends with his singing. He is tremendously witty and has
complete license to speak his mind: Olivia may be resigned to that when

Figure 28 Emma Thompson as Lear's fool. © Robert Barber.

she says, "There is no slander in an allowed fool / though he do nothing but rail" (1.5.93–94). When she has had enough of him, she orders him to be taken away, but he twists her words to make her seem the fool:

> *Olivia.* Take the fool away.
> *Feste.* Do you not hear, fellows? Take away the lady.
>
> (1.5.36–37)

King Lear's fool is the quintessential court jester and provides perhaps the most poignant example of this role (fig. 28). His levity adds to rather than detracts from the tragedy, lending greater pathos than if the play were all unremitting seriousness. He sings, amuses, and is licensed to tell the truth, which he does, despite the omnipresent threat of a beating, missing no opportunity to make Lear see the folly of having given away his kingdom to his daughters. Sometimes he speaks with naked honesty, as when Lear asks, "Who is it that can tell me who I am?" and he answers like an echo, "Lear's shadow" (1.4.227–28), and sometimes by means of a riddle: "The hedge-sparrow fed the cuckoo so long, / That it's had it head bit off by it young" (1.4.213–14). Or later when he and Lear are exchang-

ing jokes, he makes the king laugh and perhaps forget his sorrows for a
second, only to then bring him back down to earth with a thud of truth:

> *Fool.* I can tell why a snail has a house.
> *Lear.* Why?
> *Fool.* Why, to put's head in; not to give it away to his daughters,
>   and leave his horns without a case.
>
> (1.6.27–30)

Thersites in *Troilus and Cressida* (1602) is a kind of informal court
jester, addressing Ajax with aweless levity, calling him a "mongrel / beef-
witted lord" (2.1.12–13) and a "sodden-witted lord" (2.1.45), neither of
which causes any offense.[66] He also acts as a link between the audience
and the stage by making dry asides that are not noticed by other characters. He is very irreverent, constantly chipping in with his witty remarks
while Achilles, his master, refers to him as "fool" and tolerates a great deal
of forthright commentary. There is an easy, affectionately rude banter between them that belies the master-subordinate hierarchy:

> *Achilles.* How now, thou core of envy! Thou crusty batch of nature,
>   what's the news?
> *Thersites.* Why, thou picture of what thou seemest, and idol of
>   idiot-worshippers, here's a letter for thee.
> *Achilles.* From whence, fragment?
> *Thersites.* Why, thou full dish of fool, from Troy.
>
> (5.1.4–9)

Lavatch in *All's Well That Ends Well* (1602) is a "clown" who serves the
countess. In two scenes he appears alone with her and addresses her with
cheeky, punning prattle (2.2 and 3.2): "thou art a witty fool," says Parolles
(2.4.31), and in another scene Lavatch refers to his jester's bauble bawdily,
suggesting he could serve a lady well with it (4.5.27–28).[67] He also claims
for himself the qualities of truth teller and prophet so often ascribed to
jesters: "A prophet I, madam, and I speak the truth" (1.2.45).

The dominance of Shakespeare and the popularity of his jesters can
give the impression that English drama was overrun with his fools, when
in fact there are plays by other authors with jesters or jesterlike characters.
Robert Greene's *Friar Bacon and Friar Bongay* (1589) has Ralph Simnell
as jester to Henry III, a perky character who helps Prince Edward in his
quest for love and wears the cap and bells, asking Lacie at one point to
"buy me a thousand thousand / million of fine bels" (1.1.160–61).[68] Ben
Jonson's Carlo Buffone in *Every Man out of His Humour* (1599) uses mock-

ery to correct, although he is not paired with a king or other bigwig as a jester would be.[69] But he has all the qualities: "His Religion is railing, and his discourse Ribaldrie," and "They stand highest in his respect, whom he studies most to reproch" (Prologue, lines 28–30). He shows irreverence for all and sundry and cannot resist a joke.

Patient Grissill (1600), a joint effort by Thomas Dekker, Henry Chettle, and Haughton, has Babulo as jester to Grissill's father.[70] He addresses the marquis with plucky dismissiveness despite demands from his own master and Grissill that he show deference to the noble:

> *Janicola.* Fall on thy knees foole: see heeres our duke.
> *Babulo.* I haue not offended him, therefore Ile not ducke and he
> were ten Dukes.
>
> (1.2.286–89)

The marquis is not upset by his lack of groveling genuflection and invites him to serve him, but again Babulo is not impressed:

> *Marquis.* . . . Ile have thee live at court.
> *Babulo.* I haue a better trade sir, basketmaking.
>
> (1.2.310–11)

In John Marston's *The Malcontent* (1604), Bilioso has a jester called Passarello, or Sparrow, who informs us his master "keeps, beside me, fifteen jesters to instruct / him in the art of fooling" (1.8.43–44), although he is the only one we meet.[71] He is a wise fool, and when Bilioso shows he is impressed with the clever reasoning of his jester ("Thou canst prove anything"), Passarello proves he cannot be bribed into ego stroking anybody: "Anything but a rich knave, for I can flatter no man" (5.1.48–49).

Three plays feature Henry VIII's favorite jester, Will Somers. *When You See Me You Know Me* (1604) by Samuel Rowley is a tremendous portrayal of Somers, tallying with historical accounts of him, making the king laugh when he is in a bad mood, advising him, mocking clerics, entertaining with riddles and jokes, and occasionally taking a beating. Thomas Nash's punningly titled *Summer's Last Will and Testament* (1592) has Somers wearing the fool's coat, but there the resemblance to a jester ends, for apart from offering comments there is no interaction with a king, and the play seems more of a pastoral piece between Summer and Winter, although the epilogue is narrated by a dwarf.[72] Shakespeare's *Henry VIII* (1613) has no Will Somers, perhaps because by the time the play was written Robert Armin, the supreme actor of the Shakespearean court jester, had retired.[73] How different the play might have been but for such timing.

In the anonymous play *Misogonus* (1570), the character Cacurgus, called "jester" by one character (2.2.89), is several times referred to as "Will Summer," now a generic term, "Ha, ha! Now will I go play Will Summer again" (2.1.262).[74] His master looks for him, asking: "Did no man meet Will Summer here this way alate? / I have longed to talk with the counterfeit fool" (3.2.17–18). He is described in the dramatis personae as a *morio*, or fool, serving in the household of Philogonus, and he acts a fool but undoubtedly has the last laugh, "I have bepissed my hose . . . I laugh at the old fools so heartily" (1.1.231–32). His master thinks that he "can neither lie nor flatter" (1.1.257), an inability well suited to the profession of court jester, and Cacurgus does live up to this role. He keeps the audience amused with his sardonic asides, he sings, he wears the jester's costume—"one would take him for a fool by his gown and his cap" (3.2.142)—and he is also adviser and confidant with ready access to the master:

> Yourself may judge that by my foolish weed.
> Both my cap and my coat he bestowed on me.
> Nay, I am become his counselor. I can tell you news.
> Whatsoever he speaks he gives me leave to hear;
> My company at no time he will refuse.
>
> (1.1.321–25)

The court jester on the English stage had a career that was as brief as it was glorious. By the mid-seventeenth century there is little sign of him, a fact that was lamented in a play of 1662, *Thorney Abbey,* which harks back to happier days when a playwright would have known better than to portray a king without a jester, and which mentions by name some of the greatest historical jesters in England:

> They are all fools in the *Tragedy;* and you are fools that come to see the *Tragedy;* and the *Poet's* a fool who made the *Tragedy,* to tell the story of a King and a Court, and leave a *fool* out on't; when in *Pacy's* and *Somer's* and *Patche's* and *Archie's* time, my venerable Predecessours, a *fool* was always the *Principal Verb.*[75]

Similarly, in *The Woman Captain* (1679) by Thomas Shadwell, a jester tries to keep a place for himself in the play but is banished in the first scene of act 1, providing an explanation for the jester's disappearance from real life as well as stage court life: fashion.

> *Sir Humphrey.* I'll keep no Fool, 'tis out of fashion for great Men to keep Fools.

Fool. Because now adays they are their own Fools, and so save
    Charges. . . .
Sir Humphrey. I'll have none, 'tis exploded ev'n upon the Stage.
Fool. But for all that *Shakespear's* Fools had more Wit than any of
    the Wits and Criticks now adays.

                        (1:20)[76]

Tom Killigrew, court jester to Charles II, like Richard Tarlton had as
much connection with the theater as the court, albeit in a different capacity. Whereas Tarlton was a comic actor, Killigrew was manager of the
Theatre Royal in addition to being master of the revels at court and king's
foole. He had a great love and knowledge of drama, music, and opera—
on 2 August 1664 Pepys mentions Killigrew's enthusiastic plans to establish an opera house performing four operas a year.[77] Pepys, a fount of information on this debonair jester, also informs us that to keep the young
actors at the theater in line he provided a prostitute for the benefit of eight
or ten of them, at 20 s. a week.[78]

    This section began and ended with two of the finest English court
jesters, both with equally strong theatrical connections: Richard Tarlton,
the most popular comic actor of his day and favorite jester to Elizabeth,
and Tom Killigrew, jester to Charles II and enthusiastic manager of one
of London's best theaters. The jesters in between belonged more exclusively to the stage, but in Touchstone, Feste, and Lear's fool we have three
jesters who are so true to life it is hard to believe they came from a quill,
albeit a rather talented one.

ACT 4: THE FOOLISH FRENCH AND THE JESTING GERMANS

Seldom will a play be performed
That will be without a Fool

*[Selten ein spil wirt gfangen an
Dass nit auch musz ein narren han]*
              Pamphile Gengenbach (1545–46)[79]

The fools of the *sotties* did not just make people laugh, they also used their
mockery to point out the failings of society and of its upper echelons in
particular, a fact Louis XII seems to have appreciated greatly despite having at least three jesters of his own. The main precursor of the *sotties* is *Le
jeu de la feuillée* (ca. 1272) by Adam de la Halle, a renowned *trouvère,* which

some argue could be considered a *sottie* itself by virtue of the important role of the dervish-fool in it, even though it was written about two centuries before the *sottie* was established as a genre.[80] By the fourteenth and fifteenth centuries the fool appears regularly in the religious miracle and morality plays, perhaps to maintain the interest of the audience while they were being edified.[81]

Like his court jester counterpart, the fool in French medieval literature was somehow on the edge of the arena of action and therefore more independent—it seems writers made more effort to vary his characterization than with most of the other roles. Alternatively, creativity was left to the initiative of the actor, with stage directions simply announcing the fool, who was then given complete freedom. For this reason the fool's role in French drama (as well as English and Samoan) was usually taken by the best actor in the company, as Rabelais's Pantagruel explains: "In this way, when it came to distributing the roles among the players, that of fool and joker was always given to the most accomplished of the troupe" ("En ceste maniere, voyons nous entre les jongleurs, a la distribution des rolles, le personnaige du Sot et du Badin estre tous jours representé par le plus perit et perfaict joueur de leur compaignie").[82]

There is one instance where the fool in a mystery acted as a court jester, in a fragment of a fifteenth-century nativity play in which the jester belongs to Herod's court and freely exercises his traditional license.[83] This is not the only time Herod is shown with a court jester. The Latin play by Nicholas Grimald, *Archipropheta* (1547), has the jester Gelasimus (with the same root as "gelastic," laughable, and the Greek word for jester, *gelatopoios*), although he is portrayed less convincingly than the Sot described above and quoted below.

> *Herod.* Silence, you foolish clot,
> You're really rousing my rage;
> I'll give you a slap in the face
> *Fool.* An' I'll hit you in the first place.
>
> [*Herod.* Taiseis vous, clotton,
> vous moy feries bien enragier;
> je te donraie ung sofflet à ton visier!
> *Sot.* Et je le vous donraie tout premier.]

(lines 111–14)[84]

The *sotties* developed from the celebrations of the *sociétés joyeuses* that sprang up in Paris and in many of the larger provincial towns, associations of citizens or wealthy farmers that would elect a prince of fools or a *mère-folle* to preside over them while members would dress up as fools either for carnivalesque processions or dramatic performances.[85] In Rouen there were the Connards, named after the *cornes* or points of the jester's cap, in Dijon the Infanterie Dijonnaise, and in Paris the Enfants sans Souci. In a typical *sottie* the fools never act as themselves, their foolish costumes being overlaid with the costume of a prelate or dignitary or whoever else the play intends to mock. It is usually at the end of the play that the pope, king, or bishop will be exposed for the fool he is. The fools therefore are representative of a specific vice or an institution given to such a vice.[86]

These societies were the secular relations of the medieval Feast of Fools, with the difference that the feast was limited to once a year. This is a distinction that brings the societies closer to the court jester and gives them far greater freedom. The license belonging to a specific festival is much easier to control than when it is instituted at all times and places. The plays that grew out of this made good use of the jester's cover to criticize the authorities, secular and ecclesiastical. By the late fifteenth century the *sociétés joyeuses* were using the jester's costume in their plays and were performing *sotties* together with moralities and farces.[87]

A *sottie* by André de la Vigne, *Sotise à huit personnaiges* (ca. 1507), has Sot Corrompu alluding to the fact that the king had replaced his chancellor with the bishop of Paris instead of the man the Sot would have liked to see, the worthy Cardinal Briçonnet:[88]

> Oh, how the king must have turned a deaf ear
> Not to have appointed as his chancellor
> The man who by great good fortune happens to collar
> The saintliness and goodness of a first-class scholar.

> [O que le roy a esté sourd
> Qu'il n'aye faict chancelier
> Cil que faict grand chance lyer
> Tant sainct, tant bon, tant sçavant homme.]

> (lines 668–71)

The *Farce morale de troys pelerins et malice* (1523) uses the fools to satirize Louise de Savoie (1476–1531), the king's mother who twice acted as regent during his reign and who was blamed for many of the problems afflicting France under François I. In 1516 the king arrested three *sottie* actors, one of whom had played the part of Louise using the guise of Mère Sotte to mock the government. The arrests did not succeed in silencing other actors, simply making them more subtle in their attacks.[89] The play ends with the second fool excoriating rich men

> Who have eaten many a sumptuous meal
> And yet couldn't walk a single step
> Except to dance with a pretty coquette:
> It is they who Disorder at liberty have set.
>
> [Qui ont mengé maint bon repas
> Et ne seroyent marcher un pas,
> Synon danser aveq fillete:
> Se sont ceulx qui Desordre ont faicte.]

(lines 242–45)

The *Sottie nouvelle à six personnaiges du roy des sotz* (ca. 1545) is unusual in that it has one *sot* who takes the name of a historical court jester, Triboulet, who entertained François I.[90] Triboulet was also the name of Roi René's pin-headed jester and seems to have been something of a generic term for jester, much as Patch became in England. In the play he serves the king of fools, although neither he nor any of the other fools is particularly amusing, perhaps because, as Picot suggests, the play had been mutilated by censors.[91]

These French fools flourished when court jesters were at the zenith of their influence, and the two complemented each other. They provided a licensed outlet for popular criticism of abuses of power, borrowing their freedom of speech from court colleagues. The *sotties* were most popular during the fourteenth and fifteenth centuries but were still performed in Paris as late as 1632.[92] The jester's license appropriated by the fools of the *sotties* is described in a scene from *Le triomphe de l'abbaye des Conards*, which states that the stage fools could say anything without incurring the wrath of the king, "Et Conards sont permis tout dire. . . . Sans encourir du prince l'ire."[93]

Of the German carnival plays, the *Fastnachtspiele*, there are two that feature a court jester. Hans Sachs (1494–1576), the most renowned author of the genre, wrote *The Doctor with the Big Nose (Der Doctor mit der Grosen Nase)*, which has a jester called Jeckle Narr, his name being a combination of the Low and High German words for fool, *Geck* and *Narr*. He stands out in Sachs's plays because he is "permitted to comment upon and criticise his master's actions in a manner not permitted to other courtiers."[94] The doctor is the real fool, and his big nose is meant to symbolize this. He is learned but condescending to his friend, the jester's master, and disparaging about life in the country even though he is enjoying his friend's hospitality. Despite this he is treated courteously, and the jester is warned not to make any jokes about his nose, being dismissed when he pretends to honor the doctor by referring to his nose. This happens again and again, and the third time the jester feigns indifference to the nose:

> Little Sir, I couldn't care a jot
> Whether you have a nose or not;
> Whether it's big or whether it's small
> Shouldn't be something I'd notice at all.
>
> [Herlein, mich gar nit mer anficht,
> Dw habst ein nassen oder nicht.
> Sie sey geleich gros oder klein,
> Sols von mir vnpekreet sein.] [95]

(lines 279–82)

Another of Hans Sachs's *Fastnachtspiele* concerns Neidhart Fuchs, the historical, musical "merry counselor" of Duke Otto the Merry of Austria, known as the "Farmers' Enemy" (Der Baurenfeind) on account of his constant joking at their expense. In the play, *Neudhard and the Violet (Neudhart mit dem Feuhel),* he serves Duke Friedrich of Austria in an action-packed tale of revenge and counterrevenge, with the farmers trying to beat him. The play opens innocently enough with Neidhart finding the first violet of the spring, which he covers with his hat while he goes to fetch the duchess to show it to her (fig. 29). Three farmers who hate him because he hunts through their fields decide this is their chance to dish out some retribution. They pick the violet, and one of them replaces it with his own freshly deposited turd (fig. 30). The duchess arrives with her retinue to view the violet and is somewhat astonished by what she finds. Neidhard begs forgiveness, assuring her it must have been the doing of a farmer. Farmers: 1, jester: 0.

There follows a marvelous scene in which the farmers add insult to injury by tying the violet to a stick and dancing and singing around it (fig. 31). Neidhart rallies some rabble from the court to fight them, thereby seizing possession of the by now shrinking violet, which he finally presents to the duchess (fig. 32). Farmers: 1, jester: 1. The farmers then approach the duke, whom they know to be a lecher who could never say no to some nooky. They inform him that Neidhart's wife is the most beautiful woman in Austria and is in love with him. Farmers: 2, jester: 1. The duke summons Neidhart and tells him he plans to visit him at home. The

Figure 29 Neudhard finds a violet and . . .

Figure 30 The duchess has a shock

jester sniffs out the plot and uses a stock jester joke to thwart the intended seduction, saying he is delighted while explaining that his wife is very deaf and so the duke must shout when he speaks to her. He similarly warns his wife of the duke's deafness, and there results such a shouting match that nobody can understand a word of what is said and any romance is presumably killed. Farmers: 2, jester: 2.[96]

Figure 31 The farmers dance in triumph . . .

Figure 32 Until Neudhard sorts them out

The fools of the French and German stage are not as likely to be full-blown court jesters as the English, nor are they readily admitted to serious or tragic drama. Nevertheless, they fulfilled the jester's functions and, in the case of the *sotties,* would even wear his traditional costume, which the English stage jester was less likely to do.

ACT 5: VIDUSAKA, OR WHEN IS A COURT JESTER NOT A COURT JESTER?

One who looks to people's pleasure, can imitate manners of all people, resorts to various [means] and mixes with women, is ready-witted in disclosures made through Pleasantry, or in Covert Pleasure and is clever, and can give censure through his words, is to be known as a Jester *(vidusaka).*

Bharata-Muni [ascribed], *The Natyasastra* (ca. 200 B.C.)[97]

Dhananjaya describes the Vidusaka as one among the companions of the hero, playing the role of a jester by evoking laughter and fun. Sagaranandin says that the Vidusaka is to be identified with the friend and companion of the kings; and is declared as their minister of humour, and has access to the inner apartments.

G. K. Bhat, *The Vidusaka*[98]

These two descriptions of the *vidusaka,* one of the stock characters of classical Sanskrit drama, could be applied to the court jester everywhere. He is funny, down-to-earth, and irreverent but not unkind; he companions the king as a friend and confidant despite his formally inferior status and addresses him with insolent familiarity, mocking him and acting as "a photographic negative of his master, a shadow to the king's reality, resonating on a different, utterly human wavelength."[99] He also has many of the physical aspects associated with jesters, being of a dwarfish or grotesque appearance. He could be found in both court and society, as in medieval Europe, which was awash with town and guild fools very much resembling their court counterparts: "It is thus not true that the *vidusakas* are Fools who attended the courts of kings *only.* They are mere comedians, who *made their livelihood by their witticisms and also by friendly advice. . . ,* real characters in social life in the 2nd century B.C. and . . . not merely dramatic invention."[100]

There seems to be considerable resistance among some Sanskrit scholars to the idea of the *vidusaka* as a court jester, although it is not at all clear why. Perhaps they believe that the court jester is principally a European phenomenon that we should not try to foist on other cultures. Coulson refers categorically to "the Clown (who is *not* a jester or intentionally funny person)," without then attempting to qualify his assertion, and Kuiper argues extensively on the issue despite dismissing it as being "at best of minor importance."[101]

The *vidusaka* could have the appearance of the dwarf, hunchback, or otherwise abnormal physique so often associated with the jester, as a contrast to the king's physical wholeness or as a deflector of malevolent forces. This latter aspect may account for why the *vidusaka* and the court jesters we know of were Brahmans, since to act as scapegoat for the king's impurity, a man had to be a Brahman.[102] The classic handbook of drama, the *Natyasastra* (ca. 200 B.C.), prescribes the *vidusaka*'s appearance, at least in theory, and shows the possible permutations of comic grotesqueness:

> Also the gait of the vidusaka has three comical properties . . . his corporeal defects (and movements), his talk and because of his costume and make-up. He has protruding teeth, is bald-headed, hunchbacked and lame and has a distorted face. When he makes his entrance in such a way, the laughter is due to his "limbs." When, however, he walks like a bird, looking up and down, he is (also), owing to his taking excessively wide strides, laughable due to his limbs. Laughter due to words is the effect of incoherent talk.[103]

That jesters around the world were often dwarfs and would certainly not be barred from the position of jester on account of a hunchback, that such people lived in the courts of India and are identified with the similarly deformed and comic *vidusaka*, who had all the characteristics of a jester, suggests that the dwarfs in the Indian courts could be a pool from which jesters might emerge.[104] Dwarfs and hunchbacks would not be employed in court to bake bread on some sort of equal opportunities scheme. Political correctness is a recent phenomenon, and it was common for dwarfs to be employed because of and not in spite of their "vertically challenged" appearance.

The *vidusaka* of the Kerala drama of Kutiyattam comes even closer to the court jester than his predecessor in the classical Sanskrit drama. He is grotesque in appearance and often deformed or disabled, and he "treats the audience to a feast of satirical and ironic comment, self-conscious parody, and spontaneous wit." Some of the plays featuring this sharper kind of *vidusaka* were written by the poet Tolan, himself known as the jester of the eleventh-century king Kulasekharavarman. In addition, the folk clowns of the south Indian stage still exist and feature many qualities of the court jester.[105]

Kuiper acknowledges Birbal as a court jester but expresses surprise that a great poet, Tenali Ramakrsna, could have metamorphosed into a court jester in popular (and enduring) Tamil legend.[106] We have seen the overlap of poet and jester, and Tenali Ramakrsna may have been a poet who encompassed the jester, like Friedrich Taubmann in Germany and George Buchanan in Britain. As with Buchanan, the legends surrounding him may have enveloped a nugget of true anecdote in layers of embellishment.

It seems there are many indications suggesting the existence of court jesters in India, and if the term *vidusaka* is used only in the context of drama that does not mean there was no court equivalent. Kalidasa (fl. before the fifth century A.D.), the dramatist whose *vidusaka* characters seem more consistently and convincingly jesterlike than many others, was a poet and ambassador of the court with considerable knowledge of court life, and it is likely that royal palaces included theaters.[107] A dramatist who knew the workings of the court and a court that supported the theater makes the creation of a completely fictitious comical companion to the king, with no parallel in real court life, somewhat improbable. It is hard to believe that a king would foster dwarfs in his court and plays with a dwarfish jester to a king without there being some resemblance between the two. Siegel refers to a man who sounds to all intents and purposes like a jester, enjoying ready access to the king, and who was "adept at singing, dancing, and playing various instruments; he was always after strange women; he was very clever at telling dirty jokes, and skilful at making puns, riddles, and such; he knew how to lampoon people and to make folks roar with laughter."[108]

Finally, circumstantial evidence in favor of real court jesters in India: the extreme unlikelihood that a highly sophisticated understanding of his functions, identical to notions of the court jester elsewhere, would have developed in legendary and literary isolation from the society that fostered it rather than reflecting a very real and universal phenomenon. "We must assume that the fool is ancient. The professional fool and the court-jester were known in ancient India; the tradition continues. We are told that king Amanullah of Afghanistan [r. 1919–29] maintained, with no sense of incongruity, at once a private broadcasting station and a court-jester."[109]

Perhaps it is time to let the *vidusaka* speak for himself, since one jester can plead the case for his own existence better than a hundred dry scholars can prove or refute it. And oh, how much more entertainingly! I came to the *vidusaka* completely ignorant of him and with only average insight into India, and it was the jester in him that drew me. I've been all over the world of jesters, and despite reading the *vidusaka*'s words through a window of translation and unfamiliar culture, he remains for me one of the freshest and funniest of stage fools. In Kalidasa's *Sakuntala and the Ring of*

Recollection (Abhijnanasakuntala) he is called Madhavya, and in their first
scene together he blames the king who made him go hunting so that now
his limbs ache, claiming he is in such pain that he cannot lift an arm to
salute his royal master:

> *Madhavya.* Dear friend, since my hands can't move to greet you, I
>   have to salute you with my voice.
> *King.* How did you cripple your limbs?
> *Madhavya.* Why do you ask why I cry after throwing dust in my
>   eyes yourself?
>
> (103)[110]

Like Touchstone in *As You Like It,* he is bored by the delights of the pastoral idyll, and he admonishes the king for his rural pursuits: "You neglect
the business of being a king and live like a woodsman in this awful camp"
(2:103). In *Urvasi Won by Valour (Vikramorvasiya)* the jester not only is the
confidant and constant companion of the king, he also shows great kindness to the queen and sympathy for her predicament as the king falls in
love elsewhere. At the same time, he comforts the king in his torment
while also mocking him. When the king gives a long-winded description
of his love agony, the jester brings him right down to earth:

> *King.* First Love's five arrows destroyed my mind
> when I could not turn it from this wild craving;
> now winds from the sandal hills torment me further
> as they fragrantly waft through the mango grove,
> stripping withered leaves, and revealing tender buds.
> *Little Man.* Oh, stop wailing.
>
> (193)

When the queen catches the king red-handed with a letter from Urvasi he panics, asking Little Man what the next move is. "What does the
thief answer when he's caught with the goods?" he quips, which does not
amuse the king, "Fool, this is no time for joking!" (202).[111] This exchange
is echoed in *Malavika and Agnimitra (Malavikaagnimitra),* in which the
second queen catches the king wooing his new love and gives him a piece
of her mind. The jester turns it into a joke: "Sir, think of some reply. Even
a burglar caught in the act would say 'I'm just practising window repair!'"
(285).[112] *Vidusakas* do show kindness to kings but do not take their love
affairs too seriously: "Oh Lord! Thank God! After frolicking a long time
with Urvasi around paradise grove and who-knows-where-else, my dear

friend has finally returned" (*Urvasi*, 239), often equating regal heartache to the jester's ever-griping stomach:

> *King.* Enough, friend, I need compassion!
> *Gautama.* And so do I! The pit of my stomach burns like a cooking
>   pot in the market.
>
> (*Malavika*, 273)

In *The Little Clay Cart (Mycchakatika)*, attributed to Sudraka, the *vidusaka* Maitreya shows perhaps even greater familiarity, loyalty, and irreverence than Kalidasa's jesters. He stands by his master even when the latter has lost his fortune through excessive generosity and becomes the victim of injustice, like a lighthearted version of *King Lear* with a happy ending. Like Kalidasa's jesters, he helps his master in matters of love, although in this play the lady concerned has more character than Kalidasa's heroines, who—to the uninitiated at least—seem all sweetness, light, and melon-sized breasts with not a great deal else to distinguish between them.

Maitreya's use of language is also distinctive—generally more colorful and straightforward than that of the other characters. His comments are a refreshing reprieve from some of the more opulently romantic speech in the play. His metaphors are striking and earthbound and contrast with the more conventional and high-flown imagery elsewhere. In act 3 Carudatta, in the full flush of love, returns from a concert with Maitreya and sings the praises of Rebhila. As always, the jester reins in grandiloquence:

> *Carudatta.* Ah, Rebhila sang splendidly, splendidly! Yes, the vina is
>   the pearl that did not grow in the sea. . . .
> *Maitreya.* Hey, come on! Let's go home!
> *Carudatta.* Ah, splendidly indeed did Rebhila sing.
> *Maitreya.* Me, two things always make me laugh, a woman speak-
>   ing Sanskrit and a man wailing a song. I positively did not like it!
>
> (83)[113]

If the irreverent humor, the clear-sightedness, a determination to speak his mind, loyalty and familiarity shown to his master, and his frequently dwarfish or grotesque appearance are not sufficient grounds to see in the *vidusaka* a court jester, then a terra-cotta plaque might tilt the balance (fig. 33). The plaque, dating from the Gupta period (fourth to sixth century) features a *vidusaka* wearing a *three-cornered cap*, "who on the basis of his quaint cap may be identified as a jester," albeit without bells on the points, and he also wore *wooden ears*.[114] If these bear only coincidental resemblance to the European cap and bells of the jester, the *vidusaka* is

Figure 33 Vidusaka

nevertheless a delightful and convincing court jester in his own right and part of a wider body of evidence for the existence of jesters in the courts of India.

ACT 6: MODERN TIMES

> The prevalence of fool figures on the modern stage is so great that this image may very likely constitute the central "concrete poetic image" of man in the twentieth century. Certainly the fool has found a resonance in the modern imagination which he has not enjoyed for four hundred years.
>
> Ellanor Pruitt,
> "The Figure of the Fool in Contemporary Theatre"[115]

Although the court jester disappeared from the European stage from the seventeenth century, he has reappeared in modern Western drama, as well as in other spheres of art and literature, pointing to a renaissance of his popularity in Western society that has been building up for perhaps the past 150 years.[116] Archy, jester to James I and Charles I, kicks off the trend in *Charles the First* (1824), a dramatic fragment by Shelley in which Charles gives an eloquent speech in defense of his jester when Archbishop Laud complains about his subversive mockery:

> What, my Archy?
> He mocks and mimics all he sees and hears,
> Yet with a quaint and graceful licence. . . .

He lives in his own world; and, like a parrot . . .
Blasphemes with a bird's mind: his words, like arrows
Which know no aim beyond the archer's wit,
Strike sometimes what eludes philosophy. . . .
He weaves about himself a world of mirth
Out of the wreck of ours.

(360)[117]

On the modern French stage there are several instances of real court jesters' serving as inspiration for a theatrical fool, all in plays by Victor Hugo: Triboulet in *Le roi s'amuse* (1832), which became the basis for Verdi's *Rigoletto;* the four jesters in *Cromwell* (1827), who is said to have kept jesters in real life; and Angeli, the last jester at the French court, in *Marion de Lorme* (1829).[118] As a depiction of a court jester Hugo's Triboulet is not very convincing, and perhaps he used him only to lend added pathos to the tragedy. The jester himself says very little that singles him out as a funnyman.

Cromwell has four fools who dress in different versions of the jester's motley complete with cap and bells. Each carries a wooden sword, and Trick also has the jester's *marotte.* They all sing, and one of Trick's songs has the topsy-turvy element of the jester, turning the world's norms on their head with "Pygmy titans and giant dwarfs" ("Titans pygmées, / Et nains géants!") (1:641). The jesters mock the Puritans, saying that it is the duty of every jester to make a thorough study of Puritan jargon: "Il faut que tout bouffon / Du jargon puritain fasse une étude à fond" (1:646).

They think Charles II would be less boring than Cromwell and reassure themselves that if Cromwell does not need them anymore they have only to wait for Charles to become king again ("Soyez tranquilles tous. / Que Charles deux revienne, il lui faudra des fous") (1:651). They have very little exchange with Cromwell, and most of their dialogues are with each other: "Hey! Each to his own. He reigns, we laugh" ("Hé! chacun nos métiers. / Il règne: nous rions") (1:650). They stress the irony of their being the fools who are less foolish than their master:

> *Elespuru.* We, the fools of Cromwell!
> *Gramadoch.* Ill spoken, Elespuru. We are his jesters, but he is
> our fool.

> [*Elespuru.* Nous, les fous de Cromwell!
> *Gramadoch.* Mal dit, Elespuru.
> Nous sommes ses bouffons; mais il est notre fou.]

(1:651)

Their presence seems to be more to edify than to amuse the audience, for although they have the appearance of jesters, and caper and sing, their words are not generally funny. They are also uncharacteristic in that they observe Cromwell while feeling little but scorn for him. Looking at the fools of *Cromwell* and *Le roi s'amuse*, it seems Hugo did not have a very good grasp of what made them tick—his jesters lack the wit, warmth, and color of many of their literary and historical colleagues and seem bland and two-dimensional in comparison.

Angeli in *Marion de Lorme* does not behave obviously like a jester until the scene he shares with the king (4.8): "Come. You who are never frightened of my majesty, / Light in my soul a ray of gaiety" ("Viens.— Toi qui n'as jamais peur de ma majesté, / Fais luire dans mon âme un rayon de gaîté"). However, he does later rise to the requirements of a jester in a powerful speech that obtains a reprieve for two people about to be executed (1:1098).

Another early example of the revival of the court jester on stage is Alfred de Musset's *Fantasio* (1833). The play features two court jesters: St. John, who has died but who lives on in the memory of the princess, and Fantasio, a down-and-out dandy who steps into St. John's shoes to avoid creditors. St. John was physically more of a jester than Fantasio, who has to wear a wig and pretend to be a hunchback to look the part. The princess was very close to the old jester, and her tenderness to him is reminiscent of the warm relationship between Cordelia and Lear's fool. The king cannot believe she is mourning so much "the death of my fool? A hunchback court jester almost blind?" ("la mort de mon bouffon? d'un plaisant de Cour bossu et presque aveugle?") (278), but her governess understands her reasons (296), likening him to the historical jester Triboulet.[119]

On the German stage there was not much outside the *Fastnachtspiele* that resembled the court jester until the German romantics began to use jesters to mock German society in such plays as Ludwig Tieck's *Puss-in-Boots*, in which the court jester is something of a simpleton who can nevertheless occasionally outwit others; he is named after the folk fool Hanswurst. Georg Buchner's *Leonce and Lena* (1836) has Valerio as the jester for whom the power and weight of a Shakespearean court jester has been claimed.[120]

Valerio is not formally designated a jester, but he certainly acts the part. He is forever mocking and having his say, pointing out the folly of his masters, occasionally in the most point-blank terms: "Your Highness would seem to be well on the way to becoming a perfect head-case" (83).

He implies that the king is a cuckold, a favorite joke of Middle Eastern jesters. When Prince Leonce runs away, Valerio accompanies him as the Fool followed Lear on his wanderings. He is full of puns and wry comments and, like Lear's fool, thinks his master is mad although he refuses to abandon him (2.2). When Leonce works himself into a melancholic passion and decides to commit suicide, Valerio puts a stop to his melodramatic leanings, to the great disappointment of Leonce: "The fool has ruined everything with his yellow waistcoat and sky-blue breeches" (95).[121]

Frank Wedekind's *King Nicolo* (1901) has a dethroned king forced to disguise himself as a beggar and begin wandering with his daughter until the new king, Pietro, makes him his court jester in a speech that summarizes on the one hand the lowly status of the court jester and on the other his tremendous power in standing between the king and the rest of the world:

> There is a position next to the throne that until today I have left unfilled, since I did not wish to make room for folly, and for which even the greatest amount of wisdom is inadequate. You must take this post. You will have even less power or rights than the lowliest of my subjects, but your great thinking must stand between me and the people, between me and the royal counselors, and you will be allowed even to push with impunity between me and my child. . . . I appoint you my court jester—follow me!

> [Dicht naben dem Thron steht ein Posten leer, den ich bis heute unbesetzt ließ, weil ich der Torheit keinen Platz einräumen will, wo auch die größte Menge von Klugheit zu gering ist. Du aber sollst diesen Posten einnehmen. Rechtlos und machtlos sollst du sein gegenüber dem letzten Bürger meines Staates! Aber deine hohe Denkungsart soll zwischen mir und dem Volke stehen, zwischen mir und den Räten der Krone, sie soll sich ungestraft zwischen mich und mein Kind drängen dürfen. . . . Ich ernenne dich zu meinem Hofnarren.—Folge mir!] (1:581)[122]

In *Escurial*, by Michel de Ghelderode (1929), the jester Folial changes places with the king in a game. Then, in a most unjesterly fashion, Folial almost succeeds in having the king as "jester" strangled. During their role reversal, the "jester" confesses that he had the queen poisoned because he suspected she was having an affair with the real jester. After the queen dies, the roles revert and the real king has Folial strangled, then suffers pangs of regret: "My fool, my poor fool! . . . A queen, Father, is not hard to find, but a clown . . ." (178).[123]

Folial is a competent jester unafraid of his king, "I know how to speak to kings and to dogs" (167). The exchange of roles between the king and the jester is a recurrent theme. However, on a deeper level he contravenes some vital aspects of the jester's nature. A jester would not generally become deeply involved in the plot and intrigue of court life, although there are exceptions. A modern novel based on Shakespeare's *Hamlet* has Hamlet's mother involved in a rather sordid affair with Yorick, and there was one historical jester who lacked the existential detachment that is a defining characteristic of the jester.[124] The Chinese Jester Shi had an affair with one of the royal concubines, aiding and abetting her scheming both by advising her how to manipulate people and by using his jester's immunity on her behalf.[125]

The theme of the fool informs much of W. B. Yeats's writing, and fool characters occur in several of his plays. There is one who is like a jester, although he seems subordinate to no one and is almost godlike: Red Man in *The Green Helmet* (1910). He is a powerful character, a juggler and jester who suggests there is more to him than simply being the *passe-temps* performer of "a drinking joke and a gibe and a juggler's feat, that / is all / To make the time go quickly." He offers the green helmet of the title as a prize for the greatest king, perhaps showing something of the jester's right to judge the worth of a monarch. In the end he decides to bestow it on the third competing king, Cuchulain, giving as his criteria the qualities of a lover of life and a courageously laughing heart, qualities not alien to court jesters:

> And I choose the laughing lip
> That shall not turn from laughing, whatever rise or fall;
> The heart that grows no bitterer although betrayed by all;
> The hand that loves to scatter; the life like a gambler's throw;
> And these things I make prosper, till a day come that I know,
> When heart and mind shall darken that the weak may end the
> strong,
> And the long-remembering harpers have matter for their song.
>
> (243)[126]

More recently the jester has cropped up in a genre of play known as Holocaust drama, inspired by the hell of ghetto and concentration camp, with the fools driving the horror home all the more for their quirky, capering manner. Like real court jesters, they come in an assortment of physical deformities and mental oddities and use riddles, songs, puns, and poems to make their point. Yankele in Harold and Edith Lieberman's *Throne of Straw* (1972) runs rings around Rumkowski, the head of the Judenrat, who is convinced that cooperating with the Nazis will save the day. Dancing around him, Yankele challenges: "Court Jew, Council Jew. Do you think you can pull us through, this time?" (133–34). Rumkowski dismisses the mad jester: "Why must you make a fool of yourself in public?" and Yankele rebounds with, "So you don't fool the public and yourself?" (134). He is dismissed as a mindless fool by the chief of the Jewish police:

> *Rabinowitz.* We all know what's in your mind: nothing.
> *Yankele.* Nothing? Nothing is more corrupting than the illusion of
> power. [To Rumkowski] Your plumage casts no shadow and
> your throne is made of straw.
>
> (134)

Yankele mockingly mimics Rumkowski's assertion that if they comply with Nazi demands and keep people healthy enough to work and therefore be of use, everything will work out:

> "Don't listen to irresponsible voices
> They'll only get you in trouble."
> Just follow blindly all his orders
> And your trouble will be double.
> *(He dances a mime of meek obedience.)*
> But some of his subjects won't buy it
> They weren't about to stay quiet
> So he found a sure way to keep their mouths shut
> By increasing everyone's diet.
> *(Speaks directly to the audience.)*
> After all—a full mouth can't scream.[127]

In Shimon Wincelberg's *Resort 76* (ca. 1964), another Holocaust jester cracks more jokes and is closer to the archetypal jester in appearance, wearing motley rags while he himself is "a small, bent, hook-nosed man with a wild, wiry shock of red hair and the large, staring, shrewd, hooded eyes and nutcracker jaws of a Punch puppet" (43).[128] The play is set in the Lodz ghetto and is an adaptation of a work by a survivor of the ghetto. It is the fool who sees most clearly the writing on the wall and who laughs loudest about it. One character has enough Aryan blood to be released from the ghetto and falls down in thankful prayer while Yablonka quips,

"Ah, if my poor parents had known what a useful thing it would be one day to be baptized . . . they would have held me under till I drowned" (104). Like a good jester, he never loses his sense of humor, no matter how grim life is:

> *Krause.* Will you leave me alone, you old idiot?
>
> *Yablonka.* Sir, I may be an idiot, but I'm not old. There's some uncertainty about my age, because I had a brother who looked just like me, and to this day even I am not sure which one of us was shot during the roundup. It could be *I'm* the one who's dead, and my mother didn't have the heart to tell me.
>
> (47)

EPILOGUE

> Another actor said, "When I was young and was learning the actor's art, my master used to say to me, "Take heed and learn well how thou mayest become used to do the exact opposite of the words which are spoken to thee, that is to say, if people say unto thee, Go, thou must come, and when they say unto thee, Come, thou must go." And in the morning he himself used to say, "Good evening," and in the evening, "Good morning." And it came to pass one day that having been into the king's presence and made him laugh, the king commanded them to write him an order on the Treasury to give him a thousand pieces of silver.
>
> Gregory Jan Mar Bar-Hebraeus,
> *The Laughable Stories* (thirteenth century) [129]

This Middle Eastern anecdote sums up the overlap of the actor and the jester in court—actors often displayed qualities of the court jester whether by acting his part on stage or by using his techniques to have their say. Two Italian court jesters had nicknames that also reflected the crossover —Dolcibene, jester to Holy Roman Emperor Charles IV of Bohemia, was known as "King of the Jesters and Actors of Italy" ("re dei buffoni e delli istrioni d'Italia"), and Scocola, the great jester of Ferrara, was called the "Sweetest Actor" ("soavissimo istrione"). Luzio and Renier comment that it is sometimes hard to distinguish between the actor and the jester, and they refer to Ercole Albergati, jester to the marchioness of Mantua and also an inventor of theatrical tricks and no mediocre actor. [130]

In drama the court jester or clown was often a bridge between the characters in the play and the audience. He belonged to the play and often had a central role in it, but he was also detached, and his asides could make it seem he was more aware of the presence of an audience than any of the other characters. This is exactly what court jesters did in real life—they could be at the nub of the action and then suddenly stand outside it with their dispassionate observations.

In Europe the court jester and the stage jester existed more or less side by side. In France and Germany there were amateur fool activities and societies, either taking part in carnivals or putting on dramatic productions. France had highly visible amateur fool societies from the late Middle Ages based on locality or profession, and these were largely responsible for performing the satirical fool plays, the *sotties.* Although medieval England also had amateur fools, albeit more loosely organized than in France, the connection between the court jester and the stage flourished most vibrantly from the Renaissance, reaching its apogee in the jesters of Shakespeare. The last notable court jester in England, Tom Killigrew, had his feet firmly planted in both camps, even though all around him were signs of the jester's declining fortunes in both arenas. In India too the court jester seems to have existed concomitantly with the stage jester, the *vidusaka,* although it is not clear that they were interchangeable in the same way that some European and Chinese jesters were, skipping from court to stage and back again.

In ancient Greece and Rome it could be argued that the comic mimes *were* the principal court jesters. Not only might they be invited to provide impromptu entertainment at the banquets of the wealthy, they were also more than willing to shout their extemporized mockeries of influential people from the stage even when they could be severely punished for it. In Rome, when punishment meant exile, they strode out of the city and made their way across the empire, thereby perhaps sowing the seeds of the medieval armies of entertainers—jesters in particular. In addition, many of the functions, techniques, and attitudes of court jesters can be seen in the quick-lipped slaves of Plautus.

If the Roman comic mimes can be posited as the precursors of the court jester in Europe, in China the reverse might be true. The Chinese jesters relied more than jesters elsewhere on the dramatic medium of short, unscripted playlets or skits to convey their jesting correctives and gratuitous mockery. In this respect they were always closer to being actors than European jesters, who tended to address their monarchs singly and without recourse to dramatic constructs.

There are numerous Chinese jesters who did this too, but a large number of anecdotes about them are of a collective nature and have something of protodrama about them, contributing to the foundations of a full-blown theatrical tradition. With the rise of a fully developed dramatic art in China, the court jester started to merge with the professional theater and household actor. He in his turn took up the jester's baton right into the twentieth century, unlike the European theatrical court jesters, who followed their real counterparts and faded from view for a while before reemerging with a vengeance in the past two centuries.

Interestingly, the order of appearance in China (jesters first, actors later) is matched in Samoa. In the past, high chiefs each had one or two "quick flyers" *(salelelisi)* who had the official license accorded jesters elsewhere and who would attach themselves to a chief as they felt like it. There are no longer any such formal jesters, but the theater of Samoa does have a genre of comic interlude called "house of the spirits" *(fale aitu)*, performed in the same way as the Chinese jester skits or the Commedia dell'Arte plays, with a plot being worked out orally and then rehearsed and performed with a great deal of improvisation. The leading comedian is thought to be a phantom, "for it is the ghost who delivers the punchlines which carry social or political criticism home to the particular figure(s) being lampooned."[131] A novel way of acquiring a jester's license to mock with impunity—pretend to be dead.

The place of the court jester on stage was as important as his place in real court life, even if it was less long-lived. There is perhaps no better persona in whom to invest existential questioning and impartial observation —jesters are adept at being involved and detached simultaneously, living at the very heart of the action while remaining in a symbolic sense peripheral: "Every organism, whether individual, corporate, natural or political, needs to be challenged and renewed continually in order to survive, and artists, in their portrayals of this process or its failure, have frequently assigned the role of harbinger of the process to a court fool figure of some sort."[132]

The Fool is not a philosophy, but a quality of consciousness of life, an endless regard for human identity; all this lives in the fun of the Fool. The Fool is the essential poetic integrity of life itself, clear and naked, overflowing in cosmic fun; not the product of intellectual achievement, but a creation of the culture of the heart. A culture of the genius of life. I believe that there is in life, and in the human psyche, a certain quality, an inviolate eternal innocence, and this quality I call the Fool. It is a continuous wisdom and compassion that heals with fun and magic. It is the joy of the original Adam in men.

Cecil Collins, *The Vision of the Fool* [1]

Old Baldy Chun-yu laughed like hell, the King of Qi ran riot
   beyond belief;
Jester Meng shook his head in song and the firewood-hawker
   picked up a fief.
One shout from Jester Twisty Pole and wretched guards gained
   sweet relief.
Were all these not great men too?!!

Sima Qian, "Biographies of Jesters" [2]

7

Stultorum Plena Sunt Omnia, or Fools Are Everywhere

A CAVALCADE OF CAVORTING FOOLS

Foolery, sir, does walk about the orb like the sun, it shines everywhere.
William Shakespeare, *Twelfth Night* (3.1.39–40)

We have all seen how an appropriate and well-timed joke can sometimes influence even grim tyrants. . . . The most violent tyrants put
up with their clowns and fools, though these often made them the
butt of open insults.
Desiderius Erasmus, *Praise of Folly*[3]

The court jester is a universal phenomenon.[4] He crops up in every court
worth its salt in medieval and Renaissance Europe, in China, India, Japan,
Russia, America and Africa. A cavalcade of jesters tumble across centuries
and continents, and one could circle the globe tracing their footsteps. But
to China the laurels. China has undoubtedly the longest, richest, and most
thoroughly documented history of court jesters. From Twisty Pole and
Baldy Chunyu to Moving Bucket and Newly Polished Mirror, it boasts
perhaps more of the brightest stars in the jester firmament than any other
country, spanning a far wider segment of time (figs. 35 and 36). The jester's
decline began with the rise of the stage actor as the Chinese theater became
fully established during the Yuan dynasty. In many respects actors seem to
have taken up the jester's baton not only in entertaining their patrons, but
also in offering criticism and advice no less clear for being couched in wit.
Perhaps only in ancient Rome did jesters and actors overlap so much.

In comparison with those of China, the numerous jesters of Europe,
although flourishing for some four hundred years, are something of a daz-
zling display of shooting stars. Perhaps because the European court jesters

Figure 34 Folly governeth the world . . .

were so inextricably linked with the tradition of folly that straddled the Middle Ages and the Renaissance, their time was relatively short-lived, and they died out more or less as the fashion for folly faded. But for as long as they lasted, which was no mere blip, their influence permeated court life. It is a common belief that Europe was the center of the court jester's cosmos, providing the control against which other jesters, such as they are, may be measured. Yet in a sense Europe is the exception rather than the rule, precisely because the fortunes of the European court jesters rose and

Figure 35, 36 A Chinese jester?

fell with the tsunami-scale wave of medieval and Renaissance fool mania that engulfed the Continent. The concept of folly with all its variegated hues permeated Europe at all levels for several centuries, and it is against this backdrop of colorful and often contradictory manifestations of "folly" that the European jester must be seen. There were certainly jesters before the tidal wave began to swell, but it is on its crest that we see them come surfing in.

Within Europe, I have placed greatest emphasis on the jesters of England and France, although it is hard to think of a country that did not have them. In Italy the great families of the principal city-states kept jesters—the Medicis, Sforzas, and d'Estes—while some popes also were enthusiastic jester keepers. There are anecdotes pointing to jesters in Austria, Bohemia, Holland, Hungary, Ireland, Poland, Portugal, Russia, and Scotland as well as indications that the Scandinavian courts fostered them.[5] Jesters thrived in Germany, where the medieval obsession with folly was perhaps most deeply ingrained, whereas in both Italy and Spain they seem to have flourished more with the Renaissance, when the vogue for dwarfs and jesters, natural or artificial, reached fever pitch.

In Spain their popularity was recorded primarily in art, with Velázquez leading the pack (fig. 37), and even the Italians—themselves no laggards in their enthusiasm—were astonished at the mania for them there.[6] A Castilian dictionary of 1674 says that *truhanes,* the term used for artificial fools in Spanish, were "admitted to the palaces of kings and the houses of great lords and have license to say whatever pleases them, even the truth" ("admitido en los palacios de los reyes, y en las casas de los grandes señores,

Figure 37 A Velázquez natural (detail sketch)

y tiene licencia de dezir lo que se le antojare, aunque es verdad").[7] Nobles from the provinces wishing to make an impression at court would keep open table for courtiers, during which "it was also considered politic to honour the royal buffoons" because of the influence they could exercise.[8]

A town might have a jester who would be salaried rather than being the equivalent of the ubiquitous village idiot. For several centuries a number of French towns, principally Lille, paid somebody an annual fee to act as jester during festivities or public ceremonies, and he would lead any religious or carnivalesque processions. Such a person could belong to the town's wealthy bourgeoisie. Those towns that could not afford to maintain a jester would simply hire the services of one for the period of the festival.[9] The custom of municipal fools flourished even more widely in Germany, where the "trick player" (Possenreisser) was in charge of farcical entertainments and the "saying sayer" (Spruchsprecher) was expected to amuse the audience with satirical couplets.[10]

Professional guilds were known to appoint a guild jester, and a tavern might also have a jester who would be provided with free meals if he could attract more clients, a famous example being John Stone, who entertained drinkers in a tavern in Elizabethan London.[11] There was even a regimental jester (Lustig) in the eighteenth-century Swiss army who would march at the front of the soldiers, making them laugh, cajoling them out of deserting, and cheering them up when the food, the irons, or the arrogance of their officers wore them down.[12]

In other parts of the world there have existed many of the ideas about folly found in Europe during the Middle Ages and the Renaissance. Perhaps the idea of the fool as a sinner is more uniquely a product of Christianity, but the potential sanctity and occasional lucidity of madness, the paradox of the wisdom of folly, and the value of allowing certain members of society the right to turn the world on its head are concepts by no means alien to other cultures. Confucius was admonished by a madman whose words were included in the major Confucian classic. Holy fools were widespread, and many Daoist and Zen Buddhist monks seem to have had something of the jester in their mirthful irreverence toward authority and their refusal to follow the crowd. Court jesters and ritual clowns everywhere have enjoyed all the license granted to the European jester shielded by his "folly."

Outside Europe, however, these ideas existed alongside others over millennia, being durably but less densely woven into the fabric of society. The closest parallels to Europe in having madmen as jesters, or men feigning madness, can be found in the courts of caliphs and sultans.[13] But

Figure 38 Gopal strikes again

Europe seems unique in the intensity of its obsession with the concept of folly, which in a sense "burned out," though not without leaving its mark. If the jester disappeared from court, he did not disappear from society, which continued to enjoy the antics and surprises of the fool and madman—in the mountebank, the clown of the fair, or the bedlamite.

Stories about court jesters abound in India, with drama, folktales and comic books (fig. 38) providing a wealth of evidence to support accounts of jesters such as Birbal or Gopal. The distinction between the historical and the legendary is not always clear, but that does not detract from the exuberance or deep-rootedness of the Indian jester tradition, and Siegel notes that "it's safe to assume that, yes, of course there were court jesters in India."[14] Pierre Loti gives a curious description of a jester at Agra as having a white marble stool to complement the mogul's black marble throne.[15]

Like India, the Middle East has a handful of jester giants to whom all jokes may be attributed and all tricks credited, such as the Turkish Nasrudin and his Arab twin Juha (or Juhi, d. 777), or the Persian Talhak (tenth century) and the Arab Ash'ab (d. 771). As with India and China, I hope that a more widespread awareness of these jesters will help obliterate a frequent Western tendency to view these huge civilizations as having somehow lacked humor. Baghdad in the first two centuries of the Abbasid caliphate (750–1258) was a hotbed of humor, as were Medina and Hijaz, and this heat radiated across the Middle Eastern world—Turkey's Suleiman the Magnificent (r. 1520–66), who ruled during the zenith of artistic, literary, and architectural achievement in the Ottoman Empire, kept jesters, and when Benjamin Disraeli visited Egypt in 1831 he saw Pasha Mohammed Ali relaxing with his jester.[16]

The most renowned jester keepers in this part of the world were undoubtedly Sultan Mahmud of Ghazna, who carved out large swaths of territory for himself and laid the foundations for the Mogul dynasty in India and is usually paired up with Talhak, and the Abbasid caliph Harun al-Rashid, who is linked with Buhlul. Less well known but perhaps more instrumental in encouraging humor and jesterdom was al-Muttawakkil (r. 847–61), during whose caliphate "the number of humorists and jesters increases . . . and their profession acquires prestige" and whose favorite jester, ʿUbada al-Mukhannath (d. 864), like Baldy Chunyu, and countless European fools, was bald as well as ribald and would caper gaily around the caliph to amuse him.[17]

In Japan the terms *kami* (a god) or *massha* (small shrine) originally referred to the attendants of wealthy men but later came to mean jester. The most common terms for the jester were "drum-carrier" *(taikomochi)* or *hokan,* a figure who from the late seventeenth century could be found in the brothel quarters or "nightless city": "As soon as the party gets livened up from the effects of liquor, and the feasting has begun to flag, the jesting and buffoonery of the *hokan* waxes fast and furious and is accompanied by droll contortions and gesticulations."[18] It seems their status declined with time, although such jesters continued to exist into the twentieth century.

These Japanese jesters do not seem to have shared the court jester's license to offer censure or advice, and it is not clear to what extent the *taikomochi* of the brothel had counterparts in court. Apart from them and Sorori, who seemed to act as a full-fledged jester to Hideyoshi, there is little evidence available concerning the jester in Japan. It is not certain that the institution of jester was confined to red-light districts, or that no details of them were recorded: there is apparently a wealth of material from the Edo period (1603–1868) that concerns jesters but that is allegedly impenetrable even to Japanese scholars.[19] Despite the paucity of evidence, I would hazard an intuitive guess that there were court jesters in Japan, and I hope that Japanese scholars may be inspired to start digging.

The film *Ran,* by Akira Kurosawa, which takes the story of *King Lear* and transplants it to medieval Japan, depicts the jester with such power and understanding that it seems unlikely the director would not have drawn on an indigenous tradition for some of his inspiration. In addition there is an obscure reference in an early seventeenth-century travelogue to a jester serving the king of an island near southern Japan: "The king of Firando

[has] a comedian or a jester to give him delight."[20] The impression that the Japanese were not impassive toward jesters is confirmed by an anecdote recounted by Flögel describing a group of ten Dutchmen captured in Japan, probably during the seventeenth century. They were each given two cups of wine to drink and then asked to behave like jesters before state counselors. They had to contort their faces, mock each other and look about wildly, crack foolish jokes, and walk around with their feet askew. The motive behind this curious order is not clear: perhaps the Japanese just wanted to have a laugh at the expense of the Westerners. We are not told how the Dutch felt about it, but the state counselors had a whale of a time.[21]

In ancient Greece and Rome the functions of the jester were fulfilled mostly by comic mime actors both on stage, where their improvisations might mock the audience or make some punning jibe at leading figures, and in a more direct sense of providing humorous and witty entertainment at the homes of the aristocracy. Slaves and parasites could also take on these aspects of the jester, but it is perhaps principally in the mimes that we see the precursors of the European court jester with his cap and bells.

In Greece there was the "laughter maker" *(gelatopoios),* a term reflected in the English word "gelastic," laughable, and in the name given to two theatrical court jesters called Gelasimus. Xenophon's *Symposium* features Philippus, the jester who began by cracking a series of jokes that fell so flat he was reduced to tears, lamenting the humorlessness of his hosts. Then, trying a different tack, he "fell to capering madly, tossing legs and arms and head together, until he was fairly tired out." He collapsed exhausted on a sofa and asked for wine, which was brought since his audience was also "parched with laughing."[22]

Although the jester died out as a court institution (if not as a function), about the sixteenth or seventeenth century in China and the early eighteenth in Europe, there have been pockets of resistance to his demise. European homes less grand than those of kings and prelates harbored jesters for a century or two longer than the courts, a domestic jester being recorded at Hilton Castle in county Durham in the eighteenth century and a Scottish jester, Shemus Anderson (d. 1833), at Murthley Castle, Perthshire. The Queen Mother's family, the Bowes-Lyons, was "the last Scottish family to maintain a full-time jester."[23] A history of the manor of Gawsworth describes a Samuel Johnson (1691–1773) as "one of the last of the paid English jesters. . . . In addition to his being employed as jester or mirth-maker by the manorial Lord of Gawsworth, he was a welcome addition at parties given by the neighbouring country families, when he had free license to bandy his witticisms, and to utter and enact anything likely to enliven the company, and to provoke mirth and laughter."[24]

In Persia the autocratic Shah Naseredin (r. 1848–96) had all his courtiers quaking except the jester Karim Shir'ei, whose name means "opium addict" but also implies someone of lazy or sleepy demeanor. Karim Shir'ei would ridicule the whole court, including the shah. Once the shah asked whether there was a shortage of food, and the jester said "Yes, I see Your Majesty is eating only five times a day." One member of the shah's entourage had the title Saheb Ekhtiyar ("Authorized" [by the shah]). When they were out traveling Karim Shir'ei's donkey stopped at a gate, and the jokester found a pretext to mock the courtier by addressing the ass: "If you want to stop you are Saheb Ekhtiyar [authorized], and if you want to go ahead, you are also Saheb Ekhtiyar [authorized]." Like many famous jesters before him, his name is still used as a peg for jibes and jokes.[25]

The courts of the Hospodars of Moldavia and Walachia kept jesters, usually Armenians, until the beginning of the nineteenth century.[26] Other recent court jesters have been described by Victorian travelers such as J. J. Jusserand, who visited the Maghreb, and Frederick Millingen, who spent time in northern Kurdistan:

> The Bey of Tunis, when I was there years ago, had fools to amuse him in the evening, who insulted and diverted him by the contrast between their permitted insolence and his real power. Among the rich Moslem women of the same city, few of whom could read, the monotony of days spent by them till death came under the shadow of the same walls, behind the same gratings, was broken by the tales of the female fool, whose duty was to enliven the harem by sallies of the strangest liberty.[27]

> Buffoonery and jokes of all sorts are very much in favour amongst the Koords, every chief having a buffoon whose duty is to keep the company merry. The Mudir of Kotur had two of these fellows, one a short and queer-looking individual called Mollah Yassin, the other a man of the name of Hadji-Khan, who was clever enough to feign to be an idiot.[28]

Another Victorian traveler, Sir Charles Dilke, described a jester belonging to a Maori chief in New Zealand, licensed to speak freely though running the risk of an occasional thwack, referring to "Porea, the jester, a half-mad buffoon, continually mimicking the chiefs and interrupting them, and being by them or their messengers as often kicked and cuffed."[29]

Although little work has been done on the subject, it seems that when Europeans first came into contact with Polynesian societies they found that some powerful chiefs also kept jesters, "court buffoons who, by oddity in dress, gait, or gesture, or by lascivious jokes, tried to excite laughter."[30] More recently Frederick Ponsonby, who worked closely with Edward VII (r. 1901–10), tells us that Chevalier Martino was officially kept as the court marine painter, "but the real reason was that he was a sort of court jester, a butt for the king's jokes. . . . Like all jesters he was really a very shrewd man, but he liked being singled out for the king's wit."[31]

Perhaps the most recent examples of the court jester are among the ritual clowns of African and American tribes whose mocking, corrective, and unbridled topsy-turvy antics have been documented by twentieth-century anthropologists. These are not all strictly speaking court jesters, in that they do not usually serve one master, belonging more to the whole tribe or village. Also, their license is often limited to specific periods, although during such festivals or rituals their freedoms and duties accord with those of the permanently privileged jester. However, there are some tribes that have had permanently appointed jesters, such as the African Wolof jesters and the Sioux "contrary," or *heyhoka*,[32] and "jesters . . . were also attached to many African monarchs. They were frequently dwarfs, and other oddities; and their duties included besides the playing of jokes, the singing of the praises of their rulers. . . . 'But it must not be thought that these bards were mere flatterers . . . they also had licence to make sharp criticisms.'"[33]

The court jester is universal not merely in having been at home in such diverse cultures and eras, but also in taking his pick from the same ragbag of traits and talents no matter when or where he occurs. Above all he used humor, whether in the form of wit, puns, riddles, doggerel verse, songs, capering antics, or nonsensical babble, and jesters were usually also musical or poetic or acrobatic, and sometimes all three. Some physical difference from the norm was common whether it was in being a dwarf or hunchback or in having a gawky or gangly physique or a loose-limbed agility—his movements might be clumsy or nimble, but they should be somehow exaggerated or unusual. There is a Ming dynasty description of a jester that captures this, for besides always hitting the mark with his gilded tongue, he would "unleash his body and fling his limbs around, drumming his feet and flapping his tongue; he was steeped in wisdom."[34] "Capering" is the word that springs to mind, perhaps a physical reflection of his verbal agility:

I have seen
Him caper upright, like a wild morisco
Shaking . . . his bells.[35]

There is a jester-actor in Cervantes' *Don Quijote de la Mancha* (1604) whose capering makes Don Quixote's horse Rocinante bolt, taking the knight with him. Cervantes' description captures his unconstrained ebullience:

> Now, whilst they were engaged in this conversation, as Fate would have it, one of the company caught them up, dressed in motley with a lot of bells about him, and carrying three full blown ox-bladders on the end of a stick. When this clown came up to Don Quixote, he began to fence with his stick, to beat the ground with his bladders, and leap into the air to the sound of his bells; and this evil apparition so scared Rocinante that he took the bit between his teeth, and started to gallop across the field with more speed than the bones of his anatomy promised.
>
> [Estando en estas pláticas, quiso la suerte que llegase uno de la companía, que venía vestido de bigiganga, con muchos cascabeles, y en la punta de un palo traía tres vejigas de vaca hinchadas; el qual moharracho, llegándose a don Quijote, comenzó a esgrimir el palo y a sacudir el suelo con las vejigas, y a dar grandes saltos, sonando las cascabeles; cuya mala visión así alborotó a Rocinante, que, sin ser poderoso a detenerle don Quijote, tomando el frene entre los dientes, dio a correr por el campo con más ligereza que jamás prometieron los huesos de su notomía.][36]

The Importance of Being Jest Earnest

But this Will Summers was of an easie nature, and tractable disposition, who . . . gained not only grace and favour from his Majesty, but a general love of the Nobility; for he was no carry-tale, nor whisperer, nor flattering insinuater, to breed discord and dissension, but an honest plain down-right, that would speak home without halting, and tell the truth of purpose to shame the Devil; so that his plainness mixt with a kind of facetiousness, and tartness with pleasantness made him very acceptable into the companies of all men.

A Pleasant History of the Life and Death of Will Summers (1676)[37]

> In short, the King liked him so well, that he did few Things without
> Archy's Advice, in so much, that he could have scarce had greater
> Power had he been made Regent of the Kingdom.
>
> *The Ass Race* (1740)[38]

Of at least equal importance with his entertainer's cap was the jester's
function as adviser and critic. This is what distinguishes him from a pure
entertainer who would juggle batons, swallow swords, or strum on a lute
or a clown who would play the fool simply to amuse people. The jester
everywhere employed the same techniques to carry out this delicate role,
and it would take an obtuse king or emperor not to realize what he was
driving at, since "other court functionaries cooked up the king's facts for
him before delivery; the jester delivered them raw."[39] An informal survey
of the man in the street has shown that most people will pinpoint the
jester's right to speak his mind as one of his salient characteristics. I have
encountered only one person who considers this to have been more myth
than reality:

> There are many stories which show a jester as the only person who
> could counsel a stubborn king, and as such the myth of the court
> jester suggests that jesters could act as a check on the whimsical
> power of absolute monarchy. . . . I have been engaged in producing
> and reproducing a common myth of jesters. Even though the jest-
> ers dance right next to the power of the king, the text has been de-
> politicized in that it has effaced the history of the fool, and elabo-
> rated on images conjured up by Erasmus, then Shakespeare, in the
> task of making jesting reasonable and responsible, and thus political
> in modern times. . . . The respected, responsible, official jesters only
> functioned in small historical windows of possibility, for example:
> fourteenth and fifteenth century Italy and around the turn of the
> seventeenth century in England.[40]

Even if the jester's famous veracity were only a myth, it would have
been established long before Erasmus. And we have seen the impressive
extent to which jesters everywhere were allowed and encouraged to offer
counsel and to influence the whims and policies of kings, by no means being limited to "small historical windows of possibility." We have seen numerous examples of a jester advising or correcting his monarch and the
recorded instances are particularly abundant in China. The Chinese records give us an idea of just how effective a jester could be in tempering

the ruler's excesses, for the occasions when his words of warning were either ignored or punished are heavily outnumbered by those when he was heeded and even rewarded.

It is in the nature of jesters to speak their minds when the mood takes them, regardless of the consequences. They are neither calculating nor circumspect, and this may account for the "foolishness" often ascribed to them. Jesters are also generally of inferior social and political status and are rarely in a position (and rarely inclined) to pose a power threat. They have little to gain by caution and little to lose by candor—apart from liberty, livelihood, and occasionally even life, which hardly seems to have been a deterrent. They are peripheral to the game of politics, and this can reassure a king that their words are unlikely to be geared to their own advancement. Jesters are not noted for flattery or fawning. The ruler can be isolated from his courtiers and ministers, who might conspire against him. The jester too can be an isolated and peripheral figure somehow detached from the intrigues of the court, and this enables him to act as a kind of confidant.

The jester also had humor at his disposal. He could soften the blow of a critical comment in a way that prevented a dignified personage from losing face. Humor is the great defuser of tense situations. Among the Murngin tribe of Australia it is the duty of the clown to act outrageously, ludicrously imitating a fight if men begin to quarrel. In making them laugh at him, he distracts their attention from their own fight and dispels their aggression.[41] Quintilian (ca. 35–100) comments on the power of jesters' humor to carry the day:

> Now, though laughter may be regarded as a trivial matter, and an emotion frequently awakened by buffoons, actors or fools, it has a certain imperious force of its own which it is very hard to resist. . . . it frequently turns the scale in matters of great importance.
>
> [Cum videatur autem res levis et quae ab scurris, mimis, insipientibus denique saepe moveatur, tamen habet vim nescio an imperiosissimam et cui repugnari minime potest. . . . Rerum autem saepe . . . maximarum momenta vertit.][42]

The foolishness of the jester, whether in his odd appearance or his levity, implies that he is not passing judgment from on high, and this may be less galling than the "holier than thou" corrective of an earnest adviser. One of the most effective techniques the jester uses to point out his master's folly is allowing him to see it for himself. Rather than contradicting the king, the jester will agree with a harebrained scheme so wholeheartedly that the suggestion is taken to a logical extreme, highlighting its stupidity. The king can then decide for himself that maybe it wasn't such a good idea after all.

The jester is in a sense on the side of the ruler. The relationship was often very close and amiable, and the jester was almost invariably a cherished rather than a tolerated presence. This leads to the kindliness of jesters: they could be biting in their attacks, but there is usually an undercurrent of good-heartedness and understanding to their words. If they talk the king out of slicing up some innocent, it is not only to save him from the king's wrath but also to save the king from himself—they can be the only ones who will tell him he suffers from moral halitosis.

The jester is also perceived as being on the side of the people, the little man fighting oppression by the powerful. By fooling wisely ("en folastrant sagement"), the jester often won favor among the people ("gaigna de grace parmy le peuple").[43] In the folk perception of southern India a king was hardly considered a king without his jester, and the continuing appeal of the court jester in India, in stories and comic books, is perhaps equaled only in Europe. He may have disappeared from the courts and corridors of power, but he still has a powerful hold on the collective imagination. Yet he is no rebel or revolutionary. His detached stance allows him to take the side of the victim in order to curb the excesses of the system without ever trying to overthrow it—his purpose is not to replace one system with another, but to free us from the fetters of all systems:

> Under the dissolvent influence of his personality the iron network
> of physical, social and moral law, which enmeshes us from the cradle
> to the grave, seems—for the moment—negligible as a web of gossamer. The Fool does not lead a revolt against the Law, he lures us
> into a region of the spirit where, as Lamb would put it, the writ does
> not run.[44]

In Europe and India the most eminent jesters were household names, as top-class comedians are today, and stories about their jokes and tricks circulated freely, as they still do in India—there is even a kind of lentil soup named after Birbal.[45] The star jesters of China may also have enjoyed this celebrity status, as Ban Gu's biography of Dongfang Shuo suggests:

> Shuo's jokes and sallies, his divinations and guesses, shallow and inconsequential though they are, were passed around among the ordi-

nary run of people, and there was no stripling or cowherd who failed to be quite dazzled by them.

朔之詼諧，逢占射覆，其事浮淺，行於眾庶，童兒牧豎莫不眩耀！[46]

"Fond Fuill Quhair Hes Thou Bene Sa Lait?" Decline and Fall?

David Lyndsay, *Ane Satyre of the Thrie Estaits*

"What! Is he really dead? Impossible! He is feigning! See the smile on his face!" said he. Then, shaking him, he cried out, "Friend, get up and speak to your friend. You cannot be dead, you who had such a joy of life!"

Tenali Rama[47]

During the seventeenth century the court jester vanished first from the English stage, where he had had a brief but resplendent career, and then from the court. The jester's entertainment value in both France and England was perhaps taken over, as in China, partly by scripted plays performed by professional actors, together with their improvisations. There are no doubt many reasons for his demise, including the rise of the theater, changes in fashion, and perhaps an increase in printed entertainment. In addition, there was a change in attitude with the Age of Reason that may have precluded a prancing, prating, but not obviously rational creature. However, even if the jester vanished from European courts, he did not vanish from society, and he lived on in fairgrounds, market squares, and carnivals.[48] *Saltimbanques,* latter-day jack-of-all-jester-trades entertainers, frequented public places, and mountebanks meandered from town to town, usually assisted by a jester who would mock the mountebank and show him up for the quack he was—mountebanks may have made more money by amusing than by curing the audience.

Brusquet, one of the most famous French court jesters, began his career as a quack doctor, and when there were accusations that his remedies had sent patients to an early grave, he pointed out that none of the dead had complained about their treatment and that their fevers had been permanently cured: "Ceux-là qui sont morts se plaignent-ils? Et ne sont-ils pas guéris de la fièvre à perpetuité?"[49] Till Eulenspiegel also did time as a hokum-locum, though he had no idea what he was doing (fig. 40). Tom Killigrew, one of England's finest jesters, once condescended to act the

Figure 39 Decline and fall?

quack, climbing onto a mountebank's stage to impersonate him for a joke. A gentleman in the audience promised him five guineas if he could cure his servant of two shortcomings: a short memory and a lying tongue. Killigrew concocted two boluses, one to be eaten immediately, the other at supper. The servant ate the first:

> But as soon as he had put it in his mouth, he roars out, "Zounds, doctor, this is a turd!" "There, now," says Killigrew, "did I not tell you I'd cure him for you? You see the first word he speaks is truth; and I'll warrant he'll never forget it as long as he lives." [50]

There was a mountebank counterpart in both the ancient Greek and ancient Chinese theaters, where there are delightful skits of comic doctors showing no concern for the successful practice of their profession. In one case they divide the body like so much human territory to be fought over, each doctor applying what he considers the best medicine to his half of the hapless patient, arguing all the while. A scene from a Chinese play of the late thirteenth or early fourteenth century has Doctors Finishmeoff and Muddly Head as the shameless lucre-lusting charlatans:

Figure 40 Hocus-pocus
hoax-'em, poke-'em,
hokum-locum

If she's restored
we'll demand a great hoard
of cash and of paper in pay;
Should she suddenly slump,
our Gladstones we'll hump
and take to our heels straight away.

『若是好了，俺兩個多多的問他要東西錢鈔。猛可裏死了，背著藥包往外就
跑。』[51]

There are many modern echoes of jesters: at a musical competition
held in Brussels in 1834, several groups of musicians arrived with their

fool, or *more majorum*.[52] The town of Knutsford still has a procession of royal jesters on May Day, and the Morris dancers seen during summer fetes have connections with fools — there is an early fifteenth-century stained-glass window of Morris dancers in the house of George Tollet in England, one of whom is indistinguishable from an archetypal jester.[53]

But if you are sick of reading and desperate to get out there and see a jester — and who would blame you — then your best chance is a carnival. Since 1882 the annual carnival in the French town of Nice is presided over by a giant mannequin of the king of the carnival, called Triboulet, name of renowned French jesters and a recent example of the interchangeable roles of king and fool.[54] And for those who laugh about Teutonic dourness, it could be argued that the carnival tradition is more densely and vibrantly thriving in German-speaking Switzerland and southern Germany than anywhere else.

In Bad Waldsee "white fools" fill the streets and chase away darkness, symbolizing light and spring. On "Fat Thursday" *(gumpiger Dunstig)* these Pied Pipers lure children out of school with their jingling bells and dancing feet, encouraging them to shout foolish verses *(Narrenspruche)*. A procession of fools' guilds *(Narrenzünfte)* is followed by fools dressed as prince and princess with jester and courtiers *(Prinzengruppe)*. The fools' white costumes are embroidered, and one of them, Narro, has colored feathers on his hood, while Faselhannes has a pointed cap with foxtails hanging for ears. Both wear bells as "a sign of joy," their tinkling a harbinger of merriment. Real present-day court jesters, they use mirrors and fool registers to offer kindly correctives:

> "The primary duty of the Faselhannes is to reflect on the events of the past year or to make a person's bad luck laughable and joyous." They do this by holding hand-mirrors up to ordinary citizens so they may examine themselves, or by carrying books for recording foolish events. The Narro also exercises the "right of the fool" to speak freely and comment on the behaviour of others . . . [but] they never approach someone aggressively.[55]

Court jesters are very much alive and kicking in the collective memory of most places that fostered them, with the exception of China, although it is hard to find adequate reasons for this Oriental amnesia. People in English-speaking countries are extremely familiar with the jester who regularly appears in films and advertisements or posters and is a prime mover and shaker in north European carnivals. Since 1950 the French town of

Antibes has annually honored the memory of Brusquet, quack turned court jester, and Turkey still has a Nasrudin festival to commemorate its greatest funster.[56] In India stories concerning the holy trinity of Birbal, Gopal, and Tenali Rama abound in comic books and folktales, and the Middle East still pegs jokes to Ash'ab, historically a court entertainer.

Several modern novels feature court jesters, including Avigdor Dagan's heartrending account of four Jewish jesters serving a Nazi concentration camp commander, while Jeffrey Farnol's *The Fool Beloved*, a novel published in the 1950s but set in Renaissance Italy, is a curlicued depiction of a wise jester called Bimbo—yes, Bimbo.[57] Alan Brownjohn's *The Way You Tell Them: A Yarn for the Nineties* has a writer known for his "dangerous" antiestablishment stance agreeing in a Faustian deal to be at the beck and call of a media tycoon as his jester. Selling his soul for a fat check, he feels no inclination to jest for others and is often miserable and humiliated, particularly when he is made to wear the red-and-yellow cap and bells in the presence of a gorgeous celebrity he fantasizes about. He is allowed to speak his mind in front of his master, an overweening manipulator, but he has become a jester against his better judgment and is somehow neutered as a man.[58]

A more convincing and funnier modern depiction of a jester concerns the wandering jester-minstrel Streetpoet in *Troubadour* by Richard Burns, set in a fictitious medieval country. He combines a jester's quick-witted trickery and kindliness, and he sets out to save the country from oppression by finding the love of the deranged emperor's life in the hope of bringing him to his senses. Although temporarily estranged from the emperor, he has been his closest confidant and later becomes so again. He also has all the pluck and nerve of a jester, and in the opening pages he manages to amuse grubby spectators by maneuvering his way out of an imminent auto-da-fé ordered by the grim, gray-masked Brotherhood. The master of the Brotherhood, burning with puritanical zeal, is kept talking until the rain soaks the pyre and Streetpoet begins firing up his inept executioner:

> "Magnificent" observed the minstrel. "They fetch us out here in this weather and then can't even light a fire. There's hospitality for you." "I'm doing my best," complained the guard. "Haven't you any fire-spell?" "No. Any more suggestions?" "Well, as you mention it, yes. You're doing it all wrong." "Me!" The guard was affronted. "Listen, mate. I've lit more auto-da-fés than you've had hot dinners." "I'd never have had a hot dinner if you'd been lighting the stove."[59]

A delightful remix of medieval Middle Eastern folktales by a Turkish American writer, Güneli Gün, has Huru, a character from Turkish folklore, woven into the *Arabian Nights*. To evade one kind of danger she becomes licensed fool to the volatile Selim I, ruler of the Ottoman Empire from 1512 to 1520, disguising herself by covering her flowing red hair with a sheep's bladder—a unique variation on the association of jesters with bladders—thus earning from Selim the sobriquet Bald Boy. This skullcap gives her a mangy appearance, which combined with her genuine stammer, lends her the physical abnormality becoming to a jester. And despite the constant threat of losing her scabby head, she nevertheless tells Selim what she thinks:

> "That does it!" said Selim. "What makes you think you're indispensable?" "No one else will tell you the truth," she said. "I love my Prince too much to let him deceive himself."[60]

Later in the book, but earlier in history, Huru, Invisible Minstrel who "sings deep in the choir of our hearts," finds herself producing ballads to the accompaniment of her magic lyre at the wedding of Caliph Harun al-Rashid in eighth-century Baghdad. And, much to her consternation, being appointed his fool. Time-warped back to the sixteenth century, her mangy guise blown, she becomes the much-loved but maltreated wife of Selim, bearing his son, Osman Kara, half-brother of Suleiman the Magnificent. Osman grows up to be the Minstrel of the Age, Sage Sultan the Fool, Divine Fool.

> Not much is known about this king among the poets. All that remain are his songs of Magical Protest. In his songs, the life of the spirit marries the life of the senses in such ecstatic purity that to hear, just once, only one deathless song, believe me, warrants the hardship of learning Turkish. . . . The Fool's songs are called Breaths, as natural to man as is breathing. Their truth was so dangerous for the social and political establishment of the time, alas, the Fool was hanged on the gall-tree for breathing so dangerously.[61]

The singing fool and the truth-telling jester are linked elsewhere. The ethnomusicologist Theodore Levin traveled extensively in Uzbekistan in search of forms of music flourishing outside the official conservatories. His enthusiastic reviewer tells us:

> Just in case you were wondering, the "fools of god" in the title refers to the Arabic word "abdal," which, when applied in a Levinesque

manner to musicians, indicates the desire to achieve something higher than simple entertainment. The fool of god, in his (or her) musical incarnation, seeks to guide humankind toward the just and the good through song and instrumental performance. Canonical Sufi tradition sets the number of contemporary *abdal* at forty, but of course many have preceded and many more will surely follow. We can only hope that Levin, or perhaps others equally well equipped (and endowed with the apparently superhuman tolerance to vodka such fieldwork requires), will teach us more about these fools, from whom we have so much to learn.[62]

There are also a number of films with court jesters, including one starring Danny Kaye, and two recent versions of the story of Robin Hood both feature court jesters. In Woody Allen's *Everything You Ever Wanted to Know about Sex but Were Afraid to Ask* (1972), Allen takes the part at the court of Henry VIII, who seems nonplussed by the accent and argot of his fool. In Kurosawa's *Ran,* the jester is magnificent and wins the all-time prize for sartorial splendor of motley.

The British media are full of references to the court jester in a modern context: a British television series, *Birds of a Feather,* won a prestigious comedy award called "the Golden Jester," and an interview with Spike Milligan states that in another age he "might have been a court jester or visionary." The American writer Hunter S. Thompson made his reputation by "attacking the power structure, 'the dangerous bunglers, ruthless swine, or both' who he felt had hijacked the American Dream," and was described as "a kind of licensed jester, a literary Lord of Misrule."[63] A photograph of Prince Charles in a comic revue in 1970 is captioned "Charles as court jester," and the author of an article titled "Jester Murdered for Mockery," about Richard de Zoysa, a journalist-playwright in Sri Lanka with close political connections who was murdered for his satire of government, comments that "he who mocks a king risks paying a high price. And while princes may have been replaced by presidents, the price does not appear to have changed much. . . . Shooting a journalist helps to shackle free speech; so does killing a court jester. Neither should ever happen in a democratic society."[64]

Despite his continuing popularity, the court jester no longer amuses or admonishes authority with his witty license, and his role has been taken over by actors, cartoonists (fig. 41), and comedians. His critical function was replaced in China in the first instance by the ad lib comments of stage actors, and in Britain particularly by satirical prints.[65] In China the satiri-

ence minister. Viscount Cranborne, the
f the Lords, will add a touch of class. But
br's claque can honestly believe that the
rm his government's prospects.

aree broad
the emer-
someone
cular mis-
e exercises
obody ex-

poseful re-
isters sack
them, and
e who do.
now Lady)
81 reshuf-
or and Ian
ut respec-
tites, Nor-
awson, the
are risky,
ɔ damage
ut they do
sertion of
This can,
he govern-

falls into
host spec-
s made by
his "back
rst type of
unless he
And Mr
ave the guts for the second type of ene-
A year ago, he fulminated semi-pri-
bastards", the Eurosceptics who threat-
his party together. Where are they now?

ne will be branded a wimp or worse.
Then, of course, he has to make the
one new appointment will help make
in Downing Street is actually acted u
Hunt, g
chairing
Chancell
ter). Ano
prove the
commun
tial star, a
so on. We
that the g
somehow
by a resh
delusion.
The p
At any or
litical pe
conscious
polling c
photogra
ministers
Only
Waldegra
Mr Patte
for every
was, two
someone
As fo
shuffling
ministers
splash, re
their pre
for the sa
consistency. So does the fact that minis
cated new briefs quickly. As they stru
blunder. Consider the cost of having,
ment and ten transport secretaries

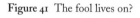

Figure 41 The fool lives on?

cal cartoon is a recent development, and humorous mockery of government has perhaps been more the province of *xiangsheng* artists and stage actors. Nowadays it is perhaps the cartoonist more than anybody who has taken over the court jester's universal mocking function and who shares the jester's compulsion to have his say even when he might suffer for it.[66]

The British cartoonist David Low used his drawings as an early warning system against Hitler, showing something of the prophetic powers attributed to jesters and, as with them, probably due more to perspicacity than to psychic ability. As early as 1936 he was ringing alarm bells about appeasement, apparently unheard, while also providing a sardonic commentary on the war once it began. An American cartoonist, Clarence

Batchelor, won a prize for an ironic caution against war, again as early as 1936.

Gardner sees humor as one of the most essential elements of democracy. Speaking of cartoon mockery of presidential campaigns in the United States, he refers to their importance in "preventing the presidential candidate from developing messianic delusions," since the presidential candidate, much like the king, is "insulated against unpleasant truths by obsequious aides who have their eyes on a White House office."[67] Like the court jester, the cartoonist can help the man in power keep a grip on reality and the limits of his own greatness by means of verbal and visual wit. At a summit between George Bush and Mikhail Gorbachev in 1990, Gorbachev's goodwill gesture was in the form a cartoon presented to Bush, just as past rulers might have exchanged jesters.[68]

The live equivalent of the court jester in modern times is perhaps the stand-up comedian, appearing on his own or with a partner. In China xiangsheng artists have a great deal in common with court jesters: "They joke, pun, sing, tell stories, do imitations, and above all satirize."[69] They use the same techniques of "misconception mode" *(cuojue shi)*, "in which the audience is kept in the dark until the punch-line liberates them," riddles, feigned naïveté in use of language, and building up the listeners' expectations only to end with an anticlimax, funny for being unexpected:

> *A.* When they got on board they were full of talk and laughter.
> *B.* Sure! They were happy!
> *A.* And in a moment were shouting and singing.
> *B.* Happy!
> *A.* Everyone together skipping and jumping!
> *B.* Happy!
> *A.* And in the end vomiting and groaning!
> *B.* Happy! (suddenly realising) Huh? Vomiting?[70]

There is much debate as to the origins of xiangsheng, with some, including the most renowned twentieth-century xiangsheng artist Hou Baolin, tracing it back to the court jesters.[71] Originally xiangsheng could be performed by one, two, or more comedians, although the double act now predominates, comprising the *dougen* or "funny man" responsible for telling the jokes and the *penggen*, who is the "straight man." The Communists felt that the satirical powers of xiangsheng should serve as a government propaganda tool, although the effect of trying to turn xiangsheng into a Party mouthpiece could castrate its comic value. Censorship notwithstanding, even scripted pieces can have enough ambiguity to allow mockery of injustices. The art has mushroomed, and pieces are performed with increasing frequency on radio and television, with amateur artists springing up across the country.

During the Third Reich it was the cabaret comedians of Berlin who were the jesters. Weiss Ferdl commented on the newly built Dachau camp, pretending to assume its barbed-wire fencing, miradors, and machine guns were intended to keep people out rather than in: "Still, I only have to say a word or two, and I'll be inside in a jiffy."[72] The night after Kristallnacht (1938) he appeared on stage draped in jewelry, and when the audience laughed at his absurd appearance, he asked them what was the matter: "Do you think I've been asleep during crystal night?"[73] Indirection is often far more effective than straightforward condemnation:

> "It's all the fault of the Jews," says the anti-Semite.
> "And the cyclists," replies the Jew.
> "Why the cyclists?"
> "Why the Jews?"[74]

Another cabaret comedian, Karl Valentin, told his audience he had seen a Mercedes limousine pull up and had been surprised when he saw it was not an SS officer who stepped out. For this he was reprimanded by the authorities, and he promised he would set the record straight. He apologized on stage for having been misleading, "The truth is, it *was* an SS officer after all."[75]

A third outspoken cabaret performer, Werner Fink, was often harassed by storm troopers. Like a good jester he would not shut up: when a Nazi called him "Jew boy," he wryly parried, "You are mistaken. I only look so intelligent."[76] And like an unfortunate minority of court jesters before him, he suffered for his brazen mockery. Hitler had grandiose architectural plans that were to be brought to life by his architect, Albert Speer, requiring whole streets to be razed. Fink started cracking jokes about this and ended up in a concentration camp; Speer tells us that "his arrest took place, incidentally, just the day before I meant to attend his show as proof that I was not offended."[77] Bad luck, old boy.

Nineteenth- and twentieth-century circus clowns also adopted some aspects of the court jester. William F. Wallett (1808–92) wore the cap and bells and was known as the "Shakespearean jester" of the circus. In 1844 he appeared before Queen Victoria and Prince Albert and thereafter billed himself as "Queen's Jester," his epitaph confirming the title: "Under the

guise of folly he preached philanthropy, extolled truth and virtue, and be-
rated vice."[78]

The Russian clowns have perhaps come closest to being society's court
jesters in the ring. Inheritors of the *skomorokhi,* the hordes of itinerant entertainers from whose ranks court jesters emerged and whose jibes at authority caused them to be banned in 1648 by Czar Alexis I (r. 1645–76),
the Russian circus clowns arose in the nineteenth century, perhaps filling
a void.[79] It began with the brothers Vladimir and Anatoly Durov (1863–
1934 and 1864–1916), who would greet the audience with "King of jesters, but never the king's jester! The Jester to His Majesty the People!" a
title that continued to be applied to circus clowns.[80] By the time Vladimir
reached the port of Archangel, he was so renowned for his piercing humor
that the police forbade him to crack topical jokes—instead he mimed his
act with a huge padlock on his mouth.[81]

The American circus clown Dan Rice (1823–1901) also crossed the line
to jesterdom. He wore the red, white, and blue costume that later came
to be associated with Uncle Sam and used sham tricks to make people see
through fraud. He mocked American politicians and American worship
of European culture and was also the unofficial jester to President Lincoln.[82] He summed up the wise fool:

> A successful clown must possess more intellect, ability, and original-
> ity than a comedian. He must be a crack mimic, an elocutionist, a
> satirist, and so ready witted that he, to the ringmaster, is a stupid fool,
> a buffoon; to the audience a wise man whose every remark is impreg-
> nated with philosophy as well as humor. This is the dual character
> of the true clown.[83]

The American comedian Will Rogers (1879–1935) acted as a kind of
jester to Woodrow Wilson, using his fooling to make pointed political
comments more palatable.[84] Like a real court jester, he had easier access to
the president than a lot of other people and would address him with great
informality, calling him "Pres." He was known for irrepressible mockery
of congressmen, exposing their self-interest and deflating their pomposity. As a latter-day jester his advice was also heeded by Franklin D. Roose-
velt, who commented, "While I had discussed European matters with
many others . . . both Americans and Foreign, Will Rogers' analysis of affairs abroad was not only more interesting, but proved to be more accurate than any other I had heard."[85]

In Britain it is Jimmy Savile who has acted the part, being known for his ability to make Prince Charles "see the absurdity of his regal expectations" and enjoying the license of the jester to speak mockingly. The modern royal household can have as much of an insulating effect on princes as in the past. Therefore an irreverent outsider who can bring the real world into the palace is no doubt a welcome and "vital requirement in the mirrored universe of royalty": "Savile, who plays the part of the court jester to the Establishment with consummate skill, is a regular visitor to Kensington and Buckingham palaces, as well as the prime minister's country residence at Chequers. *As the unofficial clown he articulates opinions which courtiers can only think.*"[86]

There has been something of a compartmentalization of the jester's functions: the clown for capering and laughable appearance, the mental patient for a disregard of social norms, the journalist as critic, and the cartoonist and comedian as mockers (and critics).[87] The demise of the court jester as a distinct profession is perhaps complete, but the need for him is not. Close to those at the apex of power, he could temper extremes of mood and rein in excessive behavior, and it is tempting to wonder how much modern committee ritual and jargon could be dispensed with if a jester was allowed to listen to the proceedings, asking the unaskable and turning each piece of "committee-speak" into a scoffing jingle.

The enlightened Swiss seem deeply aware of the contribution that jesters can still make. Recently a full-page advertisement was placed in a respected newspaper inviting applications for the post of court jester to the Swiss parliament, "to stand between the people and the politicians and between various political camps, so that politics will become more tolerable" (fig. 42). In addition, they occasionally have a cartoonist sitting in on televised debates, providing a visual, jocular running commentary of the proceedings, as jesters used to do in court. One such cartoonist sat through a World Cup football match between Switzerland and Spain and instantly summed up the Swiss trouncing by sketching a sweet, long-lashed Swiss dairy cow. He then tore off the adjacent sheet hiding a cartoon of a huge, snorting Spanish bull clambering on top of her: the Swiss were shafted in the World Cup.[88]

Monarchs and governments may still occasionally need or long for the presence of the jester that their royal predecessors enjoyed. Speer's *Inside the Third Reich* frequently refers to Hitler's "court" with Goebbels, Goering, Speer, Himmler, and others as the "courtiers," and he describes how Hitler's occasional ability to laugh meant that some sort of humor could be used to communicate serious matters to him, with Goebbels being

Petition
zur Einführung eines
Hofnarren
im
Bundeshaus

Die Politikerinnen und Politiker haben sich vom Volk entfernt, die sogenannten Volksvertreter den Kontakt zur Basis verloren. Und im Bundeshaus sagt kaum jemand mehr, was er wirklich denkt. Sondern bloss noch, was gerade opportun ist. Deshalb fordern wir den Bundesrat auf, die Stelle eines vollamtlichen Hofnarren zu schaffen und damit eine von altersher bewährte Institution wieder neu ins Leben zu rufen. Ausgestattet mit der Kompetenz, zu reden, wie ihm der Schnabel gewachsen ist. Überall dort, wo wichtige Entscheide gefällt werden: Im Parlament, an Bundesratssitzungen, in den Kommissionen. Als Vermittler zwischen Volk und Politiker und zwischen den politischen Lagern. Damit die Politik wieder erträglich wird.

Jede auf dem Bogen aufgeführte Person erhält vier Wochen lang **GRATIS** den Nebelspalter. Als Dankeschön fürs Mitmachen.

Ich unterstütze die Forderung an den Bundesrat, die Stelle eines vollamtlichen Hofnarren zu schaffen.

Name: Vorname: Strasse: PLZ/Ort:

Die ganz oder teilweise ausgefüllten Bogen werden nach Ablauf der Sammelfrist offiziell dem Bundesrat als Petition überreicht.

Bitte schicken Sie diesen Sammel-Bogen ganz oder teilweise ausgefüllt an: Nebelspalter-Verlag, Petitions-Sekretariat, 9400 Rorschach.

Informationen und zusätzliche Sammel-Bogen erhalten Sie unter Gratis-Telefon 155 26 70!

Figure 42 Advertisement for a parliamentary jester

the most proficient "court jester" to the dictator. Hard to imagine, but here it is:

> Many jokes were carefully prepared, tied up as they were with actual events, so that Hitler was kept abreast of interparty developments under the guise of foolery. Again, Goebbels was far better at this than all the others, and Hitler gave him further encouragement by showing that he was very much amused.[89]

Similarly, the need for a jester as pure entertainment value also lives on. At a banquet in Hollywood the present British queen was making polite conversation with a multimillionaire who had been allowed to sit next to her, since he had paid for the evening, despite the fact he was a crashing bore. After a while she leaned behind his back to address another guest, an actor:

> "Mr. Caine, Mr. Caine."
> "Yes, Your Majesty."
> "D'you know any jokes?"
> "Yes, Ma'am, but very few that I could tell you."
> "Have a go and then I will tell you one."[90]

The court jester is dead, long live the court jester!

FINAL FLOURISH

> Others alledge in excuse of their *practises,* that Princes in all Ages were allowed their "laughter-maker" whose *virtue* consisted in speaking any thing *without control:* That *Jesters* often *heal* what *Flatterers hurt,* so that Princes by them arrive at the notice of their Errors, seeing Jesters carry about with them an *Act of Indemnity* for whatsoever they do: That Princes, over-burdened with *States-business,* must have their *Diversions;* and that those words are not censurable for *absolutely idle,* which lead to *lawful delight.*
> Thomas Fuller, *The History of the Worthies of England* (1662)[91]

Fuller's defense of the court jester, in his passage on Tarlton, is an eloquent description of the jester's raison d'être. Rulers of the past are often viewed as variations on a theme of dictatorial tyranny and cruelty, and the past is an easy target because its people can no longer speak for themselves. In a recent interview with Ernst Gombrich this denigration of the

Figure 43 Rupert and the April Fool © Express Newspapers PLC

past is discussed. Referring to letters written by the Mantuan dukes of the Renaissance (coincidentally, one of the best sources for Italian jesters), he comments how far the letters conveyed an impression of people not dissimilar to us. This theme has recurred with astonishing regularity in the course of my research, regardless of the time or place concerned.

In observing differences of culture and era, whether to delight in or condemn, there is the risk of underestimating the similarities, which deserve as much celebration as the spice and color of the exotic. A study of the ubiquitous jester who transcends cultural and chronological divisions is a superb medium in which to highlight other universals of mankind, an ideal catalyst for bringing people geographically and historically remote so much to life as to make them seem next-door neighbors. In studying the universality of the jester it is impossible not to notice other human constants straddling centuries and continents—constants that make Us and Them ideologies, whether aimed at other nations, beliefs, or ages, seem at best simplistic and at worst myopic and crass: "Because all collectivism has its dangerous side. It leads to talk of We, We, We, Our Nation, Our Age. I very much dislike this sense of isolation and superiority. We are not all that different from our past. It was all governed, as our life is, by many accidents, tragedies, luck, and so on."[92]

In observing the jester we are given a view of those he served—principally the most powerful people in a country—which has been perhaps too readily overlooked. The presence of a jester tends to have a humanizing effect on royalty (and others), and an insight into the emotions, idiosyncrasies, moods, and affections of people who were frequently the key players in history is bound to contribute to a fuller and more complex picture of the past. The jesters of whom we have more than fleeting glimpses are quirky individuals, and through the prism of their interaction with the king we are able to see not only some of his more endearing qualities but also the singularity of people who can often seem to be only remote titles with dates attached. It is a side of history that has been widely neglected.

Pomp and ceremony were perhaps more prevalent in the past, and yet in a sense our age of apparently greater informality is more awed by ritual and formality, more taken in by it. That a personification of chaos and unpredictability was frequently invited to take part in the most formal and ritualistic occasions as a constant reminder of their limits is perhaps testimony to the expansiveness of the people who admitted them. Most people move, speak, and dress differently in a formal situation than they would at home. A jester would not. He would be consistently himself without adapting to external ritual requirements. To allow the antithesis of formality and prescribed ritual to cavort uncontrolled at its center suggests an ability to keep it in its proper existential perspective.

The nearest thing we have now is perhaps something like the drunken or eccentric tramp who wanders into a church service and parodies the proceedings, usually as an uninvited and discomfiting guest. The best front pew of Saint Giles Cathedral in Edinburgh was recently monopolized by a reeking vagrant who shuffled in with half a dozen battered shopping bags. Surly and contrary, he stood up when the congregation knelt and broke the silence of prayer with loud, incomprehensible mutterings, but nobody challenged or removed him. If anyone tried to share the pew he would complain to the sexton, who would politely ask them to move. The tramp demanded and was given a wide berth, a mirthless thorn in the side of complacency.

If a jester had been allowed to take part in arms limitation talks, laughing when somebody tried to be misleading about how many warheads his nation had, it would have been considered highly inappropriate and a diminution of the gravity of the negotiations. It might also have speeded up their successful conclusion. Nowadays most people feel greatly unsettled by a person who disrupts the orderly proceedings of formality.

Could this be a result of our having banished jesters, both natural and artificial, or the reason for it? Are we perhaps more bound by forms and rituals than our predecessors? Are we, in this regard at least, less free?

Jesters are universal, but the most universal of them must be the Middle Eastern mulla Nasrudin. Many stories show him as the jester of Tamerlane, constantly at his side, although some of the anecdotes are also ascribed to other jesters and tricksters.[93] Whether he really acted as a court jester is debatable, but he is the eternal jester in employing his irrepressible sense of humor to combat all forms of rigidity. The legendary mulla has outwitted the constraints of time, place, and possibility that most mortals are subject to.[94] He is equally at ease jesting with Tamerlane and, in the latter-day tales of Idries Shah, getting the better of a British immigration official, thereby gaining entry to the country and finding a job as a factory worker in the Midlands. His adaptability to modern British life from the medieval Middle East is impressive, as we see him cracking jokes on the underground before he turns up at a football match.[95]

Nations vie for the honor of calling him a citizen. He crops up in Turkey, where he has been claimed as a native, the Turks presenting their case more thoroughly than other countries by exhibiting his grave and holding an annual Nasrudin festival. The Sufis used his wisecracks as teaching materials, and stories about him circulate in the United States and have been published in Beijing. In the Middle Ages Nasrudin tales "were widely used to deride odious authority. In more recent times, the Mulla became a People's Hero of the USSR, when a film depicted him as scoring off again and again the wicked capitalist rulers of the country."[96] The universality of this jester extends beyond geography and history into the realm of physics. Shah notes that "the Coral Gables High-Energy Physics Conference Report uses Mulla tales to illustrate scientific phenomena which cannot be put in the limitations of ordinary technical terms."[97]

Nasrudin may be the most universal of earthbound court jesters, but the Chinese Dongfang Shuo, Han dynasty courtier and jester, Daoist immortal, and allegedly the spirit of two planets, Venus and Jupiter, goes one better. As an immortal he was difficult to pin down, and as punishment for playing with the elements he was exiled to earth, where he became a jester to Emperor Wudi of the Han.[98] After he died an astronomer noted that Jupiter, which had not been visible for forty years, suddenly reappeared, and the emperor regretted not having realized that the man who had served him for eighteen years was none other than the missing planet:[99]

One day Dongfang Shuo climbed on a cloud dragon and flew away. At that moment a crowd of people saw him ascending from the northwest and, gazing upward, were able to watch him for a long time before he was enveloped in a heavy mist that made it impossible to know what became of him.

東方朔一旦乘雲龍飛去。同時眾人見從西北上冉冉。仰望良久。大霧覆之不知所在。[46]

On the same cosmic level, a recent science fiction comic strip, *The Road to Nowhere,* has the heroes time-warped so far into the future that they reach the End of Time, where they find a king with his queen and . . . his jester, a juggling, riddling, leaping, mocking magician.[101] The court jester, it seems, is truly universal.

EPILOGUE

Future Fooling?

Plus Ça Change . . .

He travels around the world in a new wide body Boeing 767, with a
Challenger 601 and Boeing 727 as back-up. On overseas trips he has
a physician, a communications expert, a travel co-ordinator, a personal assistant, a bodyguard, and two Bedouin men whose roles are
to tell jokes in the style of traditional court jesters.

EuroBusiness, June 1999 [1]

Prince Alwaleed bin Talal bin Abdulaziz al Saud is perhaps the most
high-profile patron of jesters in the world today. The largest shareholder
in Disneyland Paris and London's Canary Wharf, he "specialises in rescu-
ing Europe's commercial follies," not to mention other commercial dam-
sels in distress such as Citicorp in the early 1990s. Not that this chivalry
has done him any harm. His current holdings and investments have been
estimated at a little over U.S. $15 billion, and in 1997 *Forbes* magazine voted
him "the world's second savviest businessman and in 1998 . . . the 13th
richest." [2]

And he keeps jesters. So where is this leading? Simply to a growing
sense that the jester is perhaps due for a renaissance, only this time he is
cropping up in commercial rather than political institutions, perhaps following a shift in the locus of power from government to big business.
Prince Alwaleed's jokers straddle the traditional and emerging roles of
the jester in that they serve a royal prince and a modern businessman
simultaneously.

The cartoonist and the stand-up comedian whom I have flagged as
filling the functions of the jester in present-day society may only be occu-
pying something of a caretaking role. My suspicion is that the corporate

jester of the future may be closer to the court jester of the past than to the cartoonists and comedians, who tend to serve a wider, societal audience, though I see no reason the two types cannot coexist. As the traditional jester would wander around a specific court, so the modern business jester ambles through a specific organization, challenging the status quo. This is not merely wishful thinking on the part of a jester lover.

The best known of these new fools was Paul Birch, officially designated corporate jester for British Airways. For a while he was allowed to ask awkward questions, to employ Edward de Bono's po (provocative operations), or as he says, "to swan around, stick my nose in other people's business, and be a pain in the arse."[3] The publicity this brought British Airways was positive, with the recruitment department having applicants say that if the company employed a jester it must be good to work for.[4]

Like many court jesters before him, however, he was dependent on the tolerance of his masters. When Bob Ayling took over, Birch was summoned by the new strategy director and told, "You've been taking the piss for the last year and it's got to stop." Birch's plea that this was his job did not receive a sympathetic hearing. Nor did his pointing out to Ayling, "You realise you can't sack me, because sacking me would show that you couldn't take it any more."[5] He was sacked. But then, when asked about his time as a corporate jester, he said that the half-life of a fool is about six to nine months. He also alluded to the jester's role as the great challenger: "People will always focus on the humour element that's inherent in the concept of the Jester; no matter how many times you explain that the main role of the Jester is to challenge. The humour is just the tool."[6]

Paul Birch may be unique in having been an officially designated corporate jester. But there is growing evidence of their informal appearance in larger businesses, though I suspect many of the best organizations have always fostered such people. I believe this is simply linked to the realization that for companies to flourish in the future will require an ever greater input of creativity, innovation, and ingenuity, since technology can be emulated so fast that business will increasingly have to rely on nimble thinking skills to keep ahead.

"Creativity" and "innovation" have become the buzzwords of fashionable management circles, but underlying it all is a very real need that the best companies genuinely try to meet. David Firth and Alan Leigh's *Corporate Fool* gives numerous examples of informal fools who fulfill all the functions of the traditional court jester—they challenge without threatening, act as confidants, ease tensions, advise and question, and are given the license to think outside that proverbial box.

"I remember a guy at my old company," says the former IT Director of a major UK electronics retailer. "He'd come along to every board meeting with ten ideas. Six of those ideas, on average, would get us nowhere—they were awful and the board happily shot them down. Two of the remaining four, if we implemented them, would probably kill the company—they were that dangerous. It was the two remaining ideas that were usually very, very hot. The thing was, he probably wouldn't have got to the two hot, money-making, process-improving ideas unless we'd given him the space and the leeway to give us six crap ideas and two deadly ones. And as for him, he had such an ability to think like a maverick that he couldn't tell the difference between the crap ideas and the great ones. But it wasn't his job to choose."[7]

Jesters are nothing if not creative, innovative, flexible, and challenging—these qualities are at the core of their being, and humor is often simply the wrapping they use to dress it up and make it acceptable. Global jokers, global capitalism? Watch this space.

APPENDIX

Table of Named Jesters

JESTER	PLACE	DATES	PATRON	COMMENTS
A Chou (Brother Clown)	China	ca. 1465–87	*Ming Xianzong	
Abu Bakr Rubabi Mandud b. 'Abdallah	Ghazna	ca. 998–1030	Sultan Mahmud	"The Rebeck Player," director of court singers, said to have served Mahmud but probably lived a century before him
Abu Dulama	Medina	8th century		Freelance jester-poet
Abu Halub	Baghdad	ca. 785	Caliph Mahdi	Stole jokes from Muzabbid
Abu Nuwas	Baghdad	756–811	Caliph Harun al-Rashid	Greatest Arabic poet of Abbasid period, occasionally acted like jester
Abu'l-Aina', Muhammed b. Qasim b. Khallad	Basra	806–95	Caliph Abu Ja'far al-Mansur	
Acedo, Don Diego de	Spain	ca. 1640	*Philip IV	Painted by Velázquez
Aedh	Ulster		Fergus	Dwarf
Aguas, Martín de	Spain	ca. 1595	*Philip II	Natural
Albergati, Ercole	Mantua	ca. 1500	Isabella d'Este	Jester-actor
Alvarado, José	Spain	ca. 1670–76	*Charles II	Natural
Ambrosio	Rome	ca. 1523–34	Pope Clement VII	
An Peixin (Fitting New Bridle)	China	889–904	*Tang Zhaozong	
Anderson, Shemus	Scotland	d. 1833	Murthley Castle	
Andrelini	France			Court poet, inherited jester post from Seigni Johan
Angeli	France	ca. 1648–1715	*Louis XIV	In Hugo's Marion de Lorme, feigned madness

Name	Country	Dates	Patron	Notes
Angoulevent	France			Real name Nicolas Joubert; aka "Prince des Sots"
Antona, Miguel de	Spain	ca. 1565–67	*Philip II	Natural; aka "El Loco"
Antonio, Don	Spain	ca. 1613	*Philip III	Dwarf, natural; aka "El Inglés"
Arcángel, El (the Archangel)	France	ca. 1679	*Charles II	Natural
Arcemalles, Maître Jehan	France	ca. 1350–64	*Jean II	Same as Johan below?
Arlotto, Piovano	Florence	1396–1483		Jester-priest
Armentieres, Colin d'	France	ca. 1383	Count of la Marche	
Armstrong, Archy	Britain	ca. 1615–40	*1. James I *2. Charles I	Dwarf, banished from court
Ash'ab	Medina	d. 771		Court entertainer became legendary jester
Austria, Don Juan de	Spain	ca. 1624–54	*Philip IV	Painted by Velázquez
Ayala, Perico de	Spain	1526	Marquis of Villena	Great friend of Zúñiga
Azhar-i Khar (Azhar the Ass)	Persia	9th century		First named Persian jester
Baltasar	Spain	ca. 1616–20	*Philip III	Dwarf, natural, French
Bañules, Antonio	Spain	ca. 1626–62	*Philip IV	Natural?
Barciacca	Italy	ca. 1509–35	Cardinal Ippolito de' Medici	
Bärenhaut	Hesse	ca. 1509–67	Landgrave Philip	
Barone, Il	Ferrara	1490	d'Este court	Would organize masquerades and other festivities
Bautista de Sevilla, Juan	Spain	ca. 1637	*Philip IV	Temporary jester?
Bayer?	Unspach		Margrave	Painter turned jester

Note: Dates given are those when jesters flourished and only occasionally refer to when they were born or died.

* = emperor, king, or queen; HRE = Holy Roman Emperor.

JESTER	PLACE	DATES	PATRON	COMMENTS
Bazan, Francisco	Spain	ca. 1675–89		Natural; aka "Soul of Purgatory" ("Anima del Purgatorio"); painted by Carreño and Francisco de Herrera
Bernadino	Ferrara	ca. 1474–1539	Isabella d'Este	Aka "The Madman" ("Il Matello")
Birbal	India	1528–83	*Akbar the Great	Poet
Blakall, Thomas	England	1485–1509	*Henry VII	
Blasco, Bernarda	Spain	ca. 1675–1702	Spanish queen	Dwarfess and natural
Boisrobert, François le Metel de	France	1592–1662	Cardinal Richelieu	Born Caen; wrote poems, letters, novels, eighteen plays
Bolla, Bartholomew	Heidelberg	ca. 1670	Duke	Born Bergamo
Bomolochus	England	ca. 1154–89	Mr. Walter Mapes	Jester to Henry II's court chaplain
Bonny, Patrick	Scotland	ca. 1580	Morton, Scottish regent	
Borcharts, Johann	Germany	ca. 1582		Court jester—a letter to his son, also a jester, is extant
Borra	Aragon	ca. 1396–1410	*Martin	Made king die laughing
Briandas	France	ca. 1538	*François I	
Brusquet	France	ca. 1559	*1. Henri II *2. François II 3. Charles IX 4. Henri III	Born Provence
Buchanan, George	England	ca. 1567–1625	*James I	Scholar, poet, courtier
Buhlul	Baghdad	d. 807	Caliph Harun al-Rashid	Aka the "Lunatic of Kufa," prototype for wise fool in Middle East

Name	Country	Dates	Patron	Notes
Caillette	France	ca. 1498–1515	*Louis XII	Natural
Calabazas, Don Juan	Spain	d. October 1639	1. Infante Cardenal *2. Philip IV	Dwarf; aka "Little Pumpkins" ("Calabacillas"), painted by Velázquez
Caldo, La	Spain	ca. 1694–96		Natural, jestress
Camber, Jemy	Scotland	ca. 1567–1603	*James VI	Natural
Capuchie	France	ca. 1547–59	*Henri II	
Carafulla	Italy	ca. 1509–35	Cardinal Ippolito de' Medici	
Cárdenas, Juan de	Spain	ca. 1624–28	*Philip IV	Natural; painted by Velázquez
Caspar dem Narren (the Fool)	Saxony	ca. 1639	Elector Johann George I	
Catalina la Portuguesa	Spain	ca. 1593–1603		Portuguese? Natural; aka "The Crazy" ("La Loca")
Catarina Matta	Ferrara	ca. 1519	1. Beatrice d'Este 2. Isabella d'Este	Isabella inherited jestress from her sister
Cathelot	France	ca. 1553–1615	Marguerite of Valois	Jestress; predecessor to La Jardinière; chalk and watercolor drawing, Clouet School, ca. 1535
Charelo, Juan	Spain	ca. 1651–58	*Philip IV	Natural
Chen Jun (Chen the Outstanding)	China	ca. 923–26	*Tang Zhuangzong	
Cheng Fuduan (Truly Assisting Uprightness)	China	ca. 780–805	*Tang Dezong	
Chicot	France	ca. 1589	*1. Henri III *2. Henri IV	Courtier, soldier
Chunyu Kun (Baldy Chunyu)	China	ca. 356–319 B.C.	*Weiwang of Qi	

* = emperor, king, or queen; HRE = Holy Roman Emperor.

JESTER	PLACE	DATES	PATRON	COMMENTS
Claus Narr (von Ranstadt)	Saxony	ca. 1480–1530	1. Elector Ernst 2. Elector Ulbrecht 3. Archbishop von Magdeburg 4. Elector Friedrich the Wise 5. Elector Johann des Betenners	Painting of him by Hans Lautensack, 1533; many books about him
Clawert, Hans	Germany	d. 1566	1. Kurfurst of Brandenburg 2. Merry councilor to Eustachius von Schlieben	Also acted as a clairvoyant and quack doctor
Clod	England	ca. 1558–1603	*Elizabeth I	
Colart	France	ca. 1422–61	*Charles VII	Aka "Monsieur de Laon"
Colquohoun, Jenny	Scotland	ca. 1542–67	*Mary	
Comendadora, La (The Commandress)	Spain	ca. 1634–36	*Philip IV	Natural
Coquerée	France	ca. 1388	House of Valois	
Coquinet	France	ca. 1342	Duke of Touraine	
Coquinet	France	ca. 1350	Louis	Same as above?
Cristóbal	Spain	ca. 1635–39	*Philip IV	Musical; aka "The Blind" ("El Ciego")
Critan	Ireland			
Crocifisso	Italy	ca. 1500		

Name	Place	Date	Patron	Notes
Crosson	France	ca. 1399	*Charles VI?	
Dagonet	England	ca. 537	*Arthur	
Dame Jehanne	France	ca. 1458	Seneschal of Beaucaire	Jestress
Danderi	Constantinople	ca. 829–42	*Theophilus	Mocked the piety of the queen
Danga	Egypt	ca. 2325–2150 B.C.	Pepi II	Allegedly a pygmy (Danga is the name of his tribe), who could "dance the God, divert the court and rejoice the heart of the King"; if he existed then he is perhaps the first court jester on record
Daroca	Spain	ca. 1621	*Philip III and/or IV	Natural
Dego	England	ca. 1492	*Henry VII	Spanish
Derry, Thomas	England	ca. 1603–25	*Anne of Denmark	
Dick	England	ca. 1485–1509	*Henry VII	Natural
Ding Xianxian	China	ca. 1101–25	*Song Huizong	Musically proficient, poet, grand commissioner of the Court Entertainments Bureau
Diodato (God-given)	Italy	ca. 1500		Prophet
Do Dera	Ireland		Lugaid MacCon	Prophet
Dolcibene (Gentle Good)	Italian	ca. 1347–78	HRE Charles IV	Wrote poems to Madonna but excommunicated for religious irreverence
Dominicus, Giovanni	Naples	ca. 1458–94	*Ferdinand I	
Don Juan of Austria	Spain	ca. 1644	*Philip IV	Painted by Velázquez, ca. 1644
Dongfang Shuo	China	154–93 B.C.	*Han Wudi	Courtier, scholar, Daoist immortal
Eltham, John of	England	ca. 1327–77	*Edward III	Natural

* = emperor, king, or queen; HRE = Holy Roman Emperor.

JESTER	PLACE	DATES	PATRON	COMMENTS
Estanislao	Spain	ca. 1563–71	HRE Charles V	Dwarf; given by King Sigismund of Poland
Faco	Rome	ca. 79	*Vespasian	Mocked Vespasian at his funeral
Faxardo, Luis	Spain	ca. 1690–93	*Charles II	Natural
Feo (Ugly)	Genoa	ca. 1500	Gian Andrea Doria	
Fetti, Fra Mariano	Italy	ca. 1500		Would run along tables at banquets; priest
Franco, Pedro	Spain	ca. 1646–60	*Philip IV	Natural
Fritella	Ferrara	ca. 1490	d'Este court	Would organize masquerades and other festivities
Fuchs, Neidhart	Austria	ca. 1330	Duke Otto the Merry	Musical; jestbook and Hans Sachs's *Fastnachtspiel* about him
Gabba	Rome	ca. 27 B.C.–A.D. 14	*Augustus	Parasite jester
Gabriel	Spain	16th century	Admiral of Castille	Aka Gabriel la Mena; very musical, gifted in extempore poetry
Gante, Manuel de	Spain	ca. 1637	*Philip IV	Natural; greatly favored by king
Gao Cuiwei (Tall Towering Mountain)	China	ca. 825–27	*Tang Jingzong	
Gasco de Guzmán, Catalina	Spain	ca. 1686–94	*Charles II	Natural, jestress; aka "the Visitor" ("La Visitor")
Geddes, James	Scotland	ca. 1542–67	*Mary	
Geffroy	France	ca. 1316–22	*Philippe V	
Giovanna Matta	Ferrara	ca. 1502	Isabella d'Este	Jestress
Giovanni Dominicus	Florence		Grand Duke Ferdinand I	
Girardot	France	ca. 13??	Duke of Burgundy	
Glorieux, Le	France		Charles, Duke of Burgundy	

Goles	Normandy	ca. 1060	William of Normandy	In *Roman de Rou* by Wace
Gollart, Françoise	France		Duchess of Brittany	Jestress
Gomez, Manuel	Spain	ca. 1642–69	*Philip IV	
Gonella	Ferrara	ca. 1440–70	Duke Niccolò d'Este	Painted by Jean Fouquet; real name Peter, an actor
Gonella	Ferrara	ca. 1450–71	Duke Borso d'Este	
Gonella	Ferrara	ca. 1352	Duke Obizzo II d'Este	
González, Estebanillo	Spain	ca. 1620	Duke of Amalfi	Wrote famous autobiography; historical or fictitious jester? debate still rages
Gopal	India		*Rama	Possibly legendary
Grant Johan le Fol	France	ca. 1375	*Charles V	Successor to Thevenin
Greffier, Le	France	ca. 1547–59	*Henri II	
Grene, Robert	England	ca. 1558–1603	*Elizabeth I	
Guillaume	France	ca. 1422–23	*1. Charles VI	
			2. Dauphin Louis	
Guillaume, Maître	France	ca. 1591	*Henri IV	Satirical pamphlets in his name; real name Guillaume le Marchand; some say he was insane
Guillaume Foirel	France	ca. 1387	*Charles VI	Same as Guillaume above?
Guillaume Fouet	France	ca. 1435	*Isabelle of Bavaria	
Guillaume Fouet	France	ca. 1342	*Jeanne de Bourgogne	
Guo Sheren	China	ca. 140–87 B.C.	*Han Wudi	Always tricked by Dongfang Shuo
Haincelin Coq	France	ca. 1380–1422	*Charles VI	

* = emperor, king, or queen; HRE = Holy Roman Emperor.

JESTER	PLACE	DATES	PATRON	COMMENTS
Hans?	France	ca. 1380–1422	*Charles VI	
Harpaste	Rome	ca. 65 A.D.	Seneca's wife	Natural, jestress
Heng Zhi (Ever Upright)	China	907–60		
Hercules?	Sweden		Admiral Bagge	
Hernandez, Madalena	Spain	ca. 1565	Princess	Natural, jestress
Hieronymus	Mantua	ca. 1600	Duke Vincentius I	Born Spain
Hinße, Claus	Pomerania	d. 1599	Duke Johann Friedrich	Died entertaining duke; Hinßendorf given to and named after him
Hitard	England	ca. 1016	*Edmund II	
Hua Maiglinni	Ireland		*Fergal of N. Ireland	Royal jester (rig-druth), a gifted minstrel
Huang Fanchuo (In Full Streamer)	China	ca. 712–56	*Tang Xuanzong	
Hudson, Sir	England	ca. 1640	*Henrietta Maria	
Ibn Hamdun	Baghdad	ca. 892–902	Caliph Mu'tadid	
Isabelica, La Chova (= corneja?)	Spain	ca. 1596–99	*Philip II	Natural, jestress
Jacominus	France	ca. 1216–72	*Henry III	
Jane	England	ca. 1553–58	*Mary Tudor	Jestress
Jardinière, La	France	ca. 1540–89	*Catherine de' Medici	Jestress; successor to Cathelot
Jardinière, La	Scotland	ca. 1542–67	*Mary Queen of Scots	Jestress
Jia Le (Joy of the Household)	China	ca. 300	Minister Wang Yan	
Jiao De (Scorching Virtue)	China	ca. 1101–25	*Song Huizong	
Jing Xinmo (Newly Polished Mirror)	China	ca. 923–26	*Tang Zhuangzong	

Name	Place	Date	Patron	Notes
Jo. Dominicus Ciaiesius	Florence		Grand Duke Ferdinand I	Poet/scholar jester
Johan, Maître	France	ca. 1328–50	*Philippe VI	Same jester as Jehan above?
Johannes	Germany?		Ubt zu Zwißsalten?	
John	England	ca. 1567–1625	*James VI and I	
John le Fol	England	ca. 1216	*1. John *2. Henry III	
John Low Muckle	Scotland	ca. 1567–1625	*James VI and I	
Johnson, Samuel	England	1691–1773	Lord Gawsworth	"Lord Flame," wrote plays
Jonas	Germany	ca. 1619–37	*Kaiser Ferdinand II	
Jonas	Germany	ca. 1630	Elector Maximilian?	Same as above?
Joseph Fröhlich (Merry Joseph)	Saxony?	ca. 1728	1. August II of Austria 2. August III of Austria	Born Bavaria; known for coarse humor; porcelain bust done by Kirchner; Meissen porcelain figure with Postmaster Schmiedel
Juan Andres	Spain	ca. 1677	*Charles II	Natural
Juan Melchor	Spain	ca. 1685–97	*Charles II	Dwarf, Portuguese
Juanillo, Don	Spain	ca. 1596–1632	*1. Philip III *2. Philip IV	Natural?
Junker (Squire) Peter	Neuburg		Duke Wolfgang	
Junker (Squire) Wießweiler	Cologne		Grave von Iseburg	
Kallenberg, Priest of	Austria	ca. 1339	Duke Otto the Merry	Priest-jester; folk fool; real name Wigand von Theben
Kathrin Lise	Saxony	ca. 1722	Duchess Weißfels	Jestress

* = emperor, king, or queen; HRE = Holy Roman Emperor.

JESTER	PLACE	DATES	PATRON	COMMENTS
Kilian	Austria?		Margrave Albrecht	
Kilian	Hungary	ca. 1439–44	*Ladislaus III	Same as above?
Killigrew, Tom	England	ca. 1660–85	*Charles II	
"King of the Samoyeds"	Russia	ca. 1696–1725	*Peter I	Polish
Kuony, Hans	Austria	ca. 1315	Duke Leopold I	Features in anonymous woodcut of 1543 as "The Warning Fool"
Lacosta	Russia	ca. 1700	Czar Peter the Great	Portuguese Jew
Laloecen	Ireland	ca. 12th century	*Rederech	Clairvoyant fool
Leppert	Saxony?	ca. 1728	August II	Born Leipzig; actor-jester
Li Jiaming (Adding Clarity Li)	China	ca. 950	*1. Nan Tang Yuanzong 2. Song Qiqiu	
Li Keji (Surpassable Li)	China	ca. 860–74	*Tang Yizong	
Lips	Baden		Margrave Philip	Mocked clergy
Liu Gansan	China	19th century		Actor
Löffler (Spooner)	Bavaria	ca. 1521–35	Duke Ludwig	Prophet; trickster; shape-shifter
Lomnae Druith (the Jester)	Ireland	ca. 626	Finn	
Lopez, Luis	Spain	ca. 1563–68	*Philip II	Natural
Lorenzo, Don	Spain	ca. 1624–25	*Philip IV	Natural?
Louviers, Guillaume de	France	ca. 1515–47	*François I	
Luo Yiqing (Light Coat Luo)	China	ca. 1031–55	*Liao Xingzong	
Macareli, Antonio	Spain	ca. 1673–93		Dwarf, natural, Italian; granted two years paid leave
Macdacherda, Comgan	Ireland			

Name	Country	Date	Patron	Notes
Manuel	Spain	ca. 1628	*Philip IV	Natural; aka "Madman of the Furies" ("Loco de las Furias")
Maria de Todo el Mundo	Spain	ca. 1666–80	*Charles II	"Mary of the Whole World"
Mariquita	Spain	ca. 1637	Simón de la Cuesta	Natural, jestress; aka "The Crazy" ("La Loca")
Marot	France	ca. 1610–43	*Louis XIII	
Marquesin	Milan	ca. 1401–66	Duke Francesco Sforza	So resembled the duke's son-in-law Malatesta that he had to leave court when he visited
Martin "le Bailli"	France		Dukes of Orléans and Angoulême	
Martinet	Germany?		Bishop of Bamberg	Dwarf
Martos, Diego de	Spain	ca. 1640–63	*Philip IV	Natural
Martyn	England	ca. 1505	*Henry VII	"The Kinges Fole"
Mathurine	France	d. pre-1627	*Henri IV	Jestress
Matthias	Germany?		Ubt zu Marchtal	
Menicucci	Florence		Grand Duke Ferdinand I	Gifted in improvization
Mertel	German	ca. 1545		Painted by Hans Mielich, 1545
Merville	France	ca. 1547–59	*Henri II	
Michael	England	ca. 1292–1358	*Isabella of France	Natural
Michael dem Narren (the Fool)	Saxony	ca. 1639	Elector Johann George I	
Michon	France	ca. 1454	Marie of Anjou	Jestress
Micton le Fol	France	ca. 1364–80	*Charles V	
Miesko	Germany	d. 1619		Jester in various courts of Stettin-Pomerania

* = emperor, king, or queen; HRE = Holy Roman Emperor.

JESTER	PLACE	DATES	PATRON	COMMENTS
Mießte (Mißte), Hans	Pomerania	ca. 1540–1619	Duke Philipp II	
Miron	Galicia	ca. 8th century	King	Italian
Monarcho	England	ca. 1558–1603	*Elizabeth I	Natural; mentioned repeatedly in king's letters; painted by Sánchez Coellos; had a guardian
Morata	Spain	ca. 1579–87	*Philip II	
Morra, Sebastian de	Spain	ca. 1648	*Philip IV	Painted by Velázquez, ca. 1648
Moynet, Jacques	France	ca. 1591	Marshal Biron	Served the marshal as jester during siege of Rouen
Muñoz, Juana	Spain	ca. 1603–43	*1. Philip III *2. Philip IV	Natural, jestress; aka "Juana the Crazy" ("Juana la Loca")
Nanino	Mantua	ca. 1512	Marquis of Mantua	Real name Antonio da Trento; threatened with manacles for overstepping the mark
Nasrudin	Turkey	ca. 1389–1405	1. Sultan Bajazet? 2. Tamerlane	Mulla-jester; famous folk fool; musical—theorbo player; numerous tales about him
Nelle	Germany	ca. 1613	*Kaiser Matthias	
Neufgermain, Louis de	France	ca. 1637	1. Duke of Orléans 2. Cardinal Richelieu	Poet-jester
Ochoa, Francisco de Ocariz y	Spain	ca. 1633–38	*Philip IV	Natural
Ottchen, Hans	Pomerania		?	
Pace	England	ca. 1558–1603	*Elizabeth I	Aka "the bitter fool"
Pache	England	ca. 1485–1509	*Henry VII	
Pape Theun	Spain	ca. 1519–58	HRE Charles V	
Patch	England	ca. 1530	Cardinal Wolsey	Natural

Patriarch of Russia	Russia	ca. 1696–1725	*Peter I	Aka "King of Siberia"
Patrick	Scotland	ca. 1306–29	*Robert the Bruce	
Patteson, William	England	ca. 1530–35	Sir Thomas More	
Pearce, Dickie	England	ca. 16??	Earl of Suffolk	
Pedrillo	Russia	ca. 1696–1725	*1. Peter I / *2. Anna Ivanova	Principal jester
Pedro, Don	Spain	ca. 1645–57	*Philip IV	Natural
Pejerón (Sagacious?)	Spain	ca. 1600	Count of Benavente	Natural; painted by Moro
Perkeo	Heidelberg	ca. 1720	Duke	Dwarf, name comes from "Perche no?"—his response whenever offered a drink; painted by Adriaen van der Werff, early eighteenth century; another painting with a baboon
Pernia, Don Cristóbal de Castañeda y	Spain	ca. 1633–49	*Philip IV	Aka "Barbarossa"; painted by Velázquez, ca. 1636–38
Pettour, Roland le	England	ca. 1154–89	*Henry II	
Pfaff Cappador	Germany	ca. 1272–92	*Kaiser Rudolph I	Possibly a priest
Phryx	Holland			Details not known
Picol, William	England	ca. 1200	*John	
Pocher (Böcher), Konrad	Pfalz, Germany		Duke? Philip the Honest	Proverb about him; natural
Polite	France	ca. 1498–1515	*Louis XII	
Pomeranus, Andreas?	France	ca. 1515–47	*François I	
Porea	New Zealand	ca. 1860	Maori chief	Natural

* = emperor, king, or queen; HRE = Holy Roman Emperor.

JESTER	PLACE	DATES	PATRON	COMMENTS
Pritschen (Plankbed?), Peter	Pfalz, Germany	ca. 1592–1610	Elector Friedrich IV	"Merry counselor"; aka a "wit-head"
Prosch, Peter	Germany	1744–1804		Wandering jester, became mad
Pußman	Prussia	ca. 1701–13	*Friedrich I	Short banishment; "Merry counselor"
Quarrey, Jehan	France	ca. 1389	Duke of Bourgogne	
Querno, Camillo	Rome	ca. 1513–21	Pope Leo X	Doggerel poet-jester
Raconis, Charles de	France	d. 16 July 1646	Cardinal Richelieu	Born Chartres; Dr. of the Sorbonne; died at Château Raconis
Rahere	England	ca. 1087–1100	*William II	Said to have founded Saint Bartholomew's Hospital
Rajagriha	China	ca. 903–18	*Wang Jian	Perhaps Indian
Ralph Stultus (Fool)	England	ca. 1199–1216	*John	
Rambouillet, Madame de	France	ca. 1528	*François I	Jestress
Ramos, Maria	Spain	ca. 1681–89	*Charles II	Natural, jestress
Rana, Juan	Spain	ca. 1651	*Philip IV	
Ravelo, Manuel	Spain	ca. 1591–1628	*1. Philip II *2. Philip III *3. Philip IV	Natural
Reyes, Mateo de los	Spain	ca. 1680–96	*Charles II	Natural; "Matthew of the Kings"
Rivera, Juan de	Spain	ca. 1676	*Charles II	Natural
Robert Buffard	England	ca. 1307–27	*Edward II	Natural
Robert Fatuus (Foolish)	England	ca. 1122–1204	*Eleanor of Aquitaine	Natural
Robert Fool	England	ca. 1364	*Edward III	Real name William Cheupaym; king provided him with maintenance for life in the abbey of Saint Albans

Name	Country	Date	Patron	Notes
Robert "Horny"	England	ca. 1087–1100	*William II	Natural
Robert le Fol	England	ca. 1314–69	Philippa of Hainault	Natural
Rocaful, Juan	Spain	ca. 1623–24	*Philip IV	
Roennu Ressammach	Ireland	12th century?	*Cathal MacFinguinne	
Rollizo, Diego Vázquez	Spain	ca. 1599–26	*1. Philip III / *2. Philip IV	Painted more than once
Roquelaure, Duke of	France	ca. 1648–1715	*Louis XIV	Dwarf-jester; known for jokes, tales and scatological humor
Rosen, Kunz von der	Austria	ca. 1493–1519	HRE Maximilian I	Portrait etching by Daniel Hopfer, ca. 1515; leads a procession in a woodcut, ca. 1518
Ruiz, Madalena	Spain	ca. 1565–1605	Princess Juana	Dwarf, natural
Saint-Flarcy, Nicolas de	France	ca. 1365	Duke of Bourgogne	
Santorbas, Pedro de	Spain	ca. 1656	*Charles V	
Sarafino, Fra	Mantua	ca. 1500	Isabella d'Este	Priest-jester; beaten; close to Isabella d'Este
Scocola	Ferrara	ca. 1450–72	Duke Borso d'Este	Dwarfish; painted with Borso in fresco by Francesco Cossa, ca. 1470
Scogin, John	England	ca. 1461–83	*Edward IV	Scholar; real or fictitious? Many jestbooks about him
Serrano, Isabel	Spain	ca. 1601–11	*Philip III	Natural, jestress, sister of María?
Serrano, Maria	Spain	ca. 1601–11	*Philip III	Natural, jestress, sister of Isabel?
Sexten	England	ca. 1509–47	*Henry VIII	
Shen Jiangao (Gradually Stretching Taller)	China	ca. 961–76	*Nan Tang Liezu	Musical
Shenton, William	England	ca. 1578	*Elizabeth I	

* = emperor, king, or queen; HRE = Holy Roman Emperor.

JESTER	PLACE	DATES	PATRON	COMMENTS
Shi Dongtong (Moving Bucket)	China	ca. 550–59	*1. Bei Qi Gaozu	
			*2. Bei Qi Wenxuandi	
Shi Luoer (Mule)	China	ca. 1321–23	*Yuan Yingzong	
Shi Yezhu (Wild Pig)	China	ca. 874–79	*Tang Xizong	
Shir'ei, Karim	Persia	ca. 1848–96	Shah Naseredin	
Sibilot	France	ca. 1574–89	*Henri III	Jestress?
Singen, Hansel von	Baden	d. 1560	Margrave Philip	
Somers, Will	England		*1. Henry VIII	Features in three plays
			*2. Mary Tudor	
			*3. Elizabeth I	
Sorori	Japan	ca. 1536–98	General Hideyoshi	Also a scabbard maker
Steffen	Germany	ca. 1711–40	HRE Charles VI	Ministers kept waiting while king saw him
Stephano, Fra	Italy	ca. 1525	Frederico d'Este	Priest-jester
Stich	Bavaria	ca. 1231	Duke Ludwig	
Stockach, Jenny von	Austria	ca. 1386	Duke Leopold the III	Prophet and adviser
Stockwell	England	ca. 1628	Sir John Oglander	"Crippled fool"
Sunzi Duo (Many Grandsons)	China	ca. 772–846?	Duke of Zhao	Poet
Talhak	Ghazna	ca. 999–1030	Sultan Mahmud	
Tan Xinpei	China	1847–1917	Empress Cixi	Actor
Tang Chaomei (Best at Mocking)	China	ca. 923–26	*Tang Zhuangzong	Poet
Tarlton, Richard	England	d. 1588?	*Elizabeth I	Actor
Taubmann, Friedrich	Weimar	1565–1613	Duke Friedrich Wilhelm	Poet-jester; musical—lute player
Taulchinne	Ireland	ca. 2d century	*Conaire	Prophet, juggler

Tenali Rama	India	ca. 1509–29	*Krsnadevaraya	May not be historical
Thevenin de St. Legier	France	d. 1375	*Charles V	
Thomas Jester	England	ca. 1509–47	*Henry VIII	
Thomasina	England	ca. 1558–1603	*Elizabeth I	Dwarf jestress
Thony	France	ca. 1547–59	1. Duke of Orléans *2. Henri II 3. François II 4. Charles IX	Portrait 1560
Thulene	France	ca. 1574–89	*Henri III	
Tolan	India	ca. 11th century?	*Kulasekharavarman	Said to be jester-poet
Triboulet	France	ca. 1460s	*René	Natural, medallion of him by F. Laurana, ca. 1461–66; marble relief also by Laurana, ca. 1460
Triboulet	France	ca. 1515	*1. Louis XII *2. François I	Chalk drawing of him by Clouet school; real name Le Ferial
Tricomini	France	ca. 1648–1775	Queen of Louis XIV	
Ußinger, Michael	Spain	ca. 1556–98	*Philip II	
Valladolid, Pablo de	Spain	d. 1648	*Philip IV	Aka "Little Pablo" ("Pablillos")
Velasquillo	Spain		Fernando	Famous in his time
Vicenta/Vicentica Ferrer	Spain	ca. 1587–1600	*1. Philip II *2. Philip III	Natural, jestress?
Vicentino	Spain	ca. 1606–9	*Philip III	
Vicorite, Le	France	ca. 1483–98	*Charles VIII	
Viso, Catalina del	Spain	ca. 1643–64	*Philip IV	Natural, jestress
Wang Ganhua (Subtle Reformer King)	China	ca. 943–61	*Nan Tang Yuanzong	Registered with music census (yue jì)

---

* = emperor, king, or queen; HRE = Holy Roman Emperor.

JESTER	PLACE	DATES	PATRON	COMMENTS
Wang Gongjin (Openly Flawless Jade)	China	ca. 1195–1224	*Song Ningzong	
Wang Jinchao (Advance Court King)	China	ca. 1621–27	*Ming Xizong	Aka "Cripple King" ("Wang Quezi")
William	England	ca. 1413–22	*Henry V	Natural
William	England	ca. 1485	*Elizabeth of York	Natural
Witasky?	Russia	ca. 1721	*Peter I	
Withastaf, Robert	England	ca. 1307–27	*Edward II	
You Meng (Jester Meng)	China	ca. 356–19 B.C.	*Weiwang of Qi	Musical (*yueren*)
You Mo (Jester Don't)	China	ca. 457–425 B.C.	Xiangzi, ruler of Zhao	
You Shi (Jester Shi)	China	ca. 676–652 B.C.	Duke of Xian	Dwarf
You Zhan (Jester Twisty Pole)	China	ca. 246–210 B.C.	*Qin Shi Huangdi	Dwarf
Zapata	Spain	ca. 1519–58	HRE Charles V	
Zhang Tingfan (Model of the Court)	China			
Zhou Ju (Prefectural Turtledove)				
Zhou Za (Going Round in Circles)	China	ca. 923–26	*Tang Zhuangzong	
Zhu Hanzhen (Upright Fellow Wish)	China	ca. 550–59	*Bei Qi Gaozu	Poet; exiled for taking bribe
Zuñiga, Don Francesillo de,	Spain	ca. 1490–ca. 1532	1. Duke of Bejar HRE Charles V	Aka "King of the Jesters" ("Rey de los bufones") and "Duke of Jerusalem"; wrote chronicle of Charles; probably born in Bejar; possibly converted Jew
Zytho	Bohemia	ca. 1389	*Wenceslaus	Tricksterlike "magical" jester

* = emperor, king, or queen; HRE = Holy Roman Emperor.

GLOSSARY OF

CHINESE CHARACTERS

A Chou	阿丑	Di	狄
An Lushan	安祿山	Ding Daquan	丁大全
An Peixin	安譬新	Ding Xianxian	丁仙現
Baoyou	寶祐	Dong Songchen	董宋臣
bingjian	兵諫	Dongchuan	東川
Bo Yi	伯夷	Dongfang Shuo	東方朔
Budai Heshang	布袋和尚	Dongwu	東武
Cai Jing	蔡京	*dougen*	逗哏
Cai Yuanzhang	蔡元長	*feng*	瘋
canjun xi	參軍戲	Feng Jiazhen	馮家禎
Cao Cao	曹操	*fengjian*	諷諫
Changjiang	長江	Feng'ao	鳳翱
changyou	倡優	Fu Jian	符堅
Changzhou	常州	Gao Cuiwei	高崔嵬
chehuangge	扯謊歌	Gao Lishi	高力士
Chen Jun	陳俊	Gaozong	高宗
Chen Mo	陳謨	Gaozu	高祖
Chenzhou	陳州	*gu*	孤
Cheng Fuduan	成輔端	Gu Wuwei	顧無為
Cheng Minzheng	程敏政	Guan Zhong	關中
Chongning	崇寧	Guangling	廣陵
chou	丑	Guangzhou	廣州
Chu	楚	*guifeng*	規諷
Chunyu Kun	淳于髡	*guijian*	規諫
Cixi	慈禧	Guo Dingwu	郭定武
cuojue shi	錯覺式	Guo Pu	郭璞
Da shaguo	打沙鍋	Guo Sheren	郭舍人

GLOSSARY OF CHINESE CHARACTERS

Han	漢	"Li sao"	離騷
Han Shan	寒山	Li Shangyin	李商隱
Han Xin	韓信	Li Shen	李紳
Hangzhou	杭州	Li Shi	李實
he	和	Li Yuanhao	李元昊
He Jiasheng	何家生	Liyuan	梨園
Hebei	河北	Lizong	理宗
Hedong	河東	Liang	梁
hou	猴	Liao	遼
hou	侯	Liezu	烈祖
hulijing	狐狸精	*linglun*	伶倫
Huan	桓	*lingren*	伶人
Huang Fanchuo	黃幡綽	Liu Bang	劉邦
Huibo ci	迴波詞	Liu Gansan	劉趕三
Huizong	徽宗	Liu Wenshu	劉文樹
huo longzi	火龍子	Liu Yi	劉誼
Ji Gong	濟功	Liu Yong	柳永
jian	諫	Liu Ziyi	劉子儀
jianguan	諫官	Lu Ruojing	陸若鏡
Jianzhou	建州	Luzhou	盧州
Jiao De	焦德	Luo Baisui	羅百歲
Jiaofang	敎坊	Luo Yiqing	羅衣輕
Jiaoyao	僬僥	Man	蠻
Jin	金	Mao	毛
Jin	晉	Meng Chang	孟昶
Jing Xinmo	鏡新蘑	Mengzi	孟子
Jingzong	敬宗	Miluo	汨羅
Jiuyou Taishi	九優太師	*mianjian*	面諫
kegua	磕瓜	Ming	明
Kong Daofu	孔道輔	*neiyou*	內優
Kong Zonghan	孔宗翰	Niu Wenshu	牛溫舒
Kongzi	孔子	*paihuai*	徘徊
kuanghuanjie	狂歡節	*paiyou*	俳優
le er wang fan	樂而忘反	*pang guan zhe qing*	旁觀者清
Li Jiaming	李家明	Pang Xun	龐勛
Li Keji	李可及	Peng Yue	彭越
Li Maozhen	李茂貞	*penggen*	捧哏

Qi	齊	*tu*	土
qishi	感施	Wangongshan	皖公山
Qin	秦	Wang Anshi	王安石
Qin Gui	秦檜	Wang Ganhua	王感化
Qing	清	Wang Gongjin	王公瑾
Qu Yuan	屈原	Wang Jian	王建
Renzong	仁宗	Wang Jinchao	王進朝
san cun she	三寸舌	Wang Kang	王亢
San xiongdi	三兄弟	Wang Luo	王洛
Shen Jiangao	申漸高	Wang Qianyou	王乾祐
Shenzong	神宗	Wang Quezi	王瘸子
Shi De	拾得	Wang Shiming	王世明
Shi Dongtong	石動筒	Wang Shipeng	王十朋
Shi Luoer	史驟兒	Wang Xiaonong	汪笑儂
Shi Miyuan	史彌遠	Wang Yan	王衍
Shi Xiaofu	時小福	Wang Yanzheng	王延政
Shi Yezhu	石野豬	Weiwang	威王
Shizong	世宗	Wenzong	文宗
Shu	蜀	Wu	吳
Shuangling ji	雙鈴記	*wu guo chi*	無過痴
Si Zhong	佀鍾	Wu Zetian	武則天
sijian	死諫	Wu Zhi	吳賢
Sizhou	泗州	Wudi	武帝
Song	宋	Wuzong	武宗
Song Qiqiu	宋齊丘	Xi Sheng	郗生
Su Dongpo	蘇東坡	Xining	熙寧
Suzong	蘇宗	Xizong	熹宗
Sunshu Ao	孫叔教	Xiangong	獻公
Sun Wu	孫污	Xianzong	憲宗
Sunzi Duo	孫子多	Xiang Yu	項羽
Tan Xinpei	譚鑫培	*xiangsheng*	相聲
tan yan wei zhong	談言微中	Xiaozong	孝宗
Tang	唐	Xingzong	興宗
Tang Chaomei	唐朝美	Xiongzhou	雄州
Tiande	天得	*Xiu ru*	繡襦
Tiansheng	天聖	*xu paiyou*	蓄俳優
Tianxi	天禧	Xuanhe	宣和

Xuanzhou	宣州	*yueji*	樂籍
Xuanzong	玄宗	*yueren*	樂人
Yan Chang	嚴昶	Zhang Chong	張崇
Yan Hui	顏回	Zhang Hei	張黑
Yan Song	嚴嵩	Zhao Ji	趙濟
Yan Yuanxian	晏元獻	Zhao Xianfang	趙仙舫
Yang Danian	楊大年	Zhaotun	趙屯
Yang Guifei	楊貴妃	Zhaozong	昭宗
Yijing	易經	Zhezong	哲宗
Ying Xiang Chi	迎祥池	Zheng Dan	鄭儋
Yizong	懿宗	*zhi*	徵
You Meng	優孟	*Zhi*	跖
You Mo	優莫	Zhonggusi	鍾鼓司
You Shi	優施	Zhongyuan	重元
"You xian shi"	遊仙詩	Zhongzong	中宗
You Zhan	優㳺	Zhou	周
youjian	優諫	Zhou Ben	周本
youling	優伶	Zhou Jiu	州鳩
youren	優人	Zhou Za	周匝
Yuan	元	Zhu Yong	朱永
Yuan Shikai	袁世凱	*zhuru*	侏儒
Yuan Yanchun	袁彥純	Zhuangzi	莊子
Yuanzong	元宗	Zhuangzong	莊宗
Yuebu	樂部	Zizhanyang	子瞻樣

ABBREVIATIONS

BJXSDG Biji xiaoshuo daguan [筆記小説大觀]. Shanghai: Jinbu Shuju.

BM   British Museum.

BN   Bibliothèque Nationale.

CSJC Congshu jicheng [叢書集成]. Ed. Wang Yunwu [王雲五]. Taibei: Yiwen Yin-shuguan, 1967–.

GJYS Gujin yishi [古今逸史]. Comp. Wu Guan [吳琯], 20 vols. Taibei: Taiwan Commercial Press, 1969.

HIST Ershisi shiji [二十四史集]. Ed. Zhang Shenshi [張沈石] and Wu Shuping [吳樹平]. Beijing:
Zhonghua Shuju, 1980.

LDXHJ Lidai xiaohua ji [歷代笑話集]. Ed. Wang Liqi [王利器]. Hong Kong: Xinyue Chubanshe, ca. 1958.

LDXS Lidai xiaoshi [歷代小史], by Wang Yunwu [王雲五]. 12 vols. Taibei: Taiwan Commercial Press, 1969.

PMLA Publications of the Modern Language Association of America.

QDYD Qingdai yandu liyuan shiliao [清代燕都梨園史料]. Ed. Zhang Cixi [張次溪]. 4 vols. 1934; sequel vol. 4, 1937. In *Zhongguo shixue congshu* [中國史學叢書]. Taibei: Xuesheng Shuju, 1964.

SBBY Sibu beiyao [四部備要]. Taibei: Zhonghua Shuju, 1965.

SBCK Sibu congkan [四部叢刊]. Shanghai: Shanghai Yinshuguan, 1919–36.

SFSW Shuofu [説郛]. 1368. Comp. Tao Zongyi [陶宗儀] (1316–1403), ed. Zhang Zongxiang [張宗祥]. Repr. of Ming ed. Shanghai: Shangwu Shudian, 1927. (Edition held in School of Oriental and African Studies.)

SFWW Shuofu [説郛]. 1368. Comp. Tao Zongyi [陶宗儀]. 1316–1403. Ed. and enl. Tao Ting [陶珽]. Zhejiang: Wanwei Shantang Kanben, 1646. (Edition held in School of Oriental and African Studies.)

SKQS Siku quanshu [四庫全書]. 1,500 vols. Shanghai: Guji Chubanshe, 1987.

TPGJ Taiping guangji [太平廣記]. 977. Comp. Li Fang [李昉] (925–96) and others. *SKQS* 1043–46.

WCXSDG   *Wuchao xiaoshuo daguan* [五朝小説大觀]. Shanghai: Saoye Shan-
          fang, 1926.

XJYK   *Xiju yuekan.* [戲劇月刊].

YMSL   *Yuan Ming shiliao biji congkan.* [元明史料筆記叢刊]. Beijing: Zhonghua
          Shuju, 1959.

YYJ   *Youyu ji* [優語集]. Comp. and ed. Ren Erbei [任二北]. Shanghai: Wenyi
          Chubanshe, 1981; repr. 1982.

ZGGD   *Zhongguo gudian xiqu lunzhu jicheng* [中國古代戲曲論著集成]. 10 vols. Beijing:
          Zhongguo Xiju Chubanshe, 1982.

NOTES

PROLOGUE

1. Laurent Joubert, *Treatise on Laughter* (1579), trans. and annot. Gregory David de Rocher (University: University of Alabama Press, 1980), 93; *Le traité du ris*, facsimile of 1579 ed. (Geneva: Saltkine Reprints, 1973), 228–29.

2. Estebanillo González, *Vida y hechos de Estebanillo González: Hombre de buen humor*, ed. Nicholas Spadaccini and Anthony N. Zahareas, 2 vols. (Madrid: Castalia, 1978), introduction, 40.

3. G. Spencer-Brown, *Laws of Form* (New York: Dutton, 1979), 109–10.

4. Ernst Gombrich, "Relativism in the Humanities: The Debate about Human Nature," in *Topics of Our Time: Twentieth Century Issues in Learning and in Art* (London: Phaidon, 1991), 42.

5. Sheila Ostrander and Lynn Schroeder, *Cosmic Memory* (London: Simon and Schuster, 1993), 176.

6. Personal communication with Sandra Billington.

7. Leonard Feinberg, ed., *Asian Laughter: An Anthology of Oriental Satire and Humor* (New York: Weatherhill, 1971), 3.

8. Although there is a good deal of work being done on the fool in the widest sense of the word, there is very little dealing specifically with the court jester. It seems that by far the most popular areas of research are literary fools, particularly Shakespearean, and various twentieth-century Western writings, with the latter tending to be more adventurous and original than the former. As for China, there seems hardly any interest in humorous subjects, apart from William Callahan's attempt to compare Chinese and Western humor in "Another Book of Laughter and Misunderstandings" (Ph.D. diss., University of Hawaii, 1992); Regina Llamas at Harvard on the role of the clown in Chinese drama; and Wei Chen-hsuan at the London School of Oriental and African Studies, on Maitreya, the Laughing Buddha.

9. Wang Guowei, "Youyu lu," in *Song Yuan xiqu shi* (Hong Kong: Taiping

Shuju, 1964), 249–66; Ren Erbei, *Youyu ji* (Shanghai: Shanghai Wenyi Chuban-she, 1981; repr. 1982).

10. The pictures included here are a drop in the ocean of those collected. I am currently working on a book to give the rest the attention they deserve: *The Court Jester in Art, Architecture, and Advertising.*

11. See "Guji liezhuan," in *Shiji*, by Sima Qian, annot. Pei Yin (Shanghai: Zhonghua Shuju, 1963), vol. 10, fol. 126, 3197–214, of which the best published translation is in *War-Lords*, by William Dolby and John Scott (Edinburgh: South-side, 1974), 157–68. Also see "Lingguan zhuan," in *Wudai shi*, by Ouyang Xiu (1007–72), *SKQS*, 279:228a–31a; "Huixie zhuan," in *Nan Tang shu*, by Ma Ling (Song), fol. 25, *SKQS*, 464:36ɪb–64a; "Lingguan zhuan," in *Liaoshi*, by Tuo Tuo (1314–55), fol. 109, *SKQS*, 289:707a–b; "Dongfang Shuo zhuan," in *Hanshu*, by Ban Gu (32–92), *HIST,* 6, fol. 65, 2841–76, trans. Burton Watson in Ban Gu, *Courtier and Commoner in Ancient China: Selections from the "History of the Former Han" by Pan Ku* (New York: Columbia University Press, 1974), 79–106. Apart from these translations of Sima Qian and Ban Gu, there is a selection in Marja Kaikkonen's excellent introduction to *Laughable Propaganda: Modern Xiangsheng as Didactic Entertainment,* Stockholm East Asian Monographs 1 (Stockholm: University of Stockholm, 1990), 21–49.

12. In J. Collier, ed., *Fools and Jesters* (London: Shakespeare Society, 1842), 1–65, and W. Carew Hazlitt, ed., *Shakespeare Jest-Books* (London: Willis and Sotheran, 1864), 2:189–260, respectively. The first edition of Tarlton was pub-lished between 1588 and 1592 but is no longer extant. The most helpful summary of various jestbooks and their editions is John Wardroper, *Jest upon Jest: A Selec-tion from the Jestbooks and Collections of Merry Tales Published from the Reign of Richard III to George III* (London: Routledge and Kegan Paul, 1970).

13. Karl Flögel, *Geschichte der Hofnarren* (Leipzig: Siegert, 1789; repr. New York: Olms, 1977); Enid Welsford, *The Fool: His Social and Literary History* (Lon-don: Faber and Faber, 1935; repr. 1968).

CHAPTER ONE

1. W. Tod Ritchie, ed., *The Bannatyne Manuscript* (Edinburgh: Scottish Text Society, 1930), vol. 4, quoted in Sandra Billington, "The Role of the Fool in En-glish Drama from the Fifteenth to the Early Sixteenth Century" (Ph.D. diss., Cambridge University, 1979), 11.

2. Horace, *Satires, Epistles and Ars Poetica,* trans. H. Rushton Fairclough, Loeb Classical Library (London: Heinemann; New York: Putnam, 1926).

3. *"Wenxuan" Li Shan zhu,* comp. Xiao Tong (501–31), annot. Li Shan (d. 689), fol. 8, *SBBY,* 560, 8a, trans. Burton Watson in *Chinese Rhyme-Prose: Poems in the Fu Form from the Han and Six Dynasties Periods* (New York: Columbia University

Press, 1971), 48. Although I am humbled by Watson's skills as a translator, I question his use of "actors" where "jesters" would have been more accurate and have adapted his beautiful translation accordingly.

4. Zhang Geng, "Shilun xiqu de qiyuan he xingcheng," *Xinjian She* 1 (1963): 59.

5. *Shuowen judu,* comp. Xu Shen (ca. 58–ca. 147), ed. Wang Jun (Shanghai: Shanghai Guji Shudian, 1983), 2:1075, 1077, and 1084.

6. I translate these terms as "actor" only when it is a professional stage or household actor performing a scripted play rather than an improvised jester skit, that is, relatively late in their history.

7. For a more detailed treatment of the Roman comic actors and their contribution to the world of jesters, see in chapter 6 below, "Act 2 Athens, Atella, and Archmimes."

8. Sergy N. Shoubinsky, "Court Jesters and Their Weddings in the Reigns of Peter the Great and Anna Ivanovna," in *Historical Narratives from the Russian,* by H. C. Romanoff (London: Rivingtons, 1871), 3–4.

9. Letters and Papers of Henry VIII, MS Public Record Office, SP.1.101, 152. Sexton is allegedly the jester of Cardinal Wolsey, better known by the common name for court fools at the time, Patch, whom Wolsey gave to Henry as a last ditch attempt to curry favor. The new young fool is said to be Will Somers, who subsequently became Henry's favorite jester. The literary references to Patch and Will's joint pranks are therefore of questionable historical accuracy. See John Southworth, *Fools and Jesters at the English Court* (Thrupp, Gloucestershire: Sutton, 1998), 70.

10. Thomas Fuller, *The History of the Worthies of England* (1662), ed. John Nichols, 2 vols. (London: Nichols, 1811), 2:311. "Happy unhappy" seems to refer to answers that hit the mark. Other accounts I have come across suggest that Tarlton started as a water carrier, and this is confirmed by Southworth, *Fools and Jesters,* 114.

11. Margaret Landon, *Anna and the King of Siam* (Garden City, NY: Garden City, 1945), 189, quoted in G. Kalff, *Opkompst, Bloei en Verdwijning van de Hofnar* (Amsterdam: De Poortpers, 1954), 26. Kalff's is one of the most neglected works of "jesterology," featuring in the bibliography of only one (Dutch) writer, even though he has included a great range of primary source materials not used elsewhere, thereby contributing some excellent new evidence to the field.

12. Flögel, *Geschichte der Hofnarren,* 207 and 302.

13. *A Pleasant History of the Life and Death of Will Summers: How He Came First to Be Known at Court, and by What Means He Got to Be King Henry the Eighth's Jester, with the Entertainment That His Cousin Patch, Cardinal Wolsey's Fool, Gave Him at His Lord's House, and How the Hogsheads of Gold Were Known by This Means* (London: Vere and Wright, 1676; repr. James Caulfield, 1794), 23.

14. E. Loseth, ed., *Robert le Diable: Roman d'aventures* (Paris: Firmin Didot, 1903), lines 1030–42 and 1051–54.

15. Alfred de Musset, *Fantasio*, in *Théâtre complet*, ed. Maurice Allem (Paris: Gallimard, 1958), 276–323; Alexander Hislop, ed., *The Book of Scottish Anecdote: Humorous, Social, Legendary and Historical*, 8th ed. (Glasgow: Morison, [nineteenth century?]), 61–62.

16. Flögel, *Geschichte der Hofnarren*, 274.

17. Sir Walter Scott, *Ivanhoe* (London: Nelson, 1897), 11.

18. Flögel, *Geschichte der Hofnarren*, 284.

19. J. B. Pratt, *The Life and Death of Jamie Fleeman, the Laird of Udny's Fool*, 3d ed. (Aberdeen: Lewis Smith, 1912), 53–54.

20. Lee Siegel, *Laughing Matters: Comic Tradition in India* (Chicago: University of Chicago Press, 1987), 322.

21. Walter Kaiser, *Praisers of Folly: Erasmus, Rabelais, Shakespeare* (Cambridge: Harvard University Press, 1963), 126.

22. ʿObeyd-e Zakani, *"The Ethics of the Aristocrats" and Other Satirical Works*, trans. Hasan Javadi, Middle Eastern Series 11 (Piedmont, CA, Jahan Books, 1985), 10.

23. Olive Macleod, *Chiefs and Cities in Central Africa* (London: Blackwood, 1912), 124, quoted in Kalff, *Opkomst*, 23.

24. Zakani, *"Ethics of the Aristocrats,"* 125, and Ali Asghar Halabi, "The Development of Humour and Satire in Persia with Special Reference to ʿUbaid-i Zakani'" (Ph.D. diss., Edinburgh University, 1980), 69. Although Halabi has not hitherto been referred to in any work on court jesters, he has made a more original contribution to the subject than perhaps anyone since Flögel. He uses primary sources, as much Arabic material as Persian, and has brought to light a number of jesters and humorists previously hidden from Western eyes, adding more colorful hues to the picture of early Islamic civilization. See also Franz Rosenthal, *Humor in Early Islam* (Westport, CT: Greenwood 1976).

25. J. A. Decourdemanche, *Sottisier de Nasr-Eddin-Hodja: Bouffon de Tamerlan* (Brussels: Chez Gay et Douce, 1878), 57; Laurence Binyon, *Akbar*, 2d ed. (London: Nelson, 1939; repr. 1942), 60.

26. "Guji liezhuan," 3200.

27. *Tangwen xushi*, comp. Lu Xinyuan (Qing), fol. 5, in *Quan Tang wen*, ed. Dong Zao and others (Beijing: Zhonghua Shuju, 1983), 11:2224b–25a. For perhaps the best secondary-source comments on the musical element of Chinese jesters, see Hou Baolin and others, "'You ge'—'chang' de kesu zhi yuan," in *Xiangsheng suyuan* (Beijing: Renmin Wenxue Chubanshe, 1982), 186–90.

28. Friedrich Ebeling, *Zur Geschichte der Hofnarren: Friedrich Taubmann—ein Kulturbild* (Leipzig: Lehmann, 1887), 178, 86.

29. Shoubinsky, "Court Jesters and Their Weddings," 34.

30. Personal communication with William Dolby.

31. Hsü Tao-Ching [Xu Daojing], *The Chinese Conception of the Theater* (Seattle: University of Washington Press, 1985), 302.

32. "Huixie zhuan," *SKQS,* 464:363a.

33. "Paiyou," in *Yuefu zalu,* by Duan Anjie (ca. 830–ca. 900), *ZGGD,* 1:58.

34. *Jiegu lu,* by Nan Chuo (Tang), *SKQS,* 839:982b–83a. A *jie gu* was a drum with ivory inlay on the base, beaten with two drumsticks.

35. *Shilin bishu luhua,* by Ye Mengde (1077–1148), fol. 1, *SKQS,* 863:652a–b. *Qu* seems to indicate "lyrics" here rather than "melody," but it could mean something like "Nice tune, shame about the key!"

36. *Zhuozhong zhi,* by Liu Ruoyu (Ming), fol. 16, *CSJC,* bk. 3967, 112.

37. Charles Hucker, *A Dictionary of Official Titles in Imperial China* (Stanford: Stanford University Press, 1985), 191.

38. Anton Zijderveld, *Reality in a Looking-Glass: Rationality through an Analysis of Traditional Folly* (London: Routledge and Kegan Paul, 1982), 51. The term "minstrel" or *ministrelli,* as used in the Middle Ages, incorporated a far wider range of performing skills than the modern reader might assume. To avoid confusion, I use "minstrel" in the sense of one who concentrated on music and "entertainer" as the umbrella term for *ministrelli, jongleurs,* and related words. Constance Bullock-Davies, *Menestrellorum Multitudo: Minstrels at a Royal Feast* (Cardiff: University of Wales Press, 1978), 19.

39. Sydney Anglo, "The Court Revels of Henry VII," *Bulletin of the John Rylands Library* 43 (1960–61): 39.

40. Bullock-Davies, *Menestrellorum Multitudo,* 2; *Dictionary of National Biography,* ed. L. Stephen and S. Lee (London: Smith, Elder, 1908–9), 19:370; R. Morgan, "Old French Jogleor and Kindred Terms: Studies in Medieval Romance Lexicography," *Romance Philology* 7 (1953–54): 282–83.

41. Southworth, *Fools and Jesters,* 36. Southworth also gives clear definitions of other less well known terms for fools and jesters in England (89–90).

42. Thomas Chobham, *Thomae de Chobham "Summa confessorum,"* ed. H. Broomfield, Series Analecta Mediaevealia Namurcensia (Paris, 1968), 292, quoted in and trans. Christopher Page, *The Owl and the Nightingale: Musical Life and Ideas in France, 1100–1300* (London: Dent, 1989), 23.

43. The term "jester" probably originated with the *geste* of the *chansons de geste* sung or chanted by European entertainers, although it is hard to know at what point "jest" took on its humorous meaning.

44. For these insights I am grateful to Philip Bennett.

45. Henrik Birnbaum, "Laughter, Play and Carnival in Old Rus," in *Words*

and Images: Essays in Honour of Professor (Emeritus) Dennis Ward, ed. M. Falchikov and others (Nottingham: Astra Press, 1989), 30–31.

46. Russell Zguta, *Russian Minstrels: A History of the Skomorokhi* (Oxford: Clarendon Press, 1978), 16, 42. and 56; Birnbaum, "Laughter, Play and Carnival," 29–30.

47. Zhang Geng, "Shilun xiqu de qiyuan he xingcheng," 64.

48. Gabriel Antoine Joseph Hécart, *Stultitiana, ou Petite biographie des fous de la ville de Valenciennes* (n.p., 1823), 14.

49. In Hazlitt, *Shakespeare Jest-Books,* 2:354.

50. Zguta, *Russian Minstrels,* 21. Could there be a connection between them and the *goliardi,* the wandering scholars of medieval Europe?

51. A. Luzio and R. Renier, "Buffoni, nani e schiavi dei Gonzaga ai tempi di Isabella d'Este," *Estr. Nuova Ant.,* ser. 3 (1891), part 1, 24:624.

52. John Doran, *The History of Court Fools* (London: Bentley, 1858), 248.

53. J. C. Williams, *The Court Poet in Medieval Ireland,* Proceedings of the British Academy 57 (London: Oxford University Press, 1971), 14.

54. Ibid., 6.

55. Alan Harrison, *The Irish Trickster* (Sheffield: Sheffield Academic Press, 1989), 32.

56. Edmund Spenser, *A View of the Present State of Ireland,* in *The Prose Works,* ed. Rudolph Gottfried (Baltimore: Johns Hopkins Press, 1949), 124.

57. "The Death of Fergus Mac Leide," in *Ancient Irish Tales,* ed. Tom Peete Cross and Clark Harris Slover (Dublin: Figgis, 1936; repr. 1969), 472.

58. Ibid., 474–75.

59. Lee Milton Hollander, *The Skalds: A Selection of Their Poems* (New York: Princeton University Press, 1945), 7, 4, and 38.

60. Finnur Jónsson, *Den oldnorske og oldislandske litteraturs historie,* 3 vols. (Copenhagen: Gad, 1894–1902), 1:338, quoted in Hollander, *Skalds,* 6.

61. Hollander, *Skalds,* 161.

62. Flögel, *Geschichte der Hofnarren,* 289. For a full treatment of Taubmann's relationship with his master, see Ebeling, *Zur Geschichte der Hofnarren,* 1–160.

63. Zakani, *"Ethics of the Aristocrats,"* 9. Paul Sprachmann, "Persian Satire, Parody and Burlesque," in *Persian Literature,* ed. E. Yarshater (Albany, NY: Bibliotheca Persica, 1988), 234.

64. David Shulman, *The King and the Clown in South Indian Myth and Poetry* (Princeton: Princeton University Press, 1985), 175. This is a tremendously eloquent and insightful work; see also Vincent Smith, *Akbar the Great Mogul, 1542–1605* (Oxford: Clarendon Press, 1917), 237.

65. Siegel, *Laughing Matters*, 298.

66. W. Roscoe, *The Life and Pontificate of Leo the Tenth*, ed. T. Roscoe, 4 vols. (London: Cadell and Davies, 1846), 3:332; verses trans. Herbert Vaughan, *The Medici Popes (Leo X and Clement VII)* (London: Methuen, 1908), 168–69.

67. Samuel Rowley (d. ca. 1633), *When You See Me You Know Me* (1604) (Oxford: Oxford University Press, 1952).

68. Luis Zapata (sixteenth century), *Miscelánea de Zapata* (Madrid: Imprenta Nacional, 1859), quoted in Diane Avalle-Arce, "La 'Crónica de Carlos V' de Don Francesillo de Zuñiga: Según el manuscrito 6193 de la Biblioteca Nacional de Madrid" (Ph.D. diss., Smith College, 1975), 35. Avalle-Arce has written one of the most informative works on Spanish jesters and provides the most thoroughly annotated edition of Zuñiga's *Chronicle* available.

69. R. H. Blyth, *Japanese Humor* (Tokyo: Japan Travel Bureau, 1957), 73.

70. *Tang yulin*, by Wang Dang (fl. ca. 1110), fol. 2, *SKQS*, 1038:28b.

71. *Qiyan lu*, by Hou Bai (fl. ca. 581), *LDXHJ*, 37.

72. *Beimeng suoyan*, by Sun Guangxian (900–68), fol. 19, *SKQS*, 1036:118b.

73. *Qingyi lu*, by Tao Gu (Song), *SKQS*, 1047:841a; *Youhuan jiwen*, by Zhang Shinan (fl. 1225), fol. 2, *CSJC*, bk. 2871, 13.

74. *Kaitian chuanxin ji*, by Zheng Qi (d. 899), *SKQS*, 1042:847a.

75. *Qingyi lu*, *SKQS*, 1047:865a. *Chengxiang* can refer either to a prime minister or to the appearance of an orange. There is also a visual pun on *zi* meaning "dregs" (or "pith"?) which contains the character *zai* meaning "prime minister," the overall gist suggesting that the prime minister's power should be curtailed.

76. *Jinhuazi zabian*, by Liu Chongyuan (fl. ca. 940), fol. 1, *SKQS*, 1035:829b–30a. The empress was the wife of Emperor Gaozong (r. 650–83).

77. "Paiyoumen," in *Shihua zonggui*, by Ruan Yue (fl. ca. 1126), part 1, fol. 46, *SKQS*, 1478:646a.

78. *Jia* means "domestic" or "family," but it may also be a pun for *jia*, "to add."

79. "Huixie zhuan," *SKQS*, 464:362b–63a. There are several versions of this poem with slight differences, although the import is the same; in one, however, the emperor "was delighted, and rewarded him with a bundle of silk." *Jingkang xiangsu zaji*, by Huang Chaoying (fl. ca. 1101), fol. 7, *SKQS*, 850:418a.

80. "Huixie zhuan," *SKQS*, 464:362b; "Paiyoumen," *SKQS*, 1478:646a.

81. Estebanillo González, *Vida y hechos*, 2:475. There is much debate as to the historicity of Estebanillo and his autobiography. The historical, biographical, and geographic details of the book are very accurate. Although the debate has not been settled, I am inclined to believe he was real. See William Knapp Jones, "Estevanillo González," *Revue Hispanique* 77 (1929): 223.

82. *Su Wei Gong wenji*, by Su Xiangxian (Song), quoted in *YYJ*, 93.

83. *Dong Qi jishi,* by Fan Zhen (1007–87), *SKQS,* 1036:582a–b.

84. *Songbai leichao,* comp. Pan Yongyin (fl. ca. 1669), ed. Liu Zhuoying (Beijing: Shumu Wenxian Chubanshe, 1985), vol. 2, fol. 5, 428–29.

85. *Shiyou tanji,* by Li Zhi (1059–1109), *SKQS,* 863:172b–73a. The hat was called "Zizhan style" *(Zizhanyang),* using Su's given name.

86. *Chengzhai shihua,* by Yang Wanli (1124–1206), *SKQS,* 1480:736b–37a, my emphasis. Su Dongpo's line referred to how a monarch should rule, and the jesters simply replaced "rule" with "laugh."

87. "Weizhao," in *Guoyu,* 2 vols. (Shanghai: Shanghai Guji Chubanshe, 1978), vol. 2, quoted in Zhang Geng, "Shilun xiqu de qiyuan he xingcheng," 58–59.

88. Avigdor Dagan, *The Court Jesters,* trans. Barbara Harshav (London: Bloomsbury, 1991), 58.

89. "Zhengyu," in *Guoyu,* vol. 2, fol. 16, 518.

90. Francis Bacon, "Of Deformity," in *Essays of Francis Bacon* (London: Dent; New York: Dutton, 1906; repr. 1916), 132.

91. Personal communication with Paul Dundas. It seems the keeping of dwarfs and hunchbacks was widespread in India. Asvaghosha, *The Buddha-karita of Asvaghosha,* in *Buddhist Mahayana Texts,* ed. E. B. Cowell (1894; New York: Dover, 1969), which deals with the life of Buddha, describes "hump-backed men coming out from the great families, and troops of . . . dwarfs" (28).

92. Southworth, *Fools and Jesters,* 10–11.

93. Véronique Dasen, *Dwarfs in Ancient Egypt and Greece* (Oxford: Clarendon Press, 1993), 25–29 and 133, quoted in Southworth, *Fools and Jesters,* 10–11.

94. Edward Wood, *Giants and Dwarfs* (London: Bentley, 1868), 253–54; A. J. Wace, "Grotesques and the Evil Eye," *Annual of the British School at Athens* 10 (1903–4): 109; Richard Swiderski, "From Folk to Popular: Plastic Evil Eye Charms," in *The Evil Eye,* ed. Clarence Maloney (New York: Columbia University Press, 1976), 37.

95. Carolus, *Excerpta de legationibus* (Paris, 1609), 128, cited in Kenneth Northcott, "The Fool in Early New High German Literature: Some Observations," in *Essays in German Literature,* ed. F. Norman (London: University of London Institute of Germanic Studies, 1965), 1:30. Wood, *Giants and Dwarfs,* 241.

96. Wood, *Giants and Dwarfs,* 280.

97. For more details of paintings of dwarfs and jesters, see Erica Tietze-Conrat, *Dwarfs and Jesters in Art,* trans. E. Osborn (New York: Phaidon, 1957), and Wood, *Giants and Dwarfs,* 258.

98. Susan Miller, "How to Sell Safer Sex," *New Scientist,* 27 February 1993, 12–13.

99. Robert Armin (ca. 1568–1615), *A Nest of Ninnies* (1608), in *Fools and Jesters,* ed. J. Collier, 1–65 (London: Shakespeare Society, 1842), 16.

100. Cross and Slover, "Death of Fergus Mac Leide," 477.

101. A. Canel, *Recherches historiques sur les fous des rois de France* (Paris: Kemerre, 1873), 68 and 130.

102. Bernal Diaz de Castillo, *The Conquest of New Spain,* trans. J. M. Cohen (Harmondsworth, Middlesex: Penguin Books, 1963), 227.

103. Francisco Clavigero, *The History of Mexico,* trans. Charles Cullen, intro. B. Feldman, facsimile reprint of first ed. (London: Robinson, 1787; repr. New York: Garland, 1979), vol. 2 bk. 5, 215.

104. Joseph Pitton de Tournefort, *Relation d'un Voyage du Levant* (Lyons, 1717), quoted in Kalff, *Opkomst,* 31, my emphasis. Copper engravings of these Turkish jesters can be found in *Abbildung des turkischen Hofes nach Ferreol* (Nürnberg, 1789), 34 n. 36.

105. Landon, *Anna and the King of Siam,* 189, quoted in Kalff, *Opkomst,* 26.

106. Wood, *Giants and Dwarfs,* 257.

107. Carl Justi, "Dwarfs, Buffoons and Jesters," in *Velasquez and His Times* (London: Grevel, 1889), 435.

108. Cf. C. Charles Frankland, *Narrative of a Visit to the Courts of Russia and Sweden in the Years 1830 and 1831* (London: H. Colburn and R. Bentley, 1832), cited in Wood, *Giants and Dwarfs,* 262.

109. Geoffroy Gaimar, *Lestorie des Engles,* ed. Thomas Duffus Hardy and Charles Trice Martin, Rolls Series (London: Her Majesty's Stationery Office, 1888–89), vol. 1 (text), 168–71 and vol. 2 (translation), 126–29, quoted in Southworth, *Fools and Jesters,* 14.

110. "Nan si," in *Han Feizi,* by Han Fei (ca. 280–234 B.C.), ed. Teruo Takeuchi, 5th ed., 2 vols. (Tokyo: Meiji Shoin, 1964), 2:702–4.

111. Gaius Suetonius, "Tiberius," in *The Lives of the Caesars,* trans. J. C. Rolfe, 2 vols., Loeb Classical Library (London: Heinemann; New York: Putnam, 1914; repr. and rev. 1930), 1.3.380–81, my emphasis.

112. Tietze-Conrat, *Dwarfs and Jesters in Art,* 86.

113. David Knechtges, "Wit, Humor, and Satire in Early Chinese Literature," *Monumenta Serica* 29 (1970–71): 83 n. 18.

114. "Daozhou min," in *Bai Juyi ji,* by Bai Juyi (772–846), ed. Gu Xuejie (Beijing: Zhonghua Shuju, 1979), vol. 1, fol. 3, 68–69, trans. Arthur Waley in Feinberg, *Asian Laughter,* 70.

115. Personal communication with David McMullen.

116. Longinus, "On the Sublime," trans. T. S. Dorsch in *Classical Literary*

Criticism (Harmondsworth, Middlesex: Penguin Books, 1965), 157, quoted in Southworth, *Fools and Jesters*, 11.

117. *Miscellanea curiosa, medica, physica* (Leipzig, 1670), cited in Wood, *Giants and Dwarfs*, 286; Andrew Allen, "The Sinister Art of 'Hindering,'" *Scotsman*, 11 February 1989, 5.

118. William Shakespeare, *A Midsummer Night's Dream*, ed. Harold Brooks, 2d ed. (London: Methuen, 1979).

119. S. Linné, "Humpbacks in Ancient America," *Ethnos* 8, 4 (1943): 170–71.

120. Personal communication with Paul Dundas.

121. Welsford, *Fool*, 66–67.

122. Shulman, *King and the Clown*, 202.

123. Siegel, *Laughing Matters*, 21.

124. Bacon, "Of Deformity," 131.

125. Giacomo Leopardi, *Zibaldone* (1823), ed. F. Flora (Milan, 1938), 2:820, quoted in Kaiser, *Praisers of Folly*, 10.

126. Dagan, *Court Jesters*, 20.

127. Sebastian Brant, *Das Narrenschiff* (1494), ed. Hans-Joachim Mähl (Stuttgart: Reclam, 1964; repr. 1988); translated as *Ship of Fools* by E. Zeydel (New York: Columbia University Press, 1944; repr. New York: Dover, 1962).

128. Desiderius Erasmus, *Praise of Folly (Encomium moriae)*, in *"Praise of Folly" and Letter to Maarten van Dorp, 1515*, trans. Betty Radice, annot. A. H. T. Levi (Harmondsworth, Middlesex: Penguin Books, 1971; repr. and rev. 1993). The earliest English translation, also worth looking at, is *The Praise of Folie* (1549), trans. Sir Thomas Chaloner, ed. C. H. Miller (Oxford: Oxford University Press, 1965).

129. Brant, *Ship of Fools*, introduction, 6.

130. Quoted in Hans Wyss, *Der Narr im schweizerischen Drama des 16. Jahrhunderts* (Bern: Haupt, 1959), 126; Elsie Parsons and Ralph Beals, "The Sacred Clowns of the Pueblo and Mayo-Yaqui Indians," *American Anthropologist* 36, 4 (1934): 500.

131. Barbara Swain, *Fools and Folly during the Middle Ages and the Renaissance* (New York: Columbia University Press, 1932), 46.

132. William Shakespeare, *King Richard II*, ed. Peter Ure, 5th ed. (London: Methuen, 1961), my emphasis.

133. David Lyndsay (ca. 1490–ca. 1555), *Ane Satyre of the Thrie Estaits*, ed. James Kinsley (London: Cassell, 1954), 193.

134. BBC Radio 4, "Thought for the Day," 13 May 1992; G. P. Fedotov, The Holy Fools," in *The Russian Religious Mind*, ed. I. Meyendorff (Cambridge: Harvard University Press, 1966), 1:316–18; Birnbaum, "Laughter, Play and Carnival," 28.

135. O. F. A. Meinardus, "Zeitgenössische Gottesnarren in den Wüsten Ägyptens," *Ostkirchliche Studien* 36, 4 (1987): 301−10; Baron de Reiffenberg, "Histoire des fous en titre d'office," in *Le lundi, nouveaux récits de Marsilius Brunck* (Brussels: Hauman, 1835), 259.

136. William Shakespeare, *The Tragedy of King Lear* (1607), ed. Kenneth Muir, 9th rev. ed. (London: Methuen, 1972), 5.3.71.

137. Brenda Rae Eno, illus., *Jewish Proverbs*, (San Francisco: Chronicle Books, 1989), 20; François Rabelais, *Le tiers livre des faicts et dicts héroiques du bon Pantagruel* (1546), in *Oeuvres complètes*, ed. Pierre Jourda (Paris: Classiques Garnier, 1962), 1:589.

138. Justi, "Dwarfs, Buffoons and Jesters," 435. The three popes reigned 1572−85, 1585−90, and 1590−91, respectively.

139. William Holdsworth, *A History of English Law*, 7th rev. ed., 16 vols. (London: Methuen, 1956; repr. 1966), 1:473−74. For more on this, see also Southworth, *Fools and Jesters*, 57.

140. William Willeford, *The Fool and His Sceptre: A Study in Clowns and Jesters and Their Audience* (London: Arnold 1969), 132.

141. John Jones, Common-Place Book, BM MS Sloane 517, fol. 33.

142. T. H. Jamieson, ed., *A Banquet of Jests* (Edinburgh: William Paterson, 1872), 22−23.

143. Doran, *History of Court Fools*, 43.

144. W. Empson, "The Praise of Folly," in *The Structure of Complex Words* (London: Chatto and Windus, 1951), 110; V. Gentili, "Madmen and Fools Are a Staple Commodity: On Madness as a System in Elizabethan and Jacobean Plays," *Cahiers Elizabethains* 34 (1988): 14.

145. Daisetz T. Suzuki, *Sengai, the Zen Master* (Greenwich, CT: New York Graphic Society [1971], 134, quoted in Conrad Hyers, *Zen and the Comic Spirit* (New York: Rider, 1974), 37.

146. Catriona Kelly, *Petrushka: The Russian Carnival Puppet Theatre* (Cambridge: Cambridge University Press, 1990), 90.

147. Personal communication with Reza Sabri-Tabrizi; Halabi, "Development of Humour," 65−66.

148. Thomson, *Acts of Parliament of Scotland*, vol. 1, quoted in Pratt, *Life and Death of Jamie Fleeman*, 10−11.

149. Duchess of Orléans, *Correspondence* (Paris, 1890), 2:315, quoted in Kalff, *Opkomst*, 64.

150. Confucius (d. 479 B.C.), *The Analects of Confucius*, trans. William Dolby (Edinburgh: privately published, 1987), 18.5, p. 89.

151. Paul Radin, *The Trickster: A Study in American Indian Mythology* (London: Routledge and Kegan Paul, 1956), ix.

152. Jo Anne Kraus, "The Comedy of Paradox: Mythic and Medieval Tricksters in Narrative" (Ph.D. diss., City University of New York, 1990), 35.

153. Ibid., 27. The name can also mean "tricky one" (ibid., 43).

154. Wolfgang Lindow, ed., *Ein kurzweilig Lesen von Dil Ulenspiegel* (1515) (Stuttgart: Reclam, 1966), 72. The proverb originated with Hansel von Singen, a jester of Margrave Philipp of Baden, who objected vociferously to having to dine with two jesters belonging to other nobles who were visiting (Flögel, *Geschichte der Hofnarren,* 209).

155. Lindow, *Kurzweilig Lesen,* 72. The court jester is also called a *Spilman* (71), the same word used in Russia.

156. González, *Vida y hechos,* 1:255–57.

157. John Timpane, "The Jest of the Rogue," in "The Romance of the Rogue: The History of a Character in English Literature 1497–1632" (Ph.D. diss., Stanford University, 1980), 142.

158. Barry Lopez, *Arctic Dreams: Imagination and Desire in a Northern Landscape* (London: Picador, 1987), 24.

159. Louis Hieb, "The Hopi Ritual Clown: Life as It Should Not Be" (Ph.D. diss., Princeton University, 1972), 32.

160. A. I. Hallowell, "Bear Ceremonialism in the Northern Hemisphere," *American Anthropologist* 28, 1 (1926): 93.

161. Royal Museum of Scotland, *The Power of the Mask,* exhibition August to October 1993.

162. Clavigero, *History of Mexico,* vol. 1, bk. 7, 400.

163. Shulman, *King and the Clown,* 201.

164. Edward Gifford, "Tongan Society," *Bernice Bishop Museum Bulletin* 61 (1929): 126.

165. Geoffrey Gorer, *Africa Dances: A Book about West African Negroes* (London: Lehmann, 1949), 49, my emphasis.

166. Viviana Pâques, "Bouffons sacrés du cercle de Bougouni (Soudan français)," *Journal de la Société des Africanistes* 24 (1954): 107.

167. Lucille Charles, "The Clown's Function," *Journal of American Folklore* 58 (1945): 30.

168. Parsons and Beal, "Sacred Clowns," 507 and 499.

169. J. H. Steward, "The Ceremonial Buffoon of the American Indian," *Papers of the Michigan Academy of Science, Arts and Letters* 14 (1931): 189–90, my emphasis.

170. Adolf Bandelier, *The Delight Makers* (New York: Dodd, Mead, 1890), 138 and 46.

171. Alison Freese, "Send in the Clowns: An Ethnohistorical Analysis of the Sacred Clowns' Role in Cultural Boundary Maintenance among the Pueblo Indians" (Ph.D. diss., University of New Mexico, 1991), 112 and 1–2.

172. Personal communication with William Dolby.

173. Erminie Voegelin, "Tubatulabal Ethnography," *Anthropological Records* 2, 1 (1938): 56, my emphasis.

174. D. M. Dooling, "The Wisdom of the Contrary: A Conversation with Joseph Epes Brown," *Parabola* 4, 1 (1979): 57.

175. Hieb, "Hopi Ritual Clown," 141, 169, 38, and 198. The print is in the Gotha Schlossmuseum, Germany.

176. Freese, "Send in the Clowns," 3.

CHAPTER TWO

1. Frank Wedekind, (1864–1918), *König Nicolo, oder So is das Leben* (1901), in *Frank Wedekind: Dramen,* ed. Manfred Hahn (Berlin: Aufbau-Verlag, 1969), 1:523.

2. Rabelais, *Tiers Livre,* 1:558.

3. Desiderius Erasmus, *Adages I.i.1 to I.v.100,* in *The Collected Works of Erasmus,* vol. 31, trans. Margaret M. Phillips, annot. R. A. B. Mynors (Toronto: University of Toronto Press, 1982), adage 1.3.1, 227.

4. Erasmus, *Praise of Folly,* trans. Betty Radice, 55–56.

5. "A Sage Fool's Testament," Harl. MS 2252, fol. 85, quoted in F. J. Furnivall, ed., *A Booke of Precedence,* Ext. Series 8 (London: Early English Text Society), 77.

6. M. de Bautru, "Relation de la première conférence que j'ai eu avec M. le comte-duc, du 27 nov. 1628," Archives des Affaires Étrangères, Correspondence politique: Espagne, vol. 15, fol. 285v quoted in J. Brown and J. Elliott, "Further Observations on Velazquez's Portraits of Jesters at the Buen Retiro," *Gazette des Beaux-Arts* 98 (1981): 192.

7. I am currently working on a comprehensive history of the jester in art.

8. Willeford, *Fool and His Sceptre,* 147.

9. Quoted in Maurice Lever, "Les bouffons et le roi," *L'Histoire* 31, 2 (1981): 85.

10. Sir Philip Sidney, *An Apologie for Poetrie* (ca. 1583), quoted in John Towsen, *Clowns: A Panoramic History of Fools and Jesters; Medieval Mimes, Jongleurs and Minstrels; Pueblo Indian Delight Makers and Cheyenne Contraries; Harlequins and Pierrots; Theatrical Buffoons and Zanies; Circus Tramps, Whitefaces and Augustes* (New York: Hawthorn Books, 1976), 59.

11. Tietze-Conrat, *Dwarfs and Jesters in Art,* 66.

12. C. C. Stopes, "Elizabeth's Fools and Dwarfs," in *Shakespeare's Environment* (London: Bell, 1914), 270; Flögel, *Geschichte der Hofnarren,* 412–13; Shoubinsky, "Court Jesters and Their Weddings," 6–7.

13. Avalle-Arce, "'Crónica de Carlos V,'" 39 and 21; Flögel, *Geschichte der Hofnarren,* 370.

14. See Tietze-Conrat, *Dwarfs and Jesters in Art,* 12 and 88.

15. Kelly, *Petrushka,* 12; Henry Wadsworth Longfellow, "The Sicilian's Tale: King Robert of Sicily," in *Tales of a Wayside Inn,* in *Writings of Henry Wadsworth Longfellow* (London: Routledge, 1886), 6:46–53.

16. L. M. Hornstein, "King Robert of Sicily: Analogues and Origins," *PMLA* 79 (1968): 17.

17. Cambridge MS ff.2.38, fol. 255r–v, quoted in Billington, " Role of the Fool," 29.

18. Hector Maclean, "The King and the Fool in Wedekind's *König Nicolo,*" *Seminar* 5, 2 (1969): 24.

19. Michel de Ghelderode, *Escurial,* trans. Lionel Abel, in *Modern Theatre,* ed. Eric Bentley (New York: Doubleday, 1957), 5:161–78.

20. Ibid., 5:174–75.

21. George Buchanan, *The Witty and Entertaining Exploits of George Buchanan, Who Was Commonly Called the King's Fool* (Stirling: Randall, 1814), 11, my emphasis.

22. Maurice Lever, *Le sceptre et la marotte: Histoire des fous de cour* (Paris: Hachette, 1985), 141–43.

23. Quoted in Zakani, *"Ethics of the Aristocrats,"* 128.

24. Alexandre Dumas, *Chicot the Jester* (London: Collins Clear-Type Press, n.d.).

25. Ibid., 6.

26. Flögel, *Geschichte der Hofnarren,* 403–4.

27. Edmond L. Wright, *The Jester Hennets* (Liskeard, Cornwall: Harry Chambers/Peterloo Poets, 1981), 30.

28. Mathurin Regnier, *Satyre XIV: La folie est générale* (1613), in *Oeuvres complètes de Mathurin Regnier,* ed. Jean Plattard (Paris: Belles Lettres, 1954), 128.

29. Letter from Lady Montague concerning the dwarf-jesters of German courts, quoted in Kalff, *Opkomst,* 159.

30. "The Tale of the Hunchback with the Tailor, the Christian Broker, the Steward and the Jewish Doctor; What Followed After; and the Tales Which Each of Them Told," in *The Book of the Thousand Nights and One Nights,* trans. from the French by Powys Mathers, 2d ed. (London: Routledge and Kegan Paul, 1964), 1:179.

31. D. Williamson and L. Williamson, "George Buchanan, the King's Fool," in *A Thorn in the King's Foot: Stories of the Scottish Travelling People* (Harmondsworth, Middlesex: Penguin Books, 1987), 100.

32. Idries Shah, *The Pleasantries of the Incredible Mulla Nasrudin* (London: Octagon Press, 1983), 18; Robert Lenkewicz, "The City of Fools" (unpublished MS).

33. Ferdinand Wolf, "Ueber den Hofnarren Kaiser Karl's V Genannt el Conde Don Francés de Zuñiga und seine Chronik," in *Sitzungsberichte der Kaiserlichen Akademie der Wissenschaften: Philosophisch-Historische Classe* 2, 1 (June 1850): 27, 30, and 35.

34. "Huixie zhuan," *SKQS*, 464:362a.

35. Shah, *Pleasantries*, 157; Ida Taylor, "The Professional Fools," *Nineteenth Century and After* 62 (1907): 256.

36. Pierre de l'Estoile, *Mémoires de Pierre de l'Estoile (Journal de Henri IV: Depuis le 2 aoust 1589, jour de la mort du roy, jusques au 22 mars 1594, jour de la réduction de Paris)*, in *Collection complète des mémoires relatifs à l'histoire de France*, ed. M. Petitot (Paris: Foucault Libraire, 1825), 46:248–49.

37. Quoted in V. Cian, "Fra Serafino, buffone," *Archivo Storico Lombardo* 18 (1891): 411, trans. William Dolby.

38. Quoted in José Moreno Villa, *Locos, enanos, negros y niños palaciegos: Gente de placer que tuvieron los Austrias en la corte española desde 1563 a 1700*, Serie de Obras Originales 1 (Mexico: España en México, 1939), 25–27. Moreno Villa, archivist at the National Palace in Madrid, has done for Spain what remains to be done for the rest of Europe: a systematic trawling of court accounts for references to jesters. His work has placed on the map dozens of jesters who would otherwise have been overlooked.

39. Zakani, *"Ethics of the Aristocrats,"* 124, and personal communication with Reza Sabri-Tabrizi.

40. Zakani, *"Ethics of the Aristocrats,"* 96.

41. Halabi, "Development of Humour," 72.

42. Armin, *Nest of Ninnies*, 44.

43. J. Mathorez, "Notes sur Maître Guillaume, fou de Henri IV et de Louis XIII: Contribution à l'histoire de la presse francaise," *Revue de Livres Anciens* 1 (1913): 277.

44. Ibid., 280.

45. Estoile, *Mémoires*, 248.

46. J. Mathorez, "Histoire de Chicot, bouffon de Henri III," *Bulletin de Bibliophile*, 1914, 303.

47. G. Mongredien, "Maître Guillaume, bouffon de Henri IV," *Mercure de France*, 15 August 1939, 6.

48. "Lingguan zhuan," in *Wudai shi,* fol. 37, *SKQS,* 279:229a.

49. Ibid., 279:229b.

50. *Zizhi tongjian* (1085), by Sima Guang (1019–86), fol. 273, *SKQS,* 310: 351a–b.

51. Shoubinsky, "Court Jesters and Their Weddings," 2–3.

52. Wace (ca. 1100–ca. 1175), *Roman de rou,* ed. A. J. Holden, 3 vols. (Paris: Picard, 1970–73), vol. 2, lines 3655–62, trans. Welsford, *Fool,* 114. The duke was later William I (William the Conqueror) of England.

53. Paul Moreau, *Fous et bouffons: Étude physiologique, psychologique et historique* (Paris, 1885), 210.

54. E. Panofsky, "Conard Celtes and Kunz von der Rosen: Two Problems of Portrait Identification," *Art Bulletin* 24 (1942): 47.

55. Harrison, *Irish Trickster,* 28.

56. Myles Dillon, *Early Irish Literature* (Chicago: University of Chicago Press, 1948), 79.

57. In Cross and Slover, "Death of Fergus Mac Leide," 119.

58. *Nan Tang jinshi,* by Zheng Wenbao (953-1013), *SKQS,* 1035:927a–40, quoted in *YYJ,* 75.

59. *Beimeng suoyan,* by Sun Guangxian (900–968), *LDXS,* bk. 4, fol. 24.1.

60. *Journal de la dépense du Roi Jean en Angleterre depuis le 1er juillet 1359 jusqu'au 8 juillet 1360, jour de son débarquement à Calais,* in *Comptes de l'argenterie des rois de France au XIVe siècle* ed. Louis Douet d'Arcq (Paris: Renouard, 1851), 241–42, my emphasis.

61. Canel, *Recherches historiques,* 52.

62. "Jinyu," fol. 2, in *Guoyu,* fol. 8, 1:286.

63. "Niu Wenshu zhuan," in *Liaoshi,* fol. 86, *SKQS,* 289:625b.

64. BM Additional MSS, 19,402, fol. 79.

65. Buchanan, *Witty and Entertaining Exploits,* 22 and 7.

66. Flögel, *Geschichte der Hofnarren,* 216–17.

67. Canel, *Recherches historiques,* 38.

68. Armin, *Nest of Ninnies,* 45.

69. *Wudai shibu,* by Tao Yue (Song), fol. 2, *SKQS,* 407:657b.

70. Armin, *Nest of Ninnies,* 47; Moreau, *Fous et bouffons,* 162.

71. Zuñiga, *Crónica,* 251, quoted in Avalle-Arce, "'Crónica de Carlos V,'" 45.

72. Zuñiga, *Crónica,* quoted in Wolf, "Zuñiga," 27 and 40.

73. J. Moffitt, "Velasquez, Fools, Calabacillas and Ripa," *Pantheon* 40, 4 (1982): 83.

74. *The Oxford Classical Dictionary,* ed. Nock Cary and others (Oxford: Clarendon Press, 1949; repr. 1957), 223; Beryl Hugill, *Bring on the Clowns* (Newton Abbott, Devon: David and Charles, 1980), 26.

75. Martine Bigeard, *La folie et les fous littéraires en Espagne, 1500–1650* (Paris: Centre de Recherches Historiques, 1972), 128; Shoubinsky, "Court Jesters and Their Weddings," 2; item 1: *Chaoye qianzai bu,* anon., fol. 6, quoted in *YYJ,* 47; item 2: "Lingguan zhuan," in *Wudai shi,* fol. 37, *SKQS,* 279:229a; item 3: "Dongfang Shuo zhuan," in *Hanshu,* by Ban Gu, *HIST,* 6, fol. 65, 2843.

76. *Benshi shi,* by Meng Qi (fl. ca. 841–86), *GJYS,* 20, fol. 1, 21b–22a.

77. Ben Jonson (ca. 1573–1637), *Epicoene, or The Silent Woman,* ed. L. A. Beaurline (London: Arnold, 1967).

78. Pepys, Samuel (1633–1703), *The Diary of Samuel Pepys,* ed. Robert Latham and William Matthews, 11 vols. (London: Bell, 1976), 8:368.

79. Flögel, *Geschichte der Hofnarren,* 294.

80. Lever, *Sceptre,* 154.

81. "Le premier compte de Geoffroi de Fleuri, argentier du roi Philippe le Long, pour les six derniers mois de l'annee 1316," in *Comptes de l'argenterie,* ed. Douet d'Arcq, 9.

82. Bernard Prost and Henri Prost, eds., *Inventaires mobiliers et extraits des comptes des ducs de Bourgogne de la maison des Valois,* 3 vols. (Paris: Leroux, 1902–8), 2:476 and 529.

83. "Compte de l'argenterie d'Étienne de la Fontaine" (1 July 1351–4 February 1352), in *Comptes de l'argenterie,* ed. Douet d'Arcq, 160. See also 149–50.

84. Bullock-Davies, *Menestrellorum Multitudo,* 18.

85. C. C. Stopes, "Jane, the Queen's Fool," in *Shakespeare's Environment* (London: Bell, 1914), 264–65.

86. Ibid., 265–67, passim.

87. Stopes, "Elizabeth's Fools and Dwarfs," 272–75.

88. Prost and Prost, *Inventaires,* 2:474; "Compte de l'argenterie d'Étienne de la Fontaine," in *Comptes de l'argenterie,* ed. Douet d'Arcq, 160.

89. T. Dickson and J. B. Paul, eds., *Accounts of the Lord High Treasurer of Scotland, 1473–1580,* 13 vols. (Edinburgh: General Register House; Her Majesty's Stationery Office, 1877–1978), 11:420.

90. Doran, *History of Court Fools,* 112.

91. Catalogue des actes de François I, no. 31874, quoted in Mathorez, "Maître Guillaume," 270.

92. Item 1: Louis Douet d'Arcq, ed., Comptes de l'*hôtel des rois de France aux XIVe et XVe siècles* (Paris: Renouard, 1865), 234; item 2: Anglo, "Court Revels"

(1 August 1505), 40; item 3: ibid. (31 July 1492), 27. Anglo suggests that most of the fools mentioned in the accounts were naturals, the distinction being between those who were classed as "fole" and those who were said to have "pleyed the fole" (16). I disagree with this interpretation. The entries for "fole" apply to those that recur, suggesting that they were permanent, recognized jesters, perhaps naturals, perhaps not. The term "pleyed the fole" seems to apply to somebody who is not normally classed as a jester but suddenly behaves like one.

93. Anglo, "Court Revels": item 1 (10 June 1494), 28; item 2 (20 February 1495), 29; item 3 (2 August 1495), 29; item 4 (10–15 March 1498), 33; item 5 (2 January 1503), 39; item 6 (14 January 1508), 43; item 7 (20 March 1508), 43.

94. Ibid.: item 1 (1 January 1492), 27; item 2 (10 June 1492), 27; item 3 (7 December 1493), 28; item 4 (20 September 1497), 32; item 5 (5–11 August 1498), 33; item 6 (6 March 1506), 40.

95. Lever, *Sceptre*, 131.

96. Quoted in Luzio and Renier, "Buffoni," 35:136.

97. Cited in Moreno Villa, *Locos*, 66 and 81.

98. Blyth, *Japanese Humor*, 73.

99. *Jiangnan yeshi*, by Long Gun (Song), fol. 7, *SKQS*, 464:104a–b.

100. Hugill, *Bring on the Clowns*, 44.

101. William Somner (1598–1669), *The Antiquities of Canterbury, or A Survey of That Ancient Citie, with the Suburbs and Cathedral*, ed. Nicolas Battely, 2d ed. (London: R. Knaplock, 1703), 39, quoted in Doran, *History of Court Fools*, 99n.

102. *Rotuli Normanniae in turri londinensi asservati*, in *Mémoires de la Société des Antiquitaires de Normandie*, 15:96, cols. 1 and 2, quoted in Canel, *Recherches historiques*, 16.

103. Bigeard, *Folie*, 130; Moreno Villa, *Locos*, 33.

104. Flögel, *Geschichte der Hofnarren*, 274–75.

105. Sandra Billington, *A Social History of the Fool* (Brighton: Harvester Press, 1984), 46 and 59; Hugill, *Bring on the Clowns*, 52 and 39.

106. *Catalogue des actes d'Henri II* (Paris: Imprimerie Nationale, 1979), quoted in Lever, *Sceptre*, 192.

107. Felix Cevoule-Angles, "Jehan-Antoine Lombard, dit Brusquet, fou du roi, 1520–1565," *Bulletin de la Société d'Études Scientifiques et Archéologiques de Draguignan* 7 (1962): 98; Lever, *Sceptre*, 210; Archives Nationales, Xia 8640, part 2, fol. 13, and Xia 9256, fol. 27, quoted in Mathorez, "Chicot," 304.

108. R. A. Zimbardo, "The Book of the Duchess and the Dream of Folly," *Chaucer Review* 18, 4 (1984): 333; Moreno Villa, *Locos*, 33.

109. Lever, *Sceptre*, 122.

110. *Yutang xianhua,* by Fan Zi (Five Dynasties), quoted in *YYJ,* 58, although the quotation cannot be found in the *SFWW,* fol. 48 ed.

111. *Gushan bizhu,* by Yu Shenxing (1545–1607), ed. Lu Jinglin (Beijing: Zhonghua Shuju, 1984), fol. 6, 66.

112. M. A. Gazeau, *Les bouffons* (Paris: Hachette, 1882), 57.

113. Lever, *Sceptre,* 152; Hugill, *Bring on the Clowns,* 52.

114. Prost and Prost, *Inventaires,* 1:74–75.

115. Moreno Villa, *Locos,* 62, 73, and 91.

116. Ibid., 98 and 112–13.

117. *Encyclopaedia Britannica,* 15th ed., *Micropaedia,* s.v. "Mu'tadid, al-"; D. S. Margoliouth, "Wit and Humour in Arabic Authors," *Islamic Culture,* part 1 (1927): 525.

118. Flögel, *Geschichte der Hofnarren,* 303–4.

119. Johan Grimmelshausen (1622–76), *Simplex Simplicissimus* (1669), trans. George Schulz-Behrend (New York: Bobbs-Merrill 1965), 87.

120. *Dongguan zouji,* by Pei Tingyu (Tang), fol. 2, *SKQS,* 407:621a.

121. Flögel, *Geschichte der Hofnarren,* 185–86.

122. E. Gordon Duff, ed., *The Dialogue or Communing between the Wise King Salomon and Marcolphus* (1492), facsimile of Bodleian copy of 1492 (London: Lawrence and Bullen, 1892), 14.

123. Passage trans. Geeta Solomon, in Feinberg, *Asian Laughter,* 548.

124. Dawlatshah, *Tazkirat al-Shu'ara,* quoted in ʿObeyd-e Zakani, *"The Ethics of the Aristocrats" and Other Satirical Works,* trans. Hasan Javadi, Middle Eastern Series 11 (Piedmont, CA: Jahan Books, 1985), 10.

125. Arturo Graf, "Un buffone di Leone X," in *Attraverso il Cinquecento* (Turin: Chiantore, 1926), 302; Tomaso Garzoni, *Piazza universale,* quoted in Luzio and Renier, "Buffoni," 24:620, trans. William Dolby.

126. Moreau, *Fous et bouffons,* 187–89.

127. Ibid., 196.

128. Moreno Villa, *Locos,* 119.

129. Prost and Prost, *Inventaires,* 1:259.

130. Archives Impériales, KK 98, fol. 185, quoted in Canel, *Recherches historiques,* 103–4.

131. Edith Sitwell, *The Two Queens and the Hive* (Harmondsworth, Middlesex: Penguin Books, 1971), 173.

132. Accounts of François II, 1560, cited in Canel, *Recherches historiques,* 181.

133. Victor Hugo, *Marion de Lorme,* in *Théâtre complet,* ed. J.-J. Thierry and

J. Mélèze (Paris: Gallimard, 1963), 1:953−1144. Hugo's play is about Louis XIII, although the historical evidence is that L'Angeli was never his jester. See Canel, *Recherches historiques*, 251−52; Birnbaum, "Laughter, Play and Carnival," 30.

134. Armin, *Nest of Ninnies*, 17, 21, and 23.

135. Herbert Giles, *A Chinese Biographical Dictionary* (London: Kelly and Walsh, 1898), 804.

136. *Tie Wei Shan congtan*, by Cai Tao (d. 1126), fol. 4, *SKQS*, 1037:590b−91a.

137. Eunice de Souza, *All about Birbal* (Bombay: IBH, 1969), 36−42.

138. J. S., *England's Merry Jester, or Court, City and Country Jests* (London: J. Wilde, 1693), 74−75.

139. Walter Raleigh, ed., *Johnson on Shakespeare: Essays and Notes* (Oxford, 1946), 121, quoted in Kaiser, *Praisers of Folly*, 220.

140. Fuller, *History of the Worthies of England*, 2:312.

141. *Pleasant History of the Life and Death of Will Summers*, 14.

142. *Tie Wei Shan congtan*, by Cai Tao (d. 1126), fol. 4, *SKQS*, 1037:590b; Siegel, *Laughing Matters*, 303.

143. Armin, *Nest of Ninnies*, 43−44 and 65.

144. James Granger, *A Biographical History of England from Egbert the Great to the Revolution* (London, 1775), 1:117, quoted in *Pleasant History of the Life and Death of Will Summers*, following the frontispiece.

145. "Guji liezhuan," 3201−2, trans. Dolby and Scott, *War-Lords*, 164−66.

146. Ibid., 3202, trans. Dolby and Scott, *War-Lords*, 167.

147. Ibid., 3204.

148. Ebeling, *Zur Geschichte der Hofnarren*, 190−91.

149. Doran, *History of Court Fools*, 252.

150. *202 Jokes of Nasreddin Hodja* (Istanbul: Galeri Minyatür, n.d.), no. 75.

151. Souza, *All about Birbal*, 16−20.

152. "Tales about Tenali Rama," trans. A. Ayyar in Feinberg, *Asian Laughter*, 433.

153. Pandit S. M. Natesa Sastri, trans., *Tales of Tennalirama, the Famous Court Jester of Southern India* (Madras: Natesan, 1900), 35−38.

154. Mongredien, "Maître Guillaume," 10 and 232.

155. Melchor de Santa Cruz de Dueñas, "De Truhanes," in *Floresta Espanola* (1572), 2d ed. (Buenos Aires: Espasa-Calpe Argentina, 1947), 46.

156. *"Shi Dongtong,"* in *TPGJ*, fol. 247, *SKQS*, 1044:596a−b. The riddle seems to be onomatopoeic.

157. "Dongfang Shuo zhuan," in *Hanshu*, 6, fol. 65, 2843, trans. Watson, in Ban Gu, *Courtier and Commoner*, 81.

158. Ibid., 2844, trans. Watson, in Ban Gu, *Courtier and Commoner*, 81.

159. Ibid., 2844, trans. Watson, in Ban Gu, *Courtier and Commoner*, 82.

160. "Dongfang Shuo," *TPGJ*, fol. 174, *SKQS*, 1044:170b.

161. Chai E, *Fantianlu congchao*, fol. 14, in *Guoxue mingzhu zhenben biji huikan*, 1 (Taibei: Dingwen Shuju, 1976), 214b.

162. Shulman, *King and the Clown*, 187–88.

163. "Guji liezhuan," 3204, trans. William Dolby, "Jesters" (unpublished MS), 3–5, and Dolby and Scott, *War-Lords*, 160.

164. Harold Lieberman and Edith Lieberman, *Throne of Straw*, in *The Theatre of the Holocaust: Four Plays*, ed. and intro. Robert Skloot (Madison: University of Wisconsin Press, 1982), 113–96.

165. *"Wenxin diaolong" jinyi*, by Liu Xie (ca. 465–ca. 522), trans. Zhou Zhenfu, ed. Ji Qin (Beijing: Zhonghua Shuju, 1986), 135.

166. Fuller, *History of the Worthies of England*, 312.

167. "The Awakening of Ulster," in *Cuchulain of Muirthemne: The Story of the Men of the Red Branch of Ulster*, trans. Augusta Gregory (London: Murray, 1902), 258–59.

168. *Tarlton's Jests*, in Hazlitt, *Shakespeare Jest-Books*, 2:191.

169. Armin, *Nest of Ninnies*, 45.

170. Giles Fletcher (1549?–1611), *Of the Rus Commonwealth* (1591), ed. Albert Schmidt (Ithaca: Cornell University Press, 1966), 146–47.

171. Luzio and Renier, "Buffoni," 24:621.

172. *Yeren xianhua*, by Jing Huan (Song), in *TPGJ*, fol. 446, *SKQS*, 1046:308a.

173. "Guji liezhuan," 3204.

174. Dagan, *Court Jesters*, 19.

175. *Wenjian lu*, by Luo Dian (Song), *SFSW*, bk. 5, fol. 9, 11a–12b.

176. *Chaoye qianzai bu*, anon. (Tang), fol. 6, quoted in *YYJ*, 47. There are several other versions of this "I saw Qu Yuan" joke, including some that attribute the witticism to another jester. An early version is in the *Bei Qi shu*, by Li Baiyao (565–648), fol. 15. *SKQS*, 263:115b–21b, quoted in *YYJ*, 47.

177. Hugill, *Bring on the Clowns*, 31.

178. Zakani, *"Ethics of the Aristocrats,"* 83, with minor adaptation.

179. Siegel, *Laughing Matters*, 307.

180. Quoted in Canel, *Recherches historiques*, 298.

181. Quoted in Luzio and Renier, "Buffoni," 35:121–22, trans. William Dolby.

182. Ibid., 304.

183. Ludwig Tieck, *Puss-in-Boots (Der gestiefelte Kater)*, trans. and ed. Gerald Gillespie, Edinburgh Bilingual Library 8 (Edinburgh: Edinburgh University Press, 1974).

184. *The New London City Jester, or A Banquet of Wit, Mirth, and Fancy* (London: Roach, 1797), 52.

CHAPTER THREE

1. Erasmus, *Praise of Folly*, trans. Betty Radice, 56.

2. Umberto Eco, *The Name of the Rose*, trans. William Weaver (London: London: Pan Books, 1984), 491.

3. Williamson and Williamson, "George Buchanan," 93.

4. Souza, *All about Birbal*, 28–31 and 47.

5. Ujváry Zoltán, *Mátyás Király Gömörben* (Debrecen, Hungary, 1990), 35, trans. Elizabeth Temple.

6. For a detailed analysis of the eighty-two fine ink drawings, including comparisons with Dürer's woodcuts for Brant's *Das Narrenschiff,* see Erika Michael, "The Drawings of Hans Holbein the Younger for Erasmus' 'Praise of Folly'" (Ph.D. diss., University of Washington, 1981). They are also clearly reproduced in Erasmus, *Erasmi Roterodami Encomium Moriae; i.e. Stultitiae Laus: Praise of Folly, Published at Basle in 1515 and Decorated with the Marginal Drawings of Hans Holbein the Younger, Now Reproduced in Facsimile with an Introduction by Heinrich Alfred Schmid,* trans. Helen Tanzer (Basel, 1931).

7. Idries Shah, *The Exploits of the Incomparable Mulla Nasrudin* (London: Octagon Press, 1983), introduction.

8. Armin, *Nest of Ninnies*, 20.

9. Quoted in Hugill, *Bring on the Clowns*, frontispiece.

10. Brant, *Das Narrenschiff,* 10; Brant, *Ship of Fools,* prologue, 58.

11. Welsford, *Fool,* 319.

12. Doran, *History of Court Fools,* 53.

13. Grimmelshausen, *Simplex Simplicissimus,* 83.

14. Pepys, *Diary,* 13 February 1668, 9:66–67.

15. *L'enfant sans soucy,* quoted in Canel, *Recherches historiques,* 310.

16. Flögel, *Geschichte der Hofnarren,* 218.

17. Quoted in Maurice Lever, "Le mythe du fol," *Magazine Littéraire,* July–August 1981, 22.

18. J. E. Neale, *Queen Elizabeth* (1934; repr. London: Reprint Society, 1942),

134; John Saward, *Perfect Fools* (Oxford: Oxford University Press, 1980), ix; Flögel, *Geschichte der Hofnarren*, 74.

19. Johann Balthasar Schupps, *Salomo, oder Regenten-Spiegel,* in *Sämtliche lehrreiche Schrifften,* vol. 1 (Frankfurt, 1701), S.41.Bl.c.5a, quoted in Wyss, *Narr im schweizerischen Drama,* 32.

20. Quoted in Helen Adolph, "On Medieval Laughter," *Speculum* 22 (1947): 16; Wyss, *Narr im schweizerischen Drama,* 47; quoted in Canel, *Recherches historiques,* 5.

21. Hugill, *Bring on the Clowns,* 37.

22. Fuller, *History of the Worthies of England,* 2:312; "Guji liezhuan," 3200, trans. Dolby and Scott, *War-Lords,* 162.

23. BN MSS Français, no. 22,564, fol. 151, quoted in Mathorez, "Chicot," 45.

24. BN MS LB.507, quoted in Mathorez, "Chicot," 44, my emphasis.

25. Halabi, "Development of Humour," 60 and 72.

26. Clavigero, *History of Mexico,* vol. 1, bk. 5, 212, my emphasis.

27. *The Works of Mencius,* in *The Chinese Classics,* trans. James Legge, 2d ed. rev., 7 vols. (Taibei: Wenxing Shudian, 1966), vol. 2, bk. 1, part 2, chap. 4 161.

28. *Dongfang Shuo zhuan,* in *Hanshu,* by Ban Gu, *HIST,* 6, fol. 65, 2860, trans. Watson, in Ban Gu, *Courtier and Commoner,* 94–95.

29. Beatrice Bartlett, *Monarchs and Ministers: The Grand Council in Mid-Ch'ing China: 1723–1820* (Berkeley: University of California Press, 1991), 6.

30. "Guji liezhuan," 3197, trans. William Dolby, *Jesters,* 2.

31. *Yijian zhi* (1166), by Hong Mai (1123–1202), part 2, fol. 4, *SKQS,* 1047: 347a.

32. *Shengchao tongshi shi,* by Mao Qiling and others, fol. 6, *Xihe heji* (Xiaoshan: Lu Ning Rui Tang, 1770, 1796), bk. 94, 13a–b.

33. *Pingzhou ketan,* by Zhu Yu (fl. ca. 1110), fol. 3, *SKQS,* 1038:309b.

34. "Guji liezhuan," 3198, trans. Dolby and Scott, *War-Lords,* 160.

35. Doran, *History of Court Fools,* 71–72.

36. Idries Shah, *Wisdom of the Idiots* (London: Octagon Press, 1989), 173.

37. Moreau, *Fous et bouffons,* 216.

38. *The Jovial Jester* (London: W. Lane, 1780), 107.

39. Avalle-Arce, "'Crónica de Carlos V,'" 48; Robert Greene, "A Pleasant Tale of Will Summers," in *The Defence of Conny-Catching,* in *The Life and Complete Works of Robert Greene,* ed. A. B. Grosart (London: Huth Library, 1881–86), 11:70–72; *Pleasant History of the Life and Death of Will Summers,* 17.

40. Margoliouth, "Wit and Humour in Arabic Authors," 532.

41. *Pleasant History of the Life and Death of Will Summers,* 19–20; *The Entertaining Companion, or The Merry Jester* (London: Sympson, 1790), 17.

42. Octavius Gilchrist, "Archibald Armstrong and His Jests," *London Magazine,* September 1824, 287. Yet it is known that Archy was with Charles in Spain. Perhaps he followed later. Or could the compiler of Archy anecdotes have muddled the facts, wanting simply to attribute to Archy a technique used by other jesters?

43. Doran, *History of Court Fools,* 255.

44. Martin du Bellay, *Les mémoires de Messire Martin du Bellay,* in *Collection complète des mémoires relatifs à l'histoire de France,* ed. M. Petitot (Paris: Foucault Libraire, 1821), 17:155.

45. Estoile, *Mémoires,* 249–50.

46. "Nan er," in *Han Feizi,* by Han Fei (ca. 280–234 B.C.), fol. 37, ed. Teruo Takeuchi, 5th ed., 2 vols. (Tokyo: Meiji Shoin, 1964), 2:654.

47. Werner Mezger, *Hofnarren im Mittelalter* (Constance: Universitätsverlag Konstanz, 1981), 49.

48. Flögel, *Geschichte der Hofnarren,* 267.

49. "Zhouyu," in *Guoyu,* fol. 3, 1:131.

50. Flögel, *Geschichte der Hofnarren,* 426.

51. Shah, *Exploits,* 7.

52. Quoted in Shulman, *King and the Clown,* 196.

53. Siegel, *Laughing Matters,* 185.

54. Ayyar Panchapakesa, trans., *The Royal Jester, or Tenali Rama* (Madras: Alliance, 1947), 48–49.

55. Rajani Bannerji, trans., *Gopal the Jester* (New York: Library of Facetious Lore, 1928), 78–83.

56. Eunice de Souza, *More about Birbal* (Bombay: IBH, 1973), 11–14, quoted in Siegel, *Laughing Matters,* 310.

57. Flögel, *Geschichte der Hofnarren,* 340.

58. *Kaitian chuanxin ji,* by Zheng Qi (d. 899), quoted in *YYJ,* 44, but not found in the *SKQS* or *BJXSDG.*

59. *Duxing zazhi,* by Zeng Minxing (Song), fol. 9, *SKQS,* 1039:578b–79a.

60. Canel, *Recherches historiques,* 239.

61. *Duxing zazhi,* fol. 9, *SKQS,* 1039:579a.

62. Arthur Marx, *My Life with Groucho: A Son's Eye View* (London: Pan Books, 1991), 73.

63. Trans. Bannerji, *Gopal the Jester,* 129. The Birbal version is in Edward

Dimock, *The Thief of Love: Bengali Tales from Court and Village* (Chicago: University of Chicago Press, 1963), 183–85, and Nasrudin's in *The Turkish Jester, or The Pleasantries of Cogia Nasr Eddin Effendi,* trans. George Borrow (Ipswich: Webber, 1884), 28.

64. Buchanan, *Witty and Entertaining Exploits,* 10.

65. Ah'med el Ibchihi, *Kitab el Mostatref,* 2:105, quoted in René Basset, trans., *Mille et un contes, récits et légendes arabes,* 2 vols. (Paris: Maisonneuve, 1924), 1:438. The same story is told of Nasrudin, the mulla-jester, with a mulla being the unlucky omen.

66. Souza, *All about Birbal,* 32–35.

67. "Huixie zhuan," *SKQS,* 464:362a–b. There is another joke about a similarly ambitious prefect and would-be emperor, Wang Yanbin, also of the Five Dynasties (907–60). The jester used a pun on the Monk of Sizhou (which sounds like *si zhou,* "four provinces") and the small amount of territory in which Wang had tried to found a dynasty: "Well, I've heard of the Monk of Four Provinces, but I've never heard of the Emperor of Five Counties!" See *Nanbu xinshu,* by Qian Yi (fl. ca. 1017), fol. 10, *SKQS,* 1036:263a.

68. Shoubinsky, "Court Jesters and Their Weddings," 4–5.

69. Zoltán, *Mátyás Király Gömörben,* 120, trans. Elizabeth Temple.

70. *Langya manchao,* by Wen Lin (1445–99), *LDXS,* bk. 10, fol. 82, 2a.

71. *Xiyuan zaji,* by Xu Xian (Ming), fol. 1, *CSJC,* bk. 3913, 30–31.

72. "Coordinating commissioners of circuits" (Hucker, "Dictionary of Official Titles," 150).

73. *Pingzhou ketan,* fol. 3, *SKQS,* 1038:310a.

74. *Xihu youlan zhiyu,* by Tian Rucheng (fl. ca. 1540), fol. 2, *SKQS,* 585:307a.

75. *Suozhui lu,* by Yin Zhi (fl. ca. 1468–82), quoted in *Gushu litan,* by Li Mo (d. 1556), fol. 8, quoted in *YYJ,* 154, although it cannot be found in the *Shuofu* (sequel) fol. 7 edition.

76. *Jianhu ji,* fifth collection, fol. 3, *BJXSDG* (sequel), 4:13a.

77. "Huixie zhuan," *SKQS,* 464:362a.

78. *Yinhua lu,* by Zhao Lin (fl. ca. 844), fol. 4, *TPGJ,* fol. 164, *SKQS,* 1035:489a, my emphasis.

79. "Lingguan zhuan," in *Liaoshi,* fol. 109, *SKQS,* 289:707a.

80. Ibid., 707b.

81. *Shuiting,* by Lu Can (1494–1551), fol. 1, *Shuo ku,* comp. Wang Wenru (Taibei: Xinxing Shuju, 1963), 2:1007a.

82. Souza, *All about Birbal,* 68.

83. *Yijian zhi,* part 2, fol. 4, *SKQS,* 1047:348b.

NOTES TO PAGES 121-27

84. Pepys, *Diary*, 8 December 1666, 7:400.

85. *Xu wenxian tongkao*, by Wang Qi (fl. ca. 1565–1614), fol. 118, *SKQS*, 629:395a.

86. Doran, *History of Court Fools*, 223.

87. *The Female Jester, or Wit for the Ladies* (London: Bew and Lewis, 1780), 103, and appearing in numerous jestbooks of the same era. The same punch line is more commonly attributed to "one Pace, a bitter Jester in Queen Elizabeth's Days, [who] came to Court: Come, says the Ladies, Pace, we shall now hear of our Faults: No, says he, I don't talk ule to that which all the Town talks of." See *The Universal Jester, or A Compleat Book of Jests* (London: Harris, 1668), 85.

88. *The Delicate Jester, or Wit and Humour Divested of Ribaldry* (London: Dixwell, 1780), 39.

89. W. W. Gent, *England's Witty and Ingenious Jester*, 17th ed. (London: Gifford, 1718), 28.

90. "Guji liezhuan," 3199, trans. Dolby and Scott, *War-Lords*, 162, my emphasis.

91. "Ci she," in *"Xinxu" jinzhu jinyi*, by Liu Xiang (77–6 B.C.), commentary and trans. Lu Yuanling (Taibei: Shangwu Yinshuguan, 1975), 204, trans. William Dolby.

92. "Huixie zhuan," *SKQS*, 464:363a.

93. "Fu Jian caiji," in *Jinshu*, by Fang Xuanling (579–648) and others, fol. 113, *SKQS*, 256:808b–9a.

94. *Tang yulin*, fol. 5, *SKQS*, 1038:123a.

95. Flögel, *Geschichte der Hofnarren*, 251.

96. *Beimeng suoyan*, fol. 1, *SKQS*, 1036:3a.

97. Doran, *History of Court Fools*, 53.

98. Vivien Foster, *Pearls of Wisdom: A Book of Aphorisms* (Harmondsworth, Middlesex: Penguin Books, 1987), 358.

99. "Huixie zhuan," *SKQS*, 464:361b.

100. *Jiangbiao zhi*, by Zheng Wenshi (953-1013), *SKQS*, 464:139b.

101. An anonymous work quoted in *YYJ*, 343–44.

102. *Jiangbiao zhi*, *SKQS*, 464:139b.

103. Doran, *History of Court Fools*, 74, trans. from Flögel, *Geschichte der Hofnarren*, 177–78.

104. Mikhail Bakhtin, *Rabelais and His World*, trans. Helene Iswolsky (Cambridge MIT Press, 1968), 309.

105. "Guji liezhuan," 3202–3, trans. Dolby and Scott, *War-Lords*, 166.

106. Ibid., 3202–3, trans. Dolby, *Jesters*, 34.

107. Ibid., 3203, trans. Dolby, *Jesters*, 36–37.

108. Ibid., 3200, trans. Dolby, *Jesters*, 17.

109. Ibid., 3200, trans. Dolby and Scott, *War-Lords*, 163.

110. Ibid., 3200, trans. Dolby, *Jesters*, 19.

111. Ibid., 3200, trans. Dolby and Scott, *War-Lords*, 163–64.

112. "Lingguan zhuan," in *Wudai shi*, fol. 37, *SKQS*, 279:229a, trans. William Dolby.

113. *Wudai shi*, fol. 40, *SKQS*, 279:249b. Another version is given in *Leishuo* (fol. 12, *SKQS*, 873:205b), which attributes this to a jester from the Court Entertainments Bureau, Fitting New Bridle (An Peixin).

114. Lucille Valentino, "Playing for Power: The Meanings of Elizabethan Entertainments" (Ph.D. diss., Wayne State University, 1983), 8.

115. M. M. J. Rigollot, *Monnaies inconnues des évêques des Innocens* (Paris: Merlin, 1837), 181, pl. 38, no. 107.

116. Rabelais, *Tiers livre*, in *Oeuvres complètes*, 1:558; François Rabelais, *The Works of Rabelais*, trans. Sir Thomas Urquhart and Peter le Motteux, 2d ed. (London: Bodley Head, 1933), 2:130.

CHAPTER FOUR

1. Emyr Wyn Jones, ed., *Barn ar Egwyddorion y Llywodraeth*, in *Yr Anterliwt Goll* (Aberystwyth: Llyfrgell Cenedlaethol Cymru, 1984), 10, trans. William Dolby.

2. John Ashton, *Humour, Wit and Satire of the Seventeenth Century* (London: Chatto and Windus, 1883), 33.

3. Elie Wiesel, *Les portes de la forêt* (Paris: Éditions du Seuil, 1964), 68.

4. Lawrence Durrell, *Mountolive* (London: Faber and Faber, 1958), 47.

5. M. Larken, "An Account of the Zande," *Sudan Notes and Records*, 9–10 (1926–27): 86, cited in Charles, "Clown's Function," 30.

6. Dagan, *Court Jesters*, 48–51.

7. *Newsweek*, 1 June 1992, 1.

8. Hyers, *Zen*, 127.

9. Shulman, *King and the Clown*, 204.

10. Victor Hugo, *Cromwell*, in *Théâtre complet*, ed. J.-J. Thierry and J. Mélèze, 2 vols. (Paris: Gallimard, 1963), 1:651.

11. Nicholas Grimald, *Archipropheta*, in *The Life and Poems of Nicholas Grimald*, ed. L. R. Merrill, Yale Studies in English 69 (New Haven: Yale University Press, 1925), 4.2.32.

12. Hugill, *Bring on the Clowns*, 64.

13. *Pingzhou ketan*, fol. 3, *SKQS*, 1038:310a.

14. *Qingbo zazhi*, by Zhou Hui (1126 – after 1198), fol. 6, *SKQS*, 1039:47b.

15. Quoted in Luzio and Renier, "Buffoni," 35:116, trans. William Dolby.

16. Quoted in ibid., 35:132. I do not know who Schips was—perhaps another jester.

17. Pepys, *Diary*, 17 February 1669, 9:451–52. Rochester was later banished from court for hitting Killigrew.

18. Bannerji, *Gopal the Jester*, 118.

19. Mathorez, "Chicot," 37.

20. Canel, *Recherches historiques*, 240.

21. Lever, *Sceptre*, 115.

22. *Calendar of Letters, Despatches and State Papers . . . at Simancas*, 5, part 1, 520, quoted in Southworth, *Fools and Jesters*, 68 – 69.

23. Gilchrist, "Archibald Armstrong," 287.

24. Quoted in Zijderveld, "De Hofnar als Instituut," *Spiegel Historiael* 2 (1976): 605 – 6.

25. "Wenzong ji," in *Jiu Tang shu*, by Liu Xu (887–946), fol. 17, part 2, *HIST*, 1:544.

26. *Tang yulin*, fol. 1, *SKQS*, 1038:19a–b. It is unclear whether it was one jester or more.

27. *Guier ji*, by Zhang Duanyi (fl. ca. 1235), fol. 3, *SKQS*, 865:467b.

28. Andrew Boorde, *The Merry Jests, and Witty Shifts of Scogin* (1626), in Hazlitt, *Shakespeare Jest-Books*, 2:37–161.

29. In ibid., 2:144.

30. Jamieson, *Banquet of Jests*, 47. This describes Scogin as jester to Henry VIII even though he would likely have died before Henry was born.

31. Buchanan, *Witty and Entertaining Exploits*, 7.

32. Sa'di, *The Persian-English Gulistan, or Rose Garden of Sa'di*, trans. Edward Rehatsek (Tehran: Shargh's Press, 1967), 102.

33. Brant, *Ship of Fools*, 9, trans. Zeydel, 58.

34. "Lomna's Head," in *Gods and Fighting Men: The Story of the Tuatha de Danaan and of the Fianna of Ireland*, trans. Augusta Gregory (London: Murray, 1904), 270 –71.

35. "Lingguan zhuan," in *Liaoshi*, fol. 109, *SKQS*, 289:707a.

36. *Shu taowu*, by Zhang Tangying (1029–71), fol. 2, *SKQS*, 464:238a. Ren Erbei suggests the skit may have been aimed at Meng Chang, hence his ordering

the jester's execution. See *Tang xinong,* 2 vols. (Beijing: Zuojia Chubanshe, 1958), 2:638.

37. *Dongdu shilüe,* by Wang Cheng (1370–1415), fol. 70, *SKQS,* 382:453b–54a.

38. "Youren feng shishi," in *Wanli yehuo bian,* by Shen Defu (1578–1642), fol. 26, *YMSL,* 3:664–65.

39. Zuñiga, *Crónica,* quoted in Wolf, "Zuñiga," 24.

40. Gazeau, *Bouffons,* 130.

41. *Tongjian jishi benmo,* by Yuan Shu (Song), fol. 206, quoted in *YYJ,* 305.

42. "Youling huiyu," in *Tingshi,* by Yue Ke (1183–1234), fol. 7, *SKQS,* 1039:458b–59a.

43. "Weishu," in *Sanguo zhi,* by Chen Shou (233–97), fol. 21, *SKQS,* 254:383b–84a.

44. "Li Shi zhuan," in *Jiu Tang shu,* fol. 135, *HIST,* 6:3731.

45. Isaac Asimov, *Foundation and Empire* (London: Grafton Books, 1990), 112.

46. *Xu wenxian tongkao,* fol. 118, *SKQS,* 629:395a.

47. Philip Corbett, *The Scurra* (Edinburgh: Scottish Academic Press, 1986), 75.

48. James Henthorn Todd, *Leabhar Breathnach Annso Sis: The Irish Version of the "Historia Britonum" of Nennius* (Dublin: Irish Archaeological Society, 1848), 182, quoted in Harrison, *Irish Trickster,* 104.

49. Flögel, *Geschichte der Hofnarren,* 275. The story of the mock execution is also told of the Italian jester Gonella.

50. Ouyang Xiu, *"Lingguan zhuan,"* In *Wudai shi,* fol. 37, *SKQS,* 279:229b.

51. Richard Bjornson, "Estebanillo González: The Clown's Other Face," *Hispania* 60, 3 (1977): 438.

52. *Qiyan lu,* in *TPGJ,* fol. 247, quoted in *YYJ,* 25, although it cannot be found in *SKQS* or *LDXHJ* editions. Square brackets are for gaps filled in by me and by William Dolby, who suggested the possible parallel between *ji wu yong,* "absolutely useless," and *ji you tong* "extremely painful."

53. Shulman, *King and the Clown,* 200.

54. *Ci Liushi jiuwen,* by Li Deyu (787–849), quoted in *YYJ,* 45, although I have been unable to verify this piece.

55. *Beimeng suoyan,* fol. 15, *SKQS,* 1036:97a, and *YYJ,* 55–56. Square brackets set off phrases occurring in the *YYJ* version but not the *SKQS.*

56. *Quesao bian,* by Xu Du (fl. ca. 1147), fol. 3, *SKQS,* 863:793a.

57. Basset, *Mille et un contes,* 1:331.

58. Doran, *History of Court Fools,* 70.

59. *Rama the Jester: An Original and Up-to-Date Version of the Stories of Tenali*

Rama, or Tales of Indian Wit and Humour (Coimbatore, India: n.d.), 20, quoted in Shulman, *King and the Clown,* 190.

60. Buchanan, *Witty and Entertaining Exploits,* 4.

61. Billington, *Mock Kings in Medieval Society and Renaissance Drama* (Oxford: Clarendon Press, 1991), 93–94 and 109.

62. Scogin again preempted Buchanan, who may have borrowed the idea or had it attributed to him by the compiler of anecdotes about him. Scogin was exiled to France but returned with his shoes full of French earth, thereby circumventing the injunction to keep off English soil. Boorde, *Merry Jests,* 2:144.

63. Duff, *Communing,* xiii.

64. Ibid., xv, 3, and xvi–xxiii.

65. Ibid., 32–33.

66. Boorde, *Merry Jests,* 155.

67. William Dolby, trans., "A-Fan-T'i Stories" (Edinburgh, unpublished MS, 1999), 28.

68. Panchapakesa, *Royal Jester,* 38–39.

69. Ibid., 40. The same story is told of an unnamed jester in a book of French jokes and anecdotes—possibly plagiarized. See *Le bouffon français, ou receuil d'anecdotes* (Paris: Blankenstein, 1812).

70. Natesa Sastri, *Tales of Tennalirama,* 4–5.

71. Souza, *All about Birbal,* 50–54.

72. Buchanan, *Witty and Entertaining Exploits,* 5.

73. Williamson and Williamson, "George Buchanan," 99–100, with minor adaptations. A similar joke is attributed in many late eighteenth-century jestbooks to a French dragoon who, on finding a man in his wife's bed for the second time threw his hat out the window—with the seducer's head in it. The dragoon asks the forgiveness of Louis XIV. See *Female Jester,* 4–5.

74. Sir Anthony Weldon, *The Court and Character of King James* (London, 1650), 91–92, quoted in Southworth, *Fools and Jesters,* 141.

75. *Die Chronik der Grafen von Zimmern,* 2:131ff., quoted in Werner Mezger, *Hofnarren im Mittelalter* (Constance: Universitätsverlag Konstanz, 1981), 66.

76. Dagan, *Court Jesters,* 19–20.

77. Shah, *Exploits,* 99.

78. Personal communication with Lt. J. M. Lines, Royal Navy.

CHAPTER FIVE

1. *Guang xiaofu,* By Feng Menglong (1574–1646), *LDXHJ,* 310, trans. William Dolby.

2. Henry Cornelius Agrippa, *Of the Vanitie and Uncertaintie of Artes and Sciences, Englished by Fa. Sangent* (London, 1569), chap. 62, sig. Aa3, quoted in Goldsmith, *Wise Fools*, 1.

3. Lin Yutang, "Zarathustra and the Jester," in *The Little Critic: Essays, Satires and Sketches on China* (Shanghai: Commercial Press, 1935), 222.

4. Luzio and Renier, "Buffoni," 35:122 and 24:631.

5. Personal communication with William Dolby.

6. Zijderveld, *Reality*, 110.

7. Pratt, *Life and Death of Jamie Fleeman*, 54–55.

8. Lin Yutang, "Zarathustra and the Jester," 224.

9. Jamieson, *Banquet of Jests*, 374, my emphasis; see figure 21.

10. Southworth, *Fools and Jesters*, 79.

11. Armin, *Nest of Ninnies*, 46–47.

12. *Qiyan lu, LDXHJ*, 10–11.

13. Rosenthal, *Humor in Early Islam*, 28.

14. Basset, *Mille et un contes*, 2:372–73.

15. Shah, *Exploits*, 86.

16. Feinberg, *Asian Laughter*, 437–38.

17. Buchanan, *Witty and Entertaining Exploits*, 7.

18. Ibid., 17. This same story is often attributed to Tom Killigrew; see *Female Jester*, 42–43.

19. Buchanan, *Witty and Entertaining Exploits*, 9.

20. J. S., *England's Merry Jester*, 11. In another account of Laud's tracking down Archy, we hear of the same bolt hole: "And what will you do then? said the King. O says Archee, I'll hide my self where he shall never find me. Where's that? says the King. In the pulpit, says Archee, for I am sure he never comes there." See *Ornatissimus Joculator, or The Compleat Jester . . .* (London: Onley, 1703), 17–18. According to Southworth (*Fools and Jesters*, 147), the story of the coach horses had the king complaining about how lean one of his horses was, with Archy suggesting he need only make it a bishop to fatten it up.

21. Pratt, *Life and Death of Jamie Fleeman*, 50–51.

22. Reiffenberg, "Histoire des fous," 256.

23. Luzio and Renier, "Buffoni," 24:632–33, trans. William Dolby.

24. ʿAbd al-Qadir ibn Muluk Shah Badaoni (b. 1540), *Muntakhab-ut-Tawarikh*, trans. W. H. Lowe, vol. 2 (Calcutta: Asiatic Society, 1925), 361–62, quoted in Siegel, *Laughing Matters*, 307.

25. Decourdemanche, *Sottisier*, 60–61.

26. Flögel, *Geschichte der Hofnarren,* 272.

27. Julius Wilhelm Zincgref (1591–1635), *Der teutschen Scharpfsinnige kluge Sprüch, Apophthegmata genant* (Strasbourg, 1628), 1:388, trans. and quoted in Welsford, *Fool,* 140.

28. Welsford, *Fool,* 143–44.

29. Mel Gussow, "Clown," *New Yorker,* 11 November 1985, 59; personal communication with William Dolby.

30. Wiesel, *Zalmen, ou La folie de Dieu* (Paris: Éditions du Seuil, 1968), 78.

31. Shulman, *King and the Clown,* 251.

32. See Meinardus, "Zeitgenössische Gottesnarren"; Shah, *Wisdom of the Idiots,* 5; Idries Shah, *Special Illumination: The Sufi Use of Humour* (London: Octagon Press, 1977), 7.

33. Thomas à Kempis (1380–1471), *The Imitation of Christ,* trans. and intro. L. Sherley-Price (London: Penguin Books, 1954).

34. Saward, *Perfect Fools,* x.

35. Sa'di, *Persian-English Gulistan,* 211 and 282.

36. See Sa'di, "The Manners of Kings," 49–179, and "The Morals of Dervishes," 180–286, in *Persian-English Gulistan.*

37. *The Court Jester, or Museum of Entertainment* (London: Hamilton, 1771), 11–12. A similar anecdote is told of Alexander the Great and Diogenes; see *Wits Museum, or The New London Jester: A Collection by the Choice Spirits of the Present Age* (London: Lane, 1780), 61.

38. Fedotov, "Holy Fools," 316.

39. Saward, *Perfect Fools,* 15, 12, 20, and 23, my emphasis.

40. Solomon Volkov, ed., *Testimony: The Memoirs of Dmitri Shostakovich,* related to Solomon Volkov, trans. Antonina Bouis (London: Hamilton, 1979), xxi.

41. Saward, *Perfect Fools,* 39, from an unpublished translation by Professor MacEoin of University College, Galway.

42. Ibid., 61 and 77.

43. Ibid., 87.

44. Quoted in and trans. Ronald Walpole, "Humor and People in Twelfth Century France," *Romance Philology* 11, 3 (1957–58): 224.

45. Saward, *Perfect Fools,* 98.

46. R. H. Blyth, *Oriental Humor* (Tokyo: Hokuseido Press, 1959; repr. 1968), 86.

47. Burton Watson, trans., *Ryokan: Zen Monk-Poet of Japan* (New York: Columbia University Press, 1977), 9.

48. Blyth, *Oriental Humor,* 85.

49. Watson, *Ryokan,* 5 and 10.

50. Ibid., 1.

51. Xing Zuisheng (Wang Kangnian), *Zhuangxie xuanlu* (Taibei: Xin Wenfeng Chuban Gongsi, 1978), 2:207.

52. E. K. Chambers, *The Medieval Stage,* 2 vols. (Oxford: Clarendon Press, 1903), 1:325.

53. M. Willson Disher, *Clowns and Pantomimes* (London: Constable, 1923; repr. New York: Blom, 1968), 43; Judith McCrary, *The Fool in French Medieval Drama* (Ann Arbor, MI: University Microfilms International, 1979), 35.

54. "Carnival in the Port of Spain, Trinidad," *Illustrated London News,* 5 May 1888, 496‑97.

55. Annie Sidro, *Le carnaval de Nice et ses fous: Paillassou, Polichinelle et Triboulet* (Nice: Serre, 1979), 91.

56. Siegel, *Laughing Matters,* xv and 4.

57. Jamieson, *Banquet of Jests,* 20.

58. Graf, "Buffone di Leone X," 300, trans. William Dolby.

59. *L'Hospidale de' Pazzi Incurabili* (Venice, 1617), 49, quoted in Graf, "Buffone," 300, trans. William Dolby.

60. Buchanan, *Witty and Entertaining Exploits,* 29.

61. Flögel, *Geschichte der Hofnarren,* 454, and Dietz-Rudiger Moser, "Fastnacht und Fastnachtspiel: Bemerkungen zum gegenwartigen Stand volkskundlicher und literarhistorischer Fastnachtsforschung," in *Popular Drama in Northern Europe in the Later Middle Ages,* ed. F. Anderson (Odense: Odense University Press, 1988), 170.

62. Luzio and Renier, "Buffoni," 35:124, trans. William Dolby.

63. Zimbardo, "Book of the Duchess," 333; Luzio and Renier, "Buffoni," 24:621.

64. Welsford, *Fool,* 16.

65. Herford, *Studies in the Literary Relations of England and Germany in the Sixteenth Century* (Cambridge: Cambridge University Press, 1886), 275.

66. *Der Pfarrer von Kalenberg,* in Felix Bobertag, ed., *Narrenbuch: Kalenberger, Peter Len, Neithard Fuchs, Markolf, Bruder Rausch,* in *Deutsche National-Litteratur: Historisch-Kritische Ausgabe,* ed. Joseph Kürschner (Berlin: Spemann, 1881), 2:66.

67. Hugill, *Bring on the Clowns,* 31‑32.

68. Basset, *Mille et un contes,* 1:499.

69. Borrow, *Turkish Jester,* 1‑2.

70. *Yang Qi fanghui heshang yulu,* ed. Ren Yong (Song) and others, in *Da cang*

jing, comp. J. Takakusu and K. Watanabe (Tokyo: Taisho Issdai-kyo Kanko Kwai, 1928), vol. 47, item 1994a–b, 641.

71. Rigollot, *Monnaies inconnues*, 101, pl. 24, no. 58; 107, pl. 26, no. 67 and pl. 26, no. 68; 181, pl. 38, no. 107, respectively.

72. William Willeford, *The Clown, the Kingdom and the Stage: A Study in the Forms of Our Relationship to Folly* (Zurich: Druck, 1967), 12.

73. Archibald Armstrong (fl. ca. 1620), "Archy's Dream, Sometimes Iester to His Maiestie, but Exiled the Court by *Canterburies* Malice: With a Relation for Whom an Odde Chaire Stood Voide in Hell" (1641), in *A Banquet of Jests*, ed. T. H. Jamieson (Edinburgh: William Paterson, 1872), 372.

74. Eighth-century canon, quoted in Harrison, *Irish Trickster*, 41.

75. Reiffenberg, "Histoire des fous," 260; Flögel, *Geschichte der Hofnarren*, 433.

76. Quoted in Doran, *History of Court Fools*, 87.

77. Birnbaum, "Laughter, Play and Carnival," 29.

78. Harrison, *Irish Trickster*, 40.

79. J. D. Ogilvy, "Mimi, Scurrae, Histriones: Entertainers of the Early Middle Ages," *Speculum* 38 (1963): 610.

80. Corbett, *Scurra*, 80.

81. Eco, *Name of the Rose*, 477.

82. Leszek Kolakowski, "The Priest and the Jester," trans. Pawel Mayewsky, in *The Modern Polish Mind*, ed. Maria Kuncewicz (London: Secker and Warburg, 1963), 323–24.

83. Seneca (ca. 4 B.C.– ca. A.D. 65), *The Epistles of Seneca*, trans. Richard Gummere, Loeb Classical Library (London: Heinemann; New York: Putnam, 1917), 1.50.2.

84. Francisco Núnez de Velasco, *Diálogos de contención entre la milicia y la ciencia* (Vallalodid, 1614), 206, quoted in Monique Joly, "Fragments d'un discours mythique sur le bouffon," in *Visages de la folie: 1500–1650 (Domaine hispano-italien)*, ed. A. Redondo and A. Rochon, Série Études 16 (Paris: Publications de la Sorbonne, 1981), 81.

85. Cristóval Suárez de Figueroa, *El Pasagero* (1617), ed. Rodríguez Marín (Madrid: Renacimiento, 1913), 254–55, quoted in Joly, "Fragments d'un discours mythique sur le bouffon," 89.

86. Luzio and Renier, "Buffoni," 35:116.

87. Adolfo Bartoli, "Buffoni di corte," *Fanfulla della Domenica*, 12 March 1882, 10, trans. William Dolby.

88. Luzio and Renier, "Buffoni," 35:132.

89. Article in *Dnevnik Russkogo Teatra*, quoted in Kelly, *Petrushka*, 11–12.

90. "Xie yin," by Liu Xie (ca. 465–ca. 522), in *"Wenxin diaolong" jinyi*, trans. Zhou Zhenfu, ed. Ji Ren, 130–37 (Beijing: Zhonghua Shuju, 1986), 132; trans. as "On Humor and Enigma," in *The Literary Mind and the Carving of Dragons*, trans. Vincent Yu-chung Shih [Shi Yuzhong] (New York: Columbia University Press, 1959), 80.

91. John Ford (fl. ca. 1639), *The Lover's Melancholy*, 1.2.16–18, in *John Ford*, ed. Henry Ellis (London: Fisher Unwin, 1888).

92. James Peacock, "Symbolic Reversal and Social History: Transvestites and Clowns of Java," in *The Reversible World: Symbolic Inversion in Art and Society*, ed. Barbara A. Babcock (Ithaca: Cornell University Press, 1978), 214.

93. Doran, *History of Court Fools*, 45.

94. Tieck, *Puss-in-Boots*, 2:88–89, trans. Gillespie with minor adjustments by William Dolby.

95. David Bevington, *Tudor Drama and Politics: A Critical Approach to Topical Meaning* (Cambridge: Harvard University Press, 1968), 64–65.

96. "Wan Xiao zhuan," in *Liaoshi*, fol. 85, *SKQS*, 289:621b.

97. Francis Thompson, "To the English Martyrs," in *Collected Poems*, ed. Wilfred Meynell (Sevenoaks, Kent: Fisher Press, 1992), 233.

98. Edward Hall, *Chronicle: Containing the History of England from the Reign of Henry IV to the End of the Reign of Henry VIII* (1548), ed. H. Ellis (London: Johnson, 1809), 761.

99. Ibid., 817–18.

100. Quoted in Doran, *History of Court Fools*, 152.

101. *Dictionary of National Biography*, 18:327–32.

102. Raphael Holinshed (d. 1580?), *Holinshed's Chronicles of England, Scotland and Ireland*, 3 vols. (London: Johnson, 1807–8), 1:110, quoted in Hazlitt, *Shakespeare Jest-Books*, 2:40.

103. Boorde, *Merry Jests*, 121.

104. Philip Ford, *George Buchanan: Prince of Poets* (Aberdeen: Aberdeen University Press, 1982), passim.

105. Williamson and Williamson, "George Buchanan," 100.

106. Ford, *Buchanan*, 103.

107. Panchapakesa, *Royal Jester*, 18.

108. "Kong Daofu zhuan," in *Songshi*, by Tuo Tuo (1314–55) and others, fol. 297, *SKQS*, 285:725b. The Khitan were sinicized, which is perhaps why Kong said they shared the same culture.

109. *Shengshui yantan lu*, by Wang Pizhi (fl. ca. 1082), fol. 9, *SKQS*, 1036:522a.

110. *Meixi qianji*, by Wang Shipeng (1112–71), fol. 6, *SKQS*, 1151:151a. For

other examples of disapproval of jesters' mocking Confucian themes, see *Tingshi*, fol. 13, *SKQS*, 1039:507a; and *Han Zhongxian yishi*, by Qiang Zhi (fl. ca. 1060), *LDXS* (Jing Ming Keben), bk. 22, fol. 70, 9b. It seems that the most frequent criticism of jesters in China arose when they brought Confucianism into their skits.

111. *Qiyan lu*, *LDXHJ*, 11. The joke works better in Chinese, which does not need the word "or" and does not use plurals.

112. *Qidong yeyu*, by Zhou Mi (1232 – 98), *SKQS*, 865:775a – b.

113. *Qiyan lu*, *LDXHJ*, 11, my emphasis.

114. *Zhongshan shihua*, by Liu Bin (1022 – 88), *SKQS*, 1478:268b – 69a.

115. "Dongfang Shuo zhuan," by Ban Gu, 2863, trans. Watson, in Ban Gu, *Courtier and Commoner*, 96.

116. Kenneth Mackenzie, coll. and trans., *The Marvellous Adventures and Rare Conceits of Master Tyll Owlglass* (London: Trubner, 1860), 140 – 42.

117. Ibid., 203 – 6 and 215.

118. *Qunju jieyi*, by Gao Yi (Song), *LDXHJ*, 58.

CHAPTER SIX

1. Edmund Bohun, *The Character of Queen Elizabeth, or A Full and Clear Account of Her Policies, and the Methods of Her Government both in Church and State, Her Virtues and Defects* (London: Chiswell, 1693), 252.

2. Martyr Christianus (sixteenth century), MS S.94b, 95a, quoted in Wyss, *Narr im schweizerischen Drama*, 149.

3. *Pilgrimage to Parnassus* (1599), in *The Three Parnassus Plays*, ed. J. B. Leishman (London: Nicholson and Watson, 1949), 95 – 132.

4. A. J. Krailsheimer and others, *The Continental Renaissance: 1500 – 1600* (Harmondsworth, Middlesex: Penguin Books, 1971), 509. Caputi sees the term as meaning "eve of the fast" *(fast Nacht)*, rather than "night of the fooling" *(fassen Nacht)*. Anthony Caputi, *Buffo: The Genius of Vulgar Comedy* (Detroit: Wayne State University Press, 1978), 41.

5. J. M. Barrie, *The Admirable Crichton* (London: Hodder and Stoughton, 1918), 1:27.

6. For a detailed treatment of these, see K. J. S. Gibson, "The Nature and Function of the Servants in Comedies First Performed at the Comédie Française between 1685 and 1732" (Ph.D. diss., Glasgow University, 1987), and Vivien Rubin, "Clowns in Nineteenth Century French Literature: Buffoons, Pierrots and 'Saltimbanques'" (Ph.D. diss., Berkeley: University of California, 1970).

7. Junko Sakaba Berberich, "The Idea of Rapture as an Approach to Kyogen," *Asian Theatre Journal* 6, 1 (1989): 31.

8. In *Plautus*, trans. Paul Nixon, 5 vols. Loeb Classical Library (London: Heinemann; New York: Putnam; Cambridge: Harvard University Press, 1916; repr. 1928−38), 2:185−269, 2:363−487, and 5:97−221, respectively.

9. K. Schipper, "The Divine Jester: Some Remarks on the Gods of the Chinese Marionette Theatre," *Bulletin of the Institute of Ethnology* 21 (1977?): 81−87.

10. Kelly, *Petrushka*, 100−102.

11. Metin And, *Karagoz: Turkish Shadow Theatre* (Ankara: Dost, 1987), 83−87.

12. Enrico Fulchignoni, "Oriental Influences on the Commedia dell'Arte," trans. Una Crowley, *Asian Theatre Journal* 7, 1 (1990): 39; And, *Karagoz*, 86−87 and 71.

13. Peacock, "Symbolic Reversal," 211.

14. Ward Keeler, *Javanese Shadow Plays, Javanese Selves* (Princeton: Princeton University Press, 1987), 29.

15. Hsü, *Chinese Conception of the Theatre*, 299.

16. William Dolby, *A History of the Chinese Theatre* (London: Elek 1976), 6.

17. John Hu, "Ming Dynasty Drama," in *Chinese Theater from Its Origins to the Present Day*, ed. Colin Mackerras (Honolulu: University of Hawaii Press, 1983), 83.

18. *Xiaoting zalu*, by Zhao Lian (Qing), fol. 1, in *Shuo ku*, comp. Wang Wenru, (Taibei: Xingxing Shuju, 1963), 2:1514b.

19. A. C. Scott, *Traditional Chinese Plays*, 3 vols. (Madison: University of Wisconsin Press, 1969), 2:19; Chai E, *Fantianlu congchao*, 214b.

20. Chai E, *Fantianlu congchao*, 214b,

21. Liu Zhesou, "Lun xiju gaizao shehui zhi nengli," *XJYK*, 1, 4 (1928): 2.

22. *Sijiu lu*, by Huang Zongxi (1610−95), in *Huang Zongxi quanji*, ed. Sun Jiasui (Hangzhou: Zhejiang Guji Chubanshe, 1985), 1:380−81.

23. Xing Zuisheng, *Zhuangxie xuanlu*, quoted in *YYJ*, 231.

24. "Youren yi guanxin guozhai," *Guangyi Congbao*, May 1911, quoted in *YYJ*, 319−20.

25. Zhang Geng, "Zhongguo huaju yundong shi chugao," *Xiju Bao*, 1954, 1−7, quoted in *YYJ*, 320.

26. Tai Weige, "Liyuan gushi," *XJYK* 1, 11 (1929): 3−4.

27. "Paiyou," in *Yuefu zalu*, 49, trans. William Dolby in "Early Chinese Plays and Theater," in Mackerras, *Chinese Theater*, 14.

28. A. C. Scott, *The Classical Theatre of China* (Westport, CT: Greenwood, 1957; repr. 1978), 76−77.

29. Scott, *Traditional Chinese Plays*, 2:10, 12−14.

30. Zhuang Yifu, ed., *Gudian xiqu cunmu huikao*, 3 vols. (Shanghai: Guji Chubanshe, 1982), 1:469; Fu Xihua, ed., *Yuandai zaju quanmu* (Beijing: Zuojia Chubanshe, 1957), 251.

31. Zhuang Yifu, *Gudian xiqu cunmu huikao*, 1:469.

32. Ibid., 2:577; *Guben xiqu congkan*, 2d collection, in 2 fols. (Shanghai: Shanghai Commercial Press, 1955); *Yinfengge zaju*, coll. and annot. Hu Shiying (Shanghai: Shanghai Guji Chubanshe, 1983), 173–82.

33. "Dongfang Shuo zhuan," by Ban Gu, 6:2843.

34. Zhuang Yifu, *Gudian xiqu cunmu huikao*, 1:461.

35. Allardyce Nicoll, *Masks, Mimes and Miracles* (London: Harrap, 1931), 124–25.

36. Ibid., 36, my emphasis.

37. Ibid., 25–26.

38. Horace, *Satires*, 1.5.51–70.

39. Gaius Suetonius, "The Deified Augustus," in *The Lives of the Caesars*, trans. J. C. Rolfe, 2 vols., Loeb Classical Library (London: Heinemann; New York: Putnam, 1914; repr. and rev. 1928–30), 1, 2:206–7.

40. "Hadrian," in *Scriptores historiae Augustae*, trans. David Magie, 3 vols., Loeb Classical Library (London: Heinemann; New York: Putnam, 1930), 1:78–79.

41. Suetonius, "Tiberius," 1, 3:356–57.

42. "Marcus Antoninus," in *Scriptores historiae Augustae*, 1:202–3.

43. Suetonius, "Nero," in *Lives of the Caesars*, 2, 6:156–57, my emphasis.

44. "Verus," in *Scriptores historiae Augustae*, 1:224–25.

45. Ibid., 1:224–25.

46. Suetonius, "Nero," 2, 6:156–57.

47. "Commodus Antoninus," in *Scriptores historiae Augustae*, 1.266–67; ibid., 1:270–71.

48. Nicoll, *Masks, Mimes and Miracles*, 121, 88, and 91.

49. Quoted in ibid., 127.

50. Bohun, *Character of Queen Elizabeth*, 353.

51. Document dated 16 May 1559, quoted in E. K. Chambers, *The Elizabethan Stage*, 4 vols. (Oxford: Clarendon Press, 1923; repr. 1951), vol. 4, app. D, Documents of Control, 263.

52. Olive Busby, *Studies in the Development of the Fool in Elizabethan Drama* (New York: Oxford University Press, 1923), 5.

53. Stowe, *Annales* (1583), quoted in Hazlitt, *Shakespeare Jest-Books*, 2:254.

54. *Dictionary of National Biography*, 19:369–71; Taylor, "Professional Fools," 260.

55. David Wiles, *Shakespeare's Clown Actor and Text in the Elizabethan Playhouse* (Cambridge: Cambridge University Press, 1987), 15.

56. Ahuva Belkin, "'Here's My Coxcomb': Some Notes on the Fool's Dress," *Assaph*, sec. C, no. 1 (1984): 40–54, and Leslie Hotson, *Shakespeare's Motley* (London: Hart-Davis, 1952).

57. Robert Armin, *Tarlton's News out of Purgatory*, in *The Collected Works of Robert Armin*, intro. J. Feather, 2 vols. (New York: Johnson Reprint Corporation, 1972), vol. 1, introduction.

58. Armin, *Nest of Ninnies*, xi.

59. W. J. Lawrence, "On the Underrated Genius of Dick Tarleton," in *Speeding up Shakespeare* (London: Argonaut Press, 1937), 18.

60. John Skelton (ca. 1460–1529), *Magnificence*, ed. Paula Neuss (Manchester: Manchester University Press, 1980).

61. F. Mares, "The Origin of the Figure Called the Vice," *Huntingdon Library Quarterly* 22 (1958): 13–16.

62. Busby, *Development of the Fool*, 38.

63. Charles Felver, *Robert Armin: Shakespeare's Fool*, Research Series 5 (Kent, OH: Kent State University Bulletin, 1961), iii.

64. Guy Butler, "Shakespeare and Two Jesters," *Hebrew University Studies in Literature and the Arts* 11 (1983): 164.

65. *The Oxford English Dictionary* (Oxford: Clarendon, 1959), s.v. "touchstone."

66. William Shakespeare, *Troilus and Cressida* (1602), ed. Kenneth Palmer (London: Methuen, 1982).

67. William Shakespeare, *All's Well That Ends Well* (1602), ed. G. K. Hunter, 3d ed. rev. (London: Methuen, 1959; repr. 1962).

68. Robert Greene, *Friar Bacon and Friar Bongay*, in *The Plays and Poems of Robert Greene*, ed., intro., and annot. J. Churton Collins (Oxford: Clarendon Press, 1905), 2:14–78.

69. Ben Jonson, *Every Man out of His Humour* (Oxford: Oxford University Press, 1920).

70. Thomas Dekker (ca. 1572–1632) and others, *Patient Grissill*, in *The Dramatic Works of Thomas Dekker*, ed. Fredson Bowers (Cambridge: Cambridge University Press, 1953), 1:207–98.

71. John Marston (ca. 1575–1634), *The Malcontent*, ed. Bernard Harris (London: A. and C. Black, 1987).

72. Thomas Nash (1567–1601), *Summer's Last Will and Testament*, in *Complete Works*, ed. R. McKerrow, 5 vols. (Oxford: Blackwell, 1958), 3:227–95.

73. William Shakespeare, *Henry VIII*, ed. R. A. Foakes, rev. ed. (London: Methuen, 1975).

74. *Misogonus*, ed. Lester Barber (New York: Garland, 1979).

75. *Thorney Abbey*, quoted in Billington, *Social History*, 69.

76. Thomas Shadwell, *The Woman Captain*, in *The Complete Works of Thomas Shadwell*, ed. Montague Summers, 5 vols. (New York: Blom, 1968), 1:7–85.

77. Pepys, *Diary*, 5:230.

78. Ibid., 9:425, 24 January 1669.

79. *Pamphile Gengenbach* (1545–46) (Hanover, 1856), 292, quoted in Émile Picot, "La sottie en France," *Romania* 7 (1878): 246.

80. Adam de la Halle (ca. 1240–ca. 1288), *Le jeu de la feuillée*, trans. and ed. Jean Dufournet (Gand, Belgium: Éditions Scientifiques E. Story-Scientia, 1977).

81. The morality plays were "halfway between the devotion of the miracle play and the sacrilege of the sottie . . . equidistant, so to speak, from the altar and the street," Kaiser, *Praisers of Folly*, 196.

82. Rabelais, *Tiers livre*, 558. In Samoa, troupes of players putting on improvisatory plays are trained and directed by the most accomplished comedian among them. See Caroline Sinavaiana, "Traditional Comic Theatre in Samoa: A Holographic View" (Ph.D. diss., University of Hawaii, 1992), vi.

83. In Gustave Cohen, ed., *Mystères et moralités du Manuscrit 617 de Chantilly* (Paris: Champion, 1920).

84. Grimald, *Archipropheta*, 228–357.

85. *Oxford Companion to French Literature*, comp. and ed. Paul Harvey and J. E. Heseltine (Oxford: Clarendon Press, 1959), s.v. "sociétés joyeuses." Although France seems to have been the predominant arena for foolish societies, they did exist elsewhere, such as in England and in Italy, where they were called *associazioni giovanili*, one of them being known as the "Brotherhood of Idiots" ("Abbazia degli Stolti"). See Caputi, *Buffo*, 85.

86. McCrary, *Fool in French Medieval Drama*, 207–8.

87. Chambers, *Medieval Stage*, 1:384.

88. André de la Vigne, *Sotise à huit personnaiges*, in *Recueil général des sotties*, ed. Émile Picot, 3 vols. (Paris: Firmin Didot, 1912), 2:1–104.

89. *Farce morale de troys pelerins et malice*, in Picot, *Recueil général des sotties*, 2:299–300.

90. *Sottie nouvelle à six personnaiges du roy des sotz*, in Picot, *Recueil général des sotties*, 3:205–31.

91. Ibid., 3:207.

92. Picot, "Sottie," 243.

93. *Le triomphe de l'abbaye des Conards,* quoted in Rigollot, *Monnaies incon-nues,* lx.

94. Northcott, "Fool in Early New High German Literature," 30.

95. Quoted in ibid., 46. A similar story is told in *England's Merry Jester* (1693), in which the jester genuinely wishes to make amends for having humiliated the big-nosed man. He appears to believe that a voluble retraction will undo the damage and starts to shout "That Man has no Nose at all! No Nose at all! No Nose at all!" (73–74).

96. Flögel, *Geschichte der Hofnarren,* 265–66. The scorecard idea I owe to Lee Siegel. This story is later attributed, with minor amendments, to George Buchanan in *The Witty and Entertaining Exploits of George Buchanan,* 3.

97. Bharata-Muni [ascribed], *The Natyasastra: A Treatise on Ancient Indian Dramaturgy and Histrionics,* trans. Manomohan Ghosh, 2 vols. (Calcutta: Asiatic Society, 1956–61), vol. 2, chap. 35, sec. 92–93, 226.

98. G. K. Bhat, *The Vidusaka* (Ahmedabad: New Order Book Company, 1959), 103.

99. Keith Jefferds, "Vidusaka versus Fool: A Functional Analysis," *Journal of South Asian Literature* 16 (1981): 61.

100. S. N. Dasgupta, *A History of Sanskrit Drama* (Calcutta, 1962), 1:654, quoted in F. B. J. Kuiper, *Varuna and Vidusaka: On the Origin of Sanskrit Drama* (Amsterdam: North-Holland, 1979), 223–24, my emphasis.

101. Michael Coulson, ed. and trans., *Three Sanskrit Plays* (Harmondsworth, Middlesex: Penguin Books, 1981), 32; Kuiper, *Varuna and Vidusaka,* 223.

102. Kuiper, *Varuna and Vidusaka,* 202–4 and 222.

103. *Natyasastra,* chap. 13, quoted in ibid., 214–15.

104. Kuiper, *Varuna and Vidusaka,* 224.

105. Shulman, *King and the Clown,* 175 and 201.

106. Kuiper, *Varuna and Vidusaka,* 226.

107. Kalidasa, *Theater of Memory: The Plays of Kalidasa,* ed. Barbara Stoler Miller (New York: Columbia University Press, 1984), 9–11 and 17.

108. Dandin (ca. 550), *Dasakumaracarita,* 7th ed., ed. with four commentaries by Narayana Balakrsna Godabole (Bombay: Nirnaya-Sagara Press, 1913), 255; quoted in and trans. Siegel, *Laughing Matters,* 300.

109. Bhat, *Vidusaka,* 25.

110. Kalidasa, *Sakuntala and the Ring of Recollection,* in *Theater of Memory* trans. Barbara Miller, 85–176.

111. Kalidasa, *Urvasi Won by Valour,* in *Theater of Memory* trans. David Gitomer, 177–251.

112. Kalidasa, *Malavika and Agnimitra,* in *Theater of Memory* trans. Edwin Gerow, 253–312.

113. Sudraka [attrib.], *The Little Clay Cart,* in *Two Plays of Ancient India,* trans. J. A. B. van Buitenen (New York: Columbia University Press, 1964; repr. 1968). Is it coincidence that the vidusaka jester Maitreya has the same name as the laughing Buddha? A *vina* is a kind of lute.

114. V. S. Agrawala, "A Palace Amusement Scene on a Terracotta Panel from Mathura," *Journal of the India Society of Oriental Art* 10 (1942): 36–37; A. N. Upadhye, "Vidusaka's Ears," *Indian Historical Quarterly* 8, 4 (1932): 793.

115. Ellanor Pruitt, "The Figure of the Fool in Contemporary Theatre" (Ph.D. diss., Emory University, 1976), abstract.

116. For the sake of convenience, "modern" here means from the late eighteenth century, when there was a revival of court jesters and fools in European drama.

117. Percy Bysshe Shelley, *Charles the First,* in *Plays, Translations, and Longer Poems* (London: Dent, 1907; repr. 1949), 357–63.

118. In Hugo, *Théâtre complet,* 1:1321–485, 1:405–952, and 1:953–1144, respectively.

119. Alfred de Musset (1810–57), *Fantasio,* in *Théâtre complet,* ed. Maurice Allem (Paris: Gallimard, 1958), 276–323.

120. Nancy Lukens, *Buchner's Valerio and the Theatrical Fool Tradition* (Stuttgart: Heinz, 1977), 11–12.

121. Georg Buchner (1813–37), *Leonce and Lena,* in *The Plays of Georg Buchner,* trans. Victor Price (London: Oxford University Press, 1971).

122. Frank Wedekind (1864–1918), *König Nicolo, oder So ist das Leben,* in *Frank Wedekind: Dramen,* ed. Manfred Hahn (Berlin: Aufbau-Verlag, 1969), 1:519–89.

123. Michel de Ghelderode, *Escurial,* trans. Lionel Abel, in *Modern Theatre,* ed. Eric Bentley (New York: Doubleday, 1957), 5:161–78.

124. Hunter Steele, *Lord Hamlet's Castle* (London: Deutsch, 1987). Steele has done for Hamlet what Robert Nye did for Falstaff—provided a rumbustious, red-blooded account.

125. "Jinyu," fol. 2, in *Guoyu,* vol. 1, fol. 8, 286.

126. W. B. Yeats, *The Green Helmet,* in *The Collected Plays of W. B. Yeats* (London: Macmillan Papermac, 1982; repr. 1992), 221–44.

127. Lieberman and Lieberman, *Throne of Straw,* quoted in Thomas Neiheiser, "Heroes and Fools: Characterizations in Holocaust Drama" (Ph.D. diss., University of Utah, 1983), 176.

128. Shimon Wincelberg, *Resort 76,* in *The Theatre of the Holocaust: Four Plays,*

ed. and intro. Robert Skloot (Madison: University of Wisconsin Press, 1982), 39–112.

129. Gregory Jan Mar Bar-Hebraeus (b. 1226), comp., *The Laughable Stories,* trans. E. A. Wallis Budge (London: Luzac, 1897), 129.

130. Quoted in Luzio and Renier, "Buffoni," 24:627 and 629; ibid., 24:624.

131. Sinavaiana, "Traditional Comic Theatre," 50–51, vi, and 74.

132. Lukens, *Buchner's Valerio,* 13.

CHAPTER SEVEN

1. Cecil Collins, *The Vision of the Fool* (Chipping Norton, Oxfordshire: Kedros, 1981), 7.

2. "Guji liezhuan," 3203, trans. Dolby, *Jesters,* 38.

3. Erasmus, *Praise of Folly,* trans. Betty Radice, 145–47.

4. The expression used as the chapter title, "stultorum plena sunt omnia," widely used in the Middle Ages, comes from a letter by Cicero quoted in *Epistulae ad familiares,* ed. Glynn Williams (Cambridge Harvard University Press, 1959), 2.9.22.4, cited in Billington, " Role of the Fool," 48.

5. Wolf, writing in 1850, mentions a Mr. Schlager as planning to write a history of court jesters in the service of Austrian princes and nobles ("Zuñiga," 22). Did he, I wonder?

6. Justi, "Dwarfs, Buffoons and Jesters," 433.

7. Sebastian de Covarrubias Horozco, *Tesoro de la lengua castellana o espanola* (Madrid: Turner, 1984), s.v. "truhan."

8. Justi, "Dwarfs, Buffoons and Jesters," 436.

9. Lever, *Sceptre,* 69–70.

10. Ibid., 72.

11. Lever, *Sceptre,* 73; Butler, "Shakespeare and Two Jesters," 164–65.

12. Reiffenberg, "Histoire des fous," 265.

13. Halabi, "Development of Humour," 59.

14. Personal communication with Lee Siegel.

15. Pierre Loti, *L'Inde (sans les Anglais)* (Paris: Calmann-Lévy, 1903), 373.

16. Benjamin Disraeli, *Beaconsfield's Letters* (London, 1887), 86, quoted in Kalff, *Opkomst,* 31–32.

17. Halabi, "Development of Humour," 64 and 67.

18. J. E. De Becker, *The Nightless City, or The History of the Yoshiwara Yukwaku* (1899; Tokyo: Tuttle, 1971), 71 and 67.

19. Personal communication with Marguerite Wells.

20. Engels, article in *Hakluyt Society,* ser. 1, vol. 66, 77, quoted in Kalff, *Opkomst,* 24.

21. Flögel, *Geschichte der Hofnarren,* 179.

22. Xenophon (ca. 570–ca. 475 B.C.), *Symposium,* trans. O. J. Todd, Loeb Classical Library (London: Heinemann, 1922), 304.

23. Doran, *History of Court Fools,* 234–35; Sue Arnold, "Nobs and Knockers," *Sunday Observer Magazine,* 20 May 1990, 18.

24. Raymond Richards, "Samuel Johnson," in *The Manor of Gawsworth* (Manchester: Morten, 1959; repr. 1974), 225. See June Weller, *The Jester: A Story for Children,* illus. Elaine Jones (Cheshire: J. Weller, 1980), which has a jester called Lord Flame showing two young children around Gawsworth Hall.

25. Personal communication with Ali Granmayeh.

26. Doran, *History of Court Fools,* 76.

27. J. J. Jusserand, *English Wayfaring Life in the Middle Ages* (London: Fisher Unwin, 1920), 221.

28. Frederick Millingen, *Wild Life among the Koords* (London: Hurst and Blackett, 1870), 255.

29. Charles Wentworth Dilke, *Greater Britain: A Record of Travel in English-Speaking Countries during 1866 and 1867* (London: Macmillan, 1869), 263, quoted in Kalff, *Opkomst,* 23.

30. George Turner, *Samoa: One Hundred Years Ago and Long Before* (London: Macmillan, 1884), 126, quoted in Mitchell, "Introduction," 18.

31. Frederick Ponsonby, *Recollections of Three Reigns* (London: Eyre and Spottiswoode, 1951), 149.

32. Dooling, "Wisdom of the Contrary," 55–59.

33. Max Gluckman, *Politics, Law and Ritual in Tribal Society* (Oxford: Blackwell, 1965; repr. 1982), 103.

34. *Qinzhun jupin,* by Pan Zhiheng (d. 1621), *Shuofu* (sequel), fol. 44, quoted in *YYJ,* 314.

35. William Shakespeare, *King Henry VI, Part 2,* ed. Andrew Cairncross, 3d ed. rev. (London: Methuen, 1957), 3.1.364–66.

36. Miguel de Cervantes, *Don Quixote,* 10th ed. (Barcelona: Editorial Juventud, 1975), part 2, chap. 11, 613; trans. J. M. Cohen as *Don Quixote* (Harmondsworth, Middlesex: Penguin Books, 1950), 535.

37. *Pleasant History of the Life and Death of Will Summers,* 12.

38. *The Ass Race, or The Secret History of Archy Armstrong, Fool to King Charles I, Extracted from a Very Curious MSS* (London, 1740).

39. A. J. Nock, "The King's Jester: Modern Style," *Harper's Monthly Magazine,* March 1928, 481.

40. Callahan, "Another Book of Laughter," 195–202. Although this dissertation is a study of humor in China and the West, the author's reading relies heavily on somewhat limited secondary sources.

41. Charles, "Clown's Function," 28.

42. Quintilian, *The "Institutio Oratorio" of Quintilian,* trans. H. E. Butler, Loeb Classical Library (London: Heinemann; Cambridge: Harvard University Press, 1953), 6.3.8–9.

43. Étienne Pasquier in a letter to Ronsard Pasquier, in *Lettres* (Paris: Gamber, 1930), 2:100, quoted in Bakhtin, *Rabelais and His World,* 60.

44. Welsford, *Fool,* 317.

45. Personal communication with Paul Dundas.

46. "Dongfang Shuo zhuan," by Ban Gu, 2874, trans. Watson in Ban Gu, *Courtier and Commoner,* 106.

47. *Tenali Rama,* trans. in Panchapakesa, *Royal Jester,* 122.

48. Billington, *Social History,* ix.

49. Taylor, "Professional Fools," 260.

50. *Female Jester,* 44–45.

51. *Jiang sangshen Cai Shun feng mu zaju,* attrib. Liu Tangqing (fl. ca. 1279), in *Yuanquxuan waibian,* ed. Sui Shusen (Beijing: Zhonghua Shuju, 1959), 1:429, trans. William Dolby in *Eight Chinese Plays* (London: Elek 1978), 23; Nicoll, *Masks, Mimes and Miracles,* 26–27.

52. Reiffenberg, "Histoire des fous," 265.

53. Billington, *Social History,* 40; *Encyclopaedia Britannica,* 15th ed., *Micropaedia,* s.v. "Morris dance." A replica of the window is in the Kingston-upon-Thames Museum and Art Gallery, London.

54. Sidro, *Carnaval de Nice,* 91.

55. Peter Tokofsky, "The Rules of Fools: Carnival in Southwest Germany" (Ph.D. diss., University of Pennsylvania, 1992), 4, 42, 67–68, 116, 26–34, and 40–42.

56. Cevoule-Angles, "Jehan-Antoine Lombard," 98.

57. Jeffrey Farnol, *The Fool Beloved* (London: Book Club, 1950).

58. Alan Brownjohn, *The Way You Tell Them: A Yarn for the Nineties* (London: Deutsch, 1990).

59. Richard Burns, *Troubadour* (London: Unwin Paperbacks, 1988), 3.

60. Güneli Gün, *On the Road to Baghdad: A Picaresque Novel of Magical Ad-*

ventures, Begged, Borrowed, and Stolen from the Thousand and One Nights (London: Picador, 1994), 58.

61. Ibid., 360 and 357.

62. Gerald Groemer, review of Theodore Levin, *The Hundred Thousand Fools of God: Musical Travels in Central Asia (and Queens, New York)* (Bloomington: Indiana University Press, 1996).

63. Personal communication with William Dolby; Christine Doyle, "Depression: My Part in Its Downfall," *Daily Telegraph,* 13 March 1990, 19; "Hunter S. Thompson: King Hoodlum of Letters," *Independent,* 14 April 1990, 16.

64. *Sunday Times,* 22 June 1990, 3; Martin Huckerby, "Jester Murdered for Mockery," *Observer,* 1 April 1990, 15.

65. John Wardroper, *Kings, Lords and Wicked Libellers: Satire and Protest, 1760–1837* (London: Murray, 1973), 3.

66. Gerald C. Gardner, *The Mocking of the President: A History of Campaign Humor from Ike to Ronnie* (Detroit: Wayne State University Press, 1988), 14.

67. Ibid., 13.

68. *Independent,* 10 September 1990, 8.

69. Perry Link, "Popular Performing Arts," in *Stubborn Weeds: Popular and Controversial Chinese Literature after the Cultural Revolution* (London: Blond and Briggs, 1984), 252.

70. Perry Link, "The Genie and the Lamp: Revolutionary *Xiangsheng,*" in *Popular Chinese Literature and Performing Arts in the People's Republic of China, 1949–1979,* ed. Bonnie McDougall (Berkeley: University of California Press, 1984), 92–93; Ma Ji, *Stormy Petrel (Haiyan),* trans. Perry Link in "Genie and the Lamp," 104–5.

71. Hou Baolin and others, "'Paiyou': 'Dou' de zaoqi xingshi," in *Xiangsheng suyuan* (Beijing: Renmin Wenxue Chubanshe, 1982), 140–54.

72. Egon Larsen, *Wit as a Weapon: The Political Joke in History* (London: Muller, 1980), 46.

73. Ibid., 49.

74. Ibid., 73.

75. Ibid., 46.

76. Ibid., 39.

77. Albert Speer, *Inside the Third Reich,* trans. Richard and Clara Winston (London: Sphere Books, 1971), 205.

78. Quoted in Towsen, *Clowns,* 196.

79. Ibid., 309.

80. Ibid., 315 and 322.

81. Ibid., 315–16.

82. Ronald Jenkins, "Representative Clowns: Comedy and Democracy in America" (Ph.D. diss., Harvard University, 1984), 6 and 50; Towsen, *Clowns*, 130.

83. Quoted in Towsen, *Clowns*, 134.

84. Charles, "Clown's Function," 25.

85. William Richard Brown, *Imagemaker: Will Rogers and the American Dream* (Columbia: University of Missouri Press, 1970), 18, quoted in Jenkins, "Representative Clowns," 78 n. 2.

86. Andrew Morton, "The Royal Marriage: Happy Ever After?" *Sunday Times*, 23 September 1990, 7.

87. O. L. Klapp, *Heroes, Villains and Fools* (Englewood Cliffs, NJ: Prentice-Hall, 1962), 16.

88. Personal communication with Miklos Otto.

89. Speer, *Inside the Third Reich*, 185 and 187.

90. Michael Caine, *What's It All About: The Autobiography* (New York: Random House Audiobooks, 1992), side 4.

91. Fuller, *History of the Worthies of England*, 2:311.

92. Eamonn McCabe, "A Brush with History," *Guardian*, 22 May 1993, 29.

93. Decourdemanche, *Sottisier*, viii–ix.

94. Shah, *Pleasantries*, 11 and 18.

95. Ibid., 157; Shah, *The Subtleties of the Inimitable Mulla Nasrudin* (London: Octagon Press, 1983), 3 and 35.

96. Shah, *Exploits*, introduction.

97. Shah, *Pleasantries*, introduction.

98. *Han Wudi neizhuan* by Ban Gu, in *L'empereur Wou des Han dans la légende Taoiste: Han Wou-ti Nei-tchouan*, trans. K. Schipper (Paris: École Française d'Extrême-Orient, 1965), 61 and 122.

99. Lionel Giles, *A Gallery of Chinese Immortals* (London: Murray, 1948), 51.

100. *Han Wudi neizhuan*, 20.

101. Neil Gaiman and Paul Johnson, *The Road to Nowhere*, Books of Magic 4 (New York: DC Comics, 1991), 32–35.

EPILOGUE

1. Oliver Edwards and Vernon Silver, "The Prince Who Saves Europe's Capitalist Monuments," *EuroBusiness*, June 1999, 32. Thanks to Edwin Datschefski for putting this gem in my path.

2. Ibid., 30.

3. Krishna Guha, "BA's Court Jester," *Financial Times,* 12 October 1995, 18.

4. David Firth and Alan Leigh, *The Corporate Fool* (Oxford: Capstone, 1998), 122.

5. Ibid., 122–23.

6. Ibid., 124.

7. Ibid., 62.

BIBLIOGRAPHY

WESTERN LANGUAGES AND MODERN CHINESE

Abbildung des turkischen Hofes nach Ferreol. Nürnberg, 1789.

Abreu Gómez, Ermilo. "Los graciosos en el teatro de Ruiz de Alarcón." *Investigaciones Lingüísticas* 3 (1935): 189–201.

Adolph, Helen. "On Medieval Laughter." *Speculum* 22 (1947): 251–53.

Agrawala, V. S. "A Palace Amusement Scene on a Terracotta Panel from Mathura." *Journal of the India Society of Oriental Art* 10 (1942): 69–73.

Agrippa, Henry Cornelius (1486–1535). *Of the Vanitie and Uncertaintie of Artes and Sciences, Englished by Fa. Sangent.* London, 1569.

Alford, Finnegan, and Richard Alford. "A Holo-cultural Study of Humor." *Ethos* 9 (1981): 149–64.

Allen, Andrew. "The Sinister Art of 'Hindering.'" *Scotsman,* 11 February 1989, 5.

Amarasingham, L. R. "Laughter as Cure: Joking and Exorcism in a Sinhalese Curing Ritual." Ph.D. diss., Cornell University, 1973.

Amelunxen, C. *Of Fools at Court.* Trans. Rhodes Barratt. Berlin: Walter de Gruyter, 1992.

Amigos del Museo del Prado. *Monstruos, enanos y bufones en la corte de los Austrias a proposito del "Retrato de Enano" de Juan van der Hamen.* Madrid: Amigos del Museo del Prado, 1986.

Amrain, Karl. *Deutscher Schwänkerzahler des XV bis XVIII Jahrhunderts.* Leipzig: Deutsche Verlagsaktiengesellschaft, 1907.

And, Metin. *Karagoz: Turkish Shadow Theatre.* Ankara: Dost, 1987.

Anderson, F., ed. *Popular Drama in Northern Europe in the Later Middle Ages.* Odense: Odense University Press, 1988.

Anderson, L. F. *The Anglo-Saxon Scop.* Toronto: University of Toronto Press, 1903.

Anglo, Sydney. "The Court Revels of Henry VII." *Bulletin of the John Rylands Library* 43 (1960–61): 12–45.

Arden, Heather. *Fools' Plays: A Study of Satire in the Sottie.* Cambridge: Cambridge University Press, 1980.

Arewa, Ojo, and G. M. Shreve. *Zande Trickster Tales.* Vol. 1 of *The Genesis of Structures in African Narrative.* 2 vols. New York: Conch Magazine, 1975.

Arjona, J. H. "La introducción del gracioso en el teatro de Lope de Vega." *Hispanic Review* 7, 1 (1939): 1–21.

Armin, Robert (ca. 1568–1615). *The Collected Works of Robert Armin.* Intro. J. Feather. 2 vols. New York: Johnson Reprint Corporation, 1972.

———. *A Nest of Ninnies.* 1608. In *Fools and Jesters,* ed. J. Collier, 1–65. London: Shakespeare Society, 1842.

Armstrong, Archibald (fl. ca. 1620). "Archy's Dream, Sometimes Iester to His Maiestie, but Exiled the Court by *Canterburies* Malice: With a Relation for Whom an Odde Chaire Stood Voide in Hell." 1641. In *A Banquet of Jests,* ed. T. H. Jamieson, 367–74. Edinburgh: William Paterson, 1872.

———. *A Choice Banquet of Witty Jests, Rare Fancies, and Pleasant Novels.... Being an Addition to Archee's Jests, Taken out of His Closet but Never Publisht by Him in His Life Time.* London: Peter Dring, 1660.

Arnaud d'Agnel, G. *Les comptes du roi René.* 3 vols. Paris: A. Picard, 1908–10.

Arnold, Sue. "Nobs and Knockers." *Sunday Observer Magazine,* 20 May 1990, 18–19.

Aschkenasy, Nehama. "The Fool as Modern Hero: A Study of Clowning, Folly and the 'Ludic' Element in Some Modern Works." Ph.D. diss., New York University, 1977.

Ashton, John. *Humour, Wit and Satire of the Seventeenth Century.* London: Chatto and Windus, 1883.

Asimov, Isaac. *Foundation and Empire.* London: Grafton Books, 1990.

The Ass Race, or The Secret History of Archy Armstrong, Fool to King Charles I, Extracted from a MSS. London, 1740.

Asvaghosha. *The Buddha-Karita of Asvaghosha.* In *Buddhist Mahayana Texts* (1894), ed. E. B. Cowell, 1–201. New York: Dover, 1969.

Auden, W. H. "Balaam and the Ass: The Master-Servant Relationship in Literature." *Thought* 29 (1954–55): 237–70.

Avalle-Arce, Diane. "La 'Crónica de Carlos V' de Don Francesillo de Zuñiga: Según el manuscrito 6193 de la Biblioteca Nacional de Madrid." Ph.D. diss., Smith College, 1975.

Ba Gong Shan Qiao 八公山樵. "Ge chang zaji" 歌場雜記. Part 3. *Xiju Xunkan* 戲劇旬刊 14 (1936): 11.

Babcock-Abrahams, Barbara. "'A Tolerated Margin of Mess': The Trickster and His Tales Reconsidered." *Journal of the Folklore Institute* 11 (1975): 147–86.

————, ed. *The Reversible World: Essays in Symbolic Inversion.* Ithaca: Cornell University Press, 1978.

Bacon, Francis (1561–1626). "Of Deformity." In *Essays of Francis Bacon,* 131–32. London: Dent; New York: Dutton, 1906; repr. 1916.

Badaoni, ʿal-Qadir ibn Muluk Shah (b. 1540). *Muntakhab-ut-Tawarikh.* Trans. W. H. Lowe. Vol. 2. Calcutta: Asiatic Society, 1925.

Bakhtin, Mikhail. *Rabelais and His World.* Trans. Helene Iswolsky. Cambridge MIT Press, 1968.

Ban Gu 班固 (32–92). *Courtier and Commoner in Ancient China: Selections from the "History of the Former Han" by Pan Ku.* Trans. Burton Watson. New York: Columbia University Press, 1974.

Bandelier, Adolf. *The Delight Makers.* New York: Dodd, Mead, 1890.

Bannerji, Rajani, trans. *Gopal the Jester.* New York: Library of Facetious Lore, 1928.

Bar-Hebraeus, Gregory John Mar (b. 1226), comp. *The Laughable Stories.* Trans. E. A. Wallis Budge. London: Luzac, 1897.

Barnes, Margaret. *King's Fool.* London: Macdonald, 1972.

Barrie, J. M. *The Admirable Crichton.* London: Hodder and Stoughton, 1918.

Bartlett, Beatrice. *Monarchs and Ministers: The Grand Council in Mid-Ch'ing China, 1723–1820.* Berkeley: University of California Press, 1991.

Bartoli, Adolfo. "Buffoni di corte." *Fanfulla della Domenica,* 12 March 1882, 10.

Bartoli, Pietro Santi (1635–1700). *Le antiche lucerne sepolcrali figurate, raccolte dalle cave sotterranee e grotte di Roma.* Rome: Bugani, 1691.

Basset, René, trans. *Mille et un contes, récits et légendes arabes.* 2 vols. Paris: Maisonneuve 1924–26.

Basso, Ellen. *In Favor of Deceit: A Study of Tricksters in an Amazonian Society.* Tucson: University of Arizona Press, 1987.

Bataillon, M. "Estebanillo González, bouffon pour rire." In *Studies in Spanish Literature of the Golden Age Presented to E. M. Wilson,* ed. R. O. Jones, 25–44. London: Tamesis Books. 1973.

Bäurer, Hans-Gunther. *Brunnenheilige im Narrenhäs: Narrenbrunnen und närrisches Wasserbrauchtum Einst und Heute.* Constance: Südkurier, 1977.

Bautru, M. de. "Relation de la première conférence que j'ai eu avec M. le comte-duc, du 27 nov. 1628." vol. 15, fol. 285v.

Beamish, Noel de Vic. *The Queen's Jester.* London: Hale, 1969.

Beaumont, Daniel. "A Mighty and Neverending Affair: Comic Anecdote and Story in Medieval Arabic Literature." *Journal of Arabic Literature* 24 (1993): 139–59.

Bec, Pierre. *Burlesque et obscenité chez les troubadours: Le contre-texte au Moyen Âge.* Paris: Stock, 1984.

Beddoes, Thomas. *Death's Jest-Book, or The Fool's Tragedy*. Ca. 1828. In *The Works of Thomas Lovell Beddoes*, ed. and intro. H. W. Donner, 321–498. Oxford: Oxford University Press; London: Humphrey Milford, 1935.

Begeer, R. J. M. "Le bouffon Gonella peint par Jan van Eyck." *Oud Holland*, 1952, 125–43.

Belkin, Ahuva. "'Here's My Coxcomb': Some Notes on the Fool's Dress." *Assaph*, sec. C, no. 1 (1984): 40–54.

Bellay, Martin du. *Les mémoires de Messire Martin du Bellay*. 1569. In *Collection complète des mémoires relatifs à l'histoire de France*, ed. M. Petitot, vol. 17. 1st ser. 52 vols. Paris: Foucault Libraire, 1821.

Bentine, Michael. *The Reluctant Jester*. London: Corgi, 1993.

Berberich, Junko Sakaba. "The Idea of Rapture as an Approach to Kyogen." *Asian Theatre Journal* 6, 1 (1989): 31–46.

Berghe, Pierre van den. "Institutionalized Licence and Normative Stability." *Cahiers d'Études Africaines* 3, 11 (1962–63): 413–23.

Bergson, Henri. "Laughter." In *Comedy*, ed. George Meredith, 61–146. New York: Doubleday, 1956.

Bertoni, G. "Buffoni alla corte di Ferrara." *Rivista d'Italia* 6 (1903): 497–505.

Bevington, David. *Tudor Drama and Politics: A Critical Approach to Topical Meaning*. Cambridge: Harvard University Press, 1968.

Bharata-Muni [ascribed]. *The Natyasastra: A Treatise on Ancient Indian Dramaturgy and Histrionics*. Ca. 200 B.C.. Trans. Manomohan Ghosh. 2 vols. Calcutta: Asiatic Society, 1956–61.

Bhat, G. K. *The Vidusaka*. Ahmedabad: New Order Book Company, 1959.

Bigeard, Martine. *La folie et les fous littéraires en Espagne, 1500–1650*. Paris: Centre de Recherches Historiques, 1972.

Billington, Sandra. "The Fool and the Moral in English and Scottish Morality Plays." In *Popular Drama in Northern Europe in the Later Middle Ages*, ed. F. Anderson, 113–33. Odense: Odense University Press, 1988.

———. *Mock Kings in Medieval Society and Renaissance Drama*. Oxford: Clarendon Press, 1991.

———. "The Role of the Fool in English Drama from the Fifteenth to the Early Sixteenth Century." Ph.D. diss., Cambridge University, 1979.

———. *A Social History of the Fool*. Brighton: Harvester Press, 1984.

———. "'Suffer Fools Gladly': The Fool in Medieval England, and the Play *Mankind*." In *The Fool and the Trickster: Studies in Honour of Enid Welsford*, ed. Paul Williams, 36–54. Cambridge: Brewer, 1979.

Binyon, Laurence. *Akbar*. 2d ed. London: Nelson, 1939; repr. 1942.

Birbal the Witty. Illus. Ram Waeerkar. Amar Chitra Katha Series 152. Bombay: India Book House, 1982.

Birnbaum, Henrik. "Laughter, Play and Carnival in Old Rus." In *Words and Images: Essays in Honour of Professor (Emeritus) Dennis Ward,* ed. M. Falchikov and others, 21–39. Nottingham: Astra Press, 1989.

Bjornson, Richard. "Estebanillo González: The Clown's Other Face." *Hispania* 60, 3 (1977): 436–42.

Blavier, A. *Les fous littéraires.* Paris: Veyrier, 1982.

Blumenthal, W. H. *The Jaded Jester: Old Fools and New Follies.* Beaminster: J. Stevens Cox, 1965.

Blyth, R. H. *Japanese Humor.* Tokyo: Japan Travel Bureau, 1957.

———. *Oriental Humor.* Tokyo: Hokuseido Press, 1959; repr. 1968.

Bobertag, Felix, ed. *Narrenbuch: Kalenberger, Peter Len, Neithart Fuchs, Markolf, Bruder Rausch.* In *Deutsche National-Litteratur: Historisch-Kritische Ausgabe,* ed. Joseph Kürschner, vol. 2. Berlin: Spemann, 1881.

Bohun, Edmund. *The Character of Queen Elizabeth, or A Full and Clear Account of Her Policies, and the Methods of Her Government both in Church and State, Her Virtues and Defects.* London: Chiswell, 1693.

The Book of the Thousand Nights and One Night. Trans. from the French by Powys Mathers. 2d ed. 4 vols. London: Routledge and Kegan Paul, 1964.

Boorde, Andrew, comp. *The Merry Jests and Witty Shifts of Scogin.* 1626. In *Shakespeare Jest-Books,* ed. W. Carew Hazlitt, 2:37–151. 3 vols. London: Willis and Sotheran, 1864.

Borrow, George, trans. *The Turkish Jester, or The Pleasantries of Cogia Nasr Eddin Effendi.* Ipswich: Webber, 1884.

Boskin, Joseph. *Sambo: The Rise and Demise of an American Jester.* New York: Oxford University Press, 1986.

Le bouffon français, ou Recueil d'anecdotes. Paris: Blankenstein, 1812.

Bowen, Barbara, ed. *One Hundred Renaissance Jokes: An Anthology.* Birmingham, AL: Summa, 1988.

Brabant, Hyacinthe. "Les traitements burlesques de la folie aux XVIe et XVIIe siècles." In *Folie et déraison à la Renaissance,* 75–97. Brussels: Brussels University Press, 1976.

Brandon, James R., trans. and ed. *On Thrones of Gold: Three Javanese Shadow Plays.* Cambridge: Harvard University Press, 1970.

Brant, Sebastian. *Das Narrenschiff.* 1494. Ed. Hans-Joachim Mähl. Stuttgart: Reclam, 1964; repr. 1988.

———. *Ship of Fools.* 1494. Trans. E. Zeydel. New York: Columbia University Press, 1944; repr. New York: Dover, 1962.

Brewer, Ebenezer. *Brewer's Dictionary of Phrase and Fable.* 2d ed. Leicester: Galley Press, n.d.

Broder, Peggy. "Positive Folly: The Role of the Fool in the Works of W. B. Yeats." Ph.D. diss., Case Western Reserve University, 1969.

Brooks, Zoe. "Spitting Image." *Animations* 8 (1985): 46–48.

Brown, Cynthia. "Political Misrule and Popular Opinion: Double Talk and Folly in Pierre Gringore's 'Jeu du Prince des Sotz.'" *Le Moyen Français* 11 (1982): 89–111.

Brown, J. *Velasquez: Courtier and Painter.* New Haven: Yale University Press, 1986.

Brown, J., and J. Elliot. "Further Observations on Velazquez's Portraits of Jesters at the Buen Retiro." *Gazette des Beaux-Arts* 98 (1981): 191–92.

Brown, William Richard. *Imagemaker: Will Rogers and the American Dream.* Columbia: University of Missouri Press, 1970.

Browne, Edward. *The Press and Poetry of Modern Persia.* Cambridge: Cambridge University Press, 1914.

Brownjohn, Alan. *The Way You Tell Them: A Yarn for the Nineties.* London: Deutsch, 1990.

Buchanan, George. *The Witty and Entertaining Exploits of George Buchanan.* Newcastle, 1850.

———. *The Witty and Entertaining Exploits of George Buchanan, Who Was Commonly Called the King's Fool.* Stirling: Randall, 1814.

Buchner, Georg (1813–37). *Leonce and Lena.* 1836. In *The Plays of Georg Buchner,* trans. Victor Price, 73–104. London: Oxford University Press, 1971.

Bullock-Davies, Constance. *Menestrellorum Multitudo: Minstrels at a Royal Feast.* Cardiff: University of Wales Press, 1978.

Burns, Richard. *Troubadour.* London: Unwin Paperbacks, 1988.

Busby, Olive. *Studies in the Development of the Fool in Elizabethan Drama.* New York: Oxford University Press, 1923.

Butler, Guy. "Shakespeare and Two Jesters." *Hebrew University Studies in Literature and the Arts* 11 (1983): 161–204.

Caine, Michael. *What's It All About: The Autobiography.* Read by Michael Caine. New York: Random House Audiobooks, 1992.

Callahan, William. "Another Book of Laughter and Misunderstandings: A Field Guide to Chuckles, Smiles and Guffaws." Ph.D. diss., University of Hawaii, 1992.

Canel, A. *Recherches historiques sur les fous des rois de France.* Paris: Kemerre, 1873.

Cang Sheng 蒼生. "Xiangshengzhe de youmo" 相聲者的幽默. *Banyue Jukan* 半月劇刊 1, 5 (1936): 344–45.

Cao Diaosheng 曹調生, ed. *Zhongguo yinyue, wudao, xiqu renming cidian* 中國音樂舞蹈戲曲人名詞典. Beijing: Shangwu Yinshuguan, 1959.

Caputi, Anthony. *Buffo: The Genius of Vulgar Comedy.* Detroit: Wayne State University Press, 1978.

"Carnival in Port of Spain, Trinidad." *Illustrated London News,* 5 May 1888, 496–97.

Carolus. *Excerpta de Legationibus.* Paris, 1609.

Caroselli, Susan. *The Quest for Eternity: Chinese Ceramic Sculptures from the People's Republic of China.* London: Thames and Hudson, 1987.

Carter, Norman. *G-String Jesters.* London: Angus and Robertson, 1966.

Cartwright, Julia. *Isabella d'Este, Marchioness of Mantua, 1474–1539: A Study of the Renaissance.* 1907–11. 2 vols. Repr. London: John Murray, 1932.

Catalogne, M. "La gentille folle de la vieille cour." *Revue Régionaliste des Pyrenées* 37, 121–22 (1954): 36–38.

Catalogue des actes d'Henri II. Paris: Imprimerie Nationale, 1979.

Caulfield, James. *Portraits, Memoirs, and Characters, of Remarkable Persons, from the Revolution in 1688 to the End of the Reign of George II.* 4 vols. London: Young and Whiteley, 1819.

Cavendish, George (fl. ca. 1550). *The Life of Cardinal Wolsey.* Ed. R. S. Sylvester. Oxford: Early English Text Society, 1959.

Cervantes, Miguel de. *Don Quixote.* 10th ed. Barcelona: Editorial Juventud, 1975. Part 2, chap. 11 trans. J. M. Cohen as *Don Quixote.* Harmondsworth, Middlesex: Penguin Books, 1950.

———. *L'ingenieux hidalgo Don Quichote de la Manche.* Trans. Louis Viardot, illus. Gustave Doré. 2 vols. Paris: Hachette, 1863.

Cevoule-Angles, Felix. "Jehan-Antoine Lombard, dit Brusquet, fou du roi, 1520–1565." *Bulletin de la Société d'Études Scientifiques et Archéologiques de Draguignan* 7 (1962): 95–99.

Chai E 柴萼. *Fantianlu congchao* 梵天廬叢鈔. Fol. 14, In *Guoxue mingzhu zhenben huikan: Biji huikan* 國學名著珍本彙刊: 筆記彙刊, 212a–25b. Taibei: Dingwen Shuju, 1976.

Chalendar, P., and G. Chalendar. "Témoignage et folie chez Elie Wiesel." *Cahiers d'Études Juives* 86 (1987): 47–54.

Chambers, E. K. *The Elizabethan Stage.* 4 vols. Oxford: Clarendon Press, 1923; repr. 1951.

———. *The Medieval Stage.* 2 vols. Oxford: Clarendon Press, 1903.

Chambers, Tod. "Sacred Biography and Performance Community: A Dramaturgical Analysis of Urban Thai Buddhist Narrative-Celebration." Ph.D. diss., Northwestern University, 1992.

Chapman, Derek H. *King Purple's Jester.* Illus. Violet M. Morgan. London: Pleiades Books, 1947.

Charles, Lucille. "The Clown's Function." *Journal of American Folklore* 58 (1945): 25–34.

Chateau-Chalons, J. de [pseud.]. *La vérité historique sur la dame et le sire de Montsoreau, Bussy d'Amboise, et le bouffon Chicot.* Tours, 1888.

Chen Guifang 陳桂芳. "Maitreya Buddha." Trans. Peter Eberly. *Sinorama,* May 1990, 116–18.

Chettle, H. *Kind-Hartes Dreame.* 1592. Ed. G. B. Harrison. London: Bodley Head Quartos, 1923.

Chobham, Thomas (thirteenth century). *Thomae de Chobham "Summa confessorum."* Ed. H. Broomfield. Series Analecta Mediaevealia Namurcensia 25. Paris, 1968.

Christensen, Arthur. "Juhi in the Persian Literature." In *A Volume of Oriental Studies Presented to Edward G. Browne,* 129–36. Cambridge: Cambridge University Press, 1922.

———. "Les sots dans la tradition populaire des Persans." *Acta Orientalia* 1 (1923): 43–75.

Christian, Linda. "The Metamorphoses of Erasmus' 'Folly.'" *Journal of the History of Ideas* 32 (1971): 289–94.

Chuan Xihua 傳惜華, ed. *Zhongguo gudian wenxue banhua xuanji* 中國古典文學版畫選集. 2 vols. Shanghai: Renmin Meishu Chubanshe, 1981.

Churchill, Sir Winston (1874–1965). *Immortal Jester: A Treasury of the Great Good Humour of Sir Winston Churchill.* Comp. Leslie Frewin. London: Frewin, 1973.

Cian, V. "Fra Serafino, buffone." *Archivo Storico Lombardo* 18 (1891): 406–14.

Cicero (106–43 B.C.). *Epistulae ad familiares.* Ed. Glynn Williams. Vol. 2. Cambridge: Harvard University Press, 1959.

Clarke, Charles. "Shakespeare's Women: Considered as Philosophers and Jesters." *Gentlemen's Magazine* 234 (1873): 514–39.

Clavigero, Francisco (1731–87). *The History of Mexico.* Trans. Charles Cullen, intro. B. Feldman. Facsimile reprint of first ed. 2 vols. London: Robinson, 1787; repr. New York: Garland, 1979.

Cline, Paul. *Fools, Clowns and Jesters.* La Jolla, CA: Green Tiger Press, 1983.

Cohen, Gustave. "Triboulet: Acteur et auteur comique de dernier quart du XVe siècle." *Revue d'Histoire du Théâtre* 6 (1954): 291–93.

———, ed. *Mystères et moralités du Manuscrit 617 de Chantilly.* Paris: Champion, 1920.

Collins, C. *The Vision of the Fool.* Chipping Norton, Oxfordshire: Kedros, 1981.

Collins, Judith. *Cecil Collins: A Retrospective Exhibition.* London: Tate Gallery 1989.

Confucius [Kongzi] (d. 479 B.C.). *The Analects of Confucius.* Trans. William Dolby. Edinburgh: privately published, 1987.

Corbett, Deborah. "Wisdom Crieth in the Streets: A Compendium of Fools for Christ's Sake." *Epiphany* 9 (1989): 57–66.

Corbett, Philip. *The Scurra.* Edinburgh: Scottish Academic Press, 1986.

Cornford, Francis. *The Origin of Attic Comedy.* Ed. Theodor Gaster. New York: Anchor Books, 1961.

Coulson, F. Raymond. *A Jester's Jingles.* Illus. H. Jenner and J. Dodworth. London: Skeffington, 1899.

Coulson, Michael, ed. and trans. *Three Sanskrit Plays.* Harmondsworth, Middlesex: Penguin Books, 1981.

Coupe, W. A. "Observations on a Theory of Political Caricature." *Comparative Studies in Society and History* 11 (1969): 79–95.

The Court Jester, or Museum of Entertainment. London: Hamilton, 1771.

Covarrubias Horozco, Sebastian de. *Tesoro de la lengua castellana o española.* 1674. Madrid: Turner, 1984.

Cox, H. *The Feast of Fools: A Theological Essay on Festivity and Fantasy.* Cambridge: Harvard University Press, 1969.

Cramer, Thomas. "Narrenliteratur." In *Geschichte der deutschen Literatur im späten Mittelalter,* 265–77. Munich: Deutscher Taschenbuch, 1990.

Cross, Tom Peete, and Clark Harris Slover, eds. "The Death of Fergus Mac Leide." In *Ancient Irish Tales,* 471–87. Dublin: Figgis, 1936; repr. 1969.

———, eds. "The Destruction of Da Derga's Hostel." In *Ancient Irish Tales,* 93–126. Dublin: Figgis, 1936; repr. 1969.

Crumrine, N. Ross. "Capakoba, the Mayo Easter Ceremonial Impersonator: Explanations of Ritual Clowning." *Journal of Scientific Studies in Religion* 8 (1969): 1–22.

Cunliffe, Richard. "Traditional Chinese Drama and Commedia dell'Arte: A Comparison." Undergraduate diss., Department of East Asian Studies, Edinburgh University, 1989.

Dagan, Avigdor. *The Court Jesters.* Trans. Barbara Harshav. London: Bloomsbury 1991.

Dandin (ca. 550). *Dasakumaracarita.* 7th ed. Ed. with four commentaries by Narayana Balakrsna Godabale. Bombay: Nirnaya-Sagara Press, 1913.

Darmon, Pièrre. "Autrefois les nains." *L'Histoire* 19, 1 (1980): 48–57.

Dasen, Véronique. *Dwarfs in Ancient Egypt and Greece.* Oxford: Clarendon Press, 1993.

Dasgupta, S. N. *A History of Sanskrit Drama.* Calcutta, 1962.

Davidson, Hilda. *The Seer in Celtic and Other Traditions.* Edinburgh: Donald, 1989.

Dawlatshah. *Tazkirat al-Shu'ara*. 1487. Quoted in ʿObeyd-e Zakani, *"The Ethics of the Aristocrats" and Other Satirical Works*, trans. Hasan Javadi, 10. Middle Eastern Series 11. Piedmont, CA: Jahan Books, 1985.

De Becker, J. E. *The Nightless City, or The History of the Yoshiwara Yukwaku*. 1899. Tokyo: Tuttle, 1971.

Decourdemanche, J. A. *Sottisier de Nasr-Eddin-Hodja: Bouffon de Tamerlan*. Brussels: Chez Gay et Douce, 1878.

Dekker, Thomas (ca. 1572–1632), and others. *Patient Grissell*. 1600. In *The Dramatic Works of Thomas Dekker*, ed. Fredson Bowers, 1:207–98. 4 vols. Cambridge: Cambridge University Press, 1953.

Delano, Lucile. "The *Gracioso* Continues to Ridicule the Sonnet." *Hispania* 18 (1935): 383–400.

The Delicate Jester, or Wit and Humour Divested of Ribaldry. London: Dixwell, 1780.

Delthil, E. *Les fous en titre d'office du blesois: Nago et Triboulet*. Paris: Imprimerie Wattier, 1884.

Dermoriane, Hermione. *The Tightrope Walker*. London: Secker and Warburg, 1989.

Dharendorf, Ralph. "The Intellectual and Society: The Social Function of the 'Fool' in the Twentieth Century." In *On Intellectuals: Theoretical Studies, Case Studies*, ed. Philip Rieff, 49–52. Garden City, NY: Doubleday, 1969.

Diaz de Castillo, Bernal (1492–1581). *The Conquest of New Spain*. Trans. J. M. Cohen. Harmondsworth, Middlesex: Penguin Books, 1963.

Dickson, T., and J. B. Paul, eds. *Accounts of the Lord High Treasurer of Scotland, 1473–1580*, 13 vols. Edinburgh: General Register House; Her Majesty's Stationary Office, 1877–1978.

Dictionary of National Biography. Ed. L. Stephen and S. Lee. 22 vols. London: Smith, Elder, 1908–9.

Diderot, Denis (1713–84). *Le neveu de Rameau*. In *Oeuvres*, ed. André Billy, 395–474. Paris: Gallimard, 1951.

Dilke, Charles Wentworth. *Greater Britain: A Record of Travel in English-Speaking Countries during 1866 and 1867*. London: Macmillan, 1869.

Dillon, Myles. *Early Irish Literature*. Chicago: University of Chicago Press, 1948.

Dimock, Edward. *The Thief of Love: Bengali Tales from Court and Village*. Chicago: University of Chicago Press, 1963.

Disher, M. Willson. *Clowns and Pantomimes*. London: Constable, 1923; repr. New York: Blom, 1968.

Disraeli, Benjamin. *Beaconsfield's Letters*. London, 1887.

Dolby, William. *Chinese Play Summaries*, 15 vols. Edinburgh: privately published, 1986.

————. "Early Chinese Plays and Theater." In *Chinese Theater from Its Origins to the Present Day,* ed. Colin Mackerras, 7–31. Honolulu: University of Hawaii Press, 1983.

————. *A History of the Chinese Theatre.* London: Elek Books, 1976.

————. "The Origins of Chinese Puppetry." *Bulletin of the School of Oriental and African Studies* 41, 1 (1978): 97–120.

————, trans. "A-Fan-T'i Stories." Unpublished MS. Edinburgh, 1999.

————, trans. *Eight Chinese Plays.* London: Paul Elek, 1978.

Dooling, D. M. "The Wisdom of the Contrary: A Conversation with Joseph Epes Brown." *Parabola* 4, 1 (1979): 54–65.

Doran, John. *The History of Court Fools.* London: Bentley, 1858.

Doré, Gustave. *Doré's Illustrations for Rabelais: A Selection of 252 Illustrations by Gustave Doré* (New York: Dover, 1978), 145.

————. *Doré Spot Illustrations: A Treasury from His Masterworks.* Selected by Carol Grafton. New York: Dover, 1987.

Douce, Francis. *Illustrations of Shakespeare, and of Ancient Manners: With Disserations on the Clowns and Fools of Shakespeare.* London: Longman, Hurst, Rees and Orme, 1807.

Douet d'Arcq, Louis, ed. *Comptes de l'argenterie des rois de France au XIVe siècle.* Paris: Renouard, 1851.

————, ed. *Comptes de l'hôtel des rois de France aux XIVe et XVe siècles.* Paris: Renouard, 1865.

————, ed. *Nouveau recueil de comptes de l'argenterie des rois de France.* Paris: Renouard, 1874.

Douglas, Mary. "The Social Control of Cognition: Some Factors in Joke Perception." *Man* 3 (1968): 361–76.

Doyle, Christine. "Depression: My Part in Its Downfall." *Daily Telegraph,* 13 March 1990, 19.

Duff, E. Gordon, ed. *The Dialogue or Communing between the Wise King Salomon and Marcolphus.* Facsimile of Bodleian copy of 1492. London: Lawrence and Bullen, 1892.

Dula, Michael. "Laughter in the Dark: The Jester God in American Literature." Ph.D. diss., University of Virginia, 1986.

Dumas, Alexandre. *Chicot the Jester.* London: Collins Clear-Type Press, n.d.

Duncan, W. J., and J. Feisal. "No Laughing Matter: Patterns of Humor in the Workplace." *Organizational Dynamics,* [after 1987], 18–30.

Duncan, W. J., and others. "Humor and Work: Application of Joking Behaviour to Management." *Journal of Management* 16, 2 (1990): 255–78.

Dundes, A., and Hauschild, T. "Auschwitz Jokes." In *Humour in Society: Resistance and Control,* ed. Chris Powell and George Paton, 56–66. London: Macmillan, 1988.

Dupuis, Pierre. *Le remonstrance de Pierre du Puis sur le resveil de Maistre Guillaume.* Paris, 1614.

Durkan, John, and others. *George Buchanan (1506–82): Renaissance Scholar and Friend of Glasgow University.* Glasgow: Glasgow University Library, 1982.

Durrell, Lawrence. *Mountolive.* London: Faber and Faber, 1958.

Ebeling, Friedrich. *Zur Geschichte der Hofnarren: Friedrich Taubmann—ein Kulturbild.* Leipzig: Lehmann, 1887.

Eberhard, W. *Minstrel Tales from Southeastern Turkey.* Berkeley: University of California Press, 1955.

Eco, Umberto. *The Name of the Rose.* Trans. William Weaver. London: Pan Books, 1984.

Edwards, Oliver, and Vernon Silver. "The Prince Who Saves Europe's Capitalist Monuments." *EuroBusiness,* June 1999, 30–34.

Eichhorz, Werner. "Tung-fang Shuo, ein chinesischer Till Eulenspiegel." *Ostasiatische Rundschau* 11 (1930): 94–96.

Empson, W. "The Praise of Folly." In *The Structure of Complex Words,* 105–24. London: Chatto and Windus, 1951.

English, James. "The Laughing Reader: A New Direction for Studies of the Comic." *Genre* 19, 2 (1986): 129–54.

Eno, Brenda Rae, illus. *Jewish Proverbs.* San Francisco: Chronicle Books, 1989.

The Entertaining Companion, or The Merry Jester; Being a Choice Collection of the Entertaining Jests . . . with the Diverting Frolicks of King Charles and His Concubines. London: Sympson, 1790.

Erasmus, Desiderius (ca. 1466–1536). *Adages I.i.1 to I.v.100.* Trans. Margaret M. Phillips, annot. R. A. B. Mynors. In *The Collected Works of Erasmus,* vol. 31. 86 vols. Toronto: University of Toronto Press, 1974–93.

———. *Erasmi Roterodami Encomium Moriae; i.e. Stultitiae Laus: Praise of Folly, Published at Basle in 1515 and Decorated with the Marginal Drawings of Hans Holbein the Younger, Now Reproduced in Facsimile with an Introduction by Heinrich Alfred Schmid.* Trans. Helen Tanzer. Basel, 1931.

———. *The Praise of Folie.* 1549. Trans. Sir Thomas Chaloner, ed. C. H. Miller. Oxford: Oxford University Press, 1965.

———. *"Praise of Folly" and Letter to Maarten van Dorp, 1515.* Trans. Betty Radice, annot. A. H. T. Levi. Harmondsworth, Middlesex: Penguin Books, 1971; repr. and rev. 1993.

Estoile, Pierre de l'. *Mémoires de Pierre de l'Estoile (Journal de Henri IV: Depuis le 2 aoust 1589 jour de la mort du roy, jusques au 22 mars 1594, jour de la réduction de Paris.* In *Collection complète des mémoires relatifs à l'histoire de France,* ed. M. Petitot, vol. 46. Paris: Foucault Libraire, 1825.

Fabre, Daniel. *Carnaval, ou La fête à l'envers.* Paris: Gallimard, 1992.

Fang Wenxi 方問溪. "Liyuan yanyu" 梨園諺語. *XJYK*, 3, 10 (1931): 1–4.

Faral, E. *Les jongleurs en France au Moyen Âge.* Paris: Champion, 1910.

Farce morale de Troys Pelerins et Malice. 1523. In *Recueil général des sotties,* ed. Émile Picot, 2:299–321. 3 vols. Paris: Firmin Didot, 1912.

Farnol, Jeffery. *The Fool Beloved.* London: Book Club, 1950.

Fedotov, G. P. "The Holy Fools." In *The Russian Religious Mind,* ed. I. Meyendorff, 1:316–43. Cambridge: Harvard University Press, 1966.

Feinberg, Leonard, ed. *Asian Laughter: An Anthology of Oriental Satire and Humor.* New York: Weatherhill, 1971.

Felver, Charles. *Robert Armin: Shakespeare's Fool.* Research Series 5. Kent, OH: Kent State University Bulletin, 1961.

———. "Robert Armin: Shakespeare's Source for Touchstone." *Shakespeare Quarterly* 7, 1 (1956): 135–37.

The Female Jester, or Wit for the Ladies. London: Bew and Lewis, 1780.

Feng Xiaoyin 馮小隱. "Guqu suibi" 顧曲隨筆. *XJYK*, 2, 1 (1929): 5–10.

Feuerstein, Georg. *Holy Madness: The Shock Tactics and Radical Teachings of Crazy-Wise Adepts, Holy Fools, and Rascal Gurus.* New York: Arkana Books, 1992.

Feuillerat, A., and G. Feuillerat, eds. *Documents relating to the Office of the Revels in the Time of Queen Elizabeth I.* Louvain: Uystpruyst, 1908.

———, eds. *Documents relating to the Revels at Court in the Time of King Edward VI and Queen Mary.* Louvain: Uystpruyst, 1914.

Fichtner, Fritz. "Darstellungen des Kursächsischen Hofnarren J. Fröhlich." *Belvedere,* 1929.

Ficoroni, F. *Dissertatio de larvis scenicis et figuris comicis antiquorum romanorum.* Rome, 1754.

Field, Catherine. "Lily Shows Three Fingers to the Establishment." *Observer,* 3 October 1993, 20.

Firth, David, and Alan Leigh. *The Corporate Fool.* Oxford: Capstone, 1998.

Flecknoe, Richard. *The Life of Tomaso the Wanderer: An Attack upon Thomas Killigrew.* 1667. Repr. London: Dobell, 1925.

Fletcher, Dennis. "Praise of Folly: An Inaugural Lecture." Durham: Durham University Press, 1981.

Fletcher, Giles (1549?–1611). *Of the Rus Commonwealth.* 1591. Ed. Albert Schmidt. Ithaca: Cornell University Press, 1966.

Flögel, Karl. *Geschichte der Hofnarren.* Leipzig: Siegert, 1789; repr. New York: Olms, 1977.

Fo, Dario. *Comic Mysteries.* Trans. Ed Emery. In *Plays,* intro. Stuart Hood, 1:1–122. London: Methuen Drama, 1992.

Foley, Kathy. "The Clown Figure in the Puppet Theatre of West Java: The Ancestor and the Individual." In *Humor and Comedy in Puppetry: Celebration of Popular Culture,* ed. Dina and Joel Sherzer, 65–78. Bowling Green, OH: Bowling Green State University Popular Press, 1987.

Folie, folies, folly dans le monde anglo-americain aux XVIIe et XVIIIe siècles. Aix-en-Provence: Université de Provence, 1984.

Fool's Journey: Tarot Postcards. London: Aquarian Press, 1993.

Ford, John (fl. ca. 1639). *The Lover's Melancholy.* 1629. In *John Ford,* ed. Henry Ellis. London: Fisher Unwin, 1888.

Ford, Philip. *George Buchanan: Prince of Poets.* Aberdeen: Aberdeen University Press, 1982.

Foster, Vivien. *Pearls of Wisdom: A Book of Aphorisms.* Harmondsworth, Middlesex: Penguin Books, 1987.

Francis, H. S. "Portrait of a Jester, Calabazas." *Bulletin of the Cleveland Museum of Art* 53, 9 (1965): 117–23.

Frankland, C. Charles. *Narrative of a Visit to the Courts of Russia and Sweden in the Years 1830 and 1831.* London: H. Colburn and R. Bentley, 1832.

Freese, Alison. "Send in the Clowns: An Ethnohistorical Analysis of the Sacred Clowns' Role in Cultural Boundary Maintenance among the Pueblo Indians." Ph.D. diss., University of New Mexico, 1991.

French, W. *Medieval Civilisation as Illustrated by the Fastnachtspiele of Hans Sachs.* Göttingen: Vandenhoeck and Ruprecht, 1925.

Freud, Sigmund. *Jokes and Their Relation to the Unconscious.* Trans. James Strachey, ed. Angela Richards. Pelican Freud Library 6. Harmondsworth, Middlesex: Penguin Books, 1986.

Fricker, Janet. "Why Laughter Is the Best Medicine." *Focus,* May 1993, 12–15.

Friedman, Gary. "Puppets against Apartheid." *Animations* 9, 3 (1986): 48–49.

F. S. *Death in a New Dress, or Sportive Funeral Elegies; Commemorating the Renowned Lives and Lamented Deaths of These Eminent Personages: Robbin the Annyseedwater Seller, Martin Parker the Famous Poet, Archee the Late King's Jester.* London: Martin Parker, 1656.

Fu Xihua 傅惜華, ed. *Yuandai zaju quanmu* 元代雜劇全目. Beijing: Zuojia Chubanshe, 1957.

Fulchignoni, Enrico. "Oriental Influences on the Commedia dell'Arte." Trans. Una Crowley. *Asian Theatre Journal* 7, 1 (1990): 29–41.

Fuller, Thomas. *The History of the Worthies of England.* 1662. Ed. John Nichols. 2 vols. London: Nichols, 1811.

Furnivall, F. J., ed. *A Booke of Precedence.* Ext. Series 8. London: Early English Text Society, 1869.

Gabotto, F. *L'epopea del buffone.* Bra: Tipografia Stefano Racca, 1893.

Gaiman, Neil, and Paul Johnson. *The Road to Nowhere.* Books of Magic 4. New York: DC Comics, 1991.

Gaimar, Geoffroy (twelfth century). *Lestorie des Engles.* Ed. Thomas Duffus Hardy and Charles Trice Martin. Vol. 1 (text) and vol. 2 (trans.). Rolls Series. London: Her Majesty's Stationery Office, 1888–89.

Gardner, Gerald C. *The Mocking of the President: A History of Campaign Humor from Ike to Ronnie.* Detroit: Wayne State University Press, 1988.

Gautier, Edmond. "Note sur Antoine d'Anglerays dit Chicot et sa famille." *Bulletin de la Société Archéologique de Tourain* 3 (1874–76): 262–66.

Gavin, Joseph, and Walsh, Thomas. "The *Praise of Folly* in Context: The Commentary of Gerardus Listrius." *Renaissance Quarterly* 24, 2 (1971): 193–209.

Gay-Para, P. "La guerre du rire: Histoires drôle du Liban." *Cahiers de Littérature Orale,* no. 20 (1986): 103–20.

Gazeau, M. A. *Les bouffons.* Paris: Hachette, 1882.

Gelder, G. J. H. van. "Arabic Debates of Jest and Earnest." In *Dispute Poems and Dialogues in the Ancient and Medieval Near East: Forms and Types of Literary Debates in Semitic and Related Literatures,* ed. G. J. Reinink and H. L. J. Vanstiphout, 199–211. Orientalia Lovaniensia Analecta 42. Louvain: Departement Orientalistiek and Uitgeverij Peeters, 1991.

———. "Mixture of Jest and Earnest in Classical Arabic Literature." *Journal of Arabic Literature* 23 (1993): part 1, 83–108; part 2, 168–90.

Gent, W. W. *England's Witty and Ingenious Jester.* 17th ed. London: R. Gifford, 1718.

Gentili, V. "Madmen and Fools Are a Staple Commodity: On Madness as a System in Elizabethan and Jacobean Plays." *Cahiers Elizabethains* 34 (1988): 11–24.

Gerhardt, Mia I. *The Art of Story-Telling: A Literary Study of the Thousand and One Nights.* Leiden: Brill, 1963.

Ghelderode, Michel de. *Escurial.* 1929. Trans. Lionel Abel. In *Modern Theatre,* ed. Eric Bentley, 5:161–78. New York: Doubleday, 1957.

Gibson, K. J. S. "The Nature and Function of the Servants in Comedies First Performed at the Comédie Française between 1685 and 1732." Ph.D. diss., Glasgow University, 1987.

Gifford, D. J. "Iconographical Notes towards a Definition of the Medieval Fool." In *The Fool and the Trickster: Studies in Honour of Enid Welsford,* ed. Paul Williams, 18–35. Cambridge: Brewer, 1979.

Gifford, Edward. "Tongan Society." *Bernice Bishop Museum Bulletin* 61 (1929), whole issue.

Gilchrist, Octavius. "Archibald Armstrong and His Jests." *London Magazine,* September 1824, 285–89.

Giles, Herbert. *A Chinese Biographical Dictionary.* London: Kelly and Walsh, 1898.

———. "Wit and Humor." In *A History of Chinese Literature,* 430–36. Rutland, VT: Tuttle, 1973.

Giles, Lionel. *A Gallery of Chinese Immortals.* London: John Murray, 1948.

Gilmore, J. A. *The Court Jester: A New and Original Comic Opera in One Act.* Wimborne, Dorset: James Tilsed, 1912.

Girl Guides Association. *Brownie Badges 7: Collector, Dancer, Jester.* Rev ed. London: Girl Guides Association, 1978.

Gluckman, Max. *Politics, Law and Ritual in Tribal Society.* Oxford: Blackwell, 1965; repr. 1982.

GoldbergBelle, Jonathan. "The Performance Poetics of Tulubommalata: A South Indian Shadow Puppet Tradition." Ph.D. diss., University of Wisconsin, Madison, 1984.

Goldsmith, Robert. "Touchstone: Critic in Motley." *PMLA* 68 (1953): 884–95.

———. *Wise Fools in Shakespeare.* East Lansing: Michigan State University Press, 1955.

Gong Kechang 龔尅昌. "Dongfang Shuo" 東方朔. In *Zhongguo lidai zhuming wenxuejia pingzhuan* 中國歷代著名文學家評傳, ed. Lü Huijuan 呂慧鵑, sequel 1, 101–16. Jinan: Shandong Jiaoyu Chubanshe, 1988.

González, Estebanillo (b. 1608). *Vida y hechos de Estebanillo González: Hombre de buen humor.* Ed. Nicholas Spadaccini and Anthony N. Zahareas. 2 vols. Madrid: Castalia, 1978.

González, J. J. Martin. "Algunas sugerencias de los bufones de Velazquez." In *Varia Velazquena: Homenaje a Velazquez en el III centenario de su muerte, 1660–1960,* 1:250–56. Madrid: Ministerio de Educación Nacional, 1960.

Gopal the Jester. Illus. Souren Roy. Amar Chitra Katha Series 237. Bombay: India Book House, 1982.

Gorer, Geoffrey. *Africa Dances: A Book about West African Negroes.* London: Lehmann, 1949.

Gossart, Ernest. "Estevanille González, un bouffon espagnol dans les Pays Bas." *Revue de Belgique,* 2d ser., 7 (1893): 137–57 and 254–63; 8 (1893): 43–55 and 200–207.

Gosson, Stephen. *The School of Abuse, Conteining a Pleasant Invective against Poets, Pipers, Plaiers, Jesters, and Such Like Catterpillers of a Commonwelth.* London: T. Woodcocke, 1579.

Graf, Arturo. "Un buffone di Leone X." In *Attraverso il Cinquecento,* 299–319. Turin: Chiantore, 1926.

Grahame, Kenneth. *Dream Days.* Illus. Maxfield Parrish. London: John Lane, 1902.

Grainger, Boyne [pseud.]. *The Jester's Reign.* London: Laidlaw and Butchart, 1938.

Granger, James. *A Biographical History of England from Egbert the Great to the Revolution.* London, 1775.

Gray, A. K. "Robert Armine, the Foole." *PMLA* 42 (1927): 673–85.

Gray, H. D. "The Roles of William Kemp." *Modern Language Review* 25, 3 (1930): 261–73.

Green, Richard. *Poets and Princepleasers: Literature and the English Court in the Late Middle Ages.* Toronto: University of Toronto Press, 1980.

Greene, Robert. *Friar Bacon and Friar Bungay.* 1589. In *The Plays and Poems of Robert Greene.* Ed., intro., and annot. J. Churton Collins, 2:14–78. Oxford: Clarendon Press, 1905.

———. "A Pleasant Tale of Will Summers." In *The Defence of Conny-Catching,* in *The Life and Complete Works of Robert Greene,* ed. A. B. Grosart, vol. 11. London: Huth Library, 1881–86.

Gregory, Augusta, trans. "The Awakening of Ulster." In *Cuchulain of Muirthemne: The Story of the Men of the Red Branch of Ulster,* 245–67. London: Murray, 1902.

———, trans. *Gods and Fighting Men: The Story of the Tuatha de Danaan and of the Fianna of Ireland.* London: Murray, 1904.

Grimald, Nicholas (1519–1562). *Archipropheta.* Ca. 1546. In *The Life and Poems of Nicholas Grimald,* ed. L. R. Merrill, 228–357. Yale Studies in English 69. New Haven: Yale University Press, 1925.

Grimmelshausen, Johann (1622–76). *Simplex Simplicissimus.* 1669. Trans. George Schulz-Behrend. New York: Bobbs-Merrill 1965.

Gringore, Pierre (1475–ca. 1538). *Le jeu du prince des sotz.* 1512. In *Recueil général des sotties,* ed. Émile Picot, 2:105–73. 3 vols. Paris: Firmin Didot, 1912.

Grock, Wettach A. *Nit M-o-o-o-glich: Grock, King of Clowns.* Trans. Basil Creighton. London: Methuen, 1957.

Groerner, Gerald. Review of Theodore Levin, *The Hundred Thousand Fools of God: Musical Travels in Central Asia (and Queens, New York).* Bloomington: Indiana University Press, 1996.

Gudas, Rom. *The Bitter-Sweet Art: Karaghiozis, the Greek Shadow Theatre.* Athens: Gnosis 1986.

Guha, Krishna. "BA's Court Jester." *Financial Times,* 12 October 1995, 18.

Gün, Güneli. *On the Road to Baghdad: A Picaresque Novel of Magical Adventures, Begged, Borrowed, and Stolen from the Thousand and One Nights.* London: Picador, 1994.

Gussow, Mel. "Clown." *New Yorker*, 11 November 1985, 51–87.

Gutwirth, Marcel. *Laughing Matter: An Essay on the Comic.* Ithaca: Cornell University Press, 1993.

Hachimonjiya, Jisho. *The Actors Analects* [*Yakusha Rongo*]. Trans. C. J. Dunn. New York: Columbia University Press, 1969.

Halabi, A. A. "The Development of Humour and Satire in Persia with Special Reference to ʿUbaid-i Zakani'." Ph.D. diss., Edinburgh University, 1980.

Hall, Edward. *Chronicle: Containing the History of England from the Reign of Henry IV to the End of the Reign of Henry VIII.* 1548. Ed. H. Ellis. London: Johnson, 1809.

Halle, Adam de la (ca. 1240–ca. 1288). *Le jeu de la feuillée.* Ca. 1262. Trans. and ed. Jean Dufournet. Gand, Belgium: Éditions Scientifiques E. Story-Scientia, 1977.

Halliwell, James O., ed. *A New and Merrie Prognostication: Being a Metrical Satire, Suppositiously Assigned to Will Summers, the Jester, and Three Others.* London, 1623; repr. 1860.

————, ed. *Tarlton's Jests: The Humour of Queen Elizabeth I's Court Jester.* Facsimile of 1844 ed. Market Drayton, Shropshire: M. Raven, 1989.

Hallowell, A. I. "Bear Ceremonialism in the Northern Hemisphere." *American Anthropologist* 28, 1 (1926): 1–175.

Hammond, P. "Mossi Joking." *Ethnology* 3 (1964): 259–67.

Handelman, Don. "The Ritual Clown: Attributes and Affinities." *Anthropos* 76 (1981): 321–70.

Hansen, Julie. "The Philosophers of Laughter: Velazquez' Portraits of Jesters at the Court of Philip IV." Master's thesis, University of Arizona, 1990.

Harbage, Alfred. *Annals of English Drama: 975–1700.* Rev. ed. London: Methuen, 1964.

————. *Thomas Killigrew: Cavalier Dramatist, 1612–83.* Philadelphia: University of Pennsylvania Press, 1930.

Harbsmeier, Christoph. "*Confucius Ridens:* Humor in the *Analects.*" *Harvard Journal of Asiatic Studies* 50, 1 (1990): 131–61.

————. "Humor in Ancient Chinese Philosophy." *Philosophy East and West* 39, 3 (1989): 289–310.

Hardingham, E. *"The Romance of Rahere" and Other Poems.* London: E. Stock, 1896.

Harrison, Alan. *The Irish Trickster.* Sheffield: Sheffield Academic Press, 1989.

Harvey, Howard. *The Theatre of the Basoche.* Cambridge: Harvard University Press, 1941.

Haseltine, Patricia. "Ritual as Frame for the Folk Humour of the Trickster, the Fool, and the Clown." *Tamkang Review* 13, 3 (1983): 209–26.

Hastrup, Kirsten, and Jan Ovesen. "The Joker's Cycle." *Journal of the Anthropological Society of Oxford* 7, 1 (1976): 11–26.

Hazlitt, W. Carew, ed. *Shakespeare Jest-Books,* 3 vols. London: Willis and Sotheran, 1864.

Hécart, Gabriel Antoine Joseph. *Stultitiana, ou Petite biographie des fous de la ville de Valenciennes.* N.p., 1823.

Heiple, D. "El licienciado vidriera y el humor tradicional des loco." *Hispania Cincinnati* 66, 1 (1983): 17–20.

Henderson, Alexandra. "Ha, Ha, Ha! It's a Funny Way to Medidate." *Scotsman,* 4 August 1993, 9.

Herford, C. H. *Studies in the Literary Relations of England and Germany in the Sixteenth Century.* Cambridge: Cambridge University Press, 1886.

Heywood, John. *The Play of the Wether.* 1528. Ed. T. N. Lennam. Oxford: Malone Society Reprints, 1971; repr. 1977.

Hieb, Louis. "The Hopi Ritual Clown: Life as It Should Not Be." Ph.D. diss., Princeton University, 1972.

———. "Meaning and Mismeaning: Toward an Understanding of the Ritual Clown." In *New Perspectives on the Pueblos,* ed. Alfonso Ortiz, 163–95. Albuquerque: University of New Mexico Press, 1972.

Highet, Gilbert. *The Anatomy of Satire.* Princeton: Princeton University Press, 1962.

Hill, John. "An Approach to Xiangsheng through an Analysis of the Xiangsheng Sketch 'Zui Jiu' ('Getting Drunk') By Hou Baolin." Undergrad. diss., Department of East Asian Studies, Edinburgh University, 1991.

Hill, Robert H. *Tales of the Jesters.* Edinburgh: W. Blackwood, 1934.

Hillman, R. *Shakespearean Subversions: The Trickster and the Play-Text.* London: Routledge and Kegan Paul, 1992.

Hislop, Alexander, ed. *The Book of Scottish Anecdote: Humorous, Social, Legendary and Historical.* 8th ed. Glasgow: Morison, [nineteenth century?].

Hochman, Stanley, ed. *McGraw-Hill Encyclopedia of World Drama.* 5 vols. New York: McGraw-Hill, 1984.

Hodgart, Matthew. *Satire.* London: Weidenfeld and Nicolson, 1969.

Hoepffner, Ernest, ed. *La folie de Tristan de Berne.* Paris: Belles Lettres, 1934.

Holdsworth, William. *A History of English Law.* 7th rev. ed. 16 vols. London: Methuen, 1956; repr. 1966.

Holinshed, Raphael (d. 1580?). *Holinshed's Chronicles of England, Scotland and Ireland.* 1587. 3 vols. London: Johnson, 1807–8.

Hollander, Lee Milton. *The Skalds: A Selection of Their Poems.* New York: Princeton University Press, 1945.

Holzknecht, Karl. *Tudor and Stuart Plays, 1497–1642.* London: Methuen, 1963.

Horace (65–8 B.C.). *Satires, Epistles and Ars Poetica.* Trans. H. Rushton Fairclough. Loeb Classical Library. London: Heinemann; New York: Putnam, 1926.

Hornstein, L. M. "King Robert of Sicily: Analogues and Origins." *PMLA* 79 (1968): 13–21.

Horsfield, Ethel. "Mental Defectives at the Court of Philip IV, as Portrayed by Velasquez." *American Journal of Mental Deficiency,* July 1940, 152–57.

L'Hospidale de' Pazzi Incurabili. Venice, 1617.

Hotson, Leslie. *Shakespeare's Motley.* London: Hart-Davis, 1952.

Hou Baolin 侯寶林. *Hou Baolin zixuan xiangsheng ji* 侯寶林自選相聲集. Lanzhou: Gansu Renmin Chubanshe, 1987.

Hou Baolin 侯寶林, and others. "'Paiyou': 'Dou' de zaoqi xingshi" 俳優逗的早期形式. In *Xiangsheng suyuan* 相聲溯源, 140–54. Beijing: Renmin Wenxue Chubanshe, 1982.

———. "'You ge'—'chang' de kesu zhi yuan" 優歌——唱的可溯之源. In *Xiangsheng suyuan* 相聲溯源, 186–90. Beijing: Renmin Wenxue Chubanshe, 1982.

Howard, Louis G. R. *The Ballad of Rahere the Jester.* London: Houghton 1931.

"How Asia's Cartoonists Saw the Year." *Far Eastern Economic Review,* December 1991, 33–37.

Hrdlickova, Vena. "The Professional Training of Chinese Storytellers and the Storytellers' Guilds." *Archiv Orientalni* 33, 2 (1965): 225–48.

Hsia [Xia], C. T. "The Chinese Sense of Humor." *Renditions* 9 (spring 1978): 30–36.

Hsü Tao-Ching [Xu Daojing]. *The Chinese Conception of the Theatre.* Seattle: University of Washington Press, 1985.

Hu, John. "Ming Dynasty Drama." In *Chinese Theater from Its Origins to the Present Day,* ed. Colin Mackerras, 60–91. Honolulu: University of Hawaii Press, 1983.

Hu Tiancheng 胡天成 "Songdai xiju tiaoxiao huaji de jiqu mei" 宋代戲劇調笑滑稽的機趣美. *Xiqu Yanjiu* 27 (1988): 246–55.

Hucker, Charles. *A Dictionary of Official Titles in Imperial China.* Stanford: Stanford University Press, 1985.

Huckerby, Martin. "Jester Murdered for Mockery." *Observer,* 1 April 1990, 15.

Hugill, Beryl. *Bring on the Clowns.* Newton Abbott, Devon: David and Charles, 1980.

Hugo, Victor (1802–85). *Cromwell.* 1827. In *Théâtre complet,* ed. J.-J. Thierry and J. Mélèze, 1:405–952. 2 vols. Paris: Gallimard, 1963.

———. *Marion de Lorme.* 1829. In *Théâtre complet,* ed. J.-J. Thierry and J. Mélèze, 1:953–1144. 2 vols. Paris: Gallimard.

————. *Le roi s'amuse.* 1832. In *Théâtre complet,* ed. J.-J. Thierry and J. Mélèze, 1: 1321–485. 2 vols. Paris: Gallimard, 1963.

————. *Théâtre complet,* ed. J.-J. Thierry and J. Mélèze. 2 vols. Paris: Gallimard, 1963.

Hutchins, William, trans. *Nine Essays of Al-Jahiz.* American University Studies Series 7 Theology and Religion, vol. 53. New York: Peter Lang, n.d.

Hyers, M. Conrad. "The Comic Profanation of the Sacred." In *Holy Laughter: Essays on Religion in the Comic Perspective,* ed. M. Conrad Hyers, 9–27. New York: Seabury Press, 1969.

————. *Zen and the Comic Spirit.* New York: Rider, 1974.

Idema, Wilt, and Stephen West. *Chinese Theater, 1100–1450: A Source Book.* Wiesbaden: Steiner, 1982.

"In Defense of Cartoons." *Free China Review* 42, 1 (1992): 18–23.

Ives, E. W. "Tom Skelton: A Seventeenth Century Jester." *Shakespeare Survey* 13 (1960): 90–105.

Jal, Augustin. "Fous en titre d'office." In *Dictionnaire critique de biographie et d'histoire,* 596–605. Paris: Plon, 1872.

————. "Nains en titre d'office." In *Dictionnaire critique de biographie et d'histoire,* 895–97. Paris: Plon, 1872.

Jamieson, T. H., ed. *A Banquet of Jests.* 1640. Edinburgh: William Paterson, 1872.

Jefferds, Keith. "Vidusaka versus Fool: A Functional Analysis." *Journal of South Asian Literature* 16 (1981): 61–73.

Jenkins, Ronald. "The Holy Humor of Bali's Clowns." *Asia* 3 (1980): 28–35.

————. "Representative Clowns: Comedy and Democracy in America." Ph.D. diss., Harvard University, 1984.

Joly, Monique. "Fragments d'un discours mythique sur le bouffon." In *Visages de la folie: 1500–1650 (Domaine hispano-italien),* ed. A. Redondo and A. Rochon, 81–91. Série Études 16. Paris: Publications de la Sorbonne, 1981.

————. *La vraie épitaphe de Triboulet.* Lyons, 1867. Quoted in *Recueil général des sotties,* ed. Émile Picot, 3:205. 3 vols. Paris: Firmin Didot, 1912.

Jones, Emyr Wyn, ed. *Barn ar Egwyddorion y Llywodraeth.* In *Yr Anterliwt Goll.* Aberystwyth: Llyfrgell Cenedlaethol Cymru, 1984.

Jones, William Knapp. "Estevanillo González." *Revue Hispanique* 77 (1929): 201–45.

Jonson, Ben (ca. 1573–1637). *Epicoene, or The Silent Woman.* 1609. Ed. L. A. Beaurline. London: Arnold, 1967.

————. *Every Man out of His Humour.* 1599. Oxford: Oxford University Press, 1920.

Jónsson, Finnur. *Den oldnorske og oldislandske litteraturs historie.* 3 vols. Copenhagen: Gad, 1894–1902.

Joubert, Laurent (1529–83). *Le traité du ris.* Facsimile of 1579 ed. Geneva: Saltkine Reprints, 1973.

———. *Treatise on Laughter (Traité du ris).* Trans. and annot. Gregory David de Rocher. University: University of Alabama Press, 1980.

The Jovial Jester, or Tim Grin's Delight: The Most Capital Collection of Wit and Laughter Containing a Selection of Good Sayings, Witty Jests Etc. London: W. Lane, 1780.

J. S. *England's Merry Jester, or Court, City and Country Jests.* London, J. Wilde, 1693.

Jusserand, J. J. *English Wayfaring Life in the Middle Ages.* London: Fisher Unwin, 1920.

Justi, Carl. "Dwarfs, Buffoons and Jesters." In *Velazquez and His Times,* 433–51. London: Grevel, 1889.

Kaestner, Eric. *Eleven Merry Pranks of Till the Jester.* Trans. Cyrus Brooks, illus. Walter Trier. London: Enoch, 1939.

Kaikkonen, Marja. *Laughable Propaganda: Modern Xiangsheng as Didactic Entertainment.* Stockholm East Asian Monographs 1. Stockholm: University of Stockholm, 1990.

Kaiser, Walter. *Praisers of Folly: Erasmus, Rabelais, Shakespeare.* Cambridge: Harvard University Press, 1963.

Kalff, G. *Opkomst, Bloei en Verdwijning van de Hofnar.* Amsterdam: De Poortpers, 1954.

Kalidasa (fl. ca. fifth century). *Malavika and Agnimitra.* Trans. Edwin Gerow. In *Theatre of Memory: The Plays of Kalidasa,* ed. Barbara Stoler Miller, 253–312. Columbia: Columbia University Press, 1984.

———. *Sakuntala and the Ring of Recollection.* Trans. Barbara Stoler Miller. In *Theatre of Memory: The Plays of Kalidasa,* ed. Barbara Stoler Miller, 85–176. Columbia: Columbia University Press, 1984.

———. *Theater of Memory: The Plays of Kalidasa,* ed. Barbara Stoler Miller (New York: Columbia University Press, 1984), 9–11 and 17.

———. *Urvasi Won by Valor.* Trans. David Gitomer. In *Theatre of Memory: The Plays of Kalidasa,* ed. Barbara Stoler Miller, 177–251. Columbia: Columbia University Press, 1984.

Kalvodova, Dana. "Clowns in the Szechuan Theatre." *Bulletin of the School of Oriental and African Studies* 28 (1965): 356–62.

Kanlayanee, Sitasuwan. "Language Use in Kyogen." Ph.D. diss., University of Washington, 1986.

Kao, George. *Chinese Wit and Humor.* New York: Sterling, 1974.

———. "From a Chinese Thesaurus of Laughs." *Renditions* 9 (spring 1978): 37–42.

Kaser, Arthur LeRoy. *Kaser's Complete Minstrel Guide: A Collection of Minstrel Material for Every Occasion.* Chicago: Dramatic, 1934.

Kaspersen, Søren. "Bildende Kunst, Theater und Volkstümlichkeit im mittelalterlichen Dänemark: Zur Wechselwirkung von Wandmalerei und Spielkultur." In *Popular Drama in Northern Europe in the Later Middle Ages,* ed. F. Anderson, 201–50. Odense: Odense University Press, 1988.

Katz, Leslie. "The Public Share: Shakespearean Dramas and National Histories." Ph.D. diss., University of California, Berkeley, 1992.

Keeler, Ward. *Javanese Shadow Plays, Javanese Selves.* Princeton: Princeton University Press, 1987.

Keith, Carroll. "The Saintly Fool Figure in the Fiction of Dostoevsky." Ph.D. diss., University of Texas, Arlington, 1992.

Kelly, Catriona. "From Pulcinella to Petrushka." *Oxford Slavonic Papers* 21 (1988): 41–63.

———. *Petrushka: The Russian Carnival Puppet Theatre.* Cambridge: Cambridge University Press, 1990.

Kempis, Thomas à (1380–1471). *The Imitation of Christ* [*De imitatio Christi*]. 1441. Trans. and intro. L. Sherley-Price. London: Penguin Books, 1954.

Khater, Akram F. "Emile Habibi: The Mirror of Irony in Palestinian Literature." *Journal of Arabic Literature* 24 (1993): 75–94.

Killigrew, Thomas (1612–83). *Comedies and Tragedies.* Illus. William Faithorne. London: Herringman, 1664.

Kipling, Rudyard (1865–1936). "Rahere." In *Rudyard Kipling's Verse: Inclusive Edition,* 734–36. London: Hodder and Stoughton, 1933.

Kirkwood, Robert, and G. Claydon. *Jesus the Jester.* Illus. Edward McLachlan. London: Longman, 1992.

Klapp, O. L. *Heroes, Villains and Fools.* Englewood Cliffs, NJ: Prentice-Hall, 1962.

Kluyver, A., and others, eds. *Woordeboek der Nederlandsche taal.* 25 vols. The Hague: Nijhoff; Leiden: Sijthoff, 1882–1989.

Knechtges, David. "Wit, Humor, and Satire in Early Chinese Literature." *Monumenta Serica* 29 (1970–71): 79–98.

Knight. "Seventeenth Century Views of Human Folly." In *Essays in German Literature,* ed. F. Norman, 1:29–51. London: University of London Institute of Germanic Studies, 1965.

Knight, Reginald. *Our Lady's Jester: A One Act Play.* London: Pitman, 1952.

Koedood, Peter. *De hofnar: Van maatschappelijk verschijnsel tot toneelnar.* Weesp, Holland: Uitgeverij Heureka, 1983.

Koepping, Klaus-Peter. "Absurdity and Hidden Truth: Cunning Intelligence and Grotesque Body Images as Manifestations of the Trickster." *History of Religions* 24, 3 (1985): 191–214.

Köhl, Gudrun, and others. *Eulenspiegel, Hofnarren und Zwerge.* Munich: Unverhau, 1982.

Kolakowski, Leszek. "The Priest and the Jester." Trans. Pawel Mayewsky. In *The Modern Polish Mind,* ed. Maria Kuncewicz, 301–26. London: Secker and Warburg, 1963.

Koopmans, Jelle, and Paul Verhuyck, eds. *Ulenspiegel, de sa vie, de ses oeuvres: Édition critique du plus ancien Ulenspiègle français du XVIe siècle.* Antwerp: Uitgeverij Vries-Brouwers, 1988.

Krailsheimer, A. J., and others. *The Continental Renaissance: 1500–1600.* Harmondsworth, Middlesex: Penguin Books, 1971.

Kraus, Jo Anne. "The Comedy of Paradox: Mythic and Medieval Tricksters in Narrative." Ph.D. diss., City University of New York, 1990.

Kreidl, Detlev. "Le portrait de Gonella: Le dessin sous-jacent dans le tableau de Gonella." *Gazette des Beaux-Arts* 97 (1981): 5–8.

Kromm, J. E. "Hogarth's Madmen." *Journal of the Warburg and Courtauld Institute* 48 (1985): 238–42.

Kuiper, F. B. J. *Varuna and Vidusaka: On the Origin of Sanskrit Drama.* Amsterdam: North-Holland 1979.

Kunzle, D. "Brueghel's Proverb Painting and the World Upsidedown." *Art Bulletin* 59 (1977): 197–202.

———. "World Upside Down: The Iconography of a European Broadsheet Type." In *The Reversible World: Essays in Symbolic Inversion,* ed. B. Babcock-Abrahams, 39–94. Ithaca: Cornell University Press, 1978.

Lacroix, Paul. *Les deux fous—histoire de temps de François Ier (1524): Precedée d'un essai historique sur les fous des rois de France.* Paris, 1837.

Ladd, Anna. *Hieronymus Rides: Episodes in the Life of a Knight and Jester at the Court of Maximilian, King of the Romans.* London: Macmillan, 1912.

Lagerkvist, Par. *The King: A Play in Three Acts.* 1932. In *Modern Theatre: Seven Plays and an Essay,* trans. and ed. Thomas Buckman, 93–151. Lincoln: University of Nebraska Press, 1966.

Landon, Margaret. *Anna and the King of Siam.* New York, 1945.

Lao Ziwei 勞子衛. "Liyuan jiushi lazatan" 梨園舊事拉雜談. *XJYK* 2, 3 (1929): 43–47.

Larken, M. "An Account of the Zande." *Sudan Notes and Records* 9–10 (1926–27): 85–134.

Larsen, Egon. *Wit as a Weapon: The Political Joke in History.* London: Muller, 1980.

Laugh When You Can, or The Monstrous Droll Jester . . . to Which Is Added The Benevolent Jew [by C. F. Barrett] London: Ann Lemoine, 1795.

La Vigne, André de. *Sotise à huit personnages.* Ca. 1507. In *Recueil général des sotties,* ed. Émile Picot, 2:1–104. 3 vols. Paris: Firmin Didot, 1912.

Lawrence, W. J. "On the Underrated Genius of Dick Tarleton." In *Speeding up Shakespeare,* 17–38. London: Argonaut Press, 1937.

Leavitt, Sturgis. "Notes on the Gracioso as a Dramatic Critic." *Studies in Philology* 27 (1931): 315–18.

Lefebvre, Joel. *Les fols et la folie: Étude sur les genres du comique et la création littéraire en Allemagne pendant la Renaissance.* Paris: Klincksieck, 1968.

Legge, Arthur. *The Pilgrim Jester.* London: John Lane, 1908.

Legge, James, trans. *The Chinese Classics.* 2d ed. rev. 7 vols. Taibei: Wenxing Shudian, 1966.

Leishman, J. B., ed. *The Three Parnassus Plays.* London: Nicholson and Watson, 1949.

Lelievre, J. "Brusquet, le fou du roi." *Bulletin de la Société des Amis d'Anet* 15 (1962): 9–10.

Lenkewicz, Robert. "The City of Fools." Unpublished MS.

Leopardi, Giacomo. *Zibaldone.* 1823. Ed. F. Flora. Milan, 1938.

Lever, Maurice. "Les bouffons et le roi." *L'Histoire* 31, 2 (1981): 83–85.

———. "Le mythe du fol." *Magazine Littéraire,* July–August 1981, 22–24.

———. *Le sceptre et la marotte: Histoire des fous de cour.* Paris: Hachette, 1985.

Levey, Michael. *Painting at Court.* London: Weidenfeld and Nicolson, 1971.

Levin, Harry, ed. *Ben Jonson: Selected Works.* New York: Random House; London: Nonesuch Press, n.d.

Levin, Theodore. *The Hundred Thousand Fools of God: Musical Travels in Central Asia (and Queens, New York).* Bloomington: Indiana University Press, 1996.

Lévy, André. "Notes bibliographiques pour une histoire des 'histoires pour rire' en Chine." In *Études sur le conte et le roman chinois,* 67–95. Paris: École Française d'Extrême-Orient, 1971.

Ley, Charles D. *El gracioso en el teatro de la Peninsula.* Madrid: Revista de Occidente, 1954.

Li Mengren 李孟任. "Xialing Li Xiaohong zhuan" 俠令李小紅傳. *XJYK* 3, 4 (1930): 205–10.

Lieberman, Harold, and Edith Lieberman. *Throne of Straw.* 1972. In *The Theatre of the Holocaust: Four Plays,* ed. and intro. Robert Skloot, 113–96. Madison: University of Wisconsin Press, 1982.

Lin Yutang. "Chinese Realism and Humour." In *The Little Critic: Essays, Satires and Sketches on China,* 86–95. Shanghai: Commercial Press, 1935.

———. "Zarathustra and the Jester." In *The Little Critic: Essays, Satires and Sketches on China*, 220–24. Shanghai: Commercial Press, 1935.

Lindow, Wolfgang, ed. *Ein kurzweilig Lesen von Dil Ulenspiegel.* 1515. Stuttgart: Reclam, 1966.

Link, Perry. "The Genie and the Lamp: Revolutionary *Xiangsheng.*" In *Popular Chinese Literature and Performing Arts in the People's Republic of China, 1949–1979*, ed. Bonnie McDougall, 83–111. Berkeley: University of California Press, 1984.

———. "Popular Performing Arts." In *Stubborn Weeds: Popular and Controversial Chinese Literature after the Cultural Revolution*, 251–86. London: Blond and Briggs, 1984.

Linné, S. "Humpbacks in Ancient America." *Ethnos* 8, 4 (1943): 161–86.

Liu Binkun 劉斌昆. "Mantan choujue" 漫談丑角. Quoted in *YYJ*, 267.

Liu Jung-en [Liu Rongen], trans. *Six Yuan Plays.* Harmondsworth, Middlesex: Penguin Books, 1972.

Liu Xie (ca. 465–ca. 522). "On Humor and Enigma." In *The Literary Mind and the Carving of Dragons*, trans. Vincent Yu-chung Shih [Shi Yuzhong], 78–83. New York: Columbia University Press, 1959.

Liu Zhesou 劉蟄叟. "Lun xiju gaizao shehui zhi nengli" 論戲劇改造社會之能力. *XJYK* 1, 4 (1929): 1–5.

Liu Zhenjia 劉振佳. "Wo guo gulao de kuanghuanjie" 我國古老的狂歡節. *Renmin Ribao* 人民日報, 31 March 1993, 8.

Loewe, Michael. "The Office of Music, ca. 114–7 B.C.." *Bulletin of the School of Oriental and African Studies* 36 (1973): 340–51.

The London Jester, or Museum of Mirth, Wit and Humour. London: Cowie and Strange, [ca. 1830].

Longchamp, Nigel. *A Mirror for Fools.* Trans. J. H. Mozley. Oxford: Blackwell, 1961.

Longfellow, Henry Wadsworth. "The Sicilian's Tale: King Robert of Sicily." In *Tales of a Wayside Inn*, in *Writings of Henry Wadsworth Longfellow*, 6:46–53. 11 vols. London: Routledge, 1886.

Longinus. "On the Sublime." Trans. T. S. Dorsch in *Classical Literary Criticism.* Harmondsworth, Middlesex: Penguin Books, 1965.

Lopez, Barry. *Arctic Dreams: Imagination and Desire in a Northern Landscape.* London: Picador, 1987.

Lopez-Rey, Jose. "On Velasquez' Portraits of Jesters at the Buen Retiro." *Gazette des Beaux-Arts* 97 (1981): 163–66.

Loseth, E., ed. *Robert le Diable: Roman d'aventures.* Thirteenth century. Paris: Firmin Didot, 1903.

Loti, Pierre. *L'Inde (sans les Anglais).* Paris: Calmann-Lévy, 1903.

Low, David. Preface to *Jesters in Earnest: Cartoons by the Czechoslovak Artist Z. K-A Hoffmeister*. London: John Murray, 1944.

Luke, Sir Harry. "The Turkish Jester." In *An Eastern Chequerboard*. London: Lovat Dickson, 1934.

Lukens, Nancy. *Buchner's Valerio and the Theatrical Fool Tradition*. Stuttgart: Heinz, 1977.

Luzio, Alessandro, and Rodolfo Renier. "Buffoni, nani e schiavi dei Gonzaga ai tempi di Isabella d'Este." *Estr. Nuova Ant.*, ser. 3 (1891): parts 1 and 2, 34:618–50, part 3, 35:112–46.

Lyndsay, David (ca. 1490–ca. 1555). *Ane Satyre of the Thrie Estaits*. 1540. Ed. James Kinsley. London: Cassell, 1954.

Ma Er Guang Sheng 馬二光生. "Cixi miji (xu)" 慈禧秘記, *Guowen Zhoubao* 國文周報 1, 10 (1924): 13–14.

McCabe, Eamonn. "A Brush with History." *Guardian*, 22 May 1993, 29.

McCrary, Judith. *The Fool in French Medieval Drama*. Ann Arbor, MI: University Microfilms International, 1979.

McDonald, Marcia. "A Two-World Condition: The Carnival Idiom and Its Function in Four Morality Plays." Ph.D. diss., Vanderbilt University, 1984.

McGoldrick, James. "Dunbar and Skelton: A Comparative Analysis of the Satiric Court Poetry." Ph.D. diss., University of Rhode Island, 1991.

McHugh, Sheila. "The Lay of the Big Fool: Its Irish and Arthurian Sources." *Modern Philology* 42, 4 (1945): 197–211.

McKechnie, Samuel. *Popular Entertainments through the Ages*. London: Low, Marston, 1931.

Mackenzie, Kenneth, coll. and trans. *The Marvellous Adventures and Rare Conceits of Master Tyll Owlglass*. London: Trubner, 1860.

Mackerras, Colin, ed. *Chinese Theater from Its Origins to the Present Day*. Honolulu: University of Hawaii Press, 1983.

Maclean, Hector. "The King and the Fool in Wedekind's *König Nicolo*." *Seminar* 5, 2 (1969): 21–35.

McLelland, Joseph. *The Clown and the Crocodile*. Richmond, VA: John Knox Press, 1970.

Macleod, Olive. *Chiefs and Cities in Central Africa*. London: Blackwood, 1912.

Macmillan, Malcolm. *Dagonet the Jester*. London: Macmillan, 1886.

Madden, Frederick. *Privy Purse Expenses of the Princess Mary, Daughter of King Henry the Eighth, Afterwards Queen Mary*. London: Pickering, 1831.

Mahalin, Paul [Émile Blondet]. *The End of Chicot*. Trans. F. W. Reed. Typescript. Whangarai, N.Z., 1953.

Mahapatra, Sitakant. *The Jester and Other Poems*. Calcutta: Writer's Workshop, 1979.

Mahler, J. G. *The Westerners among the Figurines of the T'ang Dynasty of China*. Serie Orientale Roma 20. Rome: Istituto Italiano per il Medio ed Estremo Oriente, 1959.

Malefijt, A. M. de W. "Dutch Joking Patterns." *Transactions of the New York Academy of Sciences*, ser. 2, 30 (1968): 1181–86.

Malti-Douglas, Fedwa. "Humor." In *Structures of Avarice: The Bukhala in Medieval Arabic Literature*, 108–37. Leiden: Brill, 1985.

Mann, Thomas. *The Holy Sinner*. Trans. H. T. Lowe-Porter. London: Secker and Warburg, 1951; repr. Harmondsworth, Middlesex: Penguin Books, 1962.

Manning, Bessie. *The King's Jester: A Play for Young People*. Manchester: James Galt, 1907.

Mantzius, Karl. *The History of Theatrical Art in Ancient and Modern Times*. Trans. Louise von Cossel. 2 vols. London: Duckworth, 1903.

Mares, F. "The Origin of the Figure Called the Vice." *Huntingdon Library Quarterly* 22 (1958): 11–29.

Margoliouth, D. S. "Wit and Humour in Arabic Authors." *Islamic Culture* 1 (1927): 522–34.

Marijnissen, R. H. "Bosch and Bruegel on Human Folly." In *Folie et déraison à la Renaissance*, 41–52. Brussels: Université Libre de Bruxelles, 1976.

Marston, John (ca. 1575–1634). *The Malcontent*. 1604. Ed. Bernard Harris. London: A. and C. Black, 1987.

Marx, Arthur. *My Life with Groucho: A Son's Eye View*. London: Pan Books, 1991.

Mathorez, J. "Histoire de Chicot, bouffon de Henri III." *Bulletin de Bibliophile*, 1914, 237–48 and 297–308; 1917, 33–45.

———. "Notes sur Maître Guillaume, fou de Henri IV et de Louis XIII: Contribution à l'histoire de la presse française." *Revue de Livres Anciens* 1 (1913): 264–84.

Mayer, David. *Harlequin in His Element: The English Pantomime, 1806–36*. Cambridge: Harvard University Press, 1969.

Meinardus, O. F. A. "Zeitgenössische Gottesnarren in den Wüsten Ägyptens." *Ostkirchliche Studien* 36, 4 (1987): 301–10.

Menendez Pidal, Juan. "Don Francesillo de Zuñiga, bufón de Carlos V." *Revista de Archivos, Bibliotecas y Museos* 20 (1909): 182–200.

———. "Don Francesillo de Zuñiga, bufón de Carlos V: Cartas ineditas." *Revista de Archivos, Bibliotecas y Museos* 21 (1910): 72–95.

Menendez Pidal, Ramón. *Poesia juglaresca y juglares: Aspectos de la historia literia y cultural de España*. Buenos Aires: Espasa-Calpe, 1949.

Mercier, V. *The Irish Comic Tradition.* Oxford: Clarendon Press, 1962.

Meredith, George. *Comedy.* New York: Doubleday, 1956.

Merry, Martin [pseud.]. *The Royal Jester, or Cream of the Jest: Being a Collection of the Best Jests, Puns, Jokes.* London: F. Stamper, 1751.

Meylan, Henri, ed. *Épitres du coq à l'ane: Contribution à l'histoire de la satire au XVIe siècle.* Geneva: Droz, 1956.

Mezger, Werner. "Ein Bildprogramm zur Narrenidee: Der Ambraser Zierteller von 1528." In *Fas(t)nacht in Geschichte, Kunst und Literatur,* ed. Horst Sund, 81–113. Constance: Universitätsverlag Konstanz, 1984.

———. *Hofnarren im Mittelalter.* Constance: Universitätsverlag Konstanz, 1981.

Michael, Erika. "The Drawings of Hans Holbein the Younger for Erasmus' 'Praise of Folly.'" Ph.D. diss., University of Washington, 1981.

Miller, Arthur. *Playing for Time.* New York: Bantam Books, 1981.

Miller, Samuel. "The Clown in Contemporary Art." *Theology Today* 24 (1967): 318–27.

Miller, Susan. "How to Sell Safer Sex." *New Scientist,* 27 February 1993, 12–13.

Millingen, Frederick. *Wild Life among the Koords.* London: Hurst and Blackett, 1870.

Mirsky, Jonathan. "Not a Ghost of a Smile for Deng." *Observer,* 7 June 1992, 24.

Miscellanea curiosa, medica, physica. Leipzig, 1670.

Misogonus. 1570. Ed. Lester Barber. New York: Garland 1979.

Mitchell, William. "Introduction: Mother Folly in the Islands." In *Clowning as Critical Practice: Performance Humor in the South Pacific,* ed. William Mitchell, 3–57. Pittsburgh: University of Pittsburgh Press, 1992.

Moffitt, J. "Velasquez, Fools, Calabacillas and Ripa." *Pantheon* 40, 4 (1982): 304–9.

Monestier, Martin. *Les nains.* Les Hommes Différents. Paris: Simoën, 1977.

Mongredien, G. "Maître Guillaume, bouffon de Henri IV." *Mercure de France,* 15 August 1939, 5–26.

Moore, Ernest. "Estebanillo González's Travels in Southern Europe." *Hispanic Review,* 8, 1 (1940): 24–45.

Moore, Leslie. *The Jester.* New York: Putnam's Sons, 1915.

Moragas, J. de. "Los bufones de Velasquez." In *Medicina e historia,* ed. Rocas, 6:5–15. Barcelona, 1964.

Moreau, Paul. *Fous et bouffons: Étude physiologique, psychologique et historique.* Paris, 1885.

Moreno Villa, José. *Locos, enanos, negros y niños palaciegos: Gente de placer que tuvieron los Austrias en la corte española desde 1563 a 1700,* Serie de Obras Originales 1. Mexico: España en México, 1939.

Morgan, R. "Old French Jogleor and Kindred Terms: Studies in Medieval Romance Lexicography." *Romance Philology* 7 (1953–54): 279–325.

Morreall, John. *The Philosophy of Laughter and Humor.* Albany: State University of New York Press, 1987.

———. *Taking Laughter Seriously.* Albany: State University of New York Press, 1983.

Morris, Ivan. *The World of the Shining Prince: Court Life in Ancient Japan.* Oxford: Oxford University Press, 1964; repr. Harmondsworth, Middlesex: Penguin Books, 1979.

Morris, R. N. *Behind the Jester's Mask: Canadian Editorial Cartoons about Dominant and Minority Groups, 1960–1979.* Toronto: University of Toronto Press, 1989.

Morton, Andrew. "The Royal Marriage: Happy Ever After?" *Sunday Times,* 23 September 1990, 7.

Moser, Dietz-Rudiger. "Ein Babylon der verkehrten Welt: Über Idee, System und Gestaltung der Fastnachtsbrauche." In *Fas(t)nacht in Geschichte, Kunst und Literatur,* ed. Horst Sund, 9–57. Constance: Universitätsverlag Konstanz, 1984.

———. "Fastnacht und Fastnachtspiel: Bemerkungen zum gegenwartigen Stand volkskundlicher und literarhistorischer Fastnachtsforschung." In *Popular Drama in Northern Europe in the Later Middle Ages,* ed. F. Anderson, 165–99. Odense: Odense University Press, 1988.

Moulieras, Auguste, trans. *Les fourberies de Si Djoh'a.* Paris: Leroux, 1892.

Moxey, Keith. "Pieter Brueghel and the Feast of Fools." *Art Bulletin* 64 (1982): 640–46.

Muddock, Joyce. *Basile the Jester: A Romance of the Days of Mary Queen of Scots.* London: Chatto and Windus, 1896.

Muller, Gari. *Theater of Folly: Allegory and Satire in the Sottie.* Ann Arbor, MI, University Microfilms International, 1979.

Murray, Simon. *Legionnaire: An Englishman in the French Foreign Legion.* London: Sidgwick and Jackson, 1980.

Muscatine, Charles. *The Old French Fabliaux.* New Haven: Yale University Press, 1986.

Musset, Alfred de (1810–57). *Fantasio* (1833). In *Théâtre complet,* ed. Maurice Allem, 276–323. Paris: Gallimard, 1958.

Nachman, Steven. "Discomfiting Laughter: Schadenfreude among Melanesians." *Journal of Anthropological Research* 42 (1986): 53–67.

Nash, Thomas (1567–1601). *Summer's Last Will and Testament.* 1592. In *Complete Works,* ed. R. McKerrow, 3:227–95. 5 vols. Oxford: Blackwell, 1958.

Natesa Sastri, Pandit S. M., trans. *Tales of Tennalirama, the Famous Court Jester of Southern India.* Madras: Natesan, 1900.

Nazim, Muhammed. *The Life and Times of Sultan Mahmud of Ghazna.* Cambridge: Cambridge University Press, 1931.

Neale, J. E. *Queen Elizabeth.* 1934. London: Reprint Society, 1949.

Needham, Joseph. *China: Science and Civilisation.* Cambridge: Cambridge University Press, 1954–.

Neiheiser, Thomas. "Heroes and Fools: Characterizations in Holocaust Drama." Ph.D. diss., University of Utah, 1983.

The New London City Jester, or A Banquet of Wit, Mirth and Fancy. London: J. Roach, 1797.

The New Poetical Jester, Consisting of the Most Humorous, Entertaining and Diverting Jests, Anecdotes, Bon Mots Etc. in Verse. London: Reed, 1809.

New Testament. Jerusalem: Judaean 1970.

Newton, Douglas. *Clowns.* London: Harrap, 1958.

Nicholas, David. *The Evolution of the Medieval World: Society, Government and Thought in Europe, 312–1500.* London: Longman, 1992.

Nick, Friedrich. *Die Hof- und Volksnarren.* 2 vols. Stuttgart: Scheible, 1861.

Nicolas, Nicholas H. *Privy Purse Expenses of Elizabeth of York: Wardrobe Accounts of Edward IV.* London: Pickering, 1830.

———. *The Privy Purse Expenses of Henry the Eighth (November 1529–December 1532).* London: Pickering, 1827.

Nicoll, Allardyce. *Masks, Mimes and Miracles.* London: Harrap, 1931.

———. *The World of Harlequin; A Critical Study of the Commedia dell'Arte.* Cambridge: Cambridge University Press, 1963.

Niklaus, Thelma. *Harlequin Phoenix, or The Rise and Fall of a Bergamask Rogue.* New York: G. Braziller, 1956.

Niveson, David. "Aspects of Traditional Chinese Biography." *Journal of Asian Studies* 21 (1962): 457–63.

Nock, A. J. "The King's Jester: Modern Style." *Harper's Monthly Magazine,* March 1928, 481–88.

Northcott, Kenneth. "The Fool in Early New High German Literature: Some Observations." In *Essays in German Literature,* ed. F. Norman, 1:29–51. London: University of London Institute of Germanic Studies, 1965.

Núñez de Velasco, Francisco. *Diálogos de contención entre la milicia y la ciencia.* Valladolid, 1614.

Nungezer, Edwin. *A Dictionary of Actors and of Other Persons Associated with the Public Representation of Plays in England before 1642.* New Haven: Yale University Press, 1929.

O'Connor, John. "Physical Deformity and Chivalric Laughter in Renaissance England." *New York Literary Forum* 1 (1978): 59–71.

O'Flaherty, Wendy, trans. *Hindu Myths: A Sourcebook Translated from the Sanskrit.* Harmondsworth, Middlesex: Penguin Books, 1975.

Ogilvy, J. D. "Mimi, Scurrae, Histriones: Entertainers of the Early Middle Ages." *Speculum* 38 (1963): 603–19.

Olson, C. C. "The Minstrels at the Court of Edward III." *PMLA* 56 (1941): 601–12.

Oppenheimer, Paul, trans. *Till Eulenspiegel: His Adventures.* Oxford: Oxford University Press, 1995.

Orenstein, Claudia. "Festive Revolutions: The Politics of Popular Theatre Forms." Ph.D. diss., Stanford University, 1993.

Orléans, Duchess of. *Correspondence.* Vol. 2. Paris, 1890.

Ornatissimus Joculator, or The Compleat Jester... London: W. Onley, 1703.

Ostrander, Sheila, and Lynn Schroeder. *Cosmic Memory.* London: Simon and Schuster, 1993.

The Oxford Classical Dictionary. Ed. M. Cary and others. Oxford: Clarendon Press, 1949; repr. 1957.

The Oxford English Dictionary. Oxford: Clarendon Press, 1959.

Pächt, Otto. "Le portrait de Gonella: Le problème de son auteur." *Gazette des Beaux-Arts* 97 (1981): 1–4.

Page, Christopher. *The Owl and the Nightingale: Musical Life and Ideas in France, 1100–1300.* London: Dent, 1989.

Panchapakesa, Ayyar, trans. The Royal Jester, or Tenali Rama. Madras: Alliance, 1947.

Panofsky, E. "Conard Celtes and Kunz von der Rosen: Two Problems in Portrait Identification." *Art Bulletin* 24 (1942): 39–54.

Pâques, Viviana. "Bouffons sacré du cercle de Bougouni (Soudan français)." *Journal de la Société des Africanistes* 24 (1954): 63–110.

Parsons, Elsie, and Ralph Beals. "The Sacred Clowns of the Pueblo and Mayo-Yaqui Indians." *American Anthropologist* 36, 4 (1934): 491–514.

Pasquier, Étienne. *Lettres.* Paris: Gamber, 1930.

Peacock, James. "Symbolic Reversal and Social History: Transvestites and Clowns of Java." In *The Reversible World: Symbolic Inversion in Art and Society,* ed. Barbara A. Babcock, 209–24. Ithaca: Cornell University Press, 1978.

Pearson, Allison. "For Pete's Sake, Don't Pity Him." *Evening Standard,* 12 January 1995, 11.

Pearson, Sue. *Jolly Jester.* Woodbridge, Suffolk: Henderson, 1992.

Pelaez, Alvaro (1280?–1353). *De planctu ecclesiae.* Venice, 1560. Quoted in Ramon Menendez Pidal, *Poesia juglaresca y juglares: Aspectos de la historia literia y cultural de España,* 78. Buenos Aires: Espasa-Calpe, 1949.

Pemberton, Sir Max. *Queen of the Jesters and Her Strange Adventures in Paris.* London: C. A. Pearson, 1897.

Peppard, Murray. "'Narr' and 'Narrheit' (1795–1855): A Study of the Conception and Its Echoes up to 1855." Ph.D. diss., Yale University, 1948.

Pepys, Samuel (1633–1703). *The Diary of Samuel Pepys.* Ed. Robert Latham and William Matthews. 11 vols. London: Bell, 1976.

Petit de Julleville, Louis. *La comédie et les moeurs en France au Moyen Âge.* Paris: Cerf, 1886.

Petitot, M., ed. *Collection complète des mémoires relatifs à l'histoire de France.* 1st ser. 52 vols. Paris: Foucault Libraire, 1825.

A Phanatic Play: The First Part, as It Was Presented before and by the Lord Fleetwood . . . and Others; with Master Jester and Master Pudding. London, 1660.

Picot, Émile. "La sottie en France." *Romania* 7 (1878): 236–326.

———, ed. *Recueil général des sotties.* 3 vols. Paris: Firmin Didot, 1912.

Pieper, Josef. *In Tune with the World: A Theory of Festivity.* Trans. R. and C. Winston. New York: Harcourt, Brace and World, 1965.

Pieral. *Vu d'en bas.* Paris: Laffont, 1976.

Pierce, Charles S. "The Polished Glass: A Reading of Selected Mirror Books of the English Renaissance." Ph.D. diss., Washington State University, 1982.

Pinker, Stephen. *The Language Instinct: The New Science of Language and Mind.* Harmondsworth, Middlesex: Penguin Books, 1995.

Plautus, Titus (ca. 254–ca. 184 B.C.). *The Captives [Captivi].* In *Plautus,* trans. Paul Nixon, 1:459–567. 5 vols. Loeb Classical Library. London: Heinemann; New York: Putnam; Cambridge: Harvard University Press, 1916; repr. 1928–38.

———. *Pseudolus.* In *Plautus,* trans. Paul Nixon, 4:144–285.

———. *Stichus.* In *Plautus,* trans. Paul Nixon, 5:1–95.

———. *Three Bob Day [Trinummus].* In *Plautus,* trans. Paul Nixon 5:97–221.

———. *The Two Menaechmuses [Menaechmi].* In *Plautus,* trans. Paul Nixon 2:363–487.

———. *The Weevil [Curculio].* In *Plautus,* trans. Paul Nixon 2:185–269.

A Pleasant History of the Life and Death of Will Summers: How He Came First to Be Known at Court, and by What Means He Got to Be King Henry the Eighth's Jester; with the Entertainment That His Cousin Patch, Cardinal Wolsey's Fool, Gave Him at His Lord's House; and How the Hogsheads of Gold Were Known by This Means. London: Vere and Wright, 1676; repr. James Caulfield, 1794.

Pokora, T. "Ironical Critics at Ancient Chinese Courts (Shih chi 126)." *Oriens Extremus* 20 (1973): 49–64.

Poland, Warren. "The Gift of Laughter: On the Development of a Sense of Humor in Clinical Analysis." *Psychoanalytic Quarterly* 59 (1990): 197–225.

Poley, Stefanie. *Unter der Maske des Narren.* Stuttgart: Verlag Gerd Hatje, 1981.

Ponsonby, Frederick. *Recollections of Three Reigns.* London: Eyre and Spottiswoode, 1951.

Pratt, J. B. *The Life and Death of Jamie Fleeman, the Laird of Udny's Fool,* 3d ed. Aberdeen: Lewis Smith, 1912.

Prebble, John. *The Lion in the North.* Harmondsworth, Middlesex: Penguin Books, 1983.

Prosch, Peter (1744–1804). *Mémoires d'un bouffon.* Trans. Philippe de Laborde Pédelahore and Robert Sctrick. Paris: Éditions Phébus, 1995.

Prost, Bernard, and Henri Prost, eds. *Inventaires mobiliers et extraits des comptes des ducs de Bourgogne de la maison de Valois (1363–1477).* 3 vols. Paris: Leroux, 1902–8.

Pruitt, Ellanor. "The Figure of the Fool in Contemporary Theatre." Ph.D. diss., Emory University, 1976.

Quintilian (ca. 35–ca. 100). *The "Institutio Oratorio" of Quintilian.* Trans. H. E. Butler. 4 vols. Loeb Classical Library. London: Heinemann; Cambridge: Harvard University Press, 1953.

Rabelais, François (ca. 1494–ca. 1553). *Oeuvres de Rabelais.* Illus. Gustave Doré. 2 vols. Paris, 1883–85.

———. *Le tiers livre des faicts et dicts héroiques du bon Pantagruel* (1546). In *Oeuvres complètes,* ed. Pierre Jourda, 1:388–619. Paris: Classiques Garnier, 1962.

———. *The Works of Rabelais.* Trans. Thomas Urquhart and Peter le Motteaux. 2d ed. 2 vols. London: Bodley Head, 1933.

Radcliffe-Brown, Alfred R. "On Joking Relationships." *Africa* 13, 3 (1940): 195–210.

Radin, Paul. *The Trickster: A Study in American Indian Mythology.* London: Routledge and Kegan Paul, 1956.

Raimbault, M. "Jean-Antoine Lombard, dit Brusquet, Viguier d'Antibes en 1548." *Bulletin Historique et Philologique du Comité des Travaux Historiques et Scientifiques,* 1904, 35–42.

Raleigh, Walter, ed. *Johnson on Shakespeare: Essays and Notes.* Oxford: Oxford University Press, 1946.

Rama the Jester: An Original and Up-to-Date Version of the Stories of Tenali Rama, or Tales of Indian Wit and Humour. Coimbatore, India: n.d.

Ran, Faye. "The Tragicomic Vision: The Fool in Modern Drama, Film and Literature." Ph.D. diss., Columbia University, 1988.

Ranger, Roger. *The Covent Garden Jester, or The Rambler's Companion.* London: J. Walker, 1785.

Rao, U. V. Krishna. "Bhasa's Vidusakas." *Poona Orientalist* 18 (1953): 58–75.

Redondo, A., and A. Rochon, eds. *Visages de la folie: 1500–1650 (Domaine Hispano-Italien)*, Série Études 16. Paris: Publications de la Sorbonne, 1981.

Regnier, Mathurin (1573–1613). *Oeuvres complètes de Mathurin Regnier.* Ed. Jean Plattard. Paris: Belles Lettres, 1954.

Reiffenberg, Baron de. "Histoire des fous en titre d'office." In *Le lundi, nouveaux récits de Marsilius Brunck.* Brussels: Hauman, 1835.

Ren Erbei 任二北. *Tang xinong* 唐戲弄. 2 vols. Beijing: Zuojia Chubanshe, 1958.

———. *Youyu ji* 優語集. Shanghai: Shanghai Wenyi Chubanshe, 1981; repr. 1982.

Richards, Raymond. "Samuel Johnson." In *The Manor of Gawsworth,* 224–36. Manchester: Morten, 1959; repr. 1974.

Ricketts, Mac. "The North American Indian Trickster." *History of Religions* 5 (1965): 327–50.

Rigby, P. "Joking Relationships, Kin Categories, and Clanship among the Gogo." *Africa* 38, 2 (1968): 133–55.

Rigollot, M. M. J. *Monnaies inconnues des évêques des Innocens.* Paris: Merlin, 1837.

Ritchie, W. Tod, ed. "Colkelbie Sow." In *The Bannatyne Manuscript.* Edinburgh: Scottish Text Society, 1930.

Robey, Edward. *The Jester and the Court.* London: W. Kimber, 1976.

Robinet, Isabelle. "The Taoist Immortal: Jesters of Light and Shadow, Heaven and Earth." *Journal of Chinese Religions* 13–14 (1985–86): 87–105.

Robinson, Ian, and John Harrold. "Rupert and the April Fool." In *Rupert: The Daily Express Annual.* Exeter, Devon: Pedigree Books, 1993.

Roe, Ivan. *The Jester of God.* London: Hutchinson, 1956.

Rogers, Roland. *The Jester's Tale.* Hartland, Devon: Jamaica Press, 1984.

Rohrer, Lothar, and Walter Fröhlich. *Unsere Fasnacht: Holzschnitte zur schwäbisch-alemannischen Fasnacht von Lothar Rohrer mit "alefanzigen" Anmerkungen für Einheimische und Zugereiste von Walter Fröhlich.* Constance: Sudkurier, 1978.

Roper, William. *The Mirrour of Vertue in Worldly Greatness,or The Life of Syr Thomas More, Knight, Sometime Lord Chancellour.* 1626. London: De la More Press, 1903.

Roscoe, W. *The Life and Pontificate of Leo the Tenth.* Ed. T. Roscoe. 4 vols. London: Cadell and Davies, 1846.

Rosenthal, Franz. *Humor in Early Islam.* Westport, CT: Greenwood, 1976.

Rotuli normanniae in turri londinensi asservati. In *Mémoires de la Société des Antiquitaires de Normandie,* vol. 15.

Roux, H. le, and J. Garnier. *Acrobats and Mountebanks.* Trans. A. Morton. London: Chapman and Hall, 1890.

Roux, Louis. "Divagations sémantiques pour un siècle de raisons." In *Folie, folies, folly dans le monde anglo americain aux XVIIe et XVIIIe siècles,* 7–41. Aix-en-Provence: Université de Provence, 1984.

Rowley, Samuel (d. ca. 1633). *When You See Me You Know Me.* 1604. Oxford: Oxford University Press, 1952.

The Royal Jester, or Prince's Cabinet of Wit. London: Roach, 1792.

Royal Museum of Scotland. *The Power of the Mask.* Exhibition August to October 1993.

Rubin, Vivien. "Clowns in Nineteenth Century French Literature: Buffoons, Pierrots and 'Saltimbanques.'" Ph.D. diss., University of California, Berkeley, 1970.

Sabatini, Rafael. *Sinner, Saint and Jester: A Trilogy of Romantic Adventure. . . . Comprising the Snare, the Strolling Saint, the Shame of Motley.* London: Hutchinson, 1954.

Sabugosa, Conde de. *Bobos na Corte,* 2d ed. Lisbon, 1923.

Sachs, Hans (1494–1576). *Der Doctor mit der grosen Nase.* Quoted by Kenneth Northcott, "The Fool in Early New High German Literature: Some Observations," in *Essays in German Literature,* ed. F. Norman, 1:46. London: University of London Institute of Germanic Studies, 1965.

Sa'di Shirazi. *The Persian-English Gulistan, or Rose Garden of Sa'di.* 1258. Trans. Edward Rehatsek. Tehran: Shargh's Press, 1967.

Sakanishi, Shio, trans. *The Ink-Smeared Lady and Other Kyogen.* Rutland, VT: Tuttle, 1960.

Sakuma, N. "The Fool's Role in Shakespeare." Master's thesis, Birmingham University, 1975–76.

Salerno, Henry, trans. *Scenarios of the Commedia dell'Arte: Flaminio Scala's Il Teatro delle Favole Rappresentative.* Foreword by Kenneth McKee. New York: New York University Press, 1967.

Santa Cruz de Dueñas, Melchor de. "De Truhanes." In *Floresta Española* (1572), 45–49. 2d ed. Buenos Aires: Espasa Calpe Argentina, 1947.

Santucci, M. "Le fou dans les lettres françaises médiévales." *Les Lettre Romanes* 36, 3 (1982): 195–211.

Saward, John. *Perfect Fools.* Oxford: Oxford University Press, 1980.

Saxl, F. "Holbein's Illustrations to the *Praise of Folly* by Erasmus." *Burlington Magazine* 83 (1943): 275–79.

Scarry, Richard. *Richard Scarry's "Peasant Pig and the Terrible Dragon," with "Lowly Worm the Jolly Jester."* London: Collins, 1981.

Schipper, K. "The Divine Jester: Some Remarks on the Gods of the Chinese Marionette Theatre." *Bulletin of the Institute of Ethnology* 21 (1977?): 81–94.

Schupps, Johann Balthasar. *Salomo, oder Regenten-Spiegel.* In *Sämtliche lehrreiche Schrifften,* vol. 1. Frankfurt, 1701.

Schuyler, M. "The Origin of the Vidusaka and the Employment of This Character in the Plays of Harsadeva." *Journal of the American Oriental Society* 20, pt. 2 (1899): 338–40.

Schwammberger, A. "Von Hofnarren in und aus Franken." *Jahrbuch für Frankische Landerforschung* 34–35 (1974–75): 975–81.

Scott, A. C. *The Classical Theatre of China.* Westport, CT: Greenwood, 1957; repr. 1978.

———. *Traditional Chinese Plays.* 3 vols. Madison: University of Wisconsin Press, 1969.

Scott, Walter. *Ivanhoe.* London: Nelson, 1897.

Screech, M. A., and R. Calder. "Some Renaissance Attitudes to Laughter." In *Humanism in France at the End of the Middle Ages and in the Early Renaissance,* ed. A. H. T. Levi, 216–28. Manchester: Manchester University Press; New York: Barnes and Noble, 1970.

Scriptores historiae Augustae. Trans. David Magie. 3 vols. Loeb Classical Library. London: Heinemann; New York: Putnam, 1930.

Seneca (ca. 4 B.C.–ca. A.D. 65). *The Epistles of Seneca.* Trans. Richard Gummere, Loeb Classical Library. London: Heinemann; New York: Putnam, 1917.

Shadwell, Thomas (ca. 1642–92). *The Woman Captain.* 1679. In *The Complete Works of Thomas Shadwell,* ed. Montague Summers, 1:7–85. 5 vols. New York: Blom, 1968.

Shah, Idries. *The Exploits of the Incomparable Mulla Nasrudin.* London: Octagon Press, 1983.

———. *The Pleasantries of the Incredible Mulla Nasrudin.* London: Octagon Press, 1983.

———. *Special Illumination: The Sufi Use of Humour.* London: Octagon Press, 1977.

———. *The Subtleties of the Inimitable Mulla Nasrudin.* London: Octagon Press, 1983.

———. *The Wisdom of the Idiots.* London: Octagon Press, 1989.

Shakespeare, William. *All's Well That Ends Well.* 1602. Ed. G. K. Hunter. 3d ed. rev. London: Methuen, 1959; repr. 1962.

———. *As You Like It.* 1599. Ed. Alan Brissender. Oxford: Clarendon Press, 1993.

———. *Henry VIII.* 1613. Ed. R. A. Foakes. rev. ed. London: Methuen, 1975.

———. *King Henry VI, Part 2.* 1591. Ed. Andrew Cairncross. 3d ed. rev. London: Methuen, 1957.

———. *King Richard II*, 1597. Ed. Peter Ure. 5th ed. London: Methuen, 1961.

———. *A Midsummer Night's Dream*. 1600. Ed. Harold Brooks. 2d ed. London: Methuen, 1979.

———. *The Tragedy of King Lear*. 1607. Ed. Kenneth Muir. 9th rev. ed. London: Methuen, 1972.

———. *Troilus and Cressida*. 1602. Ed. Kenneth Palmer. London: Methuen, 1982.

———. *Twelfth Night, or What You Will*. 1600. Ed. J. M. Lothian and T. W. Craik. 2d ed. London: Methuen, 1975.

Shecter, Ben. *Hester the Jester*. Tadworth, Surrey: Windmill Press, 1979.

Shelley, Percy Bysshe. Charles the First. 1819–22. In *Plays, Translations, and Longer Poems*, 357–63. London: Dent, 1907; repr. 1949.

Sherzer, Dina, and Joel Sherzer, eds. *Humor and Comedy in Puppetry: Celebration of Popular Culture*. Bowling Green, OH: Bowling Green State University Popular Press, 1987.

Shirley, Rodney. *Early Printed World Maps: 1472–1700*. London: New Holland, 1993.

———. "Epichthonius Cosmopolites: Who Was He?" *Map Collector*, March 1982, 39–40.

Shoubinsky, Sergy N. "Court Jesters and Their Weddings in the Reigns of Peter the Great and Anna Ivanovna." In *Historical Narratives from the Russian*, by H. C. Romanoff, 1–47. London: Rivingtons, 1871.

Shulman, David. *The King and the Clown in South Indian Myth and Poetry*. Princeton: Princeton University Press, 1985.

Sidro, Annie. *Le carnaval de Nice et ses fous: Paillassou, Polichinelle et Triboulet*. Nice: Serre, 1979.

Siegel, Lee. *Laughing Matters: Comic Tradition in India*. Chicago: University of Chicago Press, 1987.

Silver, L. "Fools and Women: Profane Subjects by Lucas van Leyden." *Print Collector's Newsletter* 14, 4 (1983): 130–34.

Sima Qian (145–86 B.C. or before). "Accounts of the Jesters." Trans. William Dolby. Bilingual Series 4. Unpublished MS, Edinburgh, 1993.

———. "Jesters." In *War-Lords*, trans. William Dolby and John Scott, 157–68. Edinburgh: Southside, 1974.

Simon, John. "Hulot, or The Common Man as Observer and Critic." *Yale French Studies* 23 (1959): 18–25.

Sinavaiana, Caroline. "Traditional Comic Theater in Samoa: A Holographic View." Ph.D. diss., University of Hawaii, 1992.

Sitwell, Edith. *The Two Queens and the Hive*. Harmondsworth, Middlesex: Penguin Books, 1971.

Skelton, John (ca. 1460–1529). *Magnificence.* 1515. Ed. Paula Neuss. Manchester: Manchester University Press, 1980.

Smith, Humphrey. *To the Musicioners, the Harpers...* London, 1658.

Smith, John F. *Dick Tarleton.* Trans. E. Scheffter. 2 vols. Paris, 1858.

Smith, Vincent. *Akbar the Great Mogul, 1542–1605.* Oxford: Clarendon Press, 1917.

Smyth, D. E. "The Figure of the Fool in the Works of W. B. Yeats, Samuel Beckett and Patrick White." Ph.D. diss., London University, Birkbeck College, 1971–72.

Les sobres sotz. 1536. In *Recueil général des sotties,* ed. Émile Picot, 3:45–77. 3 vols. Paris: Firmin Didot, 1912.

Sofian, Simone. "The Role of the Comic in the 'Mystère' and the 'Miracle.'" Ph. D. diss., University of Cincinnati, 1985.

Somner, William (1598–1669). *The Antiquities of Canterbury, or A Survey of That Ancient Citie, with the Suburbs and Cathedral.* Ed. Nicolas Battely. 2d ed. London: R. Knaplock, 1703.

Sottie nouvelle à six personnaiges du roy des sotz. Ca. 1545. In *recueil général des sotties,* ed. Émile Picot, 3:205–31. Paris: Firmin Didot, 1912.

South Bank Centre. *Folly and Vice: The Art of Satire and Social Criticism.* London: South Bank Centre, 1989.

Southworth, John. *The English Medieval Minstrel.* Woodbridge, Suffolk: Boydell Press, 1989.

———. *Fools and Jesters at the English Court.* Thrupp, Gloustershire: Sutton 1998.

Souza, Eunice de. *All about Birbal.* Bombay: IBH, 1969.

———. *More about Birbal.* Bombay: IBH, 1973.

Speck, Bobbie. "Woody Allen: The Philosophical Clown." Ph.D. diss., Middle Tennessee State University, 1990.

Speer, Albert. *Inside the Third Reich.* Trans. Richard and Clara Winston. London: Sphere Books, 1971.

Spencer-Brown, G. *Laws of Form.* New York: Dutton, 1979.

Spenser, Edmund (1552?–99). *A View of the Present State of Ireland.* 1596? In *The Prose Works,* ed. Rudolph Gottfried, 39–231. Baltimore: Johns Hopkins Press, 1949.

Speroni, Charles. *Wit and Wisdom of the Italian Renaissance.* Berkeley: University of California Press, 1964.

Sprachmann, Paul. "Persian Satire, Parody and Burlesque." In *Persian Literature,* ed. E. Yarshater, 226–48. Albany, NY: Bibliotheca Persica, 1988.

Stecher, M. "La sottie française et la sotternie flamande." *Bulletin de l'Académie Royale de Belgique,* 2d ser., 43 (1877): 388–432.

Steele, Hunter. *Lord Hamlet's Castle.* London: Deutsch, 1987.

Steele, Walanne. "The Lost Paradise of the Clown: The Clown Figure in Twentieth Century German Literature." Ph.D. diss., City University of New York, 1979.

Steward, J. H. "The Ceremonial Buffoon of the American Indian." *Papers of the Michigan Academy of Science, Arts and Letters* 14 (1931): 187–207.

Stopes, C. C. "Elizabeth's Fool and Dwarfs." In *Shakespeare's Environment,* 269–75. London: Bell, 1914.

———. "Jane, the Queen's Fool." In *Shakespeare's Environment,* 258–69. London: Bell, 1914.

Stuart, John, George Burnett, and George McNeill, eds. *The Exchequer Rolls of Scotland.* 23 vols. Edinburgh: H. M. General Register House, 1878–1908.

Suárez de Figueroa, Cristóval. *El Pasagero.* 1617. Ed. Rodríguez Marín. Madrid: Renacimiento, 1913.

Sudraka [attributed]. *The Little Clay Cart* [*Mycchakatika*]. In *Two Plays of Ancient India,* trans. J. A. B. van Buitenen, 47–180. 2d ed. New York: Columbia University Press, 1964; repr. 1968.

Suetonius, Gaius (ca. 70–after 130). "The Deified Augustus." In *The Lives of the Caesars,* trans. J. C. Rolfe, 1.2.121–287. 2 vols. Loeb Classical Library. London: Heinemann; New York: Putnam, 1914; repr. and rev. 1928–30.

———. *The Lives of the Caesars.* Trans. J. C. Rolfe. 2 vols. Loeb Classical Library. London: Heinemann; New York: Putnam, 1914; repr. and rev. 1928–30.

———. "Nero." In *The Lives of the Caesars,* 2.6.85–187.

———. "Tiberius." In *The Lives of the Caesars,* 1.3.289–401.

Sund, Horst, ed. *Fas(t)nacht in Geschichte, Kunst und Literatur.* Constance: Universitätsverlag Konstanz, 1984.

Susskind, Norman. "Humor in the Chanson de Geste." *Symposium* 15, 3 (1961): 185–97.

Suzuki, Daisetz T. *Sengai, the Zen Master.* Greenwich, CT: New York Graphic Society, 1971.

Swain, Barbara. *Fools and Folly during the Middle Ages and the Renaissance.* New York: Columbia University Press, 1932.

Swiderski, Richard. "From Folk to Popular: Plastic Evil Eye Charms." In *The Evil Eye,* ed. Clarence Maloney, 28–41. New York: Columbia University Press, 1976.

Tacitus, Publius (ca. 56–ca. 117). *The Annals of Tacitus.* Trans. John Jackson. 4 vols. Loeb Classical Library. London: Heinemann; Cambridge: Harvard University Press, 1937; repr. 1951.

Tai Weige 太微閣. "Liyuan gushi" 梨園故事. *XJYK* 1, 11 (1929): 151–54.

Tang Xianzu (1550–1617). *The Peony Pavilion* [*Mudan Ting*]. 1598. Trans. Cyril Birch. Bloomington: Indiana University Press, 1980.

Tapper, Bruce. "Andhra Shadow-Play Jesters: Meaning, Iconography, and History." In *Conference on Asian Puppet Theatre*, 1–14. London: School of Oriental and African Studies, 1979.

Tarlton's Jests. 1611. In *Shakespeare Jest-Books,* ed. W. Hazlitt, 2:189–260. 3 vols. London: Willis and Sotheran, 1864.

Taylor, Ida. "The Professional Fools." *Nineteenth Century and After* 62 (1907): 254–61.

Thompson, Francis. *Collected Poems.* Ed. Wilfred Meynell. Sevenoaks, Kent: Fisher Press, 1992.

Thornbury, George. "Jester's Sermon." In *Songs of the Cavaliers and Roundheads.* London: Hurst and Blackett, 1857.

Tieck, Ludwig (1773–1853). *Puss-in-Boots* [*Der gestiefelte Kater*]. 1796. Trans. and ed. Gerald Gillespie. Edinburgh Bilingual Library 8. Edinburgh: Edinburgh University Press, 1974.

Tietze-Conrat, Erica. *Dwarfs and Jesters in Art.* Trans. E. Osborn. New York: Phaidon, 1957.

Timbs, John. *English Eccentrics and Eccentricities.* London: Chatto and Windus, 1877.

Timpane, John. "The Jest of the Rogue." In "The Romance of the Rogue: The History of a Character in English Literature, 1497–1632," 137–80. Ph.D. diss., Stanford University, 1980.

Titiev, Mischa. "Some Aspects of Clowning among the Hopi Indians." In *Themes in Culture,* ed. M. D. Zamora and others, 326–36. Quezon City, Philippines: Kayumanggi, 1971.

Todd, James Henthorn. *Leabhar Breathnach Annso Sis: The Irish Version of the "Historia Britonum" of Nennius.* Dublin: Irish Archaeological Society, 1848.

Tokofsky, Peter. "The Rules of Fools: Carnival in Southwest Germany." Ph.D. diss., University of Pennsylvania, 1992.

Tournefort, Joseph Pitton de. *Relation d'un Voyage du Levant.* Lyons, 1717. Quoted in G. Kalff, *Opkomst, Bloei en Verdwijning van de Hofnar,* 31. Amsterdam: De Poortpers, 1954.

Towsen, John. *Clowns: A Panoramic History of Fools and Jesters; Medieval Mimes, Jongleurs and Minstrels; Pueblo Indian Delight Makers and Cheyenne Contraries; Harlequins and Pierrots; Theatrical Buffoons and Zanies; Circus Tramps, White-faces and Augustes.* New York: Hawthorn Books, 1976.

Trebor, Haynes. *The Jester's Intrigue: A Comic Fantasy in One Act.* New York: Samuel French, 1930.

Trevedy, J. "Les fous et folles des ducs et duchesses de Bretagne." *Bulletin de la Société Archéologique du Finistère* 23 (1896): 30–33.

———. "Fous, folles et astrologues à la cour de Bretagne." *Bulletin de la Société Archéologique du Finistère* 18 (1891): 3–14.

Trevor-Roper, Hugh. *Princes and Artists: Patronage and Ideology at Four Habsburg Courts, 1517–1633.* London: Thames and Hudson, 1976.

Tubb, E. C. *The Jester at Scar.* London: Arrow, 1970.

Turcan, Robert. *Vivre à la cour des Césars: D'Auguste à Dioclétian: Ie–IIIe siècles.* Paris: Belles Lettres, 1987.

Turner, George. *Samoa: One Hundred Years Ago and Long Before.* London: Macmillan, 1884.

202 Jokes of Nasreddin Hodja. Istanbul: Galeri Minyatür, n.d.

Tydeman, William. "Satiric Strategies in the English Cycle Plays." In *Popular Drama in Northern Europe in the Later Middle Ages,* ed. F. Anderson, 15–39. Odense: Odense University Press, 1988.

UNESCO. "Le cirque: Un art universel." *Le Courrier de l'UNESCO* 41, 1 (1988): whole issue.

The Universal Jester, or A Compleat Book of Jests. London: Harris, 1668.

Upadhye, A. N. "Vidusaka's Ears." *Indian Historical Quarterly* 8, 4 (1932): 793.

Vaillant, George. *The Aztecs of Mexico: Origin, Rise and Fall of the Aztec Nation.* New York: Doubleday, Doran, 1941.

Valentino, Lucille. "Playing for Power: The Meanings of Elizabethan Entertainments." Ph.D. diss., Wayne State University, 1983.

Vandenbroeck, Paul. *Beeld van der Andere, Vertoog Over Het. Zelf: Over Wilden en Narren, Boeren en Bedelaars.* Exhibition at Anvers. Antwerp: Koninklijk Museum voor Schone Kunsten, 1987.

Vaughan, Herbert. *The Medici Popes (Leo X and Clement VII).* London: Methuen, 1908.

Vega, Lope de (1562–1635). *Los nobles cómo Han de Ser,* in *Obras de Lope de Vega,* 8: 101–32. 13 vols. Madrid: Sucesores de Rivadeneyra, 1930.

Voegelin, Erminie. "Tubatulabal Ethnography." *Anthropological Records* 2, 1 (1938): 1–90.

Volkov, Solomon, ed. *Testimony: The Memoirs of Dmitri Shostakovich.* Related to Solomon Volkov, trans. Antonina Bouis. London: Hamilton, 1979.

Wace (ca. 1100–ca. 1175). *Roman de rou.* Ed. A. J. Holden. 3 vols. Paris: Picard, 1970–73.

Wace, A. J. "Grotesques and the Evil Eye." *Annual of the British School at Athens* 10 (1903–4): 103–14.

Wade, Terence. "Russian Folklore and Soviet Humour." *Journal of Russian Studies* 54 (1988): 3–20.

Wager, W. *The Longer Thou Livest the More Fool Thou Art.* 1559. Ed. R. M. Benbow. London: Emerald Arnold, 1968.

Wallett, William F. *The Public Life of W. F. Wallett, the Queen's Jester: An Autobiography.* Ed. John Luntley. London: Bemrose, 1870.

Walpole, Ronald. "Humor and People in Twelfth Century France." *Romance Philology* 11, 3 (1957–58): 210–25.

Wan Fei Fang Xiaoru 皖肥方肖孺. "Liyuan cidian" 梨園詞典. *XJYK* 2, 9 (1929): 1–11.

Wang Guowei 王國維. *Wang Guowei xiqu lunwen ji* 王國維戲曲論文集. Beijing: Zhongguo Xiju Chubanshe, 1984.

———. "Youyu lu" 優語錄. In *Song Yuan xiqu shi* 宋元戲曲史, 249–66. Hong Kong: Taiping Shuju, 1964.

Wang Shifu 王實甫 (fl. ca. 1297–1307). *The Moon and the Zither: The Story of the Western Wing* [*Xixiang ji*]. Trans. Wilt Idema and Stephen West. Berkeley: University of California Press, 1991.

Wardroper, John. *Jest upon Jest: A Selection from the Jestbooks and Collections of Merry Tales Published from the Reign of Richard III to George III.* London: Routledge and Kegan Paul, 1970.

———. *Kings, Lords and Wicked Libellers: Satire and Protest, 1760–1837.* London: Murray, 1973.

Watson, Burton, trans. *Chinese Rhyme-Prose: Poems in the Fu Form from the Han and Six Dynasties Periods.* New York: Columbia University Press, 1971.

———, trans. *Ryokan: Zen Monk-Poet of Japan.* New York: Columbia University Press, 1977.

Watson, D. "Erasmus' *Praise of Folly* and the Spirit of Carnival." *Renaissance Quarterly* 32, 3 (1979): 333–53.

Watts, Leclaire. "The Clown: A Comparison of the Comic Figures of Lope de Vega and William Shakespeare." Ph.D. diss., University of Connecticut, 1966.

Wechsler, Howard. *Mirror to the Son of Heaven: Wei Cheng [Zheng] at the Court of Tang Tai-tsung [Taizong].* New Haven: Yale University Press, 1974.

Wedekind, Frank (1864–1918). *König Nicolo, oder So ist das Leben.* 1901. In *Frank Wedekind: Dramen*, ed. Manfred Hahn, 1:519–89. Berlin: Aufbau-Verlag, 1969.

Weldon, Anthony Sir. *The Court and Character of King James.* London, 1650.

Weller, June. *The Jester: A Story for Children.* Illus. Elaine Jones. Cheshire: J. Weller, 1980.

Wells, Henry. *Traditional Chinese Humour: A Study in Art and Literature.* Bloomington: Indiana University Press, 1971.

Welsford, Enid. *The Fool: His Social and Literary History.* London: Faber and Faber, 1935; repr. 1968.

Wenwu 文物, vol. 6 (1979).

The Whimsical Jester, or Rochester in High Glee, Containing Great Variety of Diverting Jests, Entertaining Stories Etc. London: W. Cavell, 1788.

Whitfield, Peter. "The Fool's Cap World, c. 1590." In *The Image of the World,* 78–79. London: British Library, 1994.

Wiesel, Elie. *Les portes de la forêt.* Paris: Éditions du Seuil, 1964.

———. *Zalmen, ou La folie de Dieu.* Paris: Éditions du Seuil, 1968.

Wiesinger, Alfons. *Narrenschmaus und Fastenspeise im schwabisch-alemannischen Brauch.* Constance: Südkurier 1980.

Wiles, David. *Shakespeare's Clown Actor and Text in the Elizabethan Playhouse.* Cambridge: Cambridge University Press, 1987.

Wilhelm, Hellmut. "The Bureau of Music of Western Han." In *Society and History: Essays in Honor of Karl August Wittfogel,* ed. G. L. Ulman, 123–35. The Hague: Mouton 1978.

Willeford, William. *The Clown, the Kingdom and the Stage: A Study in the Forms of Our Relationship to Folly.* Zurich: Druck, 1967.

———. *The Fool and His Sceptre: A Study in Clowns and Jesters and Their Audience.* London: Arnold 1969.

Williams, J. C. *The Court Poet in Medieval Ireland.* Proceedings of the British Academy 57. London: Oxford University Press, 1971.

Williams, Paul, ed. *The Fool and the Trickster: Studies in Honour of Enid Welsford.* Cambridge: Brewer, 1979.

Williams, Ursula M. *Jockin the Jester.* Illus. Barbara M. Williams. London: Chatto and Windus, 1951.

Williamson, D., and L. Williamson. "George Buchanan, the King's Fool." In *A Thorn in the King's Foot: Stories of the Scottish Travelling People,* 93–100. Harmondsworth, Middlesex: Penguin Books, 1987.

Williamson, J. Redfearn. *"The Ballad of a Jester" and Other Poems.* Darwen: J. J. Riley, 1891.

Wincelberg, Shimon. *Resort 76.* 1964. In *The Theatre of the Holocaust: Four Plays,* ed. and intro. Robert Skloot, 39–121. Madison: University of Wisconsin Press, 1982.

Wisse, Ruth. *The Schlemiel as Modern Hero.* Chicago: University of Chicago Press, 1971.

Wits Museum, or The New London Jester: A Collection by the Choice Spirits of the Present Age. London: Lane, 1780.

Wolf, Christa, and Gerhard Wolf. *Till Eulenspiegel.* Berlin: Luchterhand, 1972.

Wolf, Ferdinand. "Ueber den Hofnarren Kaiser Karl's V Genannt el Conde Don Francés de Zuñiga und seine Chronik." *Sitzungsberichte der Kaiserlichen Akademie der Wissenschaften: Philosophisch-Historische Classe* 2, 1 (June 1850): 21–63.

Wood, Edward. *Giants and Dwarfs.* London: Bentley, 1868.

Woolgar, C. M., ed. *Household Accounts from Medieval England.* Records of Social and Economic History, n.s., 18, part 2. Oxford: Oxford University Press, 1993.

Wright, Edmond L. *The Jester Hennets.* Liskeard, Cornwall: Harry Chambers/ Peterloo Poets, 1981.

Wyss, Hans. *Der Narr im schweizerischen Drama des 16. Jahrhunderts.* Bern: Haupt, 1959.

Xenophon (ca. 570–ca. 475 B.C.). *Symposium.* Trans. O. J. Todd. Loeb Classical Library. London: Heinemann, 1922.

Xie Susheng 謝素聲. "Liyun zhuilu" 梨雲綴錄. *XJYK* 2, 11 (1930), 1–9.

Xie Xingshi 謝醒石. "Lihua pianpian" 梨花片片. *XJYK* 2, 11 (1930), 1–9.

Xing Zuisheng 醒醉生 (Wang Kangnian 汪康年). *Zhuangxie xuanlu* 莊諧選錄. 2 vols. Taibei: Xin Wenfeng Chuban Gongsi, 1978.

Yan Guanglin 閻廣林 and others, eds. *Youmo xiao baike* 幽默小百科. Shanghai: Academy of Social Sciences, 1992.

Yeats, W. B. *The Green Helmet.* 1910. In *The Collected Plays of W. B. Yeats,* 221–44. London: Macmillan Papermac, 1982; repr. 1992.

Yorick, or The King's Jester. London: J. Fuller, 1761.

You Guoen 游國恩. "Lun fengci" 論諷刺. *Guowen yuekan* 國文月刊, no. 21 (1942): 4–6.

"Youren yi guanxin guozhai" 優人亦關心國債. *Guangyi Congbao* 廣益叢報, May 1911.

Young, Elizabeth. "Comedy as Social Control." In "Topeng in Bali: Change and Continuity in a Traditional Drama Genre," 196–239. Ph.D. diss., University of California, San Diego, 1980.

Young, Michael. "Bursting with Laughter: Obscenity, Values and Sexual Control in a Massim Society." *Canberra Anthropology* 1 (1977): 75–87.

Zakani, ʿObeyd-e (fourteenth century). *"The Ethics of the Aristocrats" and Other Satirical Works.* Trans. Hasan Javadi, Middle Eastern Series 11. Piedmont, CA: Jahan Books, 1985.

Zapata, Luis (sixteenth century). *Miscelánea de Zapata.* Madrid: Imprenta Nacional, 1859.

Zguta, Russell. *Russian Minstrels: A History of the Skomorokhi.* Oxford: Clarendon Press, 1978.

Zhang Cixi 張次溪. "Cheng Changgeng zhuan" 程長庚傳. *XJYK* 1, 3 (1928): 1–5.

———. "Liu Gansan zhuan" 劉趕三傳. *XJYK* 1, 11 (1929): 1–4.

———. "Shi Xiaofu zhuan" 時小福傳. *XJYK* 2, 1 (1929): 1–6.

———. "Tan Xinpei zhuan" 譚鑫培傳. *XJYK* 1, 6 (1928): 1–4.

Zhang Geng 張庚. "Shilun xiqu de qiyuan he xingcheng" 試論戲曲的起源和形成. *Xinjian She* 新建設 1 (1963): 56–73.

———. "Zhongguo huaju yundong shi chugao" 中國話劇運動史初稿. *Xiju Bao* 戲劇報, 1954, 1–7. Quoted in *YYJ*, 320.

———, ed. *Zhongguo da baike quanshu: Xiqu, quyi* 中國大百科全書戲曲曲藝. Beijing: Zhongguo Da Baike Quanshu Chubanshe, 1983.

Zhang Xiaoxia 張笑俠. "Xiangsheng" 相聲. *XJYK* 2, 4 (1929): 1–10.

Zhang Yunbai 張雲白. "Ling shi" 伶史. *XJYK* 3, 1 (1930): 1–10.

———. "Ling shi (xu)" 伶史續. *XJYK* 3, 3 (1930): 1–10.

———. "Ling shi (xu)" 伶史續. *XJYK* 3, 9 (1930): 1–11.

Zhou Yibai 周易白. *Zhongguo xiqu lunji* 中國戲曲論集. Beijing: Zhongguo Xiju Chubanshe, 1960.

Zhu Zhaonian 祝肇年. "Jicheng fengci yishu de zhandou chuantong" 繼承諷刺藝術的戰鬥傳統. *Guangming Ribao* 光明日報, 13 October 1957, 11.

Zhuang Yifu 莊一拂, ed. *Gudian xiqu cunmu huikao* 古典戲曲存目彙考. 3 vols. Shanghai: Guji Chubanshe, 1982.

Zijderveld, Anton. "De Hofnar als Instituut." *Spiegel Historiael* 2 (1976): 599–607.

———. *Reality in a Looking-Glass: Rationality through an Analysis of Traditional Folly*. London: Routledge and Kegan Paul, 1982.

Zimbardo, R. A. "The Book of the Duchess and the Dream of Folly." *Chaucer Review* 18, 4 (1984): 329–46.

Zincgref, Julius Wilhelm (1591–1635). *Der teutschen Scharpfsinnige kluge Sprüch, Apophthegmata gennant*. Strasbourg, 1628.

Zoltán, Ujváry. *Mátyás Király Gömörben*. Debrecen, Hungary, 1990.

Zuñiga, Don Francesillo de. *Crónica escandalosa seguida del epistolario festivo*. Ed. and annot. Pilar Guibelalde. Barcelona: Editorial Iberia, 1969.

CLASSICAL CHINESE WORKS (LISTED BY TITLE)

Airizhai congchao 愛日齋叢鈔. By Mr. Ye 葉 (Song). Fol. 2. *SKQS*, 854:634b–48b.

Aizi houyu 艾子後語. By Lu Zhuo 陸灼 (Ming). *LDXHJ*, 152–57.

Bai Juyi ji 白居易集. By Bai Juyi 白居易 (772–846), ed. Gu Xuejie 顧學頡. Vol. 1. Beijing: Zhonghua Shuju, 1979.

Baita sui 白獺髓. By Zhang Zhongwen 張仲文 (Song). *LDXS*, bk. 6, fol. 58, 1–8.

Beimeng suoyan 北夢瑣言. By Sun Guangxian 孫光憲 (900–68). *LDXS*, bk. 4, fol. 24, 1–7.

Bei Qi shu 北齊書. By Li Baiyao 李百藥 (565–648). Fol. 15. *SKQS*, 263:115b–21b.

Benshi shi 本事詩. By Meng Qi 孟啓 (fl. ca. 841–86). *GJYS*, 20, fol. 1, 1–22.

Bowu zhi 博物誌. Comp. Zhang Hua 張華 (232–300). *SKQS*, 1047:573a–609a.

Cangshu 藏書. By Li Zhi 李贄 (fl. ca. 1567). Vol. 2. Beijing: Zhonghua Shuju, 1959; repr. 1962.

Chang'an kanhua ji 長安看花記. By Yang Maojian 楊懋建 (Qing). In *Qingren shuohui*, comp. Lei Jin, 2d coll., bk. 10, 1a–16a. Shanghai: Saoye Shanfang, 1928.

Chaoye qianzai 朝野僉載. By Zhang Zhuo 張鷟 (ca. 657–730). *SKQS*, 1035:215a–86a.

Chaoye qianzai bu 朝野僉載補. Anon. (Tang). Fol. 6. Quoted in *YYJ*, 47.

Chengzhai shihua 誠齋詩話. By Yang Wanli 楊萬里 (1124–1206). *SKQS*, 1480: 725a–45b.

Chujing shushe lingmo 鋤經書舍零墨 (ca. 1878). By Huang Xiexun 黃燮訓 (Qing). Fol. 2. *BJXSDG*, 3d coll., bk. 190, 1a–12a.

Chuxue ji 初學記 (ca. 700). By Xu Jian 徐堅 (659–729) and others. *SKQS*, 890:1a–497a.

Ci Liushi jiuwen 次柳氏舊聞. By Li Deyu 李德裕 (787–849). *SKQS*, 1035:403a–9b.

Dong Qi jishi 東齊紀事. By Fan Zhen 范鎮 (1007–87). *SKQS*, 1036:579a–605a.

Dong Weizi wenji 東維子文集. By Yang Weizhen 揚維楨 (1296–1370). Fol. 11. *SBCK, jibu*.

Dong Zhou lieguo zhi 東周列國誌. By Feng Menglong 馮夢龍 (1574–1646) and others. 2 vols. Hong Kong: Zhonghua Shuju, 1960.

Dongdu shilüe 東都事略. By Wang Cheng 王偁 (1370–1415). *SKQS*, 382.

"Dongfang Shuo" 東方朔. In *Fengsu tongyi* 風俗通義. By Ying Shao 應劭 (fl. ca. 178). *SKQS*, 862:364b–65a.

"Dongfang Shuo" 東方朔. *TPGJ*, fol. 6. *SKQS*, 1043:32b–35a.

"Dongfang Shuo" 東方朔. *TPGJ*, fol. 174. *SKQS*, 1044:170a–b.

"Dongfang Shuo" 東方朔. *TPGJ*, fol. 245. *SKQS*, 1044:584a–85b.

Dongfang Shuo gerou yi Xi Jun 東方朔割肉遺細君. Attributed to Yang Shen 楊慎 (1488–1559). Not extant.

"Dongfang Shuo ji" 東方朔記. *SFSW*, fol. 4, 13b–14a.

Dongfang Shuo zhuan 東方朔傳. In *Hanshu* 漢書, by Ban Gu 班固 (32–92). *HIST*, 6, fol. 65, 2841–76.

"Dongfang Shuo zhuan" 東方朔傳. By Guo Xian 郭憲 (ca. 26 B.C.–ca. A.D. 55). *WCXSDG*, bk. 1, 1a–2a.

Dongfang Shuo zuopin jizhu 東方朔作品輯注. Ed. Fu Qunming 傅群明. Jinan: Qilu Shushe, 1987.

Dongguan zouji 東觀奏記. By Pei Tingyu 裴庭裕 (Tang). Fol. 2, *SKQS*, 407: 617b–23b.

Duxing zazhi 獨醒雜誌. By Zeng Minxing 曾敏行 (Song). Fol. 9, *SKQS*, 1039: 574b–80a.

"Fengjian" 諷諫. In *Chuxue ji* 初學記, by Xu Jian 徐堅 (659–729) and others, fol. 18. *SKQS*, 890:293b–95a.

Fengsu tongyi 風俗通義. By Ying Shao 應劭 (fl. ca. 178). *SKQS*, 862:349a–413a.

"Guji liezhuan" 滑稽列傳. In *Shiji* 史記, by Sima Qian 司馬遷 (145–ca. 96 B.C.), annot. Pei Yin 裴駰, vol. 10, fol. 126, 3197–214. Shanghai: Zhonghua Shuju, 1963.

Gujin tan'gai 古今譚概 (1620). Comp. Feng Menglong 馮夢龍 (1574–1646). *LDXHJ*, 335–82.

Gushan bizhu 穀山筆塵. By Yu Shenxing 於慎行 (1545–1607), ed. Lu Jinglin 呂景琳. Beijing: Zhonghua Shuju, 1984.

Gushu litan 孤樹裏談. By Li Mo 李默 (d. 1556). Fol. 8. In *Shuofu* (sequel), fol. 7. 338–40. [Details of *Shuofu* are given below under *Qinzhun jupin*.]

Guang xiaofu 廣笑府. By Feng Menglong 馮夢龍 (1574–1646). *LDXHJ*, 310–34.

Guier ji 貴耳集. By Zhang Duanyi 張端義 (fl. ca. 1235). Fol. 3. *SKQS*, 865:449a–68a.

Guitian lu 歸田錄. By Ouyang Xiu 歐陽修 (1007–72). Quoted in *Shihua zonggui* 詩話總龜, by Ruan Yue 阮閱 (fl. ca. 1126), part 1, fol. 46. *SKQS*, 1478:646b.

Guoting lu 過庭錄. By Fan Gongcheng 范公偁 (fl. ca. 1147). *SKQS*, 1038:245a–71b.

Guoyu 國語. 2 vols. Shanghai: Shanghai Guji Chubanshe, 1978.

Han Feizi 韓非子. By Han Fei 韓非 (ca. 280–234 B.C.), ed. Teruo Takeuchi 竹內照夫. 5th ed. 2 vols. Tokyo: Meiji Shoin, 1964.

Han Wu gushi 漢武故事. In "Histoire anecdotique et fabuleuse de l'empereur Wou des Han," trans. Max Kaltenmark. *Lectures Chinoises* 1 (1945): 28–91.

Han Wudi neizhuan 漢武帝内傳. By Ban Gu 班固 (32–92). In *L'empereur Wou des Han dans la legende Taoiste: Han Wou-ti Nei-tchouan*, trans. K. Schipper. Paris: École Française d'Extrême-Orient, 1965.

Han Zhongxian yishi 韓忠獻遺事. By Qiang Zhi 強至 (fl. ca. 1060). *LDXS* (Jing Ming Keben), bk. 22, fol. 70, 1a–12a.

Hanshu 漢書. By Ban Gu 班固 (32–92). *HIST*, ed.

"Huixie zhuan" 詼諧傳. In *Nan Tang shu* 南唐書, by Ma Ling 馬令 (Song), fol. 25. *SKQS*, 464:361b–64a.

Jianhu ji 堅瓠集 (Preface, 1695). By Chu Renhuo 褚人穫 (ca. 1630–ca. 1705). *BJXSDG*, bks. 89–108, and *BJXSDG* (sequel), vol. 4.

Jiang Linji zazhi 江鄰幾雜誌. By Jiang Xiufu 江休復 (1005–60). *BJXSDG*, bk. 381, 1a–18b.

Jiang sangshen Cai Shun feng mu zaju 降桑椹蔡順奉母雜劇. Attributed to Liu Tangqing 劉唐卿 (fl. ca. 1279). In *Yuanquxuan waibian* 元曲選外編, ed. Sui Shusen 隋樹森, 1:428–31. 2 vols. Beijing: Zhonghua Shuju, 1959.

Jiangbiao zhi 江表誌. By Zheng Wenshi 鄭文寶 (953–1013). *SKQS*, 464:131a–47a.

Jiangnan yeshi 江南野史. By Long Gun 龍袞 (Song). Fol. 7. *SKQS*, 464:100b–04b.

Jiaofang ji 教坊記. By Cui Lingqin 崔令欽 (fl. ca. 749). *ZGGD*, 1:3–30.

Jiegu lu 羯鼓錄. By Nan Chuo 南卓 (Tang). *SKQS*, 839:981b–87b.

Jinhuazi zabian 金華子雜編. By Liu Chongyuan 劉崇遠 (fl. ca. 940). Fol. 1. *SKQS*, 1035:823a–33a.

Jinling suoshi 金陵瑣事. By Zhou Hui 周暉 (1128–after 1198). Facsimile of Ming Wanli 明萬曆 ed., vol. 1, fol. 1, 31–161. 2 vols. Beijing: Wenxue Guji Kanxing, 1955.

Jinshu 晉書. By Fang Xuanling 房玄齡 (579–648) and others. *SKQS*, 256:1a–1006a.

Jintai canlei ji 金臺殘淚記. By Zhang Jiliang 張際亮 (1799–1843). Fol. 3, *Qingren shuohui* 清人説薈. Comp. Lei Jin 雷瑨, 2d collection, bk. 10, 1a–6a. Shanghai: Saoye Shanfang, 1928.

Jing Xinmo xijian Tang Zhuangzong 敬新磨戲諫唐莊宗. Attributed to Zhou Wenzhi 周文質 (?–1334). Not extant.

Jingkang xiangsu zaji 靖康緗素雜記. By Huang Chaoying 黃朝英 (fl. ca. 1101). Fol. 7, *SKQS*, 850:415b–19b.

Jiu Tang shu 舊唐書 (945). By Liu Xu 劉昫 (887–946). *HIST*, ed.

Jiuju congtan 舊劇叢談. By Chen Yanheng 陳彥衡 (Qing). *QDYD*, 3:1552–618.

Jushuo 劇説 (1805). By Jiao Xun 焦循 (1763–1820). Fol. 1. *ZGGD*, 8:81–102.

Kaitian chuanxin ji 開天傳信記. By Zheng Qi 鄭綮 (d. 899). *SKQS*, 1042:839a–48a.

Langya manchao 琅邪漫鈔. By Wen Lin 文林 (1445–99). *LDXS*, bk. 10, fol. 82, 1–4.

Leishuo 類説. By Zeng Zao 曾慥 (ca. 1131–93). *SKQS*, vol. 873.

Liyuan jiuhua 梨園舊話. By Juan You Yi Sou 倦游逸叟 (fl. ca. 1876). *QDYD*, 3:1491–538.

Liyuan yuan 梨園原. By Huang Fanchuo 黃旛綽 (Qing). *ZGGD*, 9:1–28.

Liangban qiuyu an suibi 兩般秋雨庵隨筆. By Liang Shaoren 梁紹壬 (1792–ca. 1819). Hong Kong: Guangzhi Shuju, 1956.

Liaoshi 遼史. By Tuo Tuo 脫脫 (1314–55) and others. *SKQS*, 289:1a–735a.

Liexian zhuan 列仙傳. Attributed to Liu Xiang 劉向 (77–6 B.C.). Fol. 2. *SKQS*, 1058:499a–507b.

"Lingguan zhuan" 伶官傳. In *Liaoshi* 遼史, by Tuo Tuo 脫脫 (1314–55) and others, fol. 109. *SKQS*, 289:707a–b.

"Lingguan zhuan" 伶官傳. In *Wudai shi* 五代史, by Ouyang Xiu 歐陽修 (1007–72) and others, fol. 37. *SKQS*, 279:228a–31a.

"Lingren zhuan" 伶人傳. In *Tangyu jizhuan* 唐餘紀傳, by Chen Ting 陳霆 (fl. ca. 1502), fol. 18, 437–70. Facsimile repr. of 1544 ed. Taibei: Taiwan Xuesheng Shuju, 1969.

Meixi qianji 梅溪前集. By Wang Shipeng 王十朋 (1112–71). Fol. 6. *SKQS*, 1151:151a–57b.

Mudan ting 牡丹亭 (1598). By Tang Xianzu 湯顯祖 (1550–1617). Ed. Xu Shuofang 徐朔方 and Yang Xiaomei 楊笑梅. Beijing: Zhonghua Shuju, 1959.

Nan Tang jinshi 南唐近事. By Zheng Wenbao 鄭文寶 (953–1013). *SKQS*, 1035:927a–40.

Nan Tang shu 南唐書. By Lu You 陸遊 (1125–1210). Fol. 17. *SKQS*, 464:484a–87b.

Nan Tang shu 南唐書. By Ma Ling 馬令 (Song). Fol. 25. *SKQS*, 464:361b–64a.

Nanbu xinshu 南部新書. By Qian Yi 錢易 (fl. ca. 1017). Fol. 10. *SKQS*, 1036:255a–64b.

Nao Zhongmou 鬧中牟. By Xu Fuzuo 徐復祚 (1560–after 1630). Not extant.

"Paiyoumen" 俳優們. In *Shihua zonggui* 詩話總龜, by Ruan Yue 阮閱 (fl. ca. 1126), part 1, fol. 46. *SKQS*, 1478:645b–46b.

Pingzhou ketan 萍州可談. By Zhu Yu 朱彧 (fl. ca. 1110). Fol. 3. *SKQS*, 1038:301a–12b.

Qidong yeyu 齊東野語. By Zhou Mi 周密 (1232–98). *SKQS*, 865:635a–851b.

Qiyan lu 啓顏錄. By Hou Bai 侯白 (fl. ca. 581). *LDXHJ*, 9–43.

Qinzhun jupin 秦準劇品. By Pan Zhiheng 潘之恆 (d. 1621). In *Shuofu* 説孚 (sequel), ed. Tao Ting 陶珽, fol. 44, 1966–69. Taibei: Xinxing Shuju, ca. 1964.

Qingbai leichao 清稗類鈔. Comp. and ed. Xu Ke 徐珂 (1869–1908). Vols. 13 and 25. Shanghai: Commercial Press, 1918.

Qingbo zazhi 清波雜誌. By Zhou Hui 周煇 (1126–after 1198). Fol. 6. *SKQS*, 1039:40a–47b.

Qingyi lu 清異錄. By Tao Gu 陶穀 (Song). *SKQS*, 1047:837a–930a.

Qingyuan dangjin 慶元黨禁. By Qiao Chuan Yi Sou 樵川逸叟 (Song). *SKQS*, 451:19a–46a.

Quan Song ci 全宋詞. Comp. and ed. Tang Guizhang 唐圭璋. Vol. 1. 5 vols. Beijing: Zhonghua Shuju, 1965.

Quan Wudai shi 全五代詩. Comp. Li Diaoyuan 李調元 (b. 1734). Fol. 87. *CSJC*, bk. 1780, 1317–31.

Quesao bian 郤掃編. By Xu Du 徐度 (fl. ca. 1147). Fol. 3. *SKQS*, 863:782a–99a.

Qunju jieyi 群居解頤. By Gao Yi 高懌 (Song). *LDXHJ*, 54–59.

Sanguo zhi 三國誌. By Chen Shou 陳壽 (233–97). *HIST*, ed.

———. *SKQS*, 254.

Shengchao tongshi shi yiji 勝朝彤史拾遺記. By Mao Qiling 毛奇齡 (1623–1716) and others. Fol. 6. *Xihe heji* 西河合集. Xiaoshan: Lu Ning Rui Tang, ca. 1770; 1796, bk. 94, 1a–20a.

Shengshui yantan lu 澠水燕談錄. By Wang Pizhi 王闢之 (fl. ca. 1082). Fol. 9. *SKQS*, 1036:516b–23b.

Shihua zonggui 詩話總龜. By Ruan Yue 阮閱 (fl. ca. 1126). Part 1, fol. 46. *SKQS*, 1478:644b–50a.

Shiji 史記. By Sima Qian (145–ca. 96 B.C.) 司馬遷. Annot. Pei Yin 裴駰. Vols. 7, 9, and 10. 10 vols. Shanghai: Zhonghua Shuju, 1963.

Shilin bishu luhua 石林避暑錄話. By Ye Mengde 葉夢得 (1077–1148). Fol. 1. *SKQS*, 863:629a–72a.

Shiyou tanji 師友談紀. By Li Zhi 李廌 (1059–1109). *SKQS*, 863:171a–89b.

Shu taowu 蜀檮杌. By Zhang Tangying 張唐英 (1029–71). Fol. 2, *SKQS*, 464: 236a–45a.

Shuyuan zaji 菽園雜記. By Lu Rong 陸容 (1436–94). Fol. 7. *YMSL*, 80–92.

Shuiting 說聽. By Lu Can 陸粲 (1494–1551). Fol. 1. *Shuo ku* 說庫, comp. Wang Wenru 王文濡, 2:1005–16. 2 vols. Taibei: Xinxing Shuju, 1963.

Shuowen judu 說文句讀. Comp. Xu Shen 許慎 (ca. 58–ca. 147), ed. Wang Jun 王筠. 4 vols. Shanghai: Shanghai Guji Shudian, 1983.

Sichao wenjian lu 四朝聞見錄. By Ye Shaoweng 葉紹翁 (fl. ca. 1220). *SKQS*, 1039:637a–768a.

Sijiu lu 思舊錄. By Huang Zongxi 黃宗羲 (1610–95). In *Huang Zongxi quanji* 黃宗羲全集, ed. Sun Jiasui 孫家遂, 1:338–95. Hangzhou: Zhejiang Guji Chubanshe, 1985.

Songbai leichao 宋稗類鈔. Comp. Pan Yongyin 潘永因 (fl. ca. 1669), ed. Liu Zhuoying 劉卓英, vol. 2, fol. 5, 369–483. 2 vols. Beijing: Shumu Wenxian Chubanshe, 1985.

Songchuang zalu 松窗雜錄. By Li Jun 李俊 (Tang). *SKQS*, 1035:557a–62a.

Songshi 宋史. By Tuo Tuo 脫脫 (1314–55) and others. *SKQS*, vols. 280–88.

Su Wei Gong wenji 蘇魏公文集. By Su Xiangxian 蘇象先 (Song).

Suxiang bi 粟香筆. By Jin Wuxiang 金武祥 (Qing). Part 3, fol. 5, 1a–11b. Shanghai: Saoye Shanfang, 1887–98.

Sui Tang yanyi 隋唐演義. By Chu Renhuo 褚人穫 (ca. 1630–ca. 1705). Taibei: Shijie Shuju, 1982.

Taiping yulan 太平御覽. Comp. Li Fang 李昉 (925–96) and others. Fol. 569. *SKQS*, 898:309a–16a.

Tang yulin 唐語林. By Wang Dang 王讜 (fl. ca. 1110). *SKQS*, 1038:1a–205b.

Tangwen xushi 唐文續拾. Comp. Lu Xinyuan 陸心源 (Qing). Fol. 5. In *Quan Tang wen* 全唐文, ed. Dong Gao 董誥 and others, 11:2222b–33b. Beijing: Zhonghua Shuju, 1983.

Tangyu jizhuan 唐餘紀傳. By Chen Ting 陳霆 (fl. ca. 1502). Facsimile reprint of 1544 ed. Taibei: Taiwan Xuesheng Shuju, 1969.

Tianqi gongci 天啓宮詞. By Jiang Zhiqiao 蔣之翹 (early to middle seventeenth century). In *Xiangyan congshu* 香艷叢書, comp. Chong Tianzi 蟲天子, fol. 4, part 3, 28a–42a. Taibei: Gujing Shuju, 1969.

Tie Wei Shan congtan 鐵圍山叢談. By Cai Tao 蔡條 (d. 1126). Fol. 4. *SKQS*, 1037: 588b–98a.

Tingshi 桯史. By Yue Ke 嶽珂 (1183–1234). *SKQS*, 1039:407a–522b.

Tongjian jishi benmo 通鑑紀事本末. By Yuan Shu 袁樞 (Song). Fol. 206. *SKQS*, vols. 346–49.

Toutao zhuozhu Dongfang Shuo 偷桃捉住東方朔. By Yang Chaoguan 楊朝觀 (1712–91). In *Yinfengge zaju* 吟風閣雜劇, coll. and annot. Hu Shiying 胡士瑩, 173–82. Shanghai: Shanghai Guji Chubanshe, 1983.

Wanli yehuo bian 萬曆野獲編. By Shen Defu 沈德符 (1578–1642). Fol. 26, *YMSL*, vol. 3.

Wenjian lu 聞見錄. By Luo Dian 羅點 (Song). *SFSW*, bk. 5, fol. 9, 11b–12a.

"Wenxin diaolong" jinyi 文心雕龍今譯. By Liu Xie 劉勰 (ca. 465–ca. 522). Trans. Zhou Zhenfu 周振甫, ed. Ji Ren 冀勤. Beijing: Zhonghua Shuju, 1986.

"Wenxuan" Li Shan zhu 文選李善注. Comp. Xiao Tong 蕭統 (501–31), annot. Li Shan 李善 (d. 689). *SBBY*, vol. 560.

Wudai shi 五代史. By Ouyang Xiu 歐陽修 (1007–72) and others. *SKQS*, 279:1–537.

Wudai shibu 五代史補. By Tao Yue 陶嶽 (Song). *SKQS*, 407:641a–83b.

Xihu youlan zhiyu 西湖遊覽誌餘. By Tian Rucheng 田汝成 (fl. ca. 1540). Fol. 2. *SKQS*, 585:291b–309b.

Xiyuan zaji 西園雜記. By Xu Xian 徐咸 (Ming). Fol. 1. *CSJC*, bk. 2913.

Xianyan changtan 閒燕常談. By Dong Yan 董弅 (Song). *WCXSDG*, bk. 23, 1a–3a.

Xiaoheng ji 小亨集. By Yang Hongdao 楊弘道 (1189–1270). Fol. 6. *SKQS*, 1198: 205b–18b.

Xiaolin 笑林. By Handan Chun 邯鄲淳 (132–early third century). Trans. William Dolby. Bilingual Series 6. Edinburgh: privately published, 1994.

Xiaoting zalu 嘯亭雜錄. By Zhao Lian 昭槤 (Qing). Fol. 1. In *Shuo ku* 説庫, comp. Wang Wenru 王文濡, 2:1512–19. 2 vols. Taibei: Xingxing Shuju, 1963.

"Xie yin" 諧隱. By Liu Xie 劉協 (ca. 465–ca. 522). In *"Wenxin diaolong" jinyi* 文心雕龍今譯, trans. Zhou Zhenfu 周振甫, ed. Ji Ren 冀勤, 130–37. Beijing: Zhonghua Shuju, 1986.

Xin Tang shu 新唐書 (1060). By Ouyang Xiu 歐陽修 (1007–72) and others. *HIST*, ed.

Xinke chuxiang yinshi dianban Dongfang Shuo toutao ji 新刻出相音釋點板東方朔偷桃記. By Wu Dexiu 吳德修 (fl. ca. 1692). *Guben xiqu congkan* 古本戲曲叢刊, 2d collection. Shanghai: Shanghai Commercial Press, 1955.

Xinren guijia lu 辛壬癸甲錄. By Yang Maojian 楊懋建 (Qing). *QDYD*, 1:569–618.

Xinshi "Xunzi" duben 新譯荀子讀本. By Xunzi 荀子 (ca. 315–ca. 230 B.C.). Annot. and ed. Wang Zhonglin 王忠林. Taibei: Sanmin Shuju, 1961; rev. and repr. 1963.

"Xinxu" jinzhu jinyi 新序今注今譯. By Liu Xiang 劉向 (77–6 B.C.). Commentary and trans. Lu Yuanling 陸元令. Taibei: Shangwu Yinshuguan, 1975.

Xu moke huixi 續墨客揮犀. By Peng Sheng 彭乘 (fl. ca. 1086). Fol. 5. In *Hanfenlou miji* 涵芬樓秘笈, comp. Sun Yuxiu 孫毓修 and others, bk. 2, 31a–41a. Shanghai: Shangwu Shudian, 1916–26.

Xu wenxian tongkao 續文獻通考. By Wang Qi 王圻 (fl. ca. 1565–1614). Fol. 118. *SKQS*, 629:390b–98b.

Yandu mingling zhuan 燕都名伶傳. By Zhang Cixi 張次溪 (Qing). *QDYD*, vol. 4 (sequel), 2129–78.

Yang Qi fa fanghui heshang yulu 楊岐發方會和尚語錄. Ed. Ren Yong 任勇 (Song) and others. In *Da cang jing* 大藏經, comp. J. Takakusu and K. Watanabe, vol. 47, item 1994a–b. Tokyo: Taisho Issdai-kyo Kanko Kwai, 1928.

Yang Wen Gong tanyuan 楊文公談苑. By Huang Jian 黃鑑 (fl. ca. 1027). *SFWW*, fol. 16, 1a–4a.

Yeren xianhua 野人閒話. By Jing Huan 景煥 (Song). *TPGJ*, fol. 446. *SKQS*, 1046:304b–11a.

Yeshi lu 也是錄. By Deng Kai 鄧凱 (Ming). In *Mingji baishi huibian* 明季稗史彙編, comp. Liu Yun Jushi 留雲居士 (Qing), 7:1a–11b. Shanghai: Tushu Jicheng Ju, 1896.

Yijian zhi 夷堅誌 (1166). By Hong Mai 洪邁 (1123–1202). Part 2, fol. 4. *SKQS*, 1047:345b–51a.

Yiling zhuan 異伶傳. By Chen Danran 陳澹然 (Qing). *QDYD*, 3:1333–54.

Yiwen leiju 藝文類聚. Comp. Ouyang Xun 歐陽詢 (1827–56) and others. Fol. 63. *SKQS*, 888:417b–30a.

Yinhua lu 因話錄. By Zhao Lin 趙璘 (fl. ca. 844). Fol. 4. *TPGJ*, fol. 164. *SKQS*, 1035:485b–91a.

"Youchang" 優倡. In *Taiping yulan* 太平御覽, comp. Li Fang 李昉 (925–96) and others. *SKQS*, 898:309a–13b.

Youhuan jiwen 遊宦紀聞. By Zhang Shinan 張世南 (fl. ca. 1225). Fol. 2. *CSJC*, bk. 2871, 9–14.

"Youling huiyu" 優伶詼語. In *Tingshi* 桯史, by Yue Ke 嶽珂 (1183–1234), fol. 7. *SKQS*, 1039:458b–59a.

"Youling yulu" 優伶語錄. In *Xiaoheng ji* 小亨集, by Yang Hongdao 楊弘道 (1189–1270), fol. 6. *SKQS*, 1198:218a–b.

"Youling zhenxi" 優伶箴戲. In *Yijian zhi* 夷堅誌, comp. Hong Mai 洪邁 (1123–1202), part 2, fol. 4, *SKQS*, 1047:345b–51a.

"Youren feng shishi" 優人諷時事. In *Wanli yehuo bian* 萬曆野獲編, by Shen Defu 沈德符 (1578–1642), fol. 26. *YMSL*, 3:664–65.

"Youxi luxu" 優戲錄序. In *Dong Weizi wenji* 東維子文集, by Yang Weizhen 楊維楨 (1296–1370), fol. 11. *SBCK, jibu* 82a.

Yutang xianhua 玉堂閒話. By Fan Zi 范資 (Five Dynasties). *SFWW*, fol. 48, 1a–5a.

Yuefu zalu 樂府雜錄. By Duan Anjie 段安節 (ca. 830–ca. 900). *ZGGD*, 1:31–89.

Zhangshi keshu 張氏可書. By Zhang Zhifu 張知甫 (fl. ca. 1126). *SKQS*, 1038:707a–14a.

Zhongshan shihua 中山詩話. By Liu Bin 劉斌 (1022–88). *SKQS*, 1478:265a–77b.

"Zhuru" 侏儒. In *Liangban qiuyu an suibi* 兩般秋雨庵隨筆, by Liang Shaoren 梁紹壬 (1792–ca. 1819), fol. 6, 55–56. Hong Kong: Guangzhi Shuju, 1956.

Zhushi 麈史. By Wang Dechen 王得臣 (1036–ca. 1115). Fol. 3. *SKQS*, 862:637a–48b.

Zhuozhong zhi 酌中誌. By Liu Ruoyu 劉若愚 (Ming). Fol. 16. *CSJC*, bk. 3967, 97–134.

Zizhi tongjian 資治通鑑 (1085). By Sima Guang 司馬光 (1019–86). Fol. 273. *SKQS*, 310:346b–64b.

MANUSCRIPTS

Archives des Affaires Étrangères, Correspondence politique: Espagne, vol. 15, fol. 285v.

Archives Impériales, KK 98, fol. 185.

Archives Nationales, Xia 8640, part 2, fol. 13.

Archives Nationales, Xia 9256, fol. 27.

Bibliothèque Impériale, MS Saint-Germain, vol. 52, no. 22.

BM Additional MSS, 19,402, fol. 79.

BM MS Royal 2.A.12, fol. 304r.

BN MS LB.507.

BN MSS Français, no. 22,564, fol. 151.

Bodleian Library, Laud. Lat. 114, fol. 71.

Cambridge MS ff.2.38, fol. 255r–v.

Catalogue des actes de François I, no. 31874.

Jones, John. Common-Place Book. BM MS Sloane, 517.

Letters and Papers of Henry VIII. MS Public Record Office, SP.1.101.

Menus plaisirs, KK 127.

"A Sage Fool's Testament" (ca. 1475). BM Harleian MS 2252, fol. 85.

Trinity College, Cambridge, MS 0.3.10, fol. 44r.

Trinity College, Cambridge, MS 0.7.46, fol. 51r.

Zuñiga, Don Francisco. Historia del emperador Carlos V. BM MS Egerton 1880,
    Plut. DXX. B.

ILLUSTRATION CREDITS

Jacket. *The Laughing Jester* (Netherlands, fifteenth century). Reproduced by permission of the National Art Museum of Sweden, Stockholm, NM 6783.

Frontispiece. Kenneth Grahame, *Dream Days,* illus. Maxfield Parrish (London: John Lane, 1902), facing 90. British Library 012322.h.9. Reproduced by permission of the British Library.

Flip art. Cartoon series of a juggling jester by Nathan Barlex. Reproduced with his kind permission.

Prologue opening. Gustave Doré (1832–83), illustration for Honoré de Balzac's *Les contes drolatiques* (1855). Reproduced from Gustave Doré, *Doré Spot Illustrations: A Treasury from His Masterworks,* selected by Carol Grafton (New York: Dover, 1987), 72.

Figure 1. *The Fool's Cap World Map* (Antwerp? ca. 1590). Recently hand-colored for Wychwood Editions, with grateful thanks to Peter Whitfield for permission to reproduce this version. Originals held in the Bodleian Library (Bodleian Douce Portfolio 142 [92]) and the Royal Geographical Society (264.h.14 [6]). See Rodney Shirley, "Epichthonius Cosmopolites: Who Was He?" *Map Collector,* March 1982, 39–40, and Shirley, *Early Printed World Maps: 1472–1700* (London: New Holland, 1993), 189–90; Peter Whitfield, "The Fool's Cap World, c. 1590," in *The Image of the World* (London: British Library, 1994), 78–79.

Figure 2. *Claus Narr and His Goslings,* in George Wither, *A Collection of Emblems* (1635), 225, poems published illustrating the copperplate designs of Crispinus Passaeus. Reproduced by permission of the Bodleian Library, University of Oxford (Mason E 105).

Figure 3. *Muzierender Narr* (late fifteenth century), copperplate engraving by Meisters des Bileam. Reproduced by permission of the Staatliche Kunsthalle, Karlsruhe, Germany.

Figure 4. Gustave Doré, *Doré's Illustrations for Rabelais: A Selection of 252 Illustrations by Gustave Doré* (New York: Dover, 1978), 145.

Figure 5. *Dwarf with Dog and Bird,* detail sketched by Robert Lenkewicz from an oil on canvas by Eugène Déveria (1805–65). Paris, Louvre. This and all subsequent sketches by Robert Lenkewicz reproduced with his kind permission.

Figure 6. Mayan pottery urn, ca. sixth century, approx. eight inches high. Sketched by Robert Lenkewicz from a photograph in Erica Tietze-Conrat, *Dwarfs and Jesters in Art,* trans. E. Osborn (New York: Phaidon, 1957), 10 and 86.

Figure 7. *The Country of Pygmies,* a drawing of tropical dwarfs from an encyclopedia, *Dushu Jicheng,* ed. Chen Menglei et al. (ca. 1726), reproduced from Joseph Needham, *China: Science and Civilisation* (Cambridge: Cambridge University Press, 1971), vol. 4, part 3, fig. 992. Reproduced by permission of Cambridge University Press.

Figure 8. *Claus Narr* (1530), attributed to Hans Lautensack (1524–63), although now thought to be a seventeenth-century copy. Oil on wood. Neuburg, Heimatsmuseum. Sketched by Robert Lenkewicz from Tietze-Conrat, *Dwarfs and Jesters,* 21 and 93.

Figure 9. *Till Eulenspiegel,* woodcut by Rudolf Warnecke. Reproduced by permission of Olaf Tamaschke and Friedlinde Warnecke-Tamaschke.

Figure 10. Medal (ca. 1461–66), struck by Francesco Laurana (1423–1502). Paris, Bibliothèque Nationale. Sketched by Robert Lenkewicz from Tietze-Conrat, *Dwarfs and Jesters,* 12 and 88.

Figure 11. *Will Sommers, Kinge Heneryes Jester,* engraving by Francis Delaram. British Museum Department of Prints and Drawings. Reproduced by permission of the British Museum.

Figure 12. *Archee the King's Jester,* British Museum Print Room, Cracherode Collection P.3.361. Reproduced by permission of the British Museum.

Figure 13. *Calabacillas* (ca. 1648), canvas by Velázquez. Madrid, Prado. Detail sketched by Robert Lenkewicz.

Figure 14. Birbal's House at Fathpur-sikri, reproduced from a photograph in Vincent Smith, *Akbar the Great Mogul, 1542–1605* (Oxford: Clarendon Press, 1917), facing 443. Reproduced by permission of Oxford University Press.

Figure 15. "Rupert and the April Fool," by Ian Robinson, illustration by John Harrold in *Rupert: The Daily Express Annual* (Exeter, Devon: Pedigree Books, 1993), 86. Reproduced by permission of Express Newspapers PLC.

Figure 16. Painted earthenware (Eastern Han 25–220), excavated in 1982 from a cliffside tomb in Xindu County, Sichuan. Sketched by Christine Otto from Susan Caroselli, ed., *The Quest for Eternity: Chinese Ceramic Sculptures from the People's Republic of China* (London: Thames and Hudson, 1987). Reproduced with her kind permission.

Figure 17. From the back cover of *Rupert: The Daily Express Annual* (Exeter, Devon: Pedigree Books, 1993). Reproduced by permission of Express Newspapers PLC.

Figure 18. Relief from the *Goldenen Dachl* by Niklaus Türing (1500). Reproduced by permission of the Tiroler Landesmuseum Ferdinandeum, Innsbruck, Austria.

Figure 19. Gustave Doré, illustration for François Rabelais, *Oeuvres de Rabelais,* 2 vols. (Paris, 1883–85), reproduced from Grafton's selection in *Doré Spot Illustrations,* 58.

Figure 20. Frontispiece reproduced in T. H. Jamieson, ed., *A Banquet of Jests* (1640) (Edinburgh: William Paterson, 1872), 367–74.

Figure 21. *How Owlglass Rebuked the Priest's Covetousness,* illustration by Alfred Crowquill, in Kenneth Mackenzie, coll. and trans., *The Marvellous Adventures and Rare Conceits of Master Tyll Owlglass* (London: Trubner, 1860), facing 209.

Figure 22. "Raja Beer Bur," British Library, India Office, Add. OR 4229. Reproduced by permission of the British Library.

Figure 23. *Dongfang Shuo Steals a Peach,* illustration in Chuan Xihua, ed., *Zhongguo gudian wenxue banhua xuanji,* 2 vols. (Shanghai: Renmin Meishu Chubanshe, 1981), 2:270.

Figure 24. Head of a mimic fool, Roman terra-cotta. From F. Ficoroni, *Dissertatio de larvis scenicis et figuris comicis antiquorum romanorum* (Rome, 1754), pl. lxxii, 2. Sketched by Ben Tunstall from Allardyce Nicoll, *Masks, Mimes and Miracles* (London: Harrap, 1931), 63. Reproduced with his kind permission.

Figure 25. A mime actor on a Roman lamp. From Pietro Santi Bartoli, *Le antiche lucerne sepolcrali figurate, raccolte dalle cave sotterranee e grotte di Roma* (Rome: Bugani, 1691), vol. 1, pl. 34. Sketched by Ben Tunstall from Nicoll, *Masks, Mimes and Miracles,* 79.

Figure 26. *Richard Tarlton.* British Museum, Harleian MS 3885.f.19 Reproduced by permission of the British Museum.

Figure 27. *Thomas King as Touchstone,* Johan Zoffany. Reproduced by permission of the Garrick Club, cat. no. 384, and E.T. Archive, London.

Figure 28. *Emma Thompson as the Fool* in the Renaissance Theatre Company production of *King Lear* (1990). Reproduced by permission of Emma Thompson and Robert Barber, copyright Robert Barber.

Figure 29. Reproduced from Felix Bobertag, ed., *Narrenbuch: Kalenberger, Peter Len, Neithart Fuchs, Markolf, Bruder Rausch,* in *Deutsche National-Literatur: Historisch-Kritische-Ausgabe,* ed. Joseph Kürchner (Berlin: Spemann, 1881), 2:154.

Figure 30. Reproduced from Bobertag, *Narrenbuch,* 155.

Figure 31. Reproduced from Bobertag, *Narrenbuch,* 158.

Figure 32. Reproduced from Bobertag, *Narrenbuch,* 247.

Figure 33. Terra-cotta plaque. Mathura Museum, no. 2795. Sketched by Christine Otto from V. S. Agrawala, "A Palace Amusement Scene on a Terracotta

Panel from Mathura," *Journal of the India Society of Oriental Art* 10 (1942): 69–73. Reproduced with her kind permission.

Figure 34. *Folly Governeth the World,* illustration by Alfred Crowquill, in Mackenzie, *Marvellous Adventures,* frontispiece.

Figure 35. Stone relief, Shanxi. From Zhang Geng, *Zhongguo da baike quanshu: Xiqu, quyi* (Beijing: Zhongguo Da Baike Quanshu Chubanshe, 1983). Reproduced by permission of the Encyclopedia of China Publishing House.

Figure 36. Stone relief, Shanxi. From Zhang Geng, *Zhongguo da baike quanshu: Xiqu, quyi* (Beijing: Zhongguo Da Baike Quanshu Chubanshe, 1983). Reproduced by permission of the Encyclopedia of China Publishing House.

Figure 37. *El niño de Vallecas* (ca. 1648), canvas by Velázquez. Madrid, Prado. Detail sketched by Robert Lenkewicz.

Figure 38. Illustration by Ram Waeerkar, in *Birbal the Witty,* Amar Chitra Katha Series 237 (Bombay: India Book House, 1982), 28, used by permission. Reproduced from Lee Siegel, *Laughing Matters: Comic Tradition in India* (Chicago: University of Chicago Press, 1987), 303.

Figure 39. François Rabelais, *Oeuvres de Rabelais,* illus. Gustave Doré, 2 vols. (Paris, 1883–85).

Figure 40. *How Owlglass Turneth Doctor,* illustration by Alfred Crowquill, in Mackenzie, *Marvellous Adventures,* facing 23.

Figure 41. John Major as a jester, illustration to the Bagehot column, *Economist,* 23 July 1994, 32. Reproduced by permission of the artist, Chris Riddell.

Figure 42. From *Neue Zürcher Zeitung,* 17 May 1994, 24. Reproduced by permission of Nebelspalter, Basel.

Figure 43. "Rupert and the April Fool," by Ian Robinson, illustration by John Harrold, in *Rupert: The Daily Express Annual* (Exeter, Devon: Pedigree Books, 1993), 90. Reproduced by permission of Express Newspapers PLC.

Epilogue opening. Gustave Doré, illustration to Xavier-Boniface Saintine (1861), *Le chemin des écoliers,* reproduced from Grafton's selection in *Doré Spot Illustrations,* 9.

Epilogue closing. Gustave Doré, illustration to Honoré de Balzac, *Les contes drolatiques* (1855), reproduced from Grafton's selection in *Doré Spot Illustrations,* 72.

INDEX

Note: Jesters are indexed according to the courts where they served rather than their origin, which is generally less clear. Therefore an Italian-born jester or a jester with a German name may be listed as Spanish. Italic page numbers refer to pages with illustrations.